W9-CLS-601

Geneva and the Consolidation of the French Protestant Movement 1564-1572

with warm regards—
for Egil Grislis,
Bob Kingdon

ROBERT M. KINGDON

Geneva and the Consolidation of the French Protestant Movement 1564-1572

A Contribution to the History of Congregationalism, Presbyterianism, and Calvinist Resistance Theory

THE UNIVERSITY OF WISCONSIN PRESS
Madison, 1967

Published in the United States of America by
The University of Wisconsin Press
Box 1379, Madison, Wisconsin 53701

Published in Switzerland by
Librairie Droz
11 rue Massot, Geneva

Library of Congress Catalog Card Number 67-24373
Printed in Switzerland

ACKNOWLEDGMENTS

This book has been in the making since 1959. In the process I have received substantial help from many people and institutions. It would be difficult and laborious to acknowledge them all. But it would be indecent not to acknowledge some of them.

Most of the information upon which the book is based was gathered during the 1960-1961 academic year, which I spent in Europe as a Fellow of the American Council of Learned Societies. My search for this information was enormously facilitated by M. Henri Naef of Geneva, and by the principal editors of the Beza correspondence, Professor Henri Meylan of Lausanne and M. Alain Dufour of Geneva. M. Naef and his family loaned to me for extended periods of time the voluminous notes which he had compiled some time ago for a projected book on the Morély quarrel. MM. Meylan and Dufour permitted me full use of the magnificent files of information gathered from all over Europe for the critical edition of the Beza correspondence, now housed in the Musée historique de la Réformation of Geneva. They have also both helped repeatedly in locating and evaluating pieces of evidence important for this study.

Most of the writing of this book was done during the 1965-1966 academic year, which I spent in Princeton, New Jersey, as a Member of the Institute for Advanced Study. It owes much to the serene surroundings, the fine facilities, and the stimulating company offered by that genial institution.

In locating the materials upon which this study is based, I was also assisted by many other people, most of them librarians and archivists, particularly in Geneva and Zurich, but also in many other places in Europe and in this country. Of these, I particularly want to mention MM. Gustave Vaucher and Louis Binz, of the Archives d'Etat de Genève, who repeatedly helped me to locate and read materials in their collections; Mr. Frank Hanlin, of the University of Iowa Library, who located and recommended purchase of rare books of importance to this study; M. Jean Rott, of the Bibliothèque nationale et universitaire de Strasbourg, who graciously supplied me with a transcript of an important unpublished letter he had recently helped to discover; Mr. Jon C. Swan, then of Amsterdam, who obtained for me a photographic copy of another important unpublished letter; the Rev. Dr. Geoffrey Nuttall, of London, and the Rev. Dr. Douglas Horton, of Randolph, New Hampshire, who both called to my attention evidences of the influences of the Morély quarrel in England and who both read that section of my final draft dealing with this connection.

In resolving some of the technical problems I encountered in this study, I was further assisted by yet other people, most of them scholars working on studies parallel to this. Of these, I particularly want to mention Mlle. E. Droz of Gy (Geneva), who helped me with some technical bibliographical problems; Professor Jean-François Bergier of Geneva, my collaborator in the critical edition of the *Registres de la Compagnie des Pasteurs de Genève au temps de Calvin*, a project related at several points to this one; Professor Natalie Z. Davis of the University of Toronto, who is working on the Reformation in Lyon; Professor Nancy Roelker of Tufts University, who is working on the career of Jeanne d'Albret; Professor E. William Monter of Northwestern University, who is working on the social history of Geneva.

In preparing the text of this book for publication, I was assisted by yet other people. Professor Felix Gilbert, of the Institute for Advanced Study, supplied a helpful critical reading of the greater part of the final draft of the book. Mr. William Lubenow, a research assistant provided to me by the University of Iowa, compiled much of the material constituting Appendix I, and helped in other ways. Mr. Malcolm Sylvers, a research assistant provided to me by the University of Wisconsin, helped me in reading proofs, compiling the index, and in yet other ways. And I was again assisted at this stage in my work by Professor Meylan, who agreed to check my transcription of the Latin letter which constitutes Appendix II, and by M. Dufour, who supplied a particularly careful and critical reading of the entire final draft of the book.

This book might have been a better one, if I had waited for even more help. Among the projects which I might have investigated, is a doctoral dissertation dealing with the Morély quarrel, which is now being prepared by Mr. Carl Weiner of Carleton College for submission to the University of Wisconsin, but which was begun years before I arrived here, which I have never seen, and about which I know very little. Another such project is an edition of Morély's *Traicté de la discipline & police chrestienne*, announced for publication in 1967 by the Librairie Slatkine of Geneva.

Many other people have helped me in less tangible ways with this book. They include students and colleagues and friends in many places in many countries. I would like to mention one of them: the late Professor Garrett Mattingly, my mentor in graduate study at Columbia University. He encouraged me powerfully in the early stages of my work on this book. Unfortunately he did not live to see any substantial part of it. I hope it is not unworthy of his memory.

Robert M. Kingdon
Madison, Wisconsin, U.S.A.
February 1967

TABLE OF CONTENTS

TABLE OF ABBREVIATIONS

ARG	*Archiv für Reformationsgeschichte*
D'Aumale, *Condé*	Duc d'Aumale, *Histoire des princes de Condé*
J. Aymon, *Synodes*	[Jean] Aymon, ed., *Tous les synodes nationaux des églises réformées de France*
Beza, *Corr.*	Théodore de Bèze, *Correspondance*, ed., by Fernand Aubert, Henri Meylan, Alain Dufour, Arnaud Tripet
BHR	*Bibliothèque d'Humanisme et Renaissance*
C. Borgeaud, *Université*	Charles Borgeaud, *Histoire de l'Université de Genève*
A. Bouvier, *Bullinger*	André Bouvier, *Henri Bullinger, le successeur de Zwingli*
BSHAG	*Bulletin, Société d'histoire et d'archéologie de Genève*
BSHPF	*Bulletin de la Société de l'histoire du protestantisme français*
Calvini Opera	*Ioannis Calvini Opera quae supersunt omnia*, ed. by Baum, Cunitz, and Reuss
A. Chandieu, *Confirmation*	[Antoine de la Roche Chandieu], *La Confirmation de la discipline ecclesiastique...* (1566)
E. Choisy, *Genève au temps de Bèze*	Eugène Choisy, *L'état chrétien calviniste à Genève au temps de Théodore de Bèze*
J. Delaborde, *Coligny*	Jules Delaborde, *Gaspard de Cologny, Amiral de France*
DNB	*Dictionary of National Biography* [British]
C. du Moulin, *Opera*	Charles du Moulin, *Omnia quae extant opera*, 1681 ed.
France protestante, 1st ed.	Eug. and Em. Haag, *La France Protestante* (1846-1858)
France protestante, 2nd ed.	The same, revised by Henri Bordier (1877-1888)
J.-A. Gautier, *Hist. de Genève*	Jean-Antoine Gautier, *Histoire de Genève des origines à l'année 1691*
P.-F. Geisendorf, *Beza*	Paul-F. Geisendorf, *Théodore de Bèze*

Geneva, Arch., PC	Archives d'État de Genève, Procès criminel
— PH	— Pièces historiques
— RC	— Registres du Conseil
— RConsistoire	— Registres du Consistoire
— RCP	— Registres de la Compagnie des Pasteurs
Geneva, BPU	Bibliothèque publique et universitaire de Genève
Geneva, LB	*Le livre des bourgeois de l'ancienne République de Genève,* ed. by Alfred L. Covelle
Geneva, LH	*Livre des habitants de Genève,* ed. by Paul-F. Geisendorf
Geneva, LR, Stelling-Michaud ed.	*Le livre du recteur de l'Académie de Genève,* ed. by S. Stelling-Michaud
Geneva, MHR	Musée historique de la Réformation, Genève
Geneva, RCP, Kingdon & Bergier, eds.	*Registres de la Compagnie des Pasteurs de Genève au temps de Calvin,* ed. by R. M. Kingdon and J.-F. Bergier
H. Heyer, *L'Egl. de Genève*	Henri Heyer, *L'Eglise de Genève*
Hist. eccl.	*Histoire ecclésiastique des églises réformées au royaume de France,* ed. by G. Baum and E. Cunitz
R. M. Kingdon, *Geneva & Coming*	Robert M. Kingdon, *Geneva and the Coming of the Wars of Religion in France*
G. V. Lechler, *Verfassung*	G. V. Lechler, *Geschichte der Presbyterial- und Synodalverfassung seit der Reformation*
E. Léonard, *Hist. gen. du prot.*	Émile G. Léonard, *Histoire générale du Protestantisme*
R. D. Linder, *Viret*	Robert Dean Linder, *The Political Ideas of Pierre Viret*
London, PRO	London, Public Record Office
MDG	*Mémoires et Documents publiés par la Société d'histoire et d'archéologie de Genève*
Mémoires de Condé	*Mémoires de Condé,* [ed. by Secousse], 1743-1745
J. Morély, *Traicté*	Jean Morély, *Traicté de la discipline & police chrestienne* (1562)
H. Næf, *Conjuration d'Amboise*	Henri Næf, *La Conjuration d'Amboise et Genève*
Paris, BiblSHPF	Paris, Bibliothèque de la Société de l'histoire du protestantisme français
J. Quick, *Synodicon*	John Quick, ed., *Synodicon in Gallia Reformata*
W. Richard, *Kirchenterminologie*	Willy Richard, *Untersuchungen zur Genesis der reformierten Kirchenterminologie der Westschweiz und Frankreichs*
A. Roget, *Hist. de Genève*	Amédée Roget, *Histoire du peuple de Genève depuis la réforme jusqu'à l'escalade*
E. Rott, *Représentation*	Edouard Rott, *Histoire de la représentation diplomatique de la France auprès des cantons suisses, de leurs alliés et de leurs confédérés*

STC	A. W. Pollard and G. R. Redgrave, *A Short-Title Catalogue of Books Printed in England, Scotland, & Ireland, and of English Books Printed Abroad, 1475-1640*
J.-A. de Thou, *Hist univ.* (1740 ed.)	Jaques-Auguste de Thou, *Histoire universelle...*, 1740 the Hague ed.
THR	*Travaux d'Humanisme et Renaissance*
H. Vuilleumier, *Hist. de l'Egl. réf. du Pays de Vaud*	Henri Vuilleumier, *Histoire de l'Eglise réformée du Pays de Vaud sous le régime bernois*
C. Waddington, *Ramus*	Charles Waddington, *Ramus (Pierre de la Ramée), sa vie, ses écrits, et ses opinions*
A. W. Whitehead, *Coligny*	A. W. Whitehead, *Gaspard de Coligny, Admiral of France*
Wing	Donald Wing, *Short-Title Catalogue of Books Printed in England, Scotland, Ireland, Wales, and British America and of English Books Printed in Other Countries, 1641-1700*

INTRODUCTION

At sundown on Saturday, May 24, 1564, John Calvin died. His chief disciple, Theodore Beza, reported: " Thus, in the same moment, that day, the sun set and the greatest light which was in this world, for the direction of the Church of God, was withdrawn to Heaven. We can well say that with this single man it has pleased God in our time, to teach us the way both to live well and to die well." [1]

John Calvin had been a long time in dying. For months reports of his imminent death had circulated from Geneva. And for months his emaciated body had been wracked by agonizing disease. Doctors had tried stern remedies. Jolting rides on horse back were prescribed, for example, as treatment for a urinary ailment.[2] But nothing worked. Calvin had become steadily weaker. Until the very end, however, his mind remained sharp and clear. His last recorded statements are of much the same character as those that marked his entire mature life. They show the same driving concern for the successful operation of the Reformed Church. They show the same sublime confidence in the rightness of his reform program. And they show the same caustic scorn for those who opposed or obstructed that program. In his last formal statement to his brethren in the Geneva Company of Pastors, for example, he had taxed their fellow townsmen as being of a " perverse and unhappy nation, and, although there have been good men, the nation is perverse and wicked." [3]

His last statements also reveal much of Calvin's thought about the problems which faced the Reformed movement during the year of his death. The problems of one particular area stand out, as they had for much of the time since the Reformed regime was consolidated in Geneva, in 1555. This area was France. Until the end, Calvin kept receiving and reporting on the political news from that country. Until the end, he kept advising the faithful

---

[1] Théodore de Bèze, *Vie de Calvin*, in *Calvini Opera*, XXI, 45. For a full description of the last months of Calvin's life, with copious quotations from relevant sources, see Emile Doumergue, *Jean Calvin, les hommes et les choses de son temps* (Lausanne and Neuilly-sur-Seine, 1899-1927), VII, 443-470.

[2] Calvin to Bullinger, 2 July 1563, in *Calvini Opera*, XX, 53-54.

[3] Jean Calvin, " Discours d'adieu aux ministres," *ibid.*, IX, 892.

in France on how to adapt themselves to an environment which continued to be basically hostile. And until the end, he maintained his correspondence with the powerful French aristocrats who were his main hope for the conversion of the entire kingdom. One of his last letters had been to his old patroness, Renée, Duchess of Ferrara. Its main purpose had been to urge the duchess to encourage her niece, the Duchess of Savoy, to make open announcement of her adhesion to the Reformed faith.[1]

These concerns of the dying Calvin, point to the central problem upon which this book, like its predecessor, *Geneva and the Coming of the Wars of Religion in France, 1555-1563* (Geneva: Droz, 1956), concentrates: the problem of the nature and extent of Geneva's role in sixteenth-century French politics. The point of departure has again been the manuscript records of the Geneva Company of Pastors, this time almost entirely unpublished, which are preserved in the Geneva *Archives d'Etat* and the Geneva *Bibliothèque publique et universitaire*. When I began work on this sequel study, I expected to find that these records would reveal a geographical broadening of the interests and activities of the Geneva Company of Pastors. For the years following Calvin's death were years of growing triumphs for the Calvinist movements outside of France, particularly in Scotland and the Low Countries. Somewhat to my surprise, I discovered that France remained the area which absorbed most of the interest of the men of Geneva. They did not ignore developments in Scotland and the Low Countries, but they did not follow them as carefully or attempt to exercise as much supervision over them as they did for France. The main geographic area which interested them outside of France was Germany. The rapid growth of a Calvinist movement in the Rhenish Palatinate, and the challenge to that movement posed by an increasingly rigid and conservative Lutheranism, created the biggest non-French problem to occupy the attention of the Genevan pastors. These facts pose a great central irony: in the areas in which the Calvinist movement received its greatest supervision from Geneva—in France and Germany—it ultimately failed; in those in which it was left relatively free to follow the lead of local Calvinists—in Scotland and the Low Countries—it scored its greatest ultimate successes. There are many possible explanations of this central irony. To some of them we shall return later. For the most part, however, this book will concentrate on the foreign problems which most preoccupied the leaders in Geneva themselves, the problems of France. The problems they dealt with in Germany are also important and interesting, and merit further study, but they can easily be set aside for separate treatment.

The precise problems which the Reformed movement faced in France in the years following Calvin's death, took, naturally enough, a somewhat different shape than they had assumed during his lifetime. Problems of organizing churches for the first time, and of acquainting the public with doctrines which were relatively new, tended to fade away. Problems of consolidating a church already established, of maintaining discipline within it, and of protecting it from the increasingly formidable challenges of a revived Roman Catholic Church and a suspicious government, became more prominent. They were to be replaced in turn, by the problems of sheer survival posed by

---

[1] Calvin to the Duchess of Ferrara, 4 April 1564, *ibid.*, XX, 278-279.

the appalling St. Bartholomew's massacres of 1572. That event provides a natural terminus to this study.

Consolidation, therefore, is the primary characteristic of the Calvinist movement in the period upon which this book concentrates. We shall begin our consideration of this period of consolidation with an analysis of the situation in Geneva itself. We shall consider both the internal development of the Geneva Company of Pastors, in these years of re-organization following Calvin's death, and the program of Genevan missionary activity, in these years clouded by increasing violence in France.

We shall then turn to rather lengthy consideration of two fundamental problems with which French Protestants wrestled during this period. One was the problem of precisely what kind of ecclesiastical structure should be built to give institutional form to the French Reformed Church. The other was the problem of precisely how that Church should relate itself to a hostile French state.

The first of these problems was the subject of an extended controversy which rocked the French Reformed Church internally for more than a decade, and which helped expose it to continually stronger external attacks for an even longer period. The parties to the internal controversy were led by Jean Morély and Theodore Beza. Jean Morély, sire de Villiers, was an active Calvinist layman. He attracted to his cause a number of clergymen and a number of other laymen, some of whom were considerably more prominent than he. The best known of them is probably Peter Ramus. These men sought substantial autonomy for local congregations in church polity, a greater role for the laity in church government, and less clerical control over the morals and ideas of ordinary church members. In short they developed a platform which we might label "Congregational." Beza, of course, was Calvin's real successor as international spiritual leader of the movement. He was supported by most of his fellow clergymen and by most of the military leaders of French Protestantism. These men sought substantial control over church affairs by regional synods, a more powerful clergy with more precisely defined functions, and the control of morals and ideas by ecclesiastical institutions on the model of the Genevan Consistory. In short they developed a platform which we might label "Presbyterian."

There are several reasons for considering this internal controversy at length. It raised issues of growing and continuing importance in later church history, particularly in the church history of Britain and America. These issues helped to define Calvinism, as separate from other Protestant movements. In consequence, these issues must be of interest today, particularly to those seeking grounds upon which Christian churches can be re-united. Even without considering more remote times and places, however, one can argue that this internal quarrel was of great importance. It absorbed much of the energies of the French Reformed leadership, both lay and clerical, for the better part of a critical decade. Even after it was ended, with Beza's complete victory, it left significant scars.

In addition, this internal controversy became well enough known outside of Reformed circles, to color Gallican and Catholic attitudes toward the Calvinist movement. Indeed it fanned a second controversy, this one between the French Reformed and certain outsiders. These outsiders were typified by Charles du Moulin, the famous French jurisconsult, who, for a time, had been a Calvinist, who drifted to other Protestant positions, and who was eventually to die, so it was claimed, back in the bosom of the Roman Catholic Church. Shortly before he died, du Moulin charged, in virulent published polemics, that Calvinism was bent on creating a "state within the state," with its own set of new and foreign ecclesiastical institutions, which would usurp important social functions heretofore reserved to the old Church and the secular government. In so doing, he attacked many of the same institutions Morély opposed. Both attacks contributed in important ways to the growing disenchantment among the French population with the Reformed Church.

Neither of these two controversies has received extended attention from scholars in any country. The nature and scope of them both, however, can be reconstructed in some detail from the surviving records, many of which are unpublished. It is upon these records that much of this study will be based.

The second fundamental problem upon which we shall concentrate was a subject of recurrent debate during the entire early history of French Calvinism. Faced with fierce persecution which was either stimulated or condoned by a hostile state, French Protestants were recurrently tempted to armed resistance. These temptations were particularly strong for the great aristocrats who provided the temporal leadership of the French Protestant party. Several times during the short span of years upon which this study concentrates, these temptations became acute. They forced decisions which raised for these leaders that great moral problem, recurrent throughout the sixteenth century, of the extent to which armed resistance to constituted political authorities can be justified. Whenever they did decide on war, they were also faced with the material problems of how to gather the armies and matériel needed to support a revolt which would have a reasonable hope of success. For help with both types of problems, they appealed to Geneva. It is upon Geneva's responses to these appeals that we shall concentrate.

There are several reasons for also considering these appeals and responses at length. They should help fill out our knowledge of the development of the Calvinist resistance theory which made such a basic contribution to the revolutionary tradition in the West. And they may provide some instructive analogues to the problems which churches of the twentieth century face in dealing with hostile states.

Altogether, I hope to illustrate, to the extent to which one striking case study can, the ways in which the ideological center of a revolution develops and behaves, in a period of extension and consolidation, once the first bloom of fanatical enthusiasm and devotion have faded.

CHAPTER I

The Geneva Company of Pastors: Internal Developments, 1564-1572

Calvin's death forced the Geneva Company of Pastors to make quickly one really crucial decision. They had to elect a new Moderator. This office was an important but delicate one. Calvinists were generally too suspicious of the episcopal system to look with favor upon the development of any office which resembled that of a bishop in concentrating considerable ecclesiastical power within the hands of one man. All the ecclesiastical powers which in the Genevan situation could be claimed by the church, therefore, were concentrated in the Company of Pastors as a body. The Moderator was simply a presiding officer, who chaired the Company's weekly meetings, and who represented it before the governing Small Council of the Genevan Republic. Calvin's forceful personality, however, had given the office an importance transcending its constitutional nature. This importance was increased by the fact that he held the office for life. Small wonder, then, that some of his more distant and less informed supporters began calling him "Bishop of Geneva." [1]

It was no doubt partly to avoid this sort of misunderstanding, and certainly to avoid the possibility of a real episcopal system ever becoming established in Geneva, that Theodore Beza insisted that the office of moderator be changed somewhat following Calvin's death. In accordance with his suggestion, it was agreed that a moderator be elected every year. Beza himself, despite his protests of his own insufficiency, was immediately elected moderator, on June 2, 1564,[2] just one week after Calvin's death. He was to hold the office without interruption until 1580, but always as a result of annual election, and occasionally over his renewed protests of his insufficiency and his argument that someone else should take the job.

No one was surprised that Beza was chosen to be Calvin's successor. He had already served as Moderator, on an interim basis, in the months of Calvin's final illness. The choice of Beza, however, suggests much and explains something of the change in temper the Calvinist movement was to undergo in

---

[1] E.g. the Church of Is sur Thil to Calvin, *Calvini Opera*, XIX, 34, 8 October 1561, addresses Calvin as " evesque et surveillant en trouppeau et esglise chrestienne de Geneve et Scindicq dicelle cité. "

[2] Geneva, RCP, Kingdon & Bergier, eds., II, 102-104, 2 June 1564.

the years following its founder's death. Calvin had been noted, as few men ever are, for the power of his intellect and the charismatic impact of his personality. Beza was also a man of intellect and personality.[1] But there were differences. Beza's formal qualifications for intellectual eminence were, if anything, superior to Calvin's. His reputation as an elegant Latin stylist was deservedly high. Montaigne regarded him as one of the greatest Latin poets of the century.[2] His knowledge of Greek was thorough and constantly useful, in his translations of Scripture, his teaching, and his scholarly publications. Linguistic competence of this sort was of prime importance to anyone making his way as a sixteenth-century intellectual. Beza was also thoroughly acquainted with the contents of the writings of antiquity. He saw to it that the new Academy of Geneva had a thoroughly classical foundation to its curriculum. Indeed, he was responsible for a return to Aristotle,[3] a striking development in the history of Protestant education, which finds its parallels in the work of Melanchthon at Wittenberg. Still, with all his gifts, Beza never became an original theologian.[4] His thought never had the independence of that of Calvin. He was almost always content to follow the thought of his master—to reaffirm, to elaborate, to codify—some would say to make more rigid—but not to modify or strike out in new directions.

Beza's personality also had a different impact. Perhaps this was because of his social background. He came from a minor noble family, headquartered in the Burgundian town of Vézelay, a family probably capable of supplying him with more money and security than Calvin's. Or perhaps Beza's personality was different for less tangible reasons. In any event, his student years, at Orleans and Paris, seem to have been pleasant and easy. Throughout his life he seems to have been more gregarious and more polished socially than the intense and somewhat awkward Calvin.

A possible further consequence of Beza's relatively high social standing, may have been his almost pathological hatred of religious groups which threatened to break the organizational unity of the Reformed churches. The lower-class origins of some of these groups may well have provided a social reinforcement to his theological revulsion against them. Not that the particular groups against which he did battle had to have lowly origins to draw his ire. As we shall see, some of the men with whom he argued most vehemently in the decade following Calvin's death, were of social origins fully as distinguished as his own. But the fear, posed by the sectarian assault on Lutheran orthodoxy in the early days of the Reformation, that the whole movement would dissolve in quarreling sects or would be wiped out by the enraged forces of social order, seems to have been even more deeply grounded in Beza than

---

[1] Most of the factual information on Beza which follows, can be found in P.-F. Geisendorf, *Beza*, the most recent good biography.

[2] Pierre Villey, *Les sources et l'évolution des Essais de Montaigne* (Paris: Hachette, 1908), vol. I, *Les sources et la chronologie des Essais*, pp. 77-78.

[3] See C. Borgeaud, *Université*, I, *passim*, particularly Beza to Ramus letter, 1 December 1570, quoted on pp. 113-114, insisting on the fundamental importance of Aristotle in the Geneva curriculum.

[4] Some would argue that his return to Aristotle and his rigidity injected a significant new degree of rationalism into Protestant theology. See Ernst Bizer, *Frühorthodoxie und Rationalismus*, vol. 71 in Karl Barth and Max Geiger, eds., *Theologische Studien* (Zürich: EVZ, 1963), especially pp. 6-15.

it was in most of the leading Reformers. From the very beginning, he had been noted as an exceedingly virulent polemicist. His polemical temper did not diminish in his years of greater responsibility as Calvin's successor.

A more certain consequence of Beza's social standing, was the entrée it gave him to the aristocratic circles which were of such vital importance to the Reformed cause. Even before Calvin's death, Beza began to replace his master as the movement's chief representative in these circles. It had been Beza, not Calvin, who went to the Court of French Navarre, to advise its leaders in a plot against the French crown.[1] It had been Beza, not Calvin, whom the powerful Protestant leaders at the Court of France had invited to lead the Protestant delegation of theologians to the Colloquy of Poissy, that signal attempt to reconcile Protestants and Catholics under the auspices of the royal court. It had been Beza, not Calvin, who had accompanied the Prince of Condé on the initial campaigns of the first war of religion in France, and who had helped represent Condé at the courts of several German Protestant princes. In the years following Calvin's death, Beza continued to play his role of key adviser to the Huguenot princes. He traveled often to France to reinforce his written advice with the effective personal persuasions of which he was capable.

The ease with which Beza was elected Moderator in 1564, however, concealed weaknesses in his position. Calvin's passing had created an important vacuum and no mere election could fill it. The strains which are placed upon any group charged with the responsibility of providing collective leadership to a dynamic and even revolutionary social movement, were soon revealed. And these strains were complicated in the Genevan situation by the delicate and not yet fully resolved problems of the precise relations between the city's ecclesiastical and political institutions. Several times during the ensuing decade, Beza's leadership of the Company of Pastors was sorely tested.

In this leadership, Beza's chief allies came to be the members of the city's governing Small Council. From the beginning ties of social position, social conservatism, and mutual respect, had brought them into an easy working partnership. His chief local opposition came from his fellow ministers. And it came from the ablest of them. Some had been closely associated with Calvin for a long time, and were Beza's equal in age and experience. Others were bright young men, with the resentment of authority not uncommon in the breed.

The first challenge which Beza had to face came from one of Calvin's most distinguished collaborators, who had played a distinguished part in the growth of the movement in France. He was Jean-Raymond Merlin, who had been Beza's colleague on the faculty of the Lausanne Academy, as teacher of Hebrew, who had moved to Geneva in the general exodus of ministers provoked by Bernese opposition to certain key Calvinist doctrines and practices, who had been sent from Geneva to serve as chaplain to Admiral Coligny, and who had assisted Jeanne d'Albret, Queen of Navarre, in establishing the

---

[1] That this was an important reason for Beza's visit to Nérac in 1560, has recently been demonstrated by Alain Dufour, " L'affaire de Maligny (Lyon, 4-5 septembre 1560) vue à travers la correspondance de Calvin et de Bèze," *Cahiers d'histoire publiés par les universités de Clermont-Lyon-Grenoble,* VIII/3 (1963), 269-280.

Reformation in her home territory of Béarn.[1] He had returned to his post in Geneva shortly after Calvin's death.

Merlin's opposition was triggered by the decisions surrounding the Company's arrangements for spiritual care to victims of the plague. A renewed epidemic hit Geneva in 1564. As was usual, plague victims were removed from the city to a special pestilential hospital outside the walls, maintained only for this purpose.[2] And as was also usual, the Company was faced with the agonizing problem of deciding how to provide consolation and to administer sacraments to those sick of the plague. After lengthy debate, the Company finally decided to maintain earlier customs, and to choose one of its number by lot for this dangerous chore. The Company also decided to exempt Beza from the lottery. This latter decision was by no means a unanimous or immediate one, however. Several members, including Beza himself, argued that no one should be exempt. They pointed to the fact that many of the most prominent Reformed leaders in other cities, men like Bucer of Strasbourg, Bullinger of Zurich, Oecolampadius of Basel, had willingly ministered to victims of plague. They pointed out that Calvin himself had done so, when minister in Strasbourg. Against these arguments stood the Genevan tradition that the Moderator be exempt. Also against them stood the city Council's strongly expressed opinion that Beza should not be permitted to incur this risk. This, indeed, is one of the earliest signs of the high esteem in which they held him and of the importance they attached to his leadership in the Reformed church. The Council was even willing to go so far as to excuse all the pastors from this dangerous duty, and to permit them to hire supernumeraries to serve in the pestilential hospital. That suggestion was quickly rejected, however.[3] The scandal raised by an earlier failure of the Genevan pastors to minister to plague victims, decades ago, had not been entirely forgotten.

Accordingly, the Company proceeded to the drawing of lots. The result of an elaborate procedure was the selection of Jean Le Gaigneux,[4] a brilliant recent addition to the pastoral corps. Le Gaigneux did not take up his functions immediately, however. He asked to be excused for a short while, until his mother should leave town, since news of this risky assignment would surely upset her. The Council found this request entirely reasonable, and granted it readily.[5] Its members soon became impatient, however, when Le Gaigneux continued to delay in assuming his new duties. And impatience turned to anger, when he finally began ministering to the plague victims by shouting at them through windows from a trellis outside their rooms, rather

---

[1] On Merlin, see *France protestante*, 1st ed., art. "Merlin."

[2] See Léon Gautier, *La médecine à Genève jusqu'à la fin du XVIIIe siècle*, MDG, XXX (1906), ch. IV and *passim*, on measures taken to deal with these epidemics. N.B. pp. 159-163 re arrangements for ministry to religious needs of plague victims.

[3] See Geneva, RCP, Kingdon & Bergier, eds., II, 106-109, August 1564, for record of these deliberations.

[4] *Ibid.*, p. 108. For more on Le Gaigneux, see *France protestante*, 1st ed., art. "Le Gaigneux."

[5] Geneva, Arch., RC, LIX, 21 August 1564, cited in E. Choisy, *Genève au temps de Bèze*, p. 14.

than actually approaching them physically.[1] Reports of this unorthodox procedure provoked one of the governing syndics of the city to speak very sharply to Pastor Raymond Chauvet, apparently acting as Moderator of the Company of Pastors while Beza was gone on a mission to Berne. This reprimand was quickly followed by one addressed to the Company as a whole, which asked them to see to it that Le Gaigneux did his duty. If they did not, the Council said that it would have to " command " the Company formally to remedy the situation.

It was this reprimand, and particularly the threat to " command " the pastors, which upset Merlin. He was so upset that he decided to denounce the government in public, in a sermon. His fellows in the Company tried to dissuade him, but to no avail. On Wednesday, October 18, 1564, he let himself go. He preached an entire sermon on relations between civil and ecclesiastical authorities. It began with a demonstration of the civil magistrate's duty " to maintain the order which God established in His Church," a demonstration supported by appeal to the example of such Old Testament kings as David, Hezekiah (" Ezechias "), Josiah (" Josias "), and Joash (" Joas "). It then turned to the dangers of " tyranny " in the government of the church, a danger illustrated by the pope's assumption of the role of " head of the church " and more recently by the King of England's claim to be " head of the Anglican Church." It then settled on the Genevan scene. Merlin claimed it was " tyranny " for the Council to grant letters for reception at communion, since a Consistory had been established to handle such matters. And he accused the Council of " pure tyranny " in its recent threat to command the Company of Pastors on a matter which was purely ecclesiastical.

The violence of Merlin's attack surprised and upset the Council. In its very next session, it voted to summon the ministers to tell them of, " the regret that Messieurs [of the Council] felt and that it has never been their intention to want to usurp the authority of the church, which they claim to maintain to the pleasure of God." [2]

Merlin's violence also upset his fellow ministers. It irritated them, too, since they had urged him not to make public his feelings on the matter. Formal action on the case, however, was not handled by either Council or Company. Instead it was turned over to the Consistory, an institution specifically created for the maintenance of ecclesiastical discipline. All the city pastors were automatically members of it. It also included the elders of the Genevan church, laymen elected annually to this office, by a procedure which made it certain that several councillors and a syndic would always be members. The Consistory met once a week to act on breaches of ecclesiastical discipline. A high percentage of its cases dealt with minor sexual offenses and breaches of the peace. But more serious cases were also referred to it, including some involving schism or heresy.

---

[1] This, and all further details of this controversy (except as noted), are taken from the official record of Merlin's trial before the Consistory, in Geneva, Arch., RConsistoire, XXI, fols. 145v.-147v., 20 October 1564.

[2] Geneva, Arch., RC, LIX, fol. 121, 19 October 1564; quoted in E. Choisy, *Genève au temps de Bèze*, p. 21. Pp. 20-24 contain a brief account of the entire Merlin affair. Cf. the account in A. Roget, *Hist. de Genève*, VII, 99-104.

A special session of the Consistory was called to consider the scandal raised by Merlin's sermon, only two days after it had been delivered. Beza, back in town now, was on hand to attend this session. After a lengthy examination of the problem, the Consistory reached the conclusion that Merlin's sermon had been unfair to the magistracy and marked a dangerous breach in ministerial discipline. It decided that Le Gaigneux had been at fault and that his colleagues probably should have done something to force him to do his duty. The councillors had only done their duty in pointing this out to the ministers. It also decided that Merlin should never have ignored the advice of the other ministers in preaching a sermon on this matter. Such departure from Company discipline could only be called schismatic. It entailed the serious risk of dividing the church and opening the door to heresy. It had to be punished. Merlin was ordered to apologize in public and to promise that he would be bound in the future by the consensus of the Company of Pastors. When he refused to do so, the Council, on the Consistory's recommendation, ordered Merlin deposed from the ministry,[1] thus ending by swift action a long and distinguished career in the service of the Reformed faith.

Deposition of Merlin only provoked fresh scandal, however. The Consistory immediately had to cope with several cases of townspeople accused of having said that Merlin had been dismissed for "having said the truth from the pulpit."[2] The most serious of these cases involved one Pierre Fort, a book dealer, nephew of the prominent local printer Artus Chauvin. Fort's case, complicated by his evasions under questioning, was finally referred to the Council for criminal proceedings.[3] To stop talk of this sort, the Council, at the Consistory's urging, authorized the ministers to explain the reasons for Merlin's dismissal fully from their pulpits on a given Sunday.[4]

Word of the deposition soon began to spread beyond Geneva, furthermore. Before long Beza received a letter about the matter from Pierre Viret, the great popular preacher of the French Reformation, their former mutual colleague in Lausanne, now serving as chief pastor of the important metropolitan church of Lyon. Viret wanted precise information on the reasons for Merlin's dismissal. He particularly wanted to know if it was for causes that would keep him from being eligible for employment by the Lyon church. Merlin himself, of course, was anxious that Viret receive a reasonably mild explanation. This put the Company in an awkward position. Finally it was decided in Consistory to send Lyon an objective account of the whole affair, without any recommendation to hire Merlin but also without any recommendation that he not be hired. Beza himself drafted the statement.[5]

---

[1] Geneva, Arch., RConsistoire, XXI, fols. 151, 26 October 1564; 156-156v., 2 November 1564; RC, LIX, fols. 134, 135, 3 November 1564.

[2] Geneva, Arch., RConsistoire, XXI, fols. 167v.-168, 30 November 1564, words attributed to Pierre Fort. For fuller record of this and other similar cases, see fols. 158v., 9 November 1564; 167-168, 170-170v., 30 November 1564.

[3] Geneva, Arch., PC, No. 1245, 30 November-4 December 1564.

[4] *Ibid.*; Geneva, Arch., RConsistoire, XXI, fol. 170 v., 30 November 1564.

[5] Geneva, Arch., RConsistoire, XXI, fols. 175-175v., 7 December 1564; 178, 14 December 1564. Cf. fols. 157v.-158, 9 November 1564, for an earlier Consistorial decision that an account of Merlin's deposition be prepared, but that he be encouraged to seek a position as pastor elsewhere.

So ended the Merlin affair. Its outcome had been a triumph for the Company of Pastors as a group, for Beza as their leader, and for the city Council. The notion that an individual pastor could preach as he alone saw fit on a political matter had been rebuffed decisively. But the notion did not die. And the Merlin affair had established a pattern of protest. Succeeding cases of trouble became critical whenever a minister attacked the city's magistrates from the pulpit. The magistrates found these attacks intensely irritating, and their reactions became increasingly harsh and arbitrary. In these succeeding cases the Company of Pastors was again called upon to punish its offending member, and almost always did so, with an alacrity which often seems somewhat forced. In several of these cases, Beza was again actually out of town, on one of his many ecclesiastical, diplomatic, or private trips, at the time the offending sermon was preached. And in every case Beza was in the middle of the controversy and had to accept a large measure of responsibility for healing divisions within the Company of Pastors and for reconciling the Company and the Council.

For the time being, however, the Company of Pastors was able to join ranks following Merlin's dismissal and assume as before its double role of governing the church of Geneva and of directing the campaign to evangelize France. Jean Le Gaigneux, the brilliant young pastor whose behavior in the plague hospital had touched off the trouble, soon returned to the city, his services no longer needed as the plague had subsided. Some of his first sermons made some suspect that he approved of the course Merlin had followed. But he managed to persuade both the Company of Pastors and the Council that this had not been his intention.[1] And he resumed his rapid rise to prominence within the Genevan pastoral corps.

It is worth observing that rise. For Le Gaigneux was to be the storm center in further controversies within the Company. In 1565, he was loaned to the important Lyon church, at their request.[2] In 1566, he was a leading candidate for a professorship in theology at the Genevan Academy, a post made famous by Calvin, which Beza now found too demanding to fill alone. This professorship finally went to Nicolas Colladon, Calvin's faithful friend and assistant and the permanent Secretary of the Company of Pastors.[3] But only two years later, in 1568, Le Gaigneux's appointment to the faculty went through, and he became Rector, the principal administrative officer of the Academy.[4] Meanwhile Le Gaigneux had distinguished himself for his zeal and energy in other fields. Twice more the plague visited Geneva, and twice more the freakish operation of the lottery chose Le Gaigneux as minister to the plague victims, in 1568 and 1569.[5] He also began to distinguish himself as a preacher, and on occasions even spoke for the Company as a whole.

The most critical of these occasions involved renewed though minor clashes between Company and Council. Most of these clashes related to the

---

[1] A. Roget, *Hist. de Genève*, VII, 103-104.

[2] Geneva, Arch., RCP, Bl, fol. [26v.], 21 December 1565.

[3] *Ibid.*, fols. [30-30v.], June 1566; quoted in C. Borgeaud, *Université*, I, 105.

[4] Geneva, LR, Stelling-Michaud, ed., pp. 78, 98; latter quoted in C. Borgeaud, *Université*, I, 106, n. 5, from an earlier ed.

[5] E. Choisy, *Genève au temps de Bèze*, pp. 15-16.

administration of justice. Even before the Merlin affair, the Company objected that the Council was treating with too much leniency violators of the city's stringent sex laws.[1] These complaints were met by adoption of more stringent laws and, for a time, some exemplary punishments. But then complaints shifted to another sector. Several very prominent people, most notably one Amblard du Fossal, accused of several kinds of misbehavior, were let off with light punishments. The pastors charged that this amounted to social discrimination, to the application of one set of laws to the common people and another more lenient set to the rich and powerful. Anyone acquainted with the bewildering variety of punishments which Genevan courts imposed for crimes which seem superficially similar, can understand these charges. In the du Fossal case, for example, in 1564 the Council had judged him worthy of death. But he had exercised his right of appeal as a citizen to the Council of 200, which met only occasionally but did have certain kinds of appellate jurisdiction, and this body had let him off with a milder punishment.[2] In most of these protests to the Small Council, the Company of Pastors acted as a body.

Action as a body became impossible, however, in a case which arose in 1570. For this case involved a relative of Theodore Beza himself. His own niece was accused of adultery, of causing the death of her new-born baby, and of blasphemy. It was the blasphemy charge which divided the ministers. Beza insisted her words were harmless. Le Gaigneux and the other ministers insisted that they were blasphemous, and deserved among blasphemies a rank "most notable and exquisite." Beza urged mercy. The other ministers insisted on exemplary punishment. And while Beza was out of town on one of his numerous trips, the Council followed his colleagues' advice. Beza renewed his complaints on his return, but by then it was too late.[3]

Perhaps it was this case which split the Company of Pastors in two. Or perhaps growing animosity between Beza on the one hand and some of his ablest colleagues on the other, would have been fanned into controversy by any similar incident. At any rate, in 1571 controversy of a really dangerous sort broke out. Two principals in this controversy, as one might expect, were Le Gaigneux and Beza. But a third may surprise by his presence. It was Nicolas Colladon.

In fact it was with Colladon that the trouble began. He had been consulted by a party to a case involving the "change" or public bank which the Genevan authorities had recently established.[4] Its functions were to help the city discharge a municipal debt to the neighboring republic of Basel by providing certain banking services to the local population. It had been granted the extraordinary right to charge interest at the rate of 10%, a rate higher than the legal maximum permitted to private individuals. The ministers, on being consulted, had apparently permitted this unorthodox procedure, relying on

---

[1] Geneva, RCP, Kingdon & Bergier, eds., II, 109, July and September 1564.

[2] E. Choisy, *Genève au temps de Bèze,* pp. 10-11. Cf. pp. 45-46, re Le Gaigneux's public criticism of lenient treatment of du Fossal when the case was re-opened in 1567.

[3] See *ibid.*, pp. 40-44, for a fully documented account of this affair.

[4] For a full and expert study of this institution, see William Monter, "Le change public à Genève, 1568-1581," *Mélanges d'histoire économique et sociale en hommage au professeur Antony Babel* (Geneva, 1963), I, 265-290.

the argument that a rate of this sort could be regarded as equivalent to a tax rather than true interest.[1]

The bank's special privileges provoked some complaints from Genevans. More were provoked by irregularities in its administration. One such complaint was brought to Colladon, by a prominent parishioner who claimed that the municipal banker had paid a sum due to him in coins which were not legal tender. Colladon brought the matter to the attention of the Consistory, in hopes of resolving the quarrel between the two men. The Consistory referred it to the Council, which ordered the complainant to prison, pending further investigation, and asked Colladon to reveal all the information which the man had supplied to him. Colladon refused. He argued that it was privileged information, confided in him as a spiritual adviser. And he felt that the guilty party in the affair was the city official involved, not the man who had talked to him.[2] This in itself angered the Council. Their anger deepened when Colladon and Le Gaigneux both criticized the government in public sermons. And their anger was not mollified by the attitude of the rest of the Company of Pastors, which rather timidly supported Colladon.

Finally tempers cooled off somewhat. Under pressure Le Gaigneux and Colladon humbly apologized and were reconciled with their brethren and their governors. This was not a new experience for Le Gaigneux, who had had to apologize in this fashion several times since 1565, and who did not seem to find the experience too trying. It was newer and more difficult for Colladon, but finally he apologized too. To prevent scandals of this sort from arising again, however, it was agreed that in the future no minister would preach on a current political topic on his own account. Not that preaching of this sort was forbidden. It simply had to be discussed in the Company as a whole, and nothing could be said in public unless the Company as a whole agreed upon it.

It was too late, however, for measures of this sort to end friction. Only a few months later Colladon and Le Gaigneux again attacked the city government from the pulpit. Again Beza was out of town, this time in La Rochelle, where he served triumphantly as Moderator of the most significant national synod of the French Reformed Church to date, in the presence of Admiral Coligny, the Queen of Navarre, and a whole host of other notables. When he returned to Geneva to find the city in renewed turmoil, he lost his temper. He appeared before the Council to denounce Colladon and Le Gaigneux. He said that he found them so " completely intractable and hopeless "[3]

---

[1] This was the first of several arguments for the legitimacy of the " change," developed in a memoir presented to the Council by the Company of Pastors at the height of the ensuing controversy, and copied in Geneva, Arch., RC, LXVI, fols. 114-115, 14 September 1571. This memoir (with certain related documents) could provide the basis for a more developed study of a part of the economic ethics of the period. Its importance was noted by Monter, article cited, *Mélanges Babel,* I, 273-274 For some useful background, see Jean-François Bergier, " Taux de l'intérêt et crédit à court terme à Genève dans la seconde moitié du XVIe siècle," *Studi in onore di Amintore Fanfani,* IV (Milan : Giuffrè, 1962), 89-119, esp. 112, ff.

[2] E. Choisy, *Genève au temps de Bèze,* pp. 46-47. Pp. 46-63 contain a documented report of the entire controversy. Cf. the account in J.-A. Gautier, *Hist. de Genève,* V, 74-80, very partial to the Council.

[3] " du tout intraitable et hors d'esperance," Geneva, Arch., RC, LXVI, fol. 73v., 22 May 1571.

that he could no longer work with them, and he asked the Council to relieve him both of his post as pastor and of his post as Moderator.

The Council, of course, refused to accept Beza's resignation. Le Gaigneux rather abruptly left town. Since the pastoral corps was already seriously short-handed and since another epidemic was about to hit the city, his departure was deeply resented, apparently even by those who had been inclined to support him. Colladon, however, once more made his peace with the Council and the Company, and resumed his normal duties.

Not for long, however. A few months later, in the fall sermon preceding the quarterly administration of communion, designed to recall to the people those sins of which they must repent, Colladon plunged into troubled waters again. He had apparently been brooding for some time about the management of the public bank. He gave vent to these broodings by including its mismanagement, and particularly the usurious interest rates it charged, as among the sins for which Genevans should seek forgiveness. This immediately alarmed the authorities. They felt that Colladon was acting as if he wanted to " incite the people to mutiny." And again Beza was furious. He quickly appeared before the Council and said again that he could no longer exercise his charge in the Genevan Church. For good measure, he added that he had argued and was willing to argue again " by the word of God that the change at ten per cent is not excessive." He obviously felt that Colladon's sermon was a personal insult to him. He pointedly said that " one of the two must be a false prophet." And he urged strong action.[1]

The Council, of course, did not need much urging. It immediately ordered Colladon jailed and proceeded to a full-scale investigation. During the investigation some tempers cooled a bit. It was suggested that Colladon had only meant to attack the " changers, " not the principal of a " change " or bank.[2] But Colladon himself refused to accept this escape route. He remained defiant and absolutely refused to repent. He also retracted his previous recantations. In the circumstances, the Council felt that there was little that could be done but to depose him from the ministry, in spite of his seventeen years of faithful and effective service.[3] The Consistory then summoned him before them and informed him of their sorrow at his rebellion. He rather tartly informed them that he was not at all sorry himself—in fact he was quite happy.[4] Although somewhat provoked, the Consistory refrained from adding the penalty of excommunication, since they felt it would serve no useful purpose. Colladon left town, to begin a new and distinguished career as pastor and professor in Lausanne.[5] He took with him all the papers of the Company of Pastors which he had accumulated in his term as Company secretary, much to the displeasure of his remaining brethren.[6]

---

[1] *Ibid.*, LXVI, fol. 104, 27 August 1571.

[2] *Ibid.*, LXVI, fol. 106v., 3 September 1571.

[3] *Ibid.*, LXVI, fols. 111v.-112, 11 September 1571. Cf. fols. 106, 107, 108, 109-110v., 3-7 September 1571, re the cross-examination of Colladon.

[4] Geneva, Arch., RConsistoire, XXVIII, fol. 84v., 13 September 1571.

[5] On which see H. Vuilleumier, *Hist. de l'Egl. réf. du Pays de Vaud*, I and II, *passim.*

[6] On which see Hippolyte Aubert, " Nicolas Colladon et les registres de la Compagnie des pasteurs et professeurs de Genève," BSHAG, II (1898-1904), 138-163.

Colladon's dismissal, like Merlin's, unsettled the city considerably. Again people were questioned and punished for saying that he had been dismissed for preaching the truth.[1] The scandal was compounded this time when one of the young pastors of the village churches, undertook to defend Colladon publicly as a "good man" ("homme de bien") who had been unjustly deposed, in the weekly Congregation, a special service of Biblical study and discussion. This young pastor was Urban Chauveton, a relative of Colladon's. At Beza's urging, the Council, acting with scandalous haste, had Chauveton arrested before the service had even ended.[2] Although Chauveton showed every sign of repentance, and although he made a public retraction of his charges in the next meeting of the Congregation, the Council deposed him too.[3] Even the pleas of the Company of Pastors for more lenient treatment, could not halt their action. And to make crystal clear to the public the reasons for Colladon's deposition, a summary statement of them was drawn up and read by the Council secretary, at the same public Congregation which heard Chauveton's recantation.[4] The statement was cleverly worded to excuse both the Council and Beza for what had happened, and to lay all the blame on Colladon alone. Chauveton's dismissal did not have quite the consequences of the dismissals of Merlin and Colladon, however. The Company of Pastors found a teaching post to keep him occupied for the time being.[5] It was felt that his repentance and his youth were extenuating factors. Moreover the Company was so seriously short of personnel, due to death, resignation, and expulsion, that they did not want to lose yet another hand. Eventually he was even admitted to the "bourgeoisie" of the Genevan Republic,[6] and sent by the Company as a missionary pastor to France.

The controversy was not completely liquidated, of course, until Le Gaigneux made his peace with the Genevan authorities. He tried to do this several times from a distance, by mail or by negotiation from towns neighboring Genevan territory. But none of these gestures succeeded. And the letters of menace from Geneva pursued him to other Reformed communities, and made it impossible for him to do anything useful or effective in them.[7] So he finally decided to meet Geneva's conditions, for the last time as it turned out. He returned to the city, humiliated himself before Council and Consistory, after some hedging accepted the charges against him as a "deserter of his church, rebel against his oath, and a calumniator,"[8] accepted his deposition

[1] E.g. Geneva, Arch., RConsistoire, XXVIII, fol. 85, 13 September 1571, case of Jaques Pertine.

[2] Geneva, Arch., RC, LXVI, fol. 116v., 21 September 1571.

[3] *Ibid.*, fols. 118, 119-119v., 123v., 126, 27 September-12 October 1571. Cf. Geneva, Arch., RConsistoire, XXVIII, fols. 88v.-89, 90, 92v., 4 October-1 November 1571, for the Consistory's excommunication of Chauveton for the same offense, soon lifted.

[4] Geneva, Arch., RC, LXVI, fols. 119v.-121v., 28 September 1571.

[5] *Ibid.*, fol. 136v., 6 November 1571.

[6] Geneva, LB, p. 303, 2 June 1578.

[7] E.g. see Geneva, Arch., RCP, B2, fol. 56, 25 December 1571, fol. 58v., 15 January 1572, re successful attempts of the Genevan Company to have Le Gaigneux disciplined in Lyon.

[8] "deserteur de son eglise, ung rebelle contre son serment, et ung calomniateur," Geneva, Arch., RConsistoire, XXVIII, fol. 156, 19 June 1572. For more on these proceedings, see *ibid.*, fols. 140v., 158-158v.; RCP, B2, fols. 60v., 61, 62, 63-67; and especially Geneva, BPU, Ms. fr. 406, fols. 70-80, an entire dossier of relevant documents.

from the ministry, but did obtain the lifting of an excommunication order which had tormented him for months.[1] The extent to which he was willing to go, in order to win admission to the communion table, provides yet another striking example of the great power of excommunication as an instrument of social discipline in that age. For Le Gaigneux's humiliation did not bring him any more tangible benefits. His career was more or less wrecked. The fact of his quarrel with Geneva had received disastrously wide publicity, since the Genevans saw to it that notice of their displeasure with him was inserted in the minutes of one of the national synods of the French Reformed Church.[2] And while the Geneva Company, once he had made his peace with them, decided not to advise any other church for or against his selection as a pastor, they did decide to provide information on the facts of his deposition[3] which seems to have proved devastating. He seems to have ended his life in complete obscurity in a little Swiss village within that area around Lausanne dependent upon Berne.

It remains for us to consider the reasons and the consequences of these upsets within the Genevan Company of Pastors. The root reason, of course, was friction between the pastors and the magistrates. It took several forms—over control of pastoral activities, over civic economic policy particularly when it raised ethical problems. But an important auxiliary reason seems to have been personality conflicts within the Company of Pastors itself. Beza's open displays of temper twice in 1571, the obvious collapse of his ability to get along with Le Gaigneux and Colladon, helped make some sort of drastic action necessary. And these personality conflicts themselves may reflect a power struggle for Calvin's mantle. Or perhaps it would be fairer to say that they reflect an honest but sharp disagreement on the precise ways in which Calvin's ideas should be perpetuated.

The consequences of these upheavals are somewhat harder to judge. But they are of importance to this study. Of particular importance are the effects of these upheavals upon the Company's campaign to evangelize France. It would be easy to conclude that internal quarrels and dismissals hurt that campaign. The men who were dismissed after all, were among the ablest the Geneva Company possessed. Some of them had already performed yeoman service in French missionary work. Nicolas Colladon, particularly, had used his strategic position as Company secretary to further the work of Calvinist missionaries in France in many important ways. Merlin, Le Gaigneux, and Colladon had also all become very important parts of the teaching program which gave most of these missionaries their basic formation. Furthermore, the most serious of these upheavals, those of 1571, came at a particularly delicate time for the French Reformed Church. It was a time of political peace, of ecclesiastical consolidation, and of renewed missionary planning. It was a time marked by the great national synods of La Rochelle and Nîmes, both landmarks in the codification of French Reformed polity. Beza had

[1] Geneva, Arch., RConsistoire, XXVIII, fols. 160-160v., 3 July 1572.

[2] Held at Nîmes, 6-8 May 1572. See article XI of the "Matieres particulieres," text in J. Aymon, *Synodes*, I, 2nd pagination, 124; also in J. Quick, *Synodicon*, I, 113.

[3] Geneva, Arch., RCP, B2, fol. 70, 8 July 1572, re Company's response to an inquiry from the Church of Tours and Admiral Coligny.

to be present at both these synods, and must have been preoccupied a good deal of the time with the preparations and consequences of their deliberations. Several former Genevan ministers joined him in these preoccupations, notably Nicolas des Gallars.

But this natural conclusion may be too easy. Even during Calvin's lifetime, the Company had lost able men and yet had consequently gained in missionary efficiency. The expulsion of a man as able and as dedicated as Sebastien Castellio, for example, did not seem to weaken the movement's drive significantly. Indeed it may have strengthened that drive. The knife with the narrowest edge often cuts most deeply. Perhaps a revolutionary movement cannot hope to succeed if its impact is blunted by disunity among its leaders, whether that disunity be traced to diversity of belief or clash in personality. Other revolutions seem to have eaten their children without noticeably bad effects. At any rate, the succeeding chapters will give us some chance to judge the missionary effectiveness of the leadership supplied by the Geneva Company of Pastors to France during this same period.

CHAPTER II

The Geneva Company of Pastors: Its Mission to France, 1563-1572

Calvin's death did not force the Geneva Company of Pastors to modify significantly the tactics of the program for the conversion of France which they had launched so promisingly under his direction. But the years of his final illness and death did witness a sharp decline in the size of that program, and there was only a modest recovery from this decline. That, at least, is the development suggested by the Registers of the Company of Pastors for these years. Unless they are grossly unrepresentative, one must conclude that many fewer missionaries were dispatched during the period. This is perhaps the most striking fact to emerge from my study of the missionaries listed in these Registers. This and other raw facts which result from that study are tabulated in Appendix I to this book. An analytical summary of them is in order at this point. It must first be noted, however, that these conclusions are highly tentative and may have to be modified by future research. In particular, the research now proceeding under the direction of Professor Stelling-Michaud, for the critical edition of the Geneva Academy's *Livre du Recteur*, may force some modifications.[1] For many of the students whose careers are being pieced together by Stelling-Michaud and his assistants became missionaries to France, informally if not formally. Yet many of them are not listed in the pages of the Registers of the Company of Pastors. Still, the list that can be culled from those pages seems to me to constitute a reasonably representative sample. It is as an analysis of this sample that I present the following findings.

From the beginning of 1563 to the end of 1572, the Registers list but thirty-one men who were sent out as missionaries: twenty-eight to France; one to neighboring Lorraine; one to the neighboring Netherlands; one to England.[2] This total contrasts significantly with the eighty-eight who were sent to France alone in the preceding seven years,[3] plus nine or ten who were sent to Piedmont.[4] It can be demonstrated that the total of eighty-eight

[1] Products of this study so far published include S. Stelling-Michaud, ed., *Le livre du recteur de l'Académie de Genève (1559-1878)*, vol. 1, *Le texte*, and vol. 2, *Notices biographiques des étudiants, A-C* (Geneva: Droz 1959, 1966, vol. XXXIII in THR).

[2] For a list of their names, see Appendix I, table 1.

[3] R. M. Kingdon, *Geneva & Coming*, Appendix I.

[4] See Geneva, RCP, Kingdon & Bergier, eds., II, 62, 64, 68, 69, 74, 79, 81, 84, 105-106, for specific examples.

is grossly incomplete. No doubt the total of thirty-one is also quite incomplete. Still, I suspect that the proportion suggested by these figures is roughly accurate.

A closer look at the figures for 1563-1572 reveals rather sharp fluctuations. Two-thirds of these thirty-one were sent out in two years—1565 (8) and 1566 (13).[1] Only in 1566 did the number even approach the number which had become minimal in the years between 1557 and 1562.[2] Never did it approach the highs of 1558 and 1559, or the even greater high of 1561, unrecorded in these Registers.[3] Furthermore it dropped off sharply following 1566. Only one man went out in 1567. None at all departed in 1568, 1569, and 1570. Only two were sent in 1571. And of the two dispatched in 1572, neither went to France. While the Company's Registers are demonstrably fragmentary, and omitted, for example, mention of literally dozens of missionaries sent out in 1561, most of the supporting evidence for these later years tends to reinforce the impression created by these figures. The surviving files of the Company's correspondence, for example, are significantly thinner for these later years, and contain many fewer requests to Geneva for pastors. Pending further research, I think it reasonable to suppose that the Geneva missionary campaign in France regained some vigor in 1565 and 1566, but that it collapsed shortly thereafter, never to regain proportions of real significance.

Explanations of this curious collapse are not hard to uncover. Some lie in the Genevan situation ; some lie in the French. Within Geneva, the quarrels we have already noted among the pastors may well have diverted some energy from the high task of converting France. The death of Calvin, in itself, had robbed the city of its greatest single attraction to the idealistic French intellectuals who had made the best prospects as missionaries. Beza never did acquire a following among them to rival Calvin's. And none of his colleagues even approached Beza's modest reputation.[4] The ravages of the plague also scared away some potential missionaries. Several times during this decade epidemic disease hit Geneva hard, particularly in 1564, and 1568-1570. Student enrollments at the university dropped sharply.[5] The unorganized group of intellectuals clustered around the university, who never bothered to enroll, almost certainly also decreased in numbers. Political uncertainties in these same years also probably scared some away. The growing coolness between Zwinglian Berne and Calvinist Geneva, and the consequent weakening of the alliance between the two republics, which was almost essentîal to Geneva's independance, raised the real possibility of an

---

[1] See Appendix I, table 2, on dates of dispatch.

[2] R. M. Kingdon, *Geneva & Coming*, Appendix VI.

[3] *Ibid.*, p. 79.

[4] An interesting example of the decline of Geneva's ecclesiastical authority after Calvin's death can apparently be found in the history of the Waldensian churches of northern Italy. Giorgio Peyrot, "Influenze franco-ginevrine nella formazione delle discipline ecclesiastiche valdesi alla metà del XVI secolo," in Delio Cantimori, et al., eds., *Ginevra e l'Italia* (Florence : Sansoni, 1959), pp. 215-285, describes in considerable detail the powerful influence of Geneva on Waldensian discipline and ecclesiology, particularly from 1558 to 1564, but suggests, pp. 282-285, that it declined sharply after 1564.

[5] Particularly in the latter period. See C. Borgeaud, *Université*, I, 118-123.

attack on the city by Savoy. Fear of such an attack became particularly acute in 1567, when the Spanish armies under the Duke of Alva, bound for the repression of Protestantism in the Netherlands, passed through Savoyard territory close to Geneva.[1] This fear was reinforced by the Bernese cession to Savoy in that same year of country districts bordering the Genevan territories which had been held by the Bernese since the beginning of the Genevan Reformation and had constituted an invaluable buffer against attack upon the republic.[2] No actual attack was launched against Geneva for decades. But its very possibility alarmed the entire Genevan community, and must have given pause to some who otherwise might have come there.

Within France, competition may have cut into the Genevan effort. A well-subsidized new Academy in Orleans, for example, headed by ex-Genevan pastor Nicolas des Gallars, promised for a while to provide an important new source of pastors. While war and the attendant political uncertainties quickly forced its dissolution, other such academies were established successfully, e.g. in Nîmes.[3] War in itself, however, probably provides the chief reason for the French failure to demand more pastors of Geneva. Each placement of a missionary depended on an invitation from a French congregation. In years of open warfare, such invitations were either not forthcoming, or could not be honored because of chaotic travel conditions. The years of Geneva missionary activity, therefore, coincide almost exactly with the years of peace within France. The first war of religion, 1562-1563, led to a sharp initial cut in the number of missionaries sent. The return of peace in the latter year led to a somewhat delayed revival, reaching its peak in 1566. But the return of war in 1567, and its continuation with only the briefest of interruptions until 1570, abruptly halted the missionary campaign. Peace again in 1571 permitted a new beginning, but it was savagely cut short by the St. Bartholomew's massacres in 1572 and the consequent return of war, this time on a more desparate and fanatical scale than ever before. This clear demonstration of the importance of peace to Calvinist evangelism, gives the lie to those who claim that Calvinism posed a military threat to Catholic France in 1572, which justified the massacres.[4]

Even when France was at peace, moreover, peace was only relative. In some provinces Calvinist evangelism could be revived without much difficulty. In others, increasingly militant and vigilant Catholic factions saw to it that everything possible was done to harass the work of the Calvinists. As a result, Calvinist activity came to be concentrated even more than before

---

[1] A. Roget, *Hist. de Genève*, VII, 207-228.

[2] *Ibid.*, VII, 229-235. For a recent study of the consequences of Savoyard re-occupation within the ceded areas, see Paul-E. Martin, *Trois cas de pluralisme confessionel aux XVIe et XVIIe siècles* (Geneva : Jullien, 1961). N.B. pp. 53-55, on 1567.

[3] P.-Daniel Bourchenin, *Etude sur les Académies protestantes en France au XVIe et au XVIIe siècle* (Paris, 1882). Pp. 97-107 sketch the history of the Academy of Nîmes. On the Academy of Orleans, see N. Weiss, " Une des premières écoles de théologie protestantes en France (Orléans 1561-1568)," BSHPF, LX (1911), 218-224.

[4] E.g. Ludwig von Pastor, *The History of the Popes*, XIX (London, 1930), 509-513, justifies, not the massacres themselves, but papal and curial rejoicing over them, on the grounds that in 1572 French Calvinism posed a direct military threat to Roman Catholics throughout Europe, and to Rome itself.

in certain provinces. Above all it came to be concentrated in the great provinces of southwestern France: Guyenne, Gascony, and Languedoc.[1] Here it was protected by the military might of the most powerful among the Huguenot aristocrats. Among these the most prominent was Jeanne d'Albret, Queen of Navarre, a convert to Calvinist Protestantism, who encouraged both morally and materially the spread of her new faith within her domains.[2] Her lands and such other portions of these provinces as the Agennais and Vivarais, attracted a substantial portion of the missionaries sent out in these years. Altogether nine went to these provinces, slightly less than a third of the total. Even as important a Catholic stronghold within this area as Bordeaux acquired a Calvinist pastor, and it got one of the most prominent, Jacques des Bordes, whose abilities had won him a post on the faculty of the Geneva Academy several years earlier.

The remainder of the missionaries were scattered widely among the provinces of France. A number continued to go to such metropolitan centers as Orleans and Lyon. The provinces of Aunis, Saintonge, and Angoumois, which provide the hinterland for La Rochelle, soon to become the chief military bastion of French Protestantism, drew a few.

Other areas surprise by their absence, however. No new missionaries are listed as being sent to Paris or anywhere in the Ile-de-France. This despite the fact that Paris had been a major center for Calvinist growth in the previous decade, and continued, as we shall see, to be of considerable importance in the internal affairs of the French Reformed Church during this decade. Parisian Calvinists did face, to be sure, growing opposition in these years, most of it directed by leaders of the capital's important university community. These leaders were importing expert Reformed Catholic controversialists such as the Jesuit Juan Maldonado,[3] seeing to it that the Paris churches were staffed with fiercely anti-Protestant preachers, securing from the courts and the crown a variety of local anti-Protestant laws.

Dauphiné was another province to which no new missionaries were dispatched, according to these registers, even though it had been an important center of early Calvinism and was strategically close to Geneva itself. However research in other materials reveals that the province did in fact continue to receive missionaries from Geneva.[4]

Underlining the importance of political factors in the geographic distribution of these missionaries, is the fact that many of them were again sent directly to the courts of powerful Huguenot noblemen. They became chaplains to these aristocrats, although most of them ministered to local congregations as well. Most prominent among the aristocrats who received chaplains from Geneva in this decade were Antoine de Croy, Prince of Porcien, and Jean d'Estrées, Baron of Dodenville. The Prince of Porcien was a nephew-in-law

---

[1] See Appendix I, table 3.

[2] [Alphonse] de Ruble, *Jeanne d'Albret et la guerre civile* (Paris, 1897), ch. 1, describes in detail the queen's role in the evangelization of Guyenne, particularly in 1561.

[3] On whose career, see *Dictionnaire de théologie catholique*, art. "Maldonat, Jean."

[4] E. Arnaud, *Histoire des protestants du Dauphiné aux XVIe XVIIe et XVIIIe siècles*, I (Paris, 1875), 210-214, supplies evidence that the Reformed churches of Dauphiné did obtain a few new pastors between 1563 and 1567, and corresponded with Geneva about some of these placements.

to the Prince of Condé and one of his principal aides in the command of the Huguenot armies; d'Estrées was a former master of the royal artillery, and proved to be only a temporary recruit to the Protestant side.[1] These particular placements, significantly, gave the Calvinists entry to provinces of considerable strategic importance. Porcien's headquarters were in Champagne, close to those of the fanatically Catholic Guise family, leaders of the political opposition. D'Estrées' headquarters were in nearby Picardy, close to the border of the Spanish Netherlands.

Of somewhat less significance, is the geography of these missionaries' places of origin.[2] A good number came from the great southern provinces, Guyenne, Gascony, and Languedoc, again nearly a third of the total. Most of these were sent straight back to their home provinces, logically enough. Certain provinces may not have supplied Geneva with the raw material for their own leadership, however. None are listed as coming from the Orleannais; none from the provinces backing La Rochelle. If such a deficit existed it was no doubt filled partly by men who came from provinces where there was relatively little continuing Calvinist strength—Burgundy, for example. Practically no missionaries seem to have come from the great cities upon which the Calvinist evangelical effort had been concentrated in the beginning.

This last fact suggests a shift in the class basis of the Calvinist ecclesiastical leadership—from urban to rural elements, perhaps, or from upper to lower classes of society. A closer look at the most accessible surviving sources of information on the actual class background of the thirty-one,[3] suggests that this may be true, but does not provide really convincing proof. A certain number of the pastors continued to come from noble families—apparently three, or about ten per cent of the total. This percentage is substantially smaller than before.[4] These nobles continued to be men of some prominence in the ministry, assigned to charges of importance. None of them reached the heights in the Calvinist hierarchy attained by nobles recruited in the preceding decades, men such as Beza and des Gallars, but then the top posts were already pre-empted by these earlier arrivals.

Probably most of the pastors continued to be of the middle classes. This is at least suggested by the fact that a full eight, somewhat less than a third of the total, seem to have been members of the Genevan bourgeoisie. Six were formally enrolled within the book which provided legal evidence of that privileged status. Of these six, five had been admitted to the bourgeoisie free of charge, for services rendered to the city, generally either in teaching or preaching, while one, Jean de Léry, had purchased his right to bourgeois status, the normal method of entry for men not in positions of special utility to the city. Two others had probably acquired the bourgeois rights through ties of blood: Paul Baduel's father, Claude, had become bourgeois on payment of fee, and in the normal course of things the rights of the position should have been inherited by his son; Estienne Digne's relative, Antoine, had similarly entered the bourgeoisie on payment of fee, and the rights of the position may well

---

[1] On these men, see *France protestante*, 2nd ed., arts. "Croy" and "Estrées."

[2] See Appendix I, table 4.

[3] Appendix I, table 5.

[4] Cf. R. M. Kingdon, *Geneva & Coming*, Appendix II.

have been passed on to Estienne as well. What little evidence we have on the background of these men suggests that they came from families of roughly the same station as those they were joining in the Genevan bourgeoisie. Jacques des Bordes, for example, was son of a public prosecutor in Bordeaux, and had been studying in medicine when he felt called to theology.[1]

It is possible that some of the thirty-one pastors came from yet humbler backgrounds. A certain number of them came from small towns in Guyenne or Gascony, where they would have had to have been bourgeois of a rather modest sort if bourgeois at all.

Whatever their ultimate class backgrounds, however, most of these missionaries had again been thoroughly trained for precisely the kind of work they were to be doing in France. A good number, thirteen to be precise, had been students in the Geneva Academy shortly before dispatch.[2] A fourteenth had been a student there at an earlier period. This adds up to nearly half of all the men listed as having been sent out. Many of these students had been sent to Geneva at the expense of local congregations in France for formation as pastors, and were returned to their sponsoring communities, after only a year or two of training. They would necessarily have been quite inexperienced. This represented some departure from earlier practice.[3] However the Genevans no longer had the option, open to them in earlier years, of sending such men to minor pastorates in the other provinces of French Switzerland for seasoning. The quarrel with Berne had made that impossible. So many more of them had to get their seasoning in France.

It was still possible for these missionaries to acquire experience in Geneva itself, or in the villages dependent on the city, however, and a significant number of them did. Seven of the thirty-one had been pastors in Geneva. Seven of them had been teachers—five in the Academy, two as tutors to children. Since several of the Academy professors also held pastoral appointments, the total who had acquired professional experience in Geneva comes to eleven. Two of the Academy professors had also served as pastors in the area around Lausanne. In addition, one man had been a pastor in France and simply came to Geneva for re-assignment. Another had been a teacher in Lorraine, and came to Geneva for a period of study, before assignment back to his original community. Adding these two to the total of eleven who had served in Geneva, we get a total of thirteen men who had some kind of practical training for the work they were about to undertake in France.

Of these thirteen, however, three had also been recent students. That means that a total of twenty-four of the thirty-one pastors were professionally prepared for their tasks—eleven by formal education alone, thirteen by formal work as teachers or preachers. In this course of preparation, twenty-three of the twenty-four had been subject to the direct supervision of the Geneva Company of Pastors. This suggests strongly that the overwhelming

---

[1] *France protestante*, 2nd ed., art. " Des Bordes " ; Viret to Calvin, a letter including a recommendation of Des Bordes, 9 April 1562, *Calvini Opera*, XIX, 379-380, quoted in C. Borgeaud, *Université*, I, 77.

[2] See Appendix I, table 6, on the missionaries' occupations at the time of assignment to France.

[3] See R. M. Kingdon, *Geneva & Coming*, ch. 2, for description of this earlier practice.

majority of the missionaries, a significantly greater percentage than in the earlier period,[1] were molded by the increasingly rigid matrix of Geneva. It can probably be assumed that most of the others were subjected to many of the same formative pressures. This smaller group of missionaries was even more clearly than before Geneva's product, accustomed to Geneva's rigid discipline.

It might be concluded that this more single-minded and disciplined group of missionaries gave the movement greater strength. Again, however, the natural conclusion may be too easy. For the French Reformed Church, in the decade following Calvin's death, was rocked by bitter internal quarrels, and plagued by increasingly effective external attacks. There is considerable evidence that both were touched off and fed, in part at least, by resentment at the rigor of Genevan discipline. It is to a detailed study of these controversies that we now turn.

[1] *Ibid.*, Appendix IV.

CHAPTER III

Arguments over French Reformed Church Organization

A. The Institutional Background

Ecclesiastical institutions were extremely important to all the churches which issued from the Calvinist movement. It can be argued, in fact, that their concern for institutions is the most important single attitude which distinguishes Calvinists from such other orthodox Protestants as Lutherans, Zwinglians, and Anglicans. All of these Protestant communions claimed that there were certain objective " marks " of the true Church of Christ, which separate it from both the Roman Catholic Church and the " heretical " sects. The most important of these " marks " were always the true preaching of God's Word and the proper administration of His sacraments. But Calvinists tended to add a third set of " marks, " in the form of certain ecclesiastical institutions whose creation, they argued, had been commanded by God. And the list of these necessary institutions tended to lengthen as the Calvinist movement matured. There was even a tendency to make of this view an article of faith. The 1559 Confession of the French Reformed Church, for example, which became normative for the French branch of the Calvinist movement and which was widely diffused even beyond the boundaries of that communion, stipulated that the true Church must possess pastors, elders, and deacons, and defined the essential functions of each.[1] We cannot be surprised, in consequence, that challenges to the institutional structure of the French Reformed Church provoked bitter controversy.

However before we can understand the nature of the particular challenges to the structure of the French Reformed Church which developed during the period upon which this study concentrates, the one from the internal " Congregational " faction led by Morély and the other from the external Gallican

[1] Article 29 (which, for " elders," uses the word " surveillans " rather than " anciens," the term that came to be generally used in France), following immediately upon a more common definition of the true Church in article 28. For a good text of these articles, see *Hist. eccl.*, I, 182. For a detailed study of this Confession, see Jacques Pannier, *Les origines de la confession de foi et la discipline des Eglises Réformées de France* (Paris: Alcan, 1936), especially p. 130 on these articles. For an impressive, yet still incomplete, demonstration that this Confession was circulated widely, perhaps more widely than any other confession of the sixteenth century, see Hannelore Jahr, *Studien zur Überlieferungsgeschichte der Confession de foi von 1559*, Bd. XVI, *Beiträge zur Geschichte und Lehre der Reformierten Kirche* (Neukirchen-Vluyn: Verlag des Erziehungsvereins, 1964), which lists no less than 219 sixteenth-century editions that contain either this Confession or the Genevan Catechism upon which it was partially based.

party typified by du Moulin, we need to know something of what was being challenged. Behind the French Reformed Church, however, as all parties to the controversies recognized, lay the Church of Geneva. Many of the institutions and practices in use among the French Reformed had been borrowed directly from Geneva. Others, developed in France alone, had nevertheless been created and consolidated under the supervision of the pastors of Geneva. It is consequently with an analysis of the institutional structure of the Reformed Church in Geneva that we must begin.

Fortunately such an analysis was prepared by the most qualified of all contemporaries, Theodore Beza. As a direct result of his quarrel with Morély and Ramus, he wrote a long letter to Heinrich Bullinger, the powerful leader of the Reformed Church of Zurich. This letter describes in detail and defends with passion the very Genevan institutions which Morély was attacking. It is long enough and substantial enough to constitute a small treatise. But it has apparently never been published. Its contents, therefore, deserve extended summary.[1]

Two sets of Genevan institutions were particularly in question. A first governed the choice of ministers, primarily the ordained pastors, or preaching ministers, and the lay elders, or administrating ministers. By the time of Calvin's death, the form of election for pastors had been pretty well established. It consisted of three principal steps : choice by the Geneva Company of Pastors, confirmation by the city's governing Small Council, and acceptance by the public. The initial choice by the Company involved a screening of possible candidates, interview of them, their preaching twice before the Company, and an investigation into their life and morals. Confirmation by the Council was based on the recommendation of two of its members who were delegated to attend a meeting of the Company at which the preferred candidate would preach for a third time. If the candidate's election was confirmed, his name was then announced in all the churches, and the general public was invited to file objections. Depending on their nature, any objections would be referred either to the Company or the Council for investigation. If there were no objections, or if objections were found to be groundless, the candidate was then installed in office.

A method of deposing pastors is built right into this procedure. If there was any serious complaint about a pastor, it would again be referred to the appropriate body : a complaint about an ecclesiastical matter, to the Company of Pastors ; a complaint about a civil matter, to the Council. If the complaint seemed to justify action, either of these bodies could proceed to deposition. But the reason for deposition was generally not to be announced to the general public.

It is clear that this method of selection is essentially one of co-optation. The Company of Pastors reserved to itself primary responsibility for choosing its own members. The Council maintained what amounted to a right of veto. The right remaining to the general public was nothing more than an opportunity to protest, with no assurance that the protest would be honored. It is

---

[1] Beza to Bullinger, 13 November 1571, in Zürich, Staatsarchiv, E II 381, fols. 1304-1309, signed original. See Appendix II for the full text of this letter. Its contents are summarized in A. Bouvier, *Bullinger*, pp. 399-401 ; an important part of Bouvier's summary is quoted in E. Léonard, *Hist. gen. du prot.*, II, 121.

a method which is commonly used when it is important to ensure professional competence. It can also easily be used to maintain a dogmatic line. As Beza himself suggested, it should not be called " democratic, " but rather " aristocratic." [1] One should note, of course, that an aristocracy so chosen is one of talent rather than of birth.

The form of election for elders was also pretty well established by the time of Calvin's death. They were elected every year, by the Council, on the nomination of the Company of Pastors. They held office for one year, but could be re-elected and normally were. The group of elders had to include two members of the Small Council, four from the less important Council of Sixty, and six from the general Council of Two Hundred, so chosen that they represented every neighborhood of the city.[2] It would not be precise to call this method of selection one of co-optation, although it did contain elements of that method. But it was obviously not a " democratic " method either. The ultimate power of choice was again in the hands of the experts in ecclesiastical matters, the pastors.

A second set of Genevan institutions at question in this quarrel were those governing the discipline of the general population. While some matters of discipline could be handled either by the Company of Pastors or the Council, many, perhaps most, were handled largely by a third institution, the Consistory. This was an institution relatively unique to Calvinist polity, and regarded with considerable suspicion by many of the Reformed in such places as Zurich and Heidelberg.[3] It was made up of the pastors and the twelve elders. The pastors of the city attended regularly. The pastors of the surrounding villages were expected to attend whenever there were charges pending against their own parishioners, and could attend at other times. The Consistory handled cases involving both heterodox religious ideas and moral lapses, including a large volume of matrimonial cases, often involving sexual irregularities. It could act on its own initiative, or on referral from either the Company or the Council. It had its own methods of punishment, the simplest of which was admonition in private, the most severe of which was excommunication. If even excommunication did not produce the desired signs of repentance within a year, the Consistory could turn the offender over to the Council for some more temporal type of punishment. If the Consistory decided that temporal punishment was justified at the beginning, along with or instead of purely ecclesiastical punishment, it would so report to the Council.

To help the Consistory in its work of maintaining discipline, its members participated in what amounted to an annual religious census of the entire city. Into every one of the *dizaines* into which the city was divided, a team consisting

---

[1] In Beza to Bullinger, 13 November 1571, cited in n. to p. 38, fol. 1306v., and p. 212, below, Beza says, approvingly, that the French " habent in genere aristocratiam Consistorii nobiscum communem," while Morély's proposals would introduce into the Church « perturbatissimam et seditiosissimam democratiam."

[2] *Ibid.*, fol. 1305, and below, p. 210, « ex ipse Senatu duo, ex LX viris quatuor, ex Diacosiis sex, et quidem ex singulis urbis regionibus." The curious word " diacosiis " is evidently a rendering into Latin of the Greek word for two hundred.

[3] For an extended comparison of disciplinary institutions in these and several other Reformed cities, see Walther Köhler, *Zürcher Ehegericht und Genfer Konsistorium*, 2 vols. (Leipzig, 1932, 1942), *Quellen und Abhandlungen zur schweizerischen Reformationsgeschichte* (II. serie der *Quellen zur schweizerischen Reformationsgeschichte*), Nos. 7, 10.

of a pastor, an elder, and a municipal *dizainier* visited every family, normally during Lent, and administered to its members a kind of dogmatic test. During the rest of the year, each individual elder was supposed to keep an eye on the inhabitants of his section of the city. He was to report all irregularities among them either to the Council or the Consistory, depending on the nature of the irregularity. The elders, in short, served as the Church's spies upon the general population.

When these Genevan ecclesiastical institutions were transplanted to France, circumstances forced a number of modifications in them. Some of these modifications Beza alludes to, in this same letter to Bullinger. Others can be pieced together from other sources.[1] They can be grouped into three general categories.

One category of modifications was in the methods of selecting pastors and elders. These changes were required, in part at least, by the fact that the Reformed churches of France were generally illegal and subject to severe persecution by the secular government, and consequently often had to operate underground. As a result, it was evidently usually impossible for their pastors and elders to be chosen by procedures in which the civil government played an important part. In those few cities where the Calvinists seized complete control, local governing councils could assume a role like that of the Genevan Small Council. And in those areas where Reformed churches flourished because of the overt support or tacit approval of a powerful local nobleman, that nobleman was likely to claim some of the powers exercised by the Genevan Council, most commonly the power to veto a selection of the minister who was to serve his own household. But in all other areas, and even in these areas, where the local government was friendly, there was a tendency to rely largely on co-optation as a method of selection. When a church was first formed, its pastor typically would be sent from some other community, preferably from Geneva itself, and its first elders and deacons would be chosen in an open election by the constituting members of the congregation.[2] But from then on, further pastors and elders would be chosen by the body of existing pastors and elders, often enlarged to include deacons.[3] This selecting body may have at first been limited to members of the community which the new ministers were

---

[1] Especially synodical acts, the most important of which are those of the 1559 First National Synod of Paris. Available texts of these minutes vary widely. Probably the most reliable of the easily available ones are those included in *Hist. eccl.*, I, 173-185 (1559 Confession of Faith), 185-190 (1559 Discipline), and in J. Quick, *Synodicon*. Cf. the more dubious texts in J. Aymon, *Synodes* ; also the selected texts and commentaries in François Méjan, *Discipline de l'Eglise Réformée de France* (Paris : " Je Sers," 1947). For general analysis of the growth of Calvinist ecclesiastical institutions in France, see G. V. Lechler, *Verfassung*, especially ch. 3, " Presbyterialordnung und Synodalverband der Kirchen unter dem Kreuz in Frankreich," pp. 64-86. For a narrative account of some of these changes in these institutions, see E. Léonard, *Hist. gen. du prot.*, II, 115-123.

[2] A procedure endorsed by the 1559 Synod, according to J. Aymon, *Synodes*, I, 2nd pagination, p. 5, art. 27, and J. Quick, *Synodicon*, 1, 5, art. 26 [sic], but not found in the *Hist. eccl.* text, as F. Méjan, *op. cit.*, p. 307, notes.

[3] Endorsed by the 1559 Synod, according to *Hist. eccl.*, I, 186, art. 6, re selection of pastors. For more general discussion, see G. V. Lechler, *Verfassung*, ch. 3, especially pp. 73 and n. 2, 74, 75.

to serve. But it was soon expanded, at least for the selection of pastors, to include all the existing pastors and many of the elders of a region.[1]

Another category of modifications was in the definition of ministerial functions. These had a tendency to shift or lapse. Again, the fact that the Reformed churches were illegal and often operating underground, helps explain the changes. Persecution forced church leaders to move often. Pastors were especially vulnerable to attack and were also in short supply. Consequently they tended to move from one place to another quite frequently. In the intervals when a given church had no pastor, some of his functions would often be shifted to its lay ministers. Deacons, for example, might conduct services at which they would pray and read Bible passages.[2] In these and other ways, deacons often rose to positions of real leadership in France, and this constituted quite a departure from practice in Geneva. There the deacons were limited to the operation of the church's charitable institutions and certain other routine chores; they were excluded from the actual government of the church.

Persecution and other forces persuaded certain French churches simply to drop functions central to the ministerial role in Geneva. Those most likely to be dropped were the disciplinary functions exercised by the pastors and elders through the Consistory. Some of the French Reformed churches assigned other duties to consistories, duties which in Geneva might be handled by the Company. Other French Reformed churches hesitated even to establish consistories at all. This hesitation is probably explained by the obvious danger that a disciplined member might revert to Catholicism and betray the entire local congregation and its leaders.

However all these changes in ministerial functions were regarded, at least by Beza and his fellow leaders in the French Reformed Church, as purely temporary.[3] They made frequent attempts, through synodical resolutions and in other ways, to reduce the powers of deacons and to require the establishment of disciplinary consistories. In short, they sought to enforce the model of Geneva.

A final category of modifications was in the institutions which exercised final control over the French Reformed churches. These changes were in part dictated by simple geography. Geneva was a single city-state, small even for that day; France was an entire nation, one of the largest of the day, even if rather haphazardly put together. If the Protestant movement in France was to attain unity, and the effective force which derives from unity, it had to create institutions charged with this function. For these there was no Genevan model. Something new had to be superimposed upon the institutions

---

[1] Procedures prescribed by the 1563 National Synod of Lyon, according to J. Aymon, *Synodes*, I, 2nd pagination, p. 34, art. 15, and J. Quick, *Synodicon*, I, 34, art. 16 [sic]; made more formal and elaborate by the 1567 National Synod of Vertueil, according to J. Aymon, *Synodes*, I, 2nd pagination, p. 73, art. 4, and J. Quick, *Synodicon*, I, 75, art. 4 of ch. 8.

[2] This practice was permitted by the 1559 Synod, according to *Hist. eccl.*, I, 188, art. 24.

[3] See Beza to Bullinger, 13 November 1571, letter cited in n. to p. 38, above, fol. 1306v., and below, p. 212, re the continuing role of disciplinary consistories, recent more precise synodical definitions of ministerial functions, and the diminishing role of deacons, all in France. See also G. V. Lechler, *Verfassung*, ch. 3, especially pp. 73-74.

developed in Geneva. Beza and the other pastors of that city, however, played an important part in the creation of these new institutions. What they helped create was a hierarchy of representative bodies.[1] On the local level, meeting the needs of a city or of a rural region of several towns, were established colloquies. On the provincial level, with boundaries determined historically by the old feudal principalities out of which France had been built and practically by the most important subdivisions of the contemporary French government, were established provincial synods. And for France as a whole was established a national synod, a first meeting of which was held in Paris in 1559. The colloquies were supposed to meet frequently, every few weeks; the provincial synods somewhat less frequently, twice a year;[2] the national synod once a year. This rule could not be hard and fast, however. All of these bodies tended to meet more frequently when there were internal problems which required resolution. And all of them tended to meet less frequently or not at all, when war or persecution forced churches in a given locality to go underground. Membership in these bodies also tended to be somewhat nebulous. The delegations to them were generally chosen by local churches. They were made up of pastors, each accompanied by one or more elders or deacons.[3] Delegates to the national synods at first came from every Reformed church that could get men to the site of meeting. Later they came to be selected at provincial synods,[4] providing, of course, that provincial synods could meet at the necessary time. In provinces where they could not, leading churches of the area might take upon themselves the task of selecting a delegation. A delegation from Geneva, occasionally headed by Beza himself, attended several of these national synods. And, when they were in attendance, the Genevans took an active part in synodical decisions. In fact at one of them, the 1571 Synod of La Rochelle, the most important in the period which were are considering, Beza was elected Moderator and presided over all the meetings.[5] In general, there was a tendency for the membership in the synods, both provincial and national, to be made up more and more of ordained pastors. There was also a tendency for lines of command and areas of jurisdiction to be drawn more and more precisely. Real precision, of the kind that would please the drafter of a modern corporate table of organization, was, of course, impossible, given the recurrent chaos into which religious wars plunged France.

These, then, were the institutions, developed in Geneva and transplanted or freshly created in France, which Morély attacked. It is now time for us to examine his attack in some detail.

---

[1] G. V. Lechler, *Verfassung*, ch. 3, especially pp. 74-78. On Geneva's role in the formation and operation of these bodies, see R. M. Kingdon, *Geneva & Coming*, pp. 45 and ff.

[2] Required by the 1559 Synod, according to *Hist. eccl.*, I, 186, art. 5.

[3] Required by the 1559 Synod, according to *ibid.*, art. 3.

[4] Required, as a temporary measure, by the 1565 National Synod of Paris, according to J. Aymon, *Synodes*, I, 2nd pagination, pp. 68-69, art. 23, and J. Quick, *Synodicon*, I, 65, ch. 10 [sic]. Cf. comments by G. V. Lechler, *Verfassung*, pp. 82-83, and E. Léonard, *Hist. gen. du prot.*, II, 117.

[5] Minutes of which can be found in J. Aymon, *Synodes*, I, 2nd pagination, pp. 98-111; J. Quick, *Synodicon*, I, 89-101.

B. The Internal Attack : Jean Morély and his Treatise on Christian Discipline

Jean Morély, sire de Villiers,[1] the leader of the first formidable internal attack upon the structure of the Calvinist Reformed Church, was an unusually articulate member of that group of noble converts who made of Calvinism a potent force in sixteenth-century European politics. He did not come from the highest ranks of the nobility, but he was of a family accustomed to service at royal courts. Both his father and his father-in-law had apparently served the court of Francis I, King of France, as physicians.[2] And Morély himself was to serve the court of Jeanne d'Albret, Queen of Navarre, as a tutor.[3] Little is known of Morély's early formation. He always claimed to be a native of Paris, and it was no doubt there that he acquired the knowledge of Latin and Greek, of Holy Scripture, and of early church history, which he was later to display in his writings.[4] About 1547, he turned Protestant.[5] Shortly thereafter, he seems to have visited Protestant Germany and Switzerland and to have entered into correspondence with Conrad Pellican, the learned Hebraist then resident in Zurich.[6] However Morély cannot have become well-known

---

[1] I was led to much of my information on Morély's career by notes which M. Henri Naef of Geneva had compiled in preparation for a book he once planned to write on Morély and which he generously loaned to me.

[2] Académie des sciences morales et politiques, *Collection des ordonnances des rois de France: Catalogue des actes de François Ier* (Paris, 1887-1908, 10 vols.), VII, 576, records payment of wages some time during the 1540-1543 period to "Jean Morély, médecin ordinaire du roi;" VIII, 119 and 174, contain 1537-1539 references to "les médecins Braillon et Morelly;" II, 44, 54, 695, and IV, 152, and VI, 362, and VII, 539, contain further references to Louis Braillon, the King's doctor, ranging from 1529 to 1540. That "Jean" was the first name of Morély's father, is established by a document in Geneva, Arch., PC, 2e série, No. 1215, dated 10 April 1560. That "Braillon" was the maiden name of his wife, is established by documents published in part in H. Naef, *Conjuration d'Amboise*, p. 472, n. 1. Other members of his family of whom I have found traces, are a brother-in-law named Du Mesnil, who tried to intercede for him in a letter of 8 December 1566, addressed to Laurent de Normandie (Geneva, BPU, Ms. fr. 446, fol. 111), and, perhaps, the Calvinist pastor François de St. Paul, of whom Morély speaks, in a letter to Beza of 20 January 1567 (*ibid.*, fol. 28), as "*mon frere*"—a phrase, however, often used figuratively by early Calvinists.

[3] See below, pp. 82-96.

[4] Most of these writings, analyzed below, are in French. However the mysterious letters to Pellican, apparently from Morély, described in n. 6 below, and an unpublished letter to Calvin and his colleagues, clearly from Morély (Geneva, BPU, Ms. fr. 446, fols. 16-17, 8 May [1564]), are in Latin and contain occasional Greek words.

[5] Morély to Beza, 20 January 1567, in Geneva, BPU, Ms. fr. 446, fol. 28v., says "depuis XX ans ou ca que graces à Dieu je suis renge en son Eglise."

[6] This follows from three letters addressed to Pellican which can now be found in the Zurich Zentralbibliothek, F-47, which Professor Henri Meylan of Lausanne has called to my attention and of which he has generously supplied me with transcripts. The first, evidently written from some place in Germany, without date, but about 1549—judging from internal evidence, is signed "Janus Morellius." The other two, written from Lausanne, apparently in 1551 or 1552, are signed "Claudius Villierius," but one of them points out that this is a change of name and it would be a plausible change for Morély, sire de Villiers. Friedrich Clemens Ebrard, *Die französisch-reformierte Gemeinde in Frankfurt am Main, 1554-1904* (Frankfurt-am-Main, 1906), p. 65, notes that one of the four elders who, with pastor Valerand Poullain, signed that Church's 1554 Confession of Faith, was named Jean Morel (Murellius), and speculates that this might be the sire de Villiers. But Morély may have moved to Geneva in February of 1554 (cf. n. 2 to p. 44 below), while the Frankfurt Confession was apparently drafted in June (Ebrard, *op. cit.*, p. 63).

to all the leaders of the Zurich Church. In 1571, Bullinger denied having ever heard of him, in an acknowledgment of Beza's lengthy report upon the entire controversy,[1] then at its climax.

Morély moved to Geneva some time in the 1550's,[2] when many other French Protestants were crowding into that city. He obtained a house in a fashionable quarter.[3] He seems to have lived in relative leisure, although he did take a number of rather mysterious business trips back into France. He never bothered to apply for entry into Geneva's select bourgeoisie.[4] He does, however, seem to have made friends in every higher stratum of local society. Some were among the bourgeoisie of the city.[5] Others were prominent in the city's pastoral corps. Calvin himself stood up as god-father at the baptism of one of Morély's sons.[6] And, naturally enough, he saw a good deal of the others in the Geneva colony of French refugee noblemen. Perhaps the most prominent of these was Antoine de Lautrec, sire de Saint-Germier, a distinguished jurisconsult who was a prominent adviser to the court of Navarre both before and after his stay in Geneva.[7]

Twice Morély got into trouble in Geneva, however, and each time it was trouble with the city's leading pastors. Each incident left its mark in legal proceedings, records of which have been preserved in the Geneva State Archives. The first incident was an aftermath of the Conspiracy of Amboise in 1560, that disastrous attempt by a group of wild young Protestant noblemen, encouraged by the Prince of Condé, to kidnap the king and slaughter his advisers of the fanatically Catholic house of Guise. Shortly after the bloody suppression of this foolhardy attempt at a coup, Morély returned to Geneva from one of his business trips to France, and began circulating a dangerous rumor. He reported that many members of the French Protestant churches believed the conspiracy had received advance approval from the pastors of Geneva, in particular from Calvin and Beza.[8] This rumor was dangerous because the Court of France was still hunting for people implicated in the plot, and could have seriously embarrassed Geneva or even threatened the city's

---

[1] Bullinger to Beza, 4 December 1571, published in A. Bouvier, *Bullinger*, p. 558: " Quae de Morellio quodam scribis, plane nova sunt nobis Neque enim unquam de illo quicquam antea audivimus, neque quis ille sit, aut quid ille vel dixerit vel scripserit, hactenus intelleximus."

[2] " Jehan Morely natifz de Paris " was enrolled as a resident on 9 February 1554, according to Geneva, Arch., RC, particuliers, VIII, fol. lv. ; " Jehan Morely, Sr de Villiers" was enrolled on 2 January 1559, according to Geneva, LH, I, 146. Perhaps this puzzling double listing can be explained by an interim move away from Geneva.

[3] Described in detail in Geneva, Arch., Notaire Ragueau, V, 77-78, 25 February 1562. It was located on the rue de la cité, near the rue de Bise and the old city walls.

[4] At least he is not listed in Geneva, LB. *Hist. eccl.*, II, 34, however, claims he was a " bourgeois de la ville de Geneve."

[5] E.g. André Blandin, with whom he had business dealings (Geneva, Arch., Notaire Ragueau, V, 77-78, 25 February 1562, and Geneva, LB, p. 240); Philibert Sarasin or Serrazin, who was god-father to Morély's son Pierre (Geneva, Arch., Baptêmes, St. Gervais, II, 25 July 1563, and Geneva, LB, p. 244).

[6] Geneva, Arch., Baptêmes, St. Pierre, I, 21 April 1555.

[7] H. Naef, *Conjuration d'Amboise*, pp. 454-455, re a trip Morély took with de Lautrec; R. M. Kingdon, *Geneva & Coming*, p. 60, for more on de Lautrec.

[8] This entire incident is described in heavily-documented detail by H. Naef, *Conjuration d'Amboise*, ch. 6, pp. 437-474.

independence if it had insisted on punishing the city's pastors. Fear of retaliation no doubt explains the sharp reaction of Calvin and Beza : they must have wanted to make it absolutely clear that they had had nothing to do with the Conspiracy. They quickly instituted legal proceedings against both Morély and a local friend of his who had also repeated the rumor, demanding a public retraction and apology.

A trial followed before the city Council, in which the charges were weighed carefully and collateral evidence was collected. While Morély granted that his story had been distorted in some ways as it was re-told around town, he insisted that in substance it was true, that the pastors of Geneva had given French Protestant leaders reason to believe that they supported the Conspiracy. A key part of his story involved a French pastor named Antoine de la Roche Chandieu, who was to become a central figure in the later dispute involving Morély. Chandieu was a brilliant young nobleman who served the crucially important Reformed church in Paris, as one of its pastors. Morély charged that Chandieu had come to Geneva, as the Conspiracy of Amboise was being planned, in order to get Calvin's advice on participation. When questioned about this charge, Calvin was hardly straightforward. He seems at first to have denied the interview took place at all,[1] although he later admitted that it had. Chandieu happened to be in the city again, however, so the councillors questioned him in person. He confirmed the fact of his interview with Calvin, but his account of it tended to exonerate Calvin from the charge of having encouraged a conspiracy of the sort actually mounted.[2] Despite this and other ambiguities in the pastors' defense, the Council ruled against Morély.[3] Any other ruling, of course, would have exposed the city to the very dangers the whole trial was probably designed to avert. The punishment imposed upon Morély was fairly light, and he seemed at the time to take it with good enough grace.

Anyone who examines the later relations between the parties to this affair, however, must suspect that the incident left an important mark upon them. Morély and Beza, in particular, were later to speak of each other with a bitterness which seems to transcend the issues that divided them. This bitterness is more striking in Morély, since his language was normally mild. Beza's epithets may perhaps be regarded as characteristic of his usual polemical style, but the relentlessness with which he was to pursue Morély suggests personal animus on his part too. Calvin and Chandieu, also, were to oppose Morély in the later controversy. Calvin died before it was well under way, however, and Chandieu left little record of his personal opinions of Morély.

The second time Morély got into trouble with the Genevan pastors, it was over his critique of Calvinist ecclesiastical institutions. This was the quarrel which was to spread to France and engulf the entire Reformed church there during the decade upon which this book concentrates. It began mildly enough, however. And it did not really begin with Morély. For Morély was not the first in Geneva to criticize Calvinist ecclesiastical institutions. Objections to them, particularly to the Consistory and the rigor with which it hounded sinners, had been voiced again and again by the native citizens of

[1] *Ibid.*, p. 460.

[2] *Ibid.*, pp. 468-470.

[3] *Ibid.*, pp. 470-471.

Geneva. On occasion their objections boiled over into minor riots, which had to be suppressed with force, in order to keep the Calvinist system intact and in operation. Some of these objections were picked up by members of the Geneva colony of French noble refugees. For example the sires de Maillanne were accused of advancing arguments which reveal in embryo views later advanced by Morély at much greater length. In 1558, the Maillanne brothers were called before both the Consistory and the Council to answer complaints that they had been criticizing the city's pastors unfairly. One of the witnesses at the Consistory's hearing on these complaints reported that, among other things, the sires de Maillanne had criticized the fact that Reformed pastors were currently being chosen by " three or four " people, which, they argued, " was not done in the time of the Apostles." [1] This particular charge does not seem to have bothered the authorities as much as others, however. In any case, the entire affair was soon cleared up without much trouble. The Maillanne brothers, however, may well have passed their complaints on to Morély. They agreed with him on other matters, it would appear, since, in 1560, one of them was arrested, like Morély, for spreading the rumor that the Genevan church had sanctioned the Conspiracy of Amboise.[2]

Morély himself went far beyond such random and casual criticisms of Calvinist ecclesiastical institutions. He developed a detailed, documented, and sophisticated general critique of these institutions, wrote it out for circulation in manuscript, and then published it as a book. Its final title was *Traicté de la discipline & police chrestienne*, or *Treatise on Christian Discipline*. It was printed in Lyon, in 1562, by the famous publishing house of the de Tournes.[3] It had apparently been largely written while Morély was still in Geneva. Its preparation had required a long period of time, interrupted, Morély reports in the book's dedicatory letter, by bouts of illness. In preparing it, he also reports, he consulted a number of people, most of whom he does not name. One of these may have been Calvin.[4] Another was clearly Pierre Viret, then principal pastor of the Reformed Church in Lyon.

To consult Viret, Morély moved to Lyon himself, and submitted to Viret's inspection a copy of his manuscript. This was a shrewd move. For Viret was probably the most popular single preacher using the French language in the Protestant cause. He was thoroughly Calvinist in his theology, and had even suffered banishment from an important post in Lausanne rather than abandon at Bernese dictation the right to preach certain Calvinist doctrines and to institute certain Calvinist disciplinary practices. But he would not take Genevan dictation either, and often acted quite independently,

---

[1] Geneva, Arch., RConsistoire, XIII, fol. 47v., 12 May 1558 [sic-vs. abridged version in *Calvini Opera*, XXI, 691], " Aussi dirent que quant ung mettoyt des ministres quil nestoyt pas beau que troys ou quatre les eslizes. Et que cela ne fesoyt pas du temps des appostres." See *Calvini Opera*, XXI, 691-695, for further texts and summaries from RC and RConsistoire on this matter.

[2] H. Naef, *Conjuration d'Amboise*, ch. 9, pp. 541-560; appendix XI, pp. 695-704.

[3] For a full bibliographical description, see Alfred Cartier, *Bibliographie des éditions des de Tournes, imprimeurs lyonnais* (Paris: Editions des bibliothèques nationales de France, 1937-1938), No. 488, II, 524-525.

[4] *France protestante*, 1st ed., VII, 505-507, reports that Morély submitted the manuscript to Calvin, but that Calvin refused to read it, saying that he did not have time to go through an entire volume on a subject already decided by the Word of God. However it supplies no source for this story.

TRAICTÉ

De la discipline & police Chrestienne.

A LYON,
PAR IAN DE TOVRNES,
M. D. LXII.

although he always remained on good personal terms with Calvin and Beza. There is reason to suspect, moreover, that Viret had some sympathy for certain of Morély's ideas.[1] Morély could have become personally acquainted with Viret in Lausanne, and he must have met him in Geneva, since Viret was one of the pastors who attended the cross-examination of Morély in his trial for circulating rumors about the Conspiracy of Amboise.[2] But Viret did not have time to read the manuscript. He did begin a reading of it, but the press of events distracted him, and, shortly before leaving Lyon for a brief trip, he returned the manuscript. Morély then arranged for the printing of his manuscript, so timing it that the book would appear just before the convening of the national Synod of the French Reformed Church which was to meet in Orleans in 1562. All this is spelled out in the book's dedicatory letter, addressed to Viret. That letter then moves on to ask that Viret lay the book before the Synod for general consideration.[3]

These maneuvers suggest that Morély did not intend his book to be a frontal attack on Calvinist ecclesiastical institutions. That impression is confirmed by a letter he sent, along with one of the first copies of the book, to Calvin.[4] It is further confirmed by the general tone of the book. Clearly Morély felt he was presenting a set of constructive suggestions for ecclesiastical reform which, after study by Calvin, Viret, and the other existing leaders of the Reformed Church, might well provide a basis for changes in existing institutions and practices. As he put it in his letter to Calvin, he hoped that his suggestions would provide a foundation of the sort described by the Apostle Paul in I Corinthians 3 : 10-13, a foundation upon which others would build. But the Reformed leaders did not accept Morély's book in this spirit. They condemned it harshly at Orleans. They condemned it in Geneva. And they condemned it again and again in the years that followed. Morély and his friends reacted by fighting back. The story of these controversies we shall take up later. First we must proceed to an analysis of the book itself, in order to understand the issues in this quarrel. Before we do that, however, I cannot help observing that the whole quarrel might conceivably have been avoided, if Calvin or Viret or some other leading pastor had taken the time to read Morély's manuscript and consider his suggestions seriously.

Our analysis of the *Treatise on Christian Discipline* must begin with Morély's dedicatory letter, addressed to Viret. For in addition to its information on the composition of the book, which we have already noted, it also contains some important observations on the total structure of the argument into which the book fits. These observations take the form of two cautions. A first is fairly routine. It points out that the book's beginning is cast in the

[1] R. D. Linder, *Viret*, pp. 89-94. See also below, p. 94.

[2] H. Naef, *Conjuration d'Amboise*, p. 458.

[3] J. Morély, *Traicté*, sigs. A-2—[A-4v.]. Note particularly, on sig. A-3v., a passage explaining why Viret had not been able to read the manuscript, partially quoted in *Hist. eccl.*, Baum & Cunitz ed., II, 34, n. 3, and, on sig. [A-4], Morély's request that Viret submit the book to the Synod. The copy of the *Traicté* which I have used throughout is the one in Geneva, BPU, Rés. 277* Dg.

[4] Morély to Calvin, 10 April [1562], from Lyon, in the private Sarrau collection of unpublished autograph letters addressed to Calvin, now being prepared for publication by Professor Rodolphe Peter and M. Jean Rott of Strasbourg. M. Rott has most generously supplied me with a complete transcript of this letter.

traditional form of a work presented to a prince, reminding such a secular ruler of his obligation to religion. Presumably, therefore, it is, in part at least, a formality and not to be taken as seriously as the rest of the book. A second caution, however, is very revealing. It announces that this book is but the first half of a more general argument. Morély feels that ecclesiastical power and civil administration are two parts of the one true Church of God. In this present book, he plans to deal only with the ecclesiastical administration of that Church. In a future sequel book, he plans to deal with the " republic." [1] This second study apparently never appeared. But the notion that ecclesiastical and civil authorities are co-ordinate branches of a single institution is an important one to keep in mind while analyzing the book which did appear. Analogies between ecclesiastical government and civil government and between ecclesiastical law and civil law are constantly in Morély's mind. So are questions of the precise relations which ought to obtain between the institutions and the laws of these two branches of the Church. Both these analogies and relations are constantly referred to in the course of Morély's argument.

The body of the treatise which did appear is sub-divided into four books. Book I argues for the necessity of ecclesiastical discipline and outlines briefly what seems to Morély to be the proper way of attaining it. Book II discusses at more length how proper discipline should be applied to prevent the spread of dangerous doctrine and to control the behavior of individual Christians. Book III discusses the different orders of the clergy and outlines what Morély feels to be the appropriate way to select them. Book IV discusses the general organization of the Church, and the auxiliary institutions it needs in its task of maintaining discipline.

Morély's argument for the necessity of discipline is drawn from his rather melancholy view of the contemporary Church. In no place, he argues, is true discipline established, not even in the most doctrinally pure of the reformed churches. The fact that these reformed churches are relatively new and bedeviled with harsh problems of organization and survival, is explanation enough for their failure to establish discipline as yet. But it cannot serve as a continuing excuse. Now that the reformed churches are established in many parts of Europe it is time that discipline be established within them. For if it is not, the Church may well fall on evil days, when the present generation of unusually fine pastors passes away, since princes are already tempted to fill the approaching vacuum by usurpation of authority properly belonging

---

[1] *Ibid.*, sig. [A-4—A-4v.], " De deux choses vous advertiray-je que le commencement de ce traicté a esté par moy accommodé, & adapté pour estre presenté à un Prince: pour lequel induire à ceste meditation avec plus grande utilité, j'ay un peu recerché de loing, & deduit plus amplement ce qui attouche l'office & devoir d'iceux, tant pour la restauration de la doctrine, que pour l'institution de la police de l'Eglise... Le second poinct duquel je desire que [vous] soyez adverti, est, par ce que ceste puissance Ecclesiastique & administration civile sont comme les deux brachs [sic] de l'Eglise, ordonnés par Dieu pour la conservation & gouvernement d'icelle, je me suis efforcé de les conjoindre ensemble en ceste meditation, lequel traicte de la Republique, pour mes domestiques occupations, & le peu de santé que j'ay eu il y a jà long temps, ay esté contraint de remettre à une autre fois."

There are also repeated later allusions to this projected sequel volume, e.g. p. 322, re a subject of which he could " reserver la consideration d'icelles, aux livres que nous avons en main de la Republique Chrestienne," and p. 342, re another subject, " De quoy nous traitterons cy apres aux livres de la Republique Chrestienne."

to the Church.[1] This is a particular danger in France, given the general rowdiness of her population and the widespread corruption in her society.[2]

Once one concedes that true discipline must be established, one must then decide upon the institution charged with this establishment. For an answer to this question, Morély turned, like any good Protestant, to the Word of God, left to us by Jesus Christ and His Apostles, written down in Holy Scripture.[3] There Morély found a clear and unequivocal answer to his question: the authority to exercise true discipline rests in the whole Church, in the entire body of believers in Christ. Any delegation of it to any less inclusive institution betrays Christ's command. In developing this argument further, Morély attacks every form of church government favored by orthodox or "magisterial"[4] churchmen of his day. A system which vests disciplinary powers in bishops or Popes, he attacks as a clear perversion of Scripture and the work of Anti-Christ. In what may well be a slap at the contemporary Anglican establishment, he says that those countries which have kept bishops and the trappings of the papal establishment, while rejecting the power of the Pope, have "deformed" rather than "reformed" the Church.[5] Further, a system which vests disciplinary powers in the entire body of the clergy, he attacks as again departing from Scripture and revealing tendencies dangerously "aristocratic" or "oligarchic."[6] This, in kernel, is the attack upon Calvinist synodical polity which he was to develop at length. Finally, a system which vests disciplinary powers in secular authorities, he argues again

---

[1] *Ibid.*, p. 26, "aucuns des Princes, considerans que si pour le present nous avons ministres d'une singuliere pieté, prudence, & scavoir, nous ne nous pouvons promettre pour l'advenir de semblables: & craignans... qu'ils entreprennent cy apres pareille authorité qu'ont faict anciennement les Evesques sur l'Eglise..., ces princes... ont eux mesmes usurpé ceste domination: ... s'attribuans à eux une puissance desmesurée d'ordonner ministres, les deposer" etc.

[2] *Ibid.*, bk. 1, ch. 11, develops this criticism of France. N.B. p. 51, "Ce que celuy craindra davantage, qui considerera le naturel du François, & l'estat present du Royaume."; p. 53, "Car chacun apperçoit la ferocité naturelle de ce peuple, & specialement la presomption de la noblesse, ... davantage un chacun apperçoit l'orgueil & avarice des riches."

[3] *Ibid.*, bk. 1, ch. 7, develops the theme that discipline must be drawn from "la parole de Dieu, telle que Jesus Christ & ses Apostres nous l'ont laissee," buttressed with copious Biblical citations.

[4] George Huntston Williams' apt adjective for that branch of the Reformation which produced the established Protestant churches. See his *The Radical Reformation* (Philadelphia: Westminster, 1962), Introduction, for his most detailed explanation of the concept.

[5] J. Morély, *Traicté*, pp. 26-27, "Il y a une autre maniere de reformation, ou plustost deformation... C'est qu'en verité l'Evangile en quelques contrees est presché tellement quellement: mais la face de l'Eglise Papistique y est demourée: les mesmes Evesques apres quelque legere declaration de foy sont remis sur le col de l'Eglise avec tous leurs revenus, ostentations de richesses, & la plus grande part de leurs ceremonies: les presentations, droicts de patronnage, ornemens, chandelles, chanteries de prestres, mais en langue vulgaire, observation d'une grande partie des jours y sont restés." At least one of the Marian exiles to Geneva, Anthony Gilby, had attacked the Henrician establishment in strikingly similar terms, as "no reformation, but a deformation," in his 1558 *Admonition*, published in John Knox, *Works*, Laing ed., IV, 563, recently quoted by M. Walzer, *The Revolution of the Saints*, p. 97.

[6] J. Morely, *Traicté*, p. 62, labels church government by consistory "un gouvernement Aristocratique"; p. 70, labels selection of clergy by co-optation, a "chose Oligarchique & pleine de danger."

departs from Scripture and leads to dangerous usurpations.[1] Here he was attacking the "Erastian" tendencies so prevalent in Germany and so widely imitated elsewhere. Only by the establishment of popular church government on the model of the Apostolic Church, Morély says, can the contemporary Church recover the ancient discipline, and restore the ancient morals.[2] He promptly anticipates the charge that such a system would lead to anarchy and license. Against this charge he advances a two-fold reply. He argues, to begin with, that the system of popular government which, he insists, prevailed during the first two centuries of the Church's existence, did in fact maintain for her the best discipline she has ever seen. He points out, further, that the Church now possesses institutions capable of eliminating anarchy by giving structure and direction to a popular ecclesiastical government: in Jesus Christ, it possesses a sole monarch; in His Word, it possesses a code of law; in the councils of properly elected pastors and "seniors" (elders) already a part of Reformed church polity, it possesses temporal institutions capable of administering that law.[3]

Having developed this argument that popular church government is the sole type authorized by Scripture, Morély then proceeds, in his book II, to discuss how such a government would function in dealing with the sins of individuals. Among these sins, he distinguishes two types which require disciplinary action: sins of belief, or heresies; and sins of action, or moral delinquencies. Of the two, heresies worry him most. Three sorts worry him particularly: those which raise questions that are "vain and of no value"; those which reject Scripture such as the doctrines of the "Anabaptists and Enthusiasts" of his own day; those which accept Scripture, but reject its true meaning.[4] Both types of sins, Morély argues, become a real menace to the Church because of improper disciplinary procedures. Striking examples of such improper procedures he finds in the patristic age, in the disciplinary actions of the earliest ecumenical councils and the first bishops. Sometimes these authorities were too harsh, sometimes they were too lenient. But all too often they permitted the threats posed by sins to get out of hand, or even stimulated trouble by untrue and unscriptural discipline.

Only by resolute action within the local congregation, Morély argues, can sins be brought under control effectively, with minimum damage to the Church. If sinful beliefs can be spotted on the local level, before they have been developed and hardened, they can often be corrected by free and open discussion. Sinful actions, also, are most easily spotted by the immediate neighbors of an individual sinner, and most easily eradicated by their speedy reactions. All such sins should be dealt with by assemblies of the entire local church membership, excluding only children below the age of fifteen,

---

[1] *Ibid.*, p. 26. Quoted above, n. 1 to p. 50.

[2] *Ibid.*, p. 32, "Reprenez donc l'ancienne discipline, & vous restituerez les mœurs anciennes."

[3] *Ibid.*, p. 32. See below, p. 57 and n. 2, for text of another part of this passage and further comment on it.

[4] *Ibid.*, pp. 100-101, "En premier lieu des questions vaines & de nulle efficace... En second lieu l'Eglise a des ennemis apperts, qui rejettent l'Escriture, comme sont aujourd'huy les Anabaptistes & Entouziastes... En tiers lieu sont ceux, lesquels approuvent bien la verité de l'Escriture, mais disputent sur l'intelligence."

women, and those merchants who speculate in foodstuffs.[1] These assemblies should be presided over by pastors skilled in the knowledge of the Gospel. Their members should take oaths to be guided in all things by the Gospel. All disciplinary decisions should be taken by these assemblies, not by the pastors alone, not by any representative body such as a consistory. In communities of normal size, the entire church membership can meet in one place to make disciplinary decisions. In abnormally big communities, like Paris, where a mass meeting would be unwieldy, neighborhood assemblies could be held, gathering together all the church members resident in one section of the city. If these disciplinary assemblies discover that they cannot resolve certain problems, they can call in outside help. They might, for example, ask the advice of the pastors in neighboring areas. If a few problems still defy solution, they can always be referred to provincial synods, or even to national or ecumenical councils.[2] Appeals of this sort are to be avoided, however, wherever possible. Every effort must be made to discipline each sinner within his own congregation.

Not only should local congregations be charged with judging each individual sinner. They should also fix each individual ecclesiastical punishment. Decisions to excommunicate sinners and decisions to absolve sinners and admit them again to the bosom of the Church, are, Morély argues, the specific responsibility of each local congregation. They should not be delegated to any ecclesiastical official or to any less inclusive institution. The temporal punishment which must often accompany ecclesiastical punishment, however, is another matter. Temporal punishment, Morély suggests, must be levied by the civil magistrate, and it must occasionally be extreme. There are times when the civil magistrate must even be asked to " punish, even with death, the heretics who make conventicles and assemblies." [3] Presumably a heretic who kept his abominations to himself was to be treated somewhat more leniently. The civil magistrate must likewise punish vice with appropriate civil penalties. He should also stand guard over the channels through which dangerous opinions can be spread, by controlling carefully such means of spreading ideas as printing, particularly the printing of Bibles.[4]

Morély summarizes this part of his argument by saying : " this power to throw out of the Church, to bar from its communion, to cut off from this body

---

[1] *Ibid.*, bk. 2, chs. 8 and 9, contain detailed recommendations on how these assemblies should be constituted and on the procedures they should use. On these specific exclusions, see pp. 119-120 : " Pourtant ces personnes sont à exclure. Premierement les enfans, & ceux qui seroyent au dessous de quinze ans, pour l'incertitude de leur jugement... aussi les femmes ausquelles sainct Paul defend de parler en l'assemblee... pareillement les marchands... qui vendent bled, & vins, & autres choses necessaires à la vie de l'homme, qui attendent la mauvaise saison pour mieux faire leur main : ou lesquels vendent à bien haut pris marchandises necessaires." This connection of congregationalism with rigid discipline was to be an important feature of later English Puritanism : see the probing analysis of M. Walzer, *The Revolution of the Saints*, pp. 219-224.

[2] *Ibid.*, p. 96, speaking of heretics, " Si encores le different ne s'appoincte, je ne trouveroye mauvais d'assembler un Concile provincial, en l'Eglise qui seroit en travail, ou nationnal, ou œcumenique & universel, s'il est possible."

[3] *Ibid.*, p. 96, " l'ayde du magistrat est grandement requis en ce faict, pour punir, voire de mort, les heretiques, qui feroyent conventicules & assemblees."

[4] *Ibid.*, p. 103, " que le Magistrat veille à ce qu'il ne s'imprime livre de l'escriture, qui ne soit approuvé du Consistoire sous grandes peines corporelles."

of the Lord, or to receive into this Church and replace in this company and community, is a sovereign power, which belongs to each Church, as to a mother of a family in her house. For this reason it cannot belong to the pastors of their right." [1]

In his book III, Morély proceeds to apply his arguments for popular government of the Church to the selection of the various orders of the clergy. He dismisses episcopal appointment of clergy out of hand, as not worth serious discussion. He then discusses in more detail the typical Calvinist method of selecting pastors in his day. This method involved, as we have seen, a preliminary recommendation by the Company of Pastors, approval by the magistrate, and final acceptance by the whole church. This he found to be defective at every step: the pastors should never act as an exclusive group, but should only act with lay advice; the magistrate has no right to meddle in decisions of this sort and, anyway, usually simply accepts the ministers' recommendation; the step of acceptance by the whole church has come to be a mere rubber-stamp procedure.[2] The whole process, as Morély pointed out with some justice, amounted to selection of pastors by co-optation.

In place of this, Morély urges selection of pastors by the entire church. Initial nominations can be made by the pastors and "seniors" (elders), but any other member of the congregation should also be free to make a nomination. The final selection from among these nominations should be made by the church as a whole, prayerfully and ever mindful of the qualifications for the ministry prescribed by the Scriptures.[3] This process seems to embody ecclesiastical democracy of a rather pure and simple sort. Morély qualifies such an impression, however, with some further recommendations. He suggests an educational requirement for the pastorate, by urging that a university with ample provision for instruction in theology be established in every province. And he injects an element of hierarchical selection, when he also suggests that each church in a university town might choose pastors for outlying towns, since the members of the central church will be in a better position to judge any candidate's specific aptitudes for the ministry. Selections of this sort, however, should be made at sessions open to representatives of the actual churches such candidates are to serve, and should take into

[1] *Ibid.*, p. 168, "Mais ceste puissance de rejetter de l'Eglise, interdire de sa communion, retrencher de ce corps du Seigneur, ou recevoir en ceste Eglise, & remettre en ceste compagnie & communauté, est une puissance souveraine, qui compete à une chacune Eglise, comme à une mere de famille en sa maison. Pourtant elle ne peut appartenir aux pasteurs de leur droit."

[2] *Ibid.*, p. 184, "Je ne parle de la Tyrannique discipline, ne de la Papistique masquee de l'Evangile, mais de celle qui est receue aux Eglises mieux reformees. Les Ministres s'assemblent seuls en leur conseil, là ils font l'election pour maintenant au mieux qu'il est possible de souhaitter... Le Ministre eleu est apres presenté au Magistrat, lequel aussi le conferme. Enquoy y a double faute : L'une, que ce n'est l'estat ne la vocation d'iceluy Magistrat, & est confondre les deux gouvernemens... La seconde faute en cecy est, que quand ainsi ne seroit, le Magistrat ne pourroit rejetter le Ministre eleu, sinon pour cause bien notable... Vray est que l'experience, maistresse de tous, a découvert l'absurdité de telle election, & induit nos bons & reverens peres en nostre Seigneur d'amender ceste faute en quelques lieux, & d'y adjouster quelque ordre... L'ordre est tel : L'election faicte comme dessus de certains personnages, & le Magistrat les ayant ja confermés le plus souvent, ils sont nommés à l'Eglise, & admoneste-on que si aucun sçayt aucune chose en eux, pourquoy ils doivent estre rejettés, qu'il le declaire au Magistrat."

[3] *Ibid.*, bk. 3, ch. 3, describes these qualifications at length.

account the requests, recommendations, and criticisms of these outlying churches.[1]

Just as the Church as a whole has the right to select its pastors, so it has a right to depose them. This is a right which Morély feels must be maintained. He would permit criticism of any pastor by anyone at any time, with safeguards against libel and license, and he would permit the initiation by any two or three complainants of proceedings which could lead to deposition and even excommunication.[2]

These principles for the selection and deposition of pastors, Morély would also apply to the selection of other orders of the clergy.[3] Of these other orders, the one to which he gives the most attention is the order of " seniors " or elders.[4] He does not accept separate orders of " bishops " or " priests," arguing these terms, in their true sense, are simply synonyms for " pastors." [5] " Seniors," like pastors, should be elected by the entire membership of each local congregation. As a group, they form a council or consistory. Their functions do not seem to differ much in Morély's schema from the administrative and disciplinary functions normally exercised by elders in contemporary Reformed practice. Yet other orders which Morély discusses include the order of deacons and deaconesses and the order of doctors or teaching clergy.[6] He also notes the importance to each church of good readers, song-leaders, and sextons.[7] In dealing with each of these other orders and offices, however, he contents himself with a brief general description of its duties. He does not discuss in separate detail the ways in which its members should be chosen or deposed.

Much of Morély's argument up to this point might make one think that he supported complete congregational autonomy, of the sort often ascribed by historians to contemporary Germanic Anabaptists and later English Independents. Such a reaction must be modified, however, by the final book of this volume, which spells out in more detail Morély's recommendations for ecclesiastical institutions of greater generality. After insisting at some length upon the importance of equality among pastors and upon the Christian humility which they must all nourish within themselves,[8] he proceeds to recommend the establishment of some representative bodies within the Church. Within each local congregation, he suggests the establishment of a council

---

[1] *Ibid.*, bk. 3, ch. 5, outlines these recommendations.

[2] *Ibid.*, bk. 3, ch. 6, especially pp. 212-213.

[3] *Ibid.*, p. 199, " Toutes lesquelles choses estans dictes principalement touchant les pasteurs & Ministres, doivent estre entendues pareillement des Diacres, docteurs, lecteurs, & autres offices de l'Eglise."

[4] Morély deliberately calls them " senieurs," rather than using the usual Reformed term " anciens," on grounds that the usual term implies an unnecessary prerequisite of advanced age for these ministers. This usage seems to be unique. W. Richard, *Kirchenterminologie*, pp. 127-131, does not list " senieur " among the variant forms for " ancien." See J. Morély, *Traicté*, bk. 3, ch. 11, for full discussion of the selection and functions of " senieurs."

[5] J. Morély, *Traicté*, p. 199, " les noms de prestre, Evesque, & pasteur signifient presque une mesme chose en substance, sinon que le nom de prestre contient davantage l'honneur de l'aage."

[6] *Ibid.*, bk. 3, chs. 12 (deacons), 13 (deaconesses), 14 (doctors). On the Reformed order of doctors, see Robert W. Henderson, *The Teaching Office in the Reformed Tradition: a history of the doctoral ministry* (Philadelphia : Westminster, 1962).

[7] *Ibid.*, bk. 3, ch. 15.

[8] *Ibid.*, bk. 4, chs. 1 and 2.

of pastors and "seniors," always meeting jointly.[1] The provision for joint meeting would leave no room, of course, for the separate Company of Pastors which was such a prominent part of Genevan church polity. But the council which Morély so describes is really the consistory of existing Reformed polity, charged more with administrative than with disciplinary responsibilities. There was precedent, furthermore, for consistories of this type in existing French practice.[2] Morély recommends that each such council be presided over by a pastor elected by the congregation for a two-year term. This term could be renewed once, and, in exceptional circumstances, more than once, but normally there should be some rotation in this office. Again, he does not really depart from existing practice, except in apparently providing for popular election of the presiding officer.

Morély then proceeds to recommend establishment of a hierarchy of representative bodies on top of these local congregations. In each local "bailliage," he recommends the selection of a presiding pastor, responsible to a "council of seniors and consistory," aided by a "certain number of [other] ministers deputed to watch over the doctrine, the morals, and scandals, as much of the other ministers as of the people." [3] Elections of these men should take place in the mother-church of each *bailliage* and should be for two-year terms, staggered in order to maintain some continuity. Here, of course, Morély was providing for an equivalent to the contemporary Reformed colloquy, without the allowances for the rights of outlying congregations one might expect from an advocate of popular government within the Church.

The next layer in the ecclesiastical hierarchy Morély recommends would be filled by provincial synods.[4] They should meet every year if possible, at least every two years, with special meetings called to deal with pressing problems. In addition to their regular duties of guarding doctrine and administering the Church, Morély would charge these provincial synods with certain political responsibilities. They would be encouraged to draft remonstrances or petitions addressed to civil magistrates, to make these secular authorities aware of their obligations as Christians. This would be "not to climb above the magistrate, or to create confusion between the two governments [ecclesiastical and secular], but if there is some great disorder in the Republic, some fury and intolerable violence, such an assembly rightly ought to make a grave and serious remonstrance, as often happened toward the first Christian emperors." [5]

[1] *Ibid.*, bk. 4, ch. 4, describes the nature of this council at length, beginning, p. 282, with "Les Pasteurs donc & les Senieurs feront un seul conseil, auquel aura la principale charge de rapporter & tenir ordre un des Pasteurs, à qui l'Eglise donnera l'authorité & charge speciale de ce faire."

[2] G. V. Lechler, *Verfassung*, ch. 3, especially pp. 73-74.

[3] J. Morély, *Traicté*, p. 283, "conseil des Senieurs & Consistoire"; p. 284, "certain nombre de Ministres deputés pour veiller sur la doctrine, sur les mœurs, & scandales, tant des autres Ministres que du peuple."

[4] *Ibid.*, bk. 4, ch. 5, describes their composition and functions.

[5] *Ibid.*, pp. 286-287, "Non pas pour enjamber par dessus le Magistrat, ou pour mettre une confusion entre les deux gouvernemens, mais que s'il y avoit quelque grand desordre en la Republique, quelque fureur & violence intolerable, à bon droit une telle assemblee devroit user de grave & serieuse remonstrance : comme souvent est advenu envers les premiers Empereurs Chrestiens."

Morély is reluctant to build his hierarchy of councils much beyond the provincial level. He is suspicious of councils of greater generality and doubts that there is real Scriptural warrant for them.[1] Furthermore, he argues that the ecumenical councils of the patristic period were responsible for all kinds of evils and usurpations, and were a general menace to the Church as a whole. He does not exclude entirely, however, the possibility of councils either on the national or universal level. He grants that there may occasionally be practical reasons for summoning them.[2] But he insists that their powers must be closely circumscribed. Above all, councils of this generality must not be allowed to legislate for the Church as a whole by issuing canons. They may discuss church matters in a general way, and they may instruct or reprimand each other. To councils on the national level, as to provincial synods, would be assigned the political duty of presenting remonstrances to their national princes, whenever that seemed desirable.

The members of the councils on each of these higher levels in Morély's hierarchy, the provincial, the national, and the universal, would select their own presiding officers. At a universal council, a new presiding officer should be selected for each session. This provision, of course, represents a departure from Morély's general insistence that church leaders be selected by the entire membership of the Church. This departure is apparently justified in his mind by practical considerations and by the fact that these councils are allowed much less power than in existing Reformed polity.

This sharp reduction in power which Morély recommends, especially the reduction in power of any national church council, may explain some of the storms which his proposal was later to raise. He was occasionally able to win the support of provincial synods. But every time his proposals were laid before a national synod of the French Reformed Church, they were decisively and vehemently rejected. One obvious explanation is that no national synod wanted to abandon the substantial powers vested in it.

Morély concludes his volume with a consideration of other institutions the Church ought to establish in order to maintain good discipline. Some type of institution, he points out, should be established to relieve the poor, and property should be set aside for its support.[3] For poverty creates temptations to vice and corruption which few can resist. But, while he discusses the appropriate arrangements for poor relief at some length, he does so without much enthusiasm. In fact many of the arrangements are designed primarily to keep the able-bodied but indolent poor from receiving aid on a regular basis, so that all the church's resources for poor relief can go to those victims of circumstance who are deserving and helpless. Morély then offers some reflections about the schools and universities which, as he had pointed out earlier, he felt to be essential for the creation of an effective pastorate.[4] He also discusses briefly provisions for securing church buildings and celebrating holy days.[5] Finally he urges that libraries be established, and that in each

[1] *Ibid.*, bk. 4, ch. 6, develops this argument.

[2] *Ibid.*, bk. 4, ch. 7 (re national councils), and 8 (re ecumenical councils).

[3] *Ibid.*, bk. 4, chs. 9-13, mix considerations on poor relief and the administration of church property.

[4] *Ibid.*, bk. 4, chs. 14-17, re education.

[5] *Ibid.*, bk. 4, ch. 18.

province an ecclesiastical history be prepared.[1] On that note the volume ends abruptly, without even a summary as a conclusion.

It is not hard to provide a summary for Morély's book, however. In brief, this was his prescription for the necessary establishment of true discipline in the Christian Church: all kinds of clerical and secular dictation must be done away with; all important decisions must be vested in the entire membership of local congregations. This was the way, he felt, that discipline had been established in the time of the Apostles. Surely it was Christ's intention that discipline should be established in the same way in the time of the Reformation.

Certain aspects of this proposal are extremely interesting, and deserve immediate further comment. Perhaps the most startling, is Morély's frank plea for " democracy " in church government. The term " democracy," was, of course, well-known to educated men in the sixteenth century, but it was not in particularly high repute. For it usually meant to them, what it had meant to the Greeks who had coined the word: government by mob-rule, in which all participated, which was without law, and which was constantly subject to the whims and fancies of unprincipled demagogues. Morély knew all this, of course, and was careful to anticipate in advance the anti-democratic criticisms which his proposal would inevitably provoke. But he could not escape the logic of the fact that the sort of church government he proposed was indeed " democratic." Twice he even used the word himself. The first time, he used it rather apologetically: " Take up therefore the ancient discipline and you will restore the ancient morals. But this democratic government (they will say) is full of confusion: and is judged by the ancients to be the worst of the good governments, only to be the best of the vicious. However I could respond with a single word to such an objection: ' O man, who are you to resist God? ' Nevertheless I shall proceed farther, and shall deny such a government, which our Lord Jesus instituted, to be a democracy and popular estate." [2] What the ancients were really objecting to, he says, was the lawlessness, the demagoguery, and the lack of real public institutions in a typical " democracy." These dangers can be overcome by the Church, since it has Christ as its king, His Word as its law, and the council of pastors and " seniors " as its moderating body.

Morély's second use of the word " democracy," is less apologetic: " That where there is a legitimate council in a republic, and democracy, in which the laws dominate and have principal power (which points we have demonstrated to be in the Church), that there all things are done more wisely, with greater maturity and consideration, than in another sort of government, whatever it be. Of which give evidence the republics which have been judged the best governed which have ever been, the Athenian and

---

[1] *Ibid.*, bk. 4, ch. 19.

[2] *Ibid.*, p. 32, " Reprenez donc l'ancienne discipline, & vous restituerez les mœurs anciennes. Mais ce gouvernement Democratique (diront-ils) est plein de confusion: & est jugé des anciens estre le pire des bons gouvernemens, seulement estre le meilleur des vicienx [sic]. Or jà soit que d'une seule parole je puisse respondre à telle objection: O homme, qui est-tu qui resistes à Dieu? Toutefois je passeray outre, & nieray un tel gouvernement que nostre Seigneur Jesus a institué, estre une democratie, & estat populaire." See also above, p. 51.

Roman, of the gravel and stones of which is drawn all that is good today in all civil government." [1]

Here Morély comes close to advocating democracy as the best form of secular government. This would be a rather startling suggestion in the sixteenth century. No doubt Morély planned to work out in more detail his ideas on that subject in his second book. Yet even in this book, the analogies between ecclesiastical and civil government were frequent and clear. It would not have been difficult for his readers to draw from his argument that God wanted democracy in the Church, the conclusion that God might not look with disfavor upon democracy in the state.[2]

A second aspect of Morély's proposal which deserves underlining, is his emphasis on the role of the local congregation. Again and again it is clear in his argument that the real " Church " is the local body of believers. Only here should decisions about doctrine and behavior normally be made. Only here should selections of clergy be made. This emphasis on congregational autonomy is, to be sure, modified by the substantial role Morély gives to the " mother-church " of each *bailliage* and province, in the decision-making processes. It is further modified by the role which he assigns to consistories, colloquies, provincial synods, and, very begrudgingly, to national synods and ecumenical councils. Nevertheless it is clear that Morély was urging considerable decentralization in church government. As much power as possible should be vested in local units. In this, Morély may have reflected, as some of his opponents were to charge, the influence of earlier Germanic Anabaptists. He may have also conceivably influenced, in turn, the practice of later English Independents.[3]

Related to Morély's desire for popular church government and for local rule, is his emphasis on lay participation in the rule of the church. Again and again he insists that pastors have no right to make certain decisions or appointments on their own authority. Again and again he insists that every organized group representing a church should include lay " seniors," and should not be restricted solely to the ordained pastors. In this, Morély was obviously attacking the contemporary Reformed institution of the Company of Pastors, which had grown so powerful in communities like Geneva.

---

[1] *Ibid.*, p. 183, " Que où il y a conseil legitime en une Republique, & democratie, en laquelle les loix dominent, & ont principale puissance (lesquels poincts nous avons demonstré estre en l'Eglise) que là toutes choses se font plus sagement, avec plus grande maturité, & consideration, qu'en autre sorte de gouvernement, quel qu'il soit. De quoy font foy les Republiques qui ont esté jugées les mieux gouvernees qui furent onques, l'Athenienne, & Romaine : du gravois & pierres desquelles tout ce qui est de bon aujourd'huy en tout gouvernement civil, est tiré."

[2] For fuller discussion of this aspect of Morély's argument and of hostile reactions to it, see Robert M. Kingdon, " Calvinism and Democracy : some political implications of debates on French Reformed Church government, 1562-1572," *American Historical Review*, LXIX (1964), 393-401. Cf. the contemporary reaction to " democracy " by Calvin, discussed by John T. McNeill, " John Calvin on Civil Government," in George L. Hunt and John T. McNeill, eds., *Calvinism and the Political Order* (Philadelphia : Westminster, 1965), ch. 2, especially pp. 37-38. McNeill's discussion is based in part on a perhaps unavoidable translation of " politia " as " democracy " which seems to me to lose the moral distinction normally drawn by the ancients and by men of the sixteenth century between good " politia " and bad " democratia." Cf. also the ambiguous reaction, similar to Morély's, of Pierre Viret, discussed by R. D. Linder, *Viret*, pp. 87-94.

[3] See below, pp. 127-135, for further consideration of this possibility.

I suspect that it was Morély's insistence on more lay participation in church government, more than any other aspect of his program, which sparked much of the bitter controversy which his proposal engendered. It must have seemed powerfully appealing to laymen, many of them of high birth and substantial education, who were becoming increasingly impatient with the increasingly rigid and arbitrary leadership supplied to the Reformed movement by its pastors. And it must have been powerfully irritating to the pastors who had devoted life, intelligence, and property, sometimes at substantial personal sacrifice, to the advancement of the Reformed cause.

A final aspect of Morély's proposal which bears underlining, is its political activism. As between those Calvinists who felt that the faithful should accept passively all the tribulations in the shape of wicked rulers and persecution to which Providence subjected them, and those who wanted to take political action to resolve such problems, Morély was clearly on the side of the activists. It is less clear, however, whether he would support violent or illegal political action. The chief kind of action he recommended was the remonstrance, which he felt the various councils of the Church should be prepared to make whenever the political situation made it necessary. Since he dwells on this duty of remonstrance particularly in his discussion of provincial synods, he may have looked upon it as primarily a way of bringing pressure to bear upon provincial governors, provincial estates, and provincial *parlements*. He does, however, also regard remonstrance as a duty of national synods.

This activism, combined with democracy, local rule, and anti-clericalism, could have made of Morély's proposal the platform for a movement of proportions that would have been truly revolutionary in the sixteenth century. However that was not to be. His proposal was in itself too tentative and modest in statement. And it never did win enough strong and aggressive support.

A more precise measure of the kind of support it was intended to win, can be gained from a study of the authorities upon which Morély based his argument. Such a study reveals that Morély was writing above all for the contemporary Protestant audience. The two bodies of authority which he cites most frequently are the books of the Bible and the records of the Patristic Church. Of the two, the Bible is clearly the more important. It was the source of which Morély was most conscious, and upon whose authority he relied most heavily. Again and again he cites Bible verses in support of arguments. The margins of his book contain constant references to specific passages in the Bible, which the accompanying text studies with care, or simply quotes, or paraphrases, or to which it merely alludes. A thorough study of Morély's use of Scripture would distract from our present analysis. It is interesting to note, however, that while he normally insisted that Scripture was the " Word of God," and should be accepted without demur, he was not completely consistent and invariable in this rule. When dealing with the selection of deaconesses, for example, he rejects St. Paul's rule that deaconesses should be widows of at least sixty years of age who had raised children. He suggests that this rule was established because of a surplus of women eager to help the early Church in its work, and that since the surplus has disappeared, so should the rule.[1]

[1] J. Morély, *Traicté*, p. 255, " Et ce donc qu'il [sainct Paul] requiert que la vefve aye soixante ans, qu'elle aye esté femme d'un mary, qu'elle aye nourry ses enfans, ne sont conditions necessaires pour tous temps en telle vocation : mais où le nombre d'icelles

Second only to the Bible among Morély's authorities are the records of the Patristic Church—both the writings of the Church Fathers themselves, and the history of the early Church's development. To this history he refers frequently, citing actions of emperors and councils, saintly bishops and scoundrelly heretics, in adducing support for his argument. The precise records from which he draws this information are not revealed. A student of patristics could no doubt ferret them out. But that, again, would distract from this analysis.

Among his Protestant audience, Morély no doubt hoped chiefly to win the educated. The elaboration of his Scriptural and patristic arguments suggests this. This impression is strengthened by his occasional references to the secular thought of the ancients. He cites Aristotle, for example, to support the argument that governments with a broad base are more likely to reach wise decisions than governments with a narrow base.[1] But he uses such direct appeals to the authority of the ancient thinkers only occasionally. They are not the standard fixture in his work that they are in so many writings of the period.

An appeal to the educated is often also an appeal to the upper ranks of society. That Morély had them primarily in mind is suggested, furthermore, at many points in his volume. While there were, of course, many parts of his proposal for popular participation in church government that would seem to have been appealing to such active and articulate members of the lower ranks of society as the printers' journeymen,[2] in general he seems to have presupposed the sort of society in which the higher orders provide ' natural ' leadership. Such a presupposition is suggested particularly by his fear that improved poor relief would encourage dangerously the undeserving poor. But it is also suggested by the emphasis on moral rigor which informs his entire argument. In any event, it is clear, as we shall soon see, that Morély in fact won his most significant support from certain great aristocrats, other members of the nobility, and their clients.

The educated Protestant audience to which Morély meant to appeal was no doubt largely that of France. His book, after all, is in French and many of his specific recommendations are clearly intended for the reformed churches of France. In fact some of them were already in use in France. If he was appealing to Frenchmen, however, he was not appealing to chauvinists among them, of the sort who would be impressed only by appeals to their own customs and to authorities from their own resident population. This, at least, is suggested by the few casual references he makes to contemporary practices and contemporary thinkers.

---

ne seroit si grand, qu'il n'y eust beaucoup à choisir, il n'y a doute qu'il ne soit permis de faire election des plus vertueuses & charitables, & qui seroyent en plus grande liberté, encores que toutes ces conditions ne s'y trouvassent."

See also Morély to Calvin, 10 April [1562], described in n. 4 to p. 48 above, for a modest and tentative but very explicit claim that his entire argument was founded on the Bible.

[1] *Ibid.*, p. 183, " Car (comme Aristote dit fort prudemment) comme un banquet, auquel plusieurs apportent leur souppe, est mieux fourny, & plus abondant, que ne seroit le banquet ordinaire d'un, ou de peu de personnes, pareillement en une grande assemblee où chacun apporte librement son advis & jugement, il y a plus de conseil, & prudence, qu'en conseil quelconque de peu de personnes."

[2] This is suggested by Natalie Zemon Davis, " Strikes and Salvation at Lyons," ARG, LVI (1965), 58, n. 34.

Among contemporary practices, for example, he speaks with special praise of one which seems to have been in use among the reformed churches of the Swiss Pays de Vaud and the Savoyard Chablais, both then controlled by the Republic of Berne. In speaking of church assemblies, he commends the practice of having local "congregations, assemblies, or colloquies" meet weekly to discuss the Scriptures and church affairs, in areas large enough to encompass about twenty pastors but small enough so that all of them can attend without inconvenience, these groups to be presided over by "deans" assisted by "jurors." [1] The only reformed churches of the French language which seem to have used at that time the titles "dean" and "juror," were those of the Pays de Vaud and the Chablais. They labeled the presiding pastor of each of their regional "classes" or colloquies a "dean," and named the pastors elected as alternates to take his place, if need arose, "jurors." [2]

Among contemporary thinkers, Morély similarly turns to men who did not live in France. One of the two he cites, to be sure, Calvin, was certainly a Frenchman, yet his most significant work was done outside his native country. The other, Martin Bucer, the reformer of Strasbourg, was a German, whose main knowledge of things French probably came from the exiles who took

---

[1] J. Morély, *Traicté*, p. 284, "Pour lesquelles raisons je desireroye que l'ordre des Eglises de par deça fust observé : c'est à sçavoir que les Eglises de chacun bailliage fussent departies en certaines congregations, assemblées ou colloques, tant pour l'interpretation de l'escriture, que nous avons dit devoir estre faicte en public, que pour leur communiquer des affaires des Eglises de leurs corps : lesquels se vuideroyent, ou par les Eglises, s'ils appartenoyent à la cognoissance d'icelles, ou entre les Pasteurs. En quoy on auroit esgard que les lieux ne fussent trop distans, à ce que les Ministres se peussent commodement assembler une fois la sepmaine, & peussent aller & venir en un jour, & despescher leurs petits affaires domestiques. Si seroit-il à souhaiter (si le pais le pouvoit souffrir) qu'il y eust en chacune telle assemblee environ vingt pasteurs : car par ce moyen il y auroit plus de conseil, & de gravité, & pour l'advenir moins de menees. En chacune telle assemblee un de ces Ministres que nous pouvons appeler surveillans, presideroit, (iceux sont communement appelés par deça Doyens) outre lesquels pour leur soulagement, & à ce que l'Eglise ne soit jamais sans personne grave & propre pour presider, & pour beaucoup d'autres affaires, on a coustume d'elire des Jurés, ce que je loue grandement, & est chose digne d'imitation."

[2] W. Richard, *Kirchenterminologie*, p. 134, re "doyen"; confirmed and amplified by a source called to my attention by Natalie Zemon Davis : Antoine du Pinet, *La conformite des eglises reformees de France et de l'eglise primitive, en police & Ceremonies* (n.p., 1564), "un Doyen & quatre jurez és Eglises de Berne [i.e. the Pays de Vaud and Chablais]... 27" (index) ; "Vray est, que par maniere d'ordre, on elit en quelques Eglises reformees, qui ne sont de ce royaume, un Doyen & quatre jurez en chasque classe et congregation des Ministres" (p. 27). Morély's reference to the practice as one current "here" ("de par deça") might lead one to assume that he meant Lyon, where the book was published, or Geneva, where he presumably wrote most of it. And the companies of pastors in both those cities did undertake activities of the sort he commends here. However the terms "doyen" and "juré" were never, to my knowledge, used in Geneva in this sense. Neither is "doyen" so used in Lyon, I am told by Mrs. Davis, who plans to include some detailed description of the Reformed Church in Lyon in her forthcoming book, *Strikes and Salvation at Lyons*. Morély's apparent allusion here to a Swiss practice is one of several considerations which lead me to discount the intriguing theory of E. Léonard, *Hist. gen. du prot.*, II, 115-123, that Morély was defending consistently but unsuccessfully an essentially French "congregationalism" against a foreign "presbyterianism" imported from Switzerland. A more telling negative consideration is the fact that the only prominent French Reformed leader of Swiss birth, Viret, was relatively sympathetic to Morély, while his most implacable opponents were all of French birth. While some of these opponents, like Beza, had, to be sure, emigrated to Geneva, others, like Chandieu, were still resident in France.

refuge in his city. Morély's reference to Calvin comes in a discussion of the ministerial order of doctors. He compares the doctor to the " prophet," as that word is used in the New Testament, explicitly adapting a definition of " prophecy " advanced by " Master John Calvin, one of the most excellent apostles the Lord has raised up in this time." [1] Morély's reference to Bucer comes toward the end of his book, in the course of a discussion on the charitable works of the church and of the proper ways to finance them. He concludes that one good way to finance churchly activity is by collections at church services, especially Sunday services. In support of this argument, he cites, with warm approval, the concurring opinion of Bucer, a " man of admirable piety, judgment, knowledge, and dexterity." [2]

The analysis of the audience for which Morély was writing tends to be reinforced, I feel, by the general tone of his work. Clearly he was appealing to others within the Calvinist tradition. Not only does he mention Calvin himself with respect and admiration. He also supports with enthusiasm such controverted Calvinist doctrines as intolerance, that typically Calvinist insistence that heresy, particularly of the Anabaptist type, must be punished rigorously, even with death.[3] Morély's own expression of Calvinism, however, is often rather uncharacteristically undogmatic. He states his entire argument with considerable modesty and frequent tentativeness. A number of times he even confesses that he can't develop his arguments skillfully, and urges that those better qualified do so.[4] This modesty of tone is indeed refreshing, in an age dominated on the intellectual plane by the shrill and arrogant certainty of men like Calvin and Erasmus. Modesty could not save Morély from controversy, however. The venomous attacks of his enemies and the enthusiastic support of his friends were soon to plunge the French Reformed Church into a prolonged struggle.

C. The Internal Quarrel:

1. *First Reactions to Morély's Proposal*

The first formal reactions to Morély's proposal materialized very quickly. They materialized at the very next meeting of the national Synod of the French Reformed Church, the meeting to which Morély had asked Viret to submit his book. This Synod met in Orleans, at the end of April, 1562, only a few weeks after the book had left the presses. It met at a time when the

[1] J. Morély, *Traicté*, p. 257, " ce mot de Prophetie (comme aussi l'expose Maistre Jean Calvin un des plus excellens Apostres que le Seigneur a suscités en ce temps, non seulement pour la restauration de son Eglise, mais aussi pour l'illustration de la doctrine & conservation d'icelle à perpetuité) signifie interpretation claire & illustre de l'escriture saincte."

[2] *Ibid.*, p. 321, " Touchant les aumosnes ordinaires des fideles en particulier, l'advis de maistre Martin Bucer homme de pieté, jugement, sçavoir, & d'exterité admirables, me semble digne d'estre ensuivy : lequel il escrit en son livre du regne de Jesus Christ : à sçavoir que és assemblees solennelles qui se font quelques jours la sepmaine, specialement le jour du repos, nous sommes tenus d'apporter au Seigneur nostre present : & ce à bon droit."

[3] See above, n. 3 to p. 52.

[4] E.g. J. Morély, *Traicté*, bk. 2, ch. 1, develops an apology of this sort at some length.

Huguenot armies were assembling in that very city, to do battle for their faith against the French crown and the Catholic Guise, in the first French war of religion. The records of this particular Synod are even less revealing than usual about the churches represented and the delegates in attendance. It seems reasonably clear, however, that attendance was poor,[1] that the sessions were brief, and that the approach of war distracted and subdued everyone involved. War did not distract them, to be sure, from even considering Morély's book. But it may have inhibited a full discussion of his proposals and it may have kept away delegates inclined to consider them with sympathy. Viret, for example, although he had planned to attend, did not in the end get to Orleans.[2]

A delegate who did get to Orleans was Antoine de la Roche Chandieu, and he was chosen to preside over the Synod's sessions. This choice may well have sealed the initial fate of Morély's proposals. For Chandieu, as we have already noted, was close to Calvin and Beza. As a witness in the Geneva trial of Morély for spreading the rumor that the city's pastors had approved in advance of the Amboise Conspiracy, Chandieu knew of the tensions between his friends and Morély. Chandieu was also to assume a leading role in certain later attempts to refute and suppress Morély's ideas.

There is little record of the Orleans Synod's discussion of Morély's book. There is ample record, however, of its decision. That decision was to condemn the book, flatly and unequivocally. It is expressed in these words:

" As to that Book entituled, *A Treatise of Christian Discipline and Polity*; composed and published by *John Morelly*, the Council judges, That as to the Points concerning the Discipline of the Church, by which he pretends to condemn and subvert the Order received in our Churches, founded upon the Word of God, that the said Book contains wicked Doctrine, and tends to the Confusion and Dissipation of the Church; and therefore the said Council cautions the Faithful to take heed of the aforesaid Doctrine." [3]

Even a condemnation this sweeping and this widely publicized was not enough to satisfy the pastors of Geneva. They determined to take direct action against Morély, using the machinery of the Genevan state and church. They got a chance to do so several weeks later, when Morély returned to Geneva. He was promptly ordered to appear before the Consistory, at the regular weekly session scheduled for Thursday, November 5, 1562. This summons seems to have frightened him right out of the city, however, for on that day the Consistory got word that he had returned to Lyon. It ordered his wife to inform her husband, by writing, that he must appear before the Consistory in a few days.[4] For months Morély ignored this peremptory summons. Then in July of 1563, he sent an application to the city councillors charged with criminal matters, asking that he be permitted to return to Geneva for business reasons, and agreeing to appear before the Consistory. On

---

[1] Chapter 2, article 1, of the acts of this Synod notes many delegates were absent. Chapter 1 names the three officers elected by the Synod and their churches. See J. Quick, *Synodicon*, I, 22; J. Aymon, *Synodes*, 2nd pagination, p. 23.

[2] See R. D. Linder, *Viret*, pp. 43-44, re Viret's movements during this period; p. 93, re his intention to go to Orleans, with some speculation as to why he did not.

[3] J. Quick, *Synodicon*, I, 27; cf. J. Aymon, *Synodes*, I, 2nd pagination, p. 29.

[4] Geneva, Arch., RConsistoire, XIX, fol. 169, 5 November 1562. Fol. 174v., 19 and 21 November 1562, notes he had still not appeared and considers further action.

Calvin's advice, these officials granted Morély's request and offered him safe-conduct.[1]

Morély returned to Geneva and duly kept his promise. Twice he appeared before the Consistory and was sharply questioned.[2] At first he offered to abandon his views, if any one of the three recognized intellectual leaders of the French Reformed movement, Farel, Viret, or Calvin, should explicitly reject them. Calvin, who attended these sessions as a member of the Consistory, refused to take up this challenge, insisting that it would be highly improper for him to usurp a position of superiority over a national synod by presuming to judge its decisions. Then Calvin, now acting as spokesman for the Consistory, tried to persuade Morély to retract. Morély replied in the classic Protestant way, by saying that he would retract only if proven wrong by the Word of God. The Consistory then shifted its attack somewhat by pointing out to Morély that he had never obtained the permission of any government to publish his book, even though in the book itself he had insisted that such permission should always be obtained for any publication dealing with religion. The Consistory next presented Morély with a short statement of the views which it required him to retract, a statement which summarized the argument of his book with reasonable fairness but great brevity. At that point, Morély asked for permission to submit a written reply, which he could presumably prepare at leisure and document. The Consistory flatly refused this request and continued to press him. He continued to ask for a chance to answer in writing. The Consistory then lost all patience. It ruled him " excommunicated, as a schismatic and man given to contentions." And it ordered him to appear before the city Council for appropriate secular action. This order seems really to have alarmed Morély, who no doubt remembered the harshness with which Genevan courts had treated others accused of religious dissent. He again left town, abruptly and secretly. Behind him, he left with his wife a letter, explaining his flight, and complaining that " the Consistory had not wanted to hear him, but before having examined the case had pronounced a sentence which he named Atrocious." [3]

The wheels of Genevan justice were not stopped or even slowed by Morély's flight. Even though he was absent, the city Council proceeded

[1] Geneva, Arch., Jur. Pen. A-3 (Livre des Criminels, 1562-1564), 1563, fol. 41v., 16 July.

[2] Geneva, Arch., RConsistoire, XX, fols. 115, 120v., 26 and 31 August 1563.

[3] All these details on the Consistory hearings can be found in *L'Extraict des procedures faites & tenues contre Jean Morelli...* (Geneva: Perrin, 1563). Key passages: re Morély's appeal to Calvin, "il luy fut dit par spectable Jean Calvin (pource que ledit Morelli promettoit d'acquiescer à ce que spectables Guillaume Farel, Pierre Viret & luy en diroyent) qu'il n'entendoit point estre arbitre par dessus le Synode, ni retracter ce qui avoit esté là determiné : pource que ce seroit usurper une superiorité qui ne luy appartenoit point " (p. 5) ; the Consistory's summary of the views Morély was to retract, " que le peuple eust la cognoissance de tout ce qui appartenoit au regime & police de l'Eglise : & que s'il y avoit des Consistoires, qu'ils ne pouvoyent rien diffinir ne quant à la doctrine, ne quant aux mœurs : mais seulement rapporter au peuple, auquel seul il appartenoit de juger " (pp. 6-7) ; the Consistory's sentence, " l'a excommunié comme schismatique & homme addonné à contentions " (p. 8) ; Morély's letter to his wife, " donne à entendre que le Consistoire ne l'a pas voulu ouir, mais devant qu'avoir cognu la cause a prononcé une sentence qu'il nomme, Atroce " (p. 9). This publication is closely based on the official records in Geneva, Arch., PC, 2nd series, No. 1256, which are partially corroborated by the sketchier account in RConsistoire, XX, fols. 115, 120v, 26 and 31 August 1563.

immediately to consider the case against him. Theodore Beza presented this case, at some length, to the councillors charged with criminal proceedings. He noted pointedly that Morély's book contained democratic ecclesiastical ideas, or, to use his own words, "a false doctrine, against this Church and other reformed ones of France... [returning] all the affairs to the people." He then told the councillors of the condemnation of Morély's book by the Orleans Synod, of the examination of Morély by the Geneva Consistory, and of his flight.[1] The councillors, after asking Calvin's advice,[2] decided to condemn Morély, and promulgated a condemnatory sentence which Calvin drafted for them.[3] This sentence declared Morély guilty of disobedience and contempt, because of his failure to appear before the Council when summoned. In punishment of these crimes, and even more to prevent any further spread of his ideas, it was ordered that his book be burned publicly. Sale, purchase, or reading of the book was henceforth prohibited, and all copies of it were to be delivered to the authorities within twenty-four hours.[4]

Even those in Geneva suspected of sympathizing with Morély were subject to harassment. Days before the Council actually condemned Morély, the Consistory, in a related case, rigorously cross-examined an apothecary named Pierre Touillet and several of his friends. They were accused of having been overly familiar with Morély and of having stored copies of his books. Touillet admitted that he had repeated Morély's rumor, that "the ministers approved the tumult of Amboise." And a friend reported that he had also said that Morély's book "seemed to him good" even though he knew it had been condemned by the Synod of Orleans. The Consistory instructed Beza to report Touillet's case to the Council.[5] Clearly the Genevan authorities meant business with their drastic prohibitions.

A final and surprising link in this chain of reactions was a decision to publish the entire Genevan proceedings against Morély. Before the year was out, François Perrin, one of Calvin's favorite printers, brought out an eleven-page pamphlet on the case. It contained a lengthy account of the Consistory's proceedings against Morély and a full text of the Council's sentence condemning him and his book.[6] Publication of this kind was really extraordinary. The

---

[1] Geneva, Arch., Jur. Pen. A-3 (Livre des Criminels, 1562-1564), 1563, fols. 55-55v., 2 September. The quoted passage: "ledit Morelli avoit faict ung livre fort pernicieux ou il y a doctrine faulse contre ceste eglise & aultres de France reformees mesmes par ledit livre il remet tous les affaires au peuple."

[2] *Ibid.*, fol. 56, 3 September 1563.

[3] *Ibid.*, fol. 58, 10 September 1563, identifies Calvin as the author of this draft; fol. 59, 14 September 1563, records some discussion of the extent to which Morély should be punished, and, 16 September 1563, records the proclamation of the sentence. PC, No. 1256, contains two drafts of the sentence, one with marginal notes in Calvin's hand.

[4] Published text of this sentence in *L'Extraict des procedures faites & tenues contre Jean Morelli...*, pp. 10-11.

[5] Geneva, Arch., RConsistoire, XX, 129-129v., 129v.-130, 9 September 1563. Touillet himself "confesse avoir dict que les ministres avoient approuves la tumulte d'Amboyse"; a witness reported "avoir ouy dire audit Touillet dudit livre quil luy sembloit bon... [even though he knew]... que ledit livre avoyt este condampne au Synode dOrleans." Touillet soon moved to France, but was pursued even there for accepting Morély's views on ecclesiastical discipline: see Church of Montauban to Ministers of Geneva, 19 November 1564, in Geneva, BPU, Ms. l. 197A, fol. 190, signed original.

[6] *L'Extraict des procedures faites & tenues contre Jean Morelli...* (Geneva: Perrin, 1563). I have used the copy in Geneva, BPU, Gf 567/Rés. 186.

L'EXTRAICT DES

Procedures ſaites &

TENVES CONTRE IEAN Morelli, natiſ de Paris, & n'agueres habitant en la ville de Geneue: touchant vn liure compoſé par luy, De la diſcipline Eccleſiaſtique, auec la ſentence des magnifiques ſeigneurs Sindiques & Conſeil dudit Geneue, prononcée & executée le ſezieme de Septembre 1563.

A GENEVE,

De l'Imprimerie de François Perrin.

M. D. LXIII.

Council normally kept all records of its legal proceedings secret,[1] and so did the Consistory. Clearly the Genevan authorities wanted to give the widest possible publicity to their condemnation of Morély.

These, then, were the first reactions to Morély's book. They show that the leadership of the French Reformed Church, vigorously led by Calvin in person, strongly seconded by Beza in Geneva and apparently by Chandieu in France, was determined to prevent any discussion of Morély's proposals, to stop all circulation of his book, and to punish him personally. If these leaders had succeeded, the controversy provoked by Morély would have never really developed. But, as so often in the sixteenth century, violent condemnations and excommunication were not enough to end the argument. They rather forced a shift in its form and its locale. Morély returned to his home near Paris. Among the Reformed in that critically important area, he won important new converts to his ideas. They helped him fan the flames of controversy to even greater heights.

2. *Morély in the Ile-de-France* [2]

Morély did not try to set ablaze the Protestant population of central France with any crusade for ecclesiastical reform immediately upon his arrival in the Paris area. On the contrary, he first tried to reconcile himself with the existing Reformed Church. He made this attempt by appearing in person at a meeting of a regional synod. This particular Synod met at La Ferté-sous-Jouarre, in April of 1564.[3] It was composed of delegates representing the provinces of Ile-de-France, Picardy, Brie, and Champagne. To the student of Calvinist politics, this Synod is interesting for more than one reason. The reason which pre-occupies us now, however, is that one of its main orders of business was a thorough re-examination of the Morély affair.

By this time Morély had obviously returned to his home. He had probably also had time, in the months since he had left Geneva, to renew his acquaintances with the nobility of the area, particularly with those devoted to the Reformed cause. The fact of his continuing excommunication seems to have weighed heavily upon him. It was to escape this dangerous spiritual punishment that he appeared before the Synod, begging for reconciliation. The Synod agreed to consider his case, and studied it with real care, probably a good deal more care than had been exercised at Orleans. Three of the pastors present at La Ferté were deputed to study Morély's book. They returned with the report that it contained a number of " errors and dangerous

[1] Which is why Jean-Jacques Rousseau, when he became embroiled with Genevan censors in the eighteenth century, seized upon this publication to build his own argument about the Genevan tradition of censorship. For more on this incident, see below, p. 137.

[2] Much of what follows in this section is drawn from an unsigned and undated but demonstrably authoritative manuscript narrative report on Morély's relations with the Reformed of the Ile-de-France from April 1564, to the middle of 1566. It can be found in the Genevan dossier of manuscripts on the Morély affair : Geneva, BPU, Ms. fr. 446, fols. 12-13v.

[3] This is one of the rare provincial synods whose minutes have been preserved. A contemporary copy of them, obtained by Sir Thomas Smith for the English government, can be found in London, Public Record Office, State Papers, Foreign, General Series, Elizabeth (S.P. 70), vol. 73, No. 469. For a summary description, see the *Calendar of State Papers, Foreign, 1564-1565*, p. 119, No. 357.

opinions," and that in it a number of Scriptural passages were " corrupted and turned from their straightforward and naive sense." [1] Antoine de la Roche Chandieu, the continuing bane of Morély's existence, who presided at this Synod as at Orleans, then entered the discussion himself. He debated at length with Morély, demonstrating to him the errors of his book. Some of the charges of error are incorporated in the minutes of the Synod, which happily have been preserved. Perhaps the most interesting charge is one which takes a sharp and dangerous political turn. Morély was told,

" that what he had written in his printed book, page 20, where it seems that he would take away the absolute power and authority of kings, is against the Word of God and the Confession of Faith of the churches." [2]

The passage under fire is probably this :

" Not that I want to say that it is for Princes to call up for their own consideration everything that concerns religion, and make themselves super-arbiters for regulating celestial doctrine according to their fantasies, (that which should not be permitted to them in political affairs), or to assume an unbounded power." [3]

Since the issue of the legitimacy of political resistance was very much in the air at this time, and was discussed in this very Synod, this charge must have been a most disturbing one. As we shall see later, moreover, a link was often drawn by contemporaries between ecclesiastical ideas which were democratic or semi-democratic, and resistance to royal authority. It is odd, however, to find orthodox Calvinists in effect criticizing a man for not being sufficiently Erastian. No wonder an English diplomat was glad to send home for his government a complete transcript of the records of this Synod.

These arguments appeared to win Morély over. He admitted that there were errors in his book, and promised to remedy the evil he had done in releasing it so hastily, by publishing a new work which would contain corrections. He agreed to submit himself to the ecclesiastical discipline then in force among the French Reformed churches, acknowledging that it was based on the Word of God. He promised to seek reconciliation with the Church of Geneva. And he drafted and signed a written recantation, which was incorporated within the Synod's minutes.[4] The Synod then ordered that, providing the Consistory of his home locality agreed, Morély was to be permitted to partake of communion. He shook hands all around, and the reconciliation seemed complete.

Only a few days later, on May 8, Morély took a first step to fulfill his promises. He wrote a long and humble letter to the pastors of Geneva, and

---

[1] Geneva, BPU, Ms. fr. 446, fol. 12 : " qu'il contenoit plusieurs erreurs et dangereuses oppinions et que beaucoup de passages de l'Escripture sainte y estoient corrumpues et destournez de leur droict et naïf sens."

[2] London, PRO, S.P. For. Eliz., 1564-5, 70, vol. 73, No. 469-I, p. [8], "ce quil a escript en son livre imprime page 20 ou il semble quil vueille oster la puissance absolue & aucto[rité] des Roys est contre la parolle de Dieu et confession de foy des Eglises."

[3] J. Morély, *Traicté*, p. 20, " Non pas que je vueille dire que ce soit aux Princes de revoquer à leur cognoissance tout le faict de la religion, & se faire superarbitres pour ordonner de la doctrine celeste à leurs fantasies, (ce que mesmes ne leur devroit estre permis és affaires politiques) ne pour entreprendre une puissance desordonnee."

[4] London, PRO, S.P. For. Eliz., 1564-5, 70, vol. 73, No. 469-1, p. [10], dated 29 April 1564.

had it sent to Calvin.[1] In this letter, he recounted the actions of the Synod of La Ferté and announced his change of heart, his decision to abjure his errors publicly, and his desire for reconciliation with the Genevan Consistory and Council. By the time this letter was written, however, Calvin was already dying. He may never have seen it. Some other hand, perhaps Beza's, scribbled some caustic marginal notes on it, and it was filed away in what was to become a very substantial bundle of papers relating to Morély.

Morély's promise to publish a corrected edition of his book was not fulfilled so quickly. Indeed there is no evidence that it was ever fulfilled. In Clermont-en-Beauvoisis, where he had settled down to live, the local Reformed minister asked him when he was going to perform this duty. He replied that he would get to work on it right away. On the strength of this promise, and by the advice of the local consistory, Morély was admitted again to communion.[2]

And so it seemed that the affair was over. But this was not to be. Two dangerous loose ends soon undid the whole settlement. One was Morély's failure to prepare his corrected edition. The other was Geneva's flat refusal to accept his apology.

It took some time for these loose ends to unravel the settlement, however. For the rest of 1564, nothing much happened. Morély kept stalling on the preparation of the correction he was to publish. And Geneva took little or no notice of his plea for reconciliation. There is apparently no reference in any of the Genevan registers to this plea, and, if any letters were sent out from Geneva in response to it, they apparently have not been preserved. If we can accept the chronology of the contemporary manuscript narrative of this stage in the quarrel, however, a letter rejecting Morély's apologies was in fact written by Pastor Colladon, on behalf of the Genevan Consistory, to the Paris Church.[3] Grounds for this rejection were that his letter of apology had not contained a sufficiently straightforward recognition of the fault he had committed in publishing his erroneous opinions, and that he had not as yet reconciled himself with the Genevan government. This Genevan rejection seems to have irritated Morély a good deal. In addition, it provided him with a talking point which was to win him considerable sympathy.

Sometime around the turn of the year, Morély moved to Paris itself. This brought his case into the immediate jurisdiction of the important Reformed Church of Paris. It also must have brought Morély into renewed conflict with his old nemesis, Antoine de la Roche Chandieu. The conflict between Morély and the Parisians reached climaxes three times during the year of 1565,

---

[1] Morély to the pastors of Geneva, 8 May [1564], in Geneva, BPU, Ms. fr. 446, fols. 16-17, signed original, with an external address to Calvin. This letter eluded the editors of the *Calvini Opera* and has apparently never been published.

[2] Geneva, BPU, Ms. fr. 446, fol. 12.

[3] *Ibid.*, re " lettres desdits freres [de Genève] escriptes a ceste esglise [de Paris] le 9 de decembre 1565, signées Colladon au nom des pasteurs et anciens du Consistoire." The date 1565 seems to be an obvious error for 1564, since the passage is immediately followed by an account of subsequent events in February 1565. However I have not only been unable to locate a copy of this letter, but have also not found mention of it in the Genevan registers, while there is record there of exchanges re Morély in December of 1565. This suggests the possibility that the writer of this narrative was mistaken, and that Geneva either did not receive or chose to ignore in 1564 this overture from Morély.

each time on the occasion of a synod held in Paris. The first two synods were provincial ones, representing only the reformed churches of the Ile-de-France. The last Synod was a national one.

Early in February the first of these synods assembled. It summoned Morély to appear in order to explain why he had not as yet fulfilled all of his promises. This summons seems to have provoked a burst of bad temper in Morély. He appeared before the Synod, all right, but he upset the brethren by telling them there was nothing in his book contrary to the Word of God, and by noting that the Synod was meeting illegally, in defiance of the king's edicts. This last shaft really horrified the Synod. It was, alas, true. Morély's temper quickly changed, however, and before long he was apologizing and retracting his statements. He meekly listened to a scolding from the Synod. After further discussions, and Morély's signature of a new retraction, which repeated the substance of the earlier one and added an explicit acceptance of the condemnations which his work had received in Orleans and Geneva, Morély was again reconciled with his fellow Protestants. The Consistory of the Paris Church, taking into account his new retraction and certain other promises he made, with some reluctance agreed to admit him to communion.[1]

And so again it seemed that the quarrel was over. To make sure that it was over, however, this first provincial Synod of 1565 took one further significant step. It decreed that " a treatise confirming the discipline received in the churches be printed." [2] This task must have been assigned to Antoine de la Roche Chandieu. At least it can be demonstrated that he was the author of the treatise which eventually appeared. Its appearance was delayed for more than a year, however, for reasons which succeeding events will help to explain.

The first of these events occurred in the month of July following, at another Synod of the province of the Ile-de-France. One of the principal items on this Synod's agenda was discussion of a letter in defense of Morély, from Odet de Coligny, the Cardinal of Châtillon. This development was dramatic and important. It meant that Morély had finally won some support, and won it in an extremely significant quarter. To understand why this should be so, we need to take a closer look at the Cardinal of Châtillon.

Two major aristocratic houses provided the political and military leadership and much of the material support for the entire early Protestant movement in France. These were the houses of Navarre and Châtillon. Of the leaders of the house of Châtillon, the one who is rightly most widely honored and most intensively studied is Gaspard de Coligny, the Admiral of France. But his two brothers were very close to the Admiral, and were often assigned important roles of their own in the intricate scenario of Huguenot politics. One of these brothers was Odet de Coligny, the Cardinal of Châtillon.[3] His title may be deceptive, for those not well acquainted with sixteenth-century ecclesiastical politics. For although he had been a prince of the Roman Catholic Church

[1] *Ibid.*, fol. 12v. A copy of the text of this new retraction, dated 12 February 1565, can be found in *ibid.*, fols. 45-46. On the question of the legality of synods, see below, pp. 160-161.

[2] *Ibid.*, fol. 12v., " un traicte confirmatif de la discipline receue des esglises seroit imprimé."

[3] For biographical information on Odet de Coligny, see *France protestante*, 2nd. ed., art. " Châtillon," and works cited in following notes.

since the age of sixteen, was Bishop of Beauvais, and held many choice benefices, Odet never became a priest. In fact he never seems to have bothered to learn much about religion at all. His appointments had been purely political, and his career, also, was purely political.

Shortly before the beginning of the first war of religion in France, Odet de Coligny had followed his brothers into the Reformed Church. His conversion became known to the general public in 1561, when he openly celebrated communion in the Protestant way in his episcopal mansion in Beauvais. It was made more or less irrevocable in 1564, when he married a noble woman of prominent family in a private ceremony.[1] In spite of his conversion, he kept as many of his former ecclesiastical titles, functions, and revenues as possible. He apparently rather enjoyed being one of history's very few Protestant cardinals. He apparently did not even object to hearing his wife addressed by the extremely exclusive if not entirely unique title of "Madame la Cardinale."[2] He was determined not to relinquish the access to the crown and to the royal councils, to which his office entitled him. And he was careful to protect an income which was truly princely, which he himself estimated, shortly before his death, to total some 120,000 livres a year.[3]

Odet de Coligny brought to the French Protestant cause two great talents. One was for shrewd and skillful diplomacy. The other was for generous but discriminating patronage of the arts. Writers as renowned as Rabelais and Ronsard had good reason for eloquently praising the munificence of his patronage.[4] Rulers as powerful and as wily as Catherine de Medicis, Regent of France, and Elizabeth I, Queen of England, had good reason for respecting his negotiating abilities. A chronicler's description of Odet at the court of England may help to explain this respect:

"He was a handsome old man, of a good stature, with a long white beard, dressed always in black, with a great cloak of velvet or satin and a long coat, without ever wearing any mark of a cardinal; in addition of a good nature, if one had not upset him. The Queen never saw him without, in greeting him, kissing him."[5]

Obviously he was a man of considerable personal charm.

---

[1] In G. Bonet-Maury, "Les origines de la réforme à Beauvais (1532-1568)," BSHPF, XXIII (1874), p. 82, re his conversion; p. 134, re his appointments of Protestant pastors in 1563; p. 137, re his marriage.

[2] Title used by Florimond de Raemond, *Histoire de la naissance, progrez et decadence de l'heresie de ce siecle* (Rouen, 1647-1648), p. 757; a passage quoted in *France protestante,* 2nd ed., IV, col. 157, art. Châtillon. I am not sure the title was actually used by contemporaries.

[3] In Ernest G. Atkinson, "The Cardinal of Châtillon in England, 1568-1571," *Proceedings of the Huguenot Society of London,* III (1888-1891), pp. 241, 246.

[4] Quoted at length in Marguerite Christol, "Odet de Coligny, Cardinal de Châtillon," BSHPF, CVII (1961), 7-12. See also in N. Weiss, "Une des premières écoles de théologie protestantes en France (Orléans 1561-1568)," BSHPF, LX (1911), pp. 223-224, re Odet de Coligny's generous patronage of students in that institution.

[5] Florimond de Raemond, *op. cit.* in n. 14, pp. 757-758: "C'estoit un beau vieillard, d'une belle taille, la barbe longue et blanche, vestu tousjours de noir, d'un grand saye de velours ou de satin, avec un long manteau, sans porter aucune marque de Cardinal; au reste d'un bon naturel, si on ne l'eust gasté. La Reine ne le voyoit jamais,' que le saluant elle ne le baisast." For more on his negotiations in England, see E. G. Atkinson, *op. cit.* in n. 3, and F. de Schickler, *Les églises du refuge en Angleterre* (Paris, 1892, 3 vols.), I, 150-155.

It was probably Odet de Coligny's reputation as a patron that led Morély to approach him. At any rate, he sent the Cardinal and his brothers a letter complaining bitterly of the rigor with which he was being treated, particularly by the Church of Paris.[1] The extent of his bitterness may well have been deepened by new letters from Geneva, addressed both to Morély personally and to the Parisian Consistory, drafted by Beza in accordance with the instructions of the Genevan Consistory.[2] These letters again rejected Morély's pleas for reconciliation, again because he had not made his peace with the Genevan government and had not as yet made as full and frank a retraction of the content of his book as the Genevans wanted. And they taxed the Parisians for having admitted him to communion before he had fully purged himself.

The Cardinal then sent the Synod a report of Morély's complaints. And he added his own sharp comment, " that it is not proper thus to hammer away and scoff at people in the Church." [3]

The provincial Synod of the Ile-de-France meeting in July of 1565, thus found itself caught for fair. It had to deal with the recent anger of the Reformed movement's spiritual leaders in Geneva. And it had to deal with the immediate anger of one of the movement's most powerful temporal leaders. The only way out seemed to be renewed negotiation with Morély. He again appeared before the Synod, and again seemed tractable enough. The Synod decided to permit him to continue receiving communion, but on condition that he take further steps to reconcile himself with the Genevan authorities. A prominent member of the clergy in Paris, who knew Geneva well since he had served as a pastor there himself, François Morel, sire de Collonges, ventured to offer Morély some advice on the drafting of his letters asking for reconciliation.

But again reconciliation failed. Morély promptly sent off yet another letter of apology to the Genevan Consistory. After stalling for several months, he also sent one to the Genevan Council.[4] Most modern readers of these letters would probably find their apologies nearly as complete and as abject as possible. But contemporaries did not think so. François Morel warned Morély that his letter to the Consistory was not satisfactory.[5] His warning turned out to be prophetic. Both the Consistory and the Council of Geneva again rejected the apologies. The Consistory also complained to the Paris Church of the way in which the whole matter was being handled.[6] Morély reacted by again becoming bitter. He prepared a number of written accounts

---

[1] Reported in Geneva, BPU, Ms. fr. 446, fol. 12v.

[2] Geneva, Arch., RConsistoire, XXII, fol. 59, 10 May 1565; fol. 65, 17 May 1565, records these instructions and discussion preceding them. For contemporary copies of the letters themselves, see Geneva, BPU, Ms. fr. 446, fols. 38-39, 17 May 1565, to Morély; fols. 40-41, 17 May 1565, to Paris Consistory.

[3] Geneva, BPU, Ms. fr. 446, fol. 12v., reports as a quotation, " qu'il ne falloit pas ainsi rebattre et baffouer les personnes en l'Esglise."

[4] *Ibid.*, fol. 19, 13 July 1565, to Consistory; fols. 20-21, 14 October 1565, to Council, signed originals.

[5] So reports *ibid.*, fol. 13.

[6] By letter drafted by Beza, 10 October 1565, according to *ibid.* The Geneva Council's rejections came later, 9 December 1565, according to *ibid.*, following discussions recorded in Geneva, Arch., Jur. Pen. A-4 (Livre des Criminels, 1565-1566), 1565, fol. 80, 6 December; fol. 81v., 10 December; RConsistoire, XXII, fol. 182, 6 December.

of the whole quarrel to date, with complaints against the rigor of both the provincial synods and the Genevans, and sent them to Protestants he thought might prove sympathetic. And he agreed to an appeal which must have been accepted with considerable relief by the bedeviled Parisians, an appeal to the next national Synod.

By the time the Fifth National Synod of the Reformed Church in France assembled in Paris, toward the end of December, 1565, the Morély affair was clearly one of the most serious and delicate facing the Church. It could not be handled in the peremptory fashion with which it had been dismissed at Orleans. The delegates accordingly gave long and serious attention to the problem. Morély himself appeared, more convinced of the rightness of his program than ever. He presented to the Synod copies of his book and of various writings in support of its argument. He also presented to the Synod accounts of the actions taken against him in Geneva and elsewhere, with his complaints about them. The Synod refused to take under consideration Morély's complaints about these various hearings and trials. But it did discuss at length his program for reform of church discipline.

It will come as no surprise to anyone who knows about the history of early French national synods, however, to learn that this Synod also eventually ruled against Morély. Almost every one of these early synods was presided over by a man either sent directly from Geneva or closely allied to the Genevan pastors. The 1565 Synod was no exception. The man elected to preside over its sessions was Nicolas des Gallars, pastor of Orleans, one of Calvin's most trusted disciples and a former member of the Genevan pastoral corps. This Synod's considered conclusion was to,

" by this present Act condemn his [Morély's] said Books and Writings, as containing evil and dangerous Opinions, subverting that Discipline which is conformable unto the Word of God, and at this day received in the Reformed Churches of this Kingdom : and whereas delivering up the Government of the Church unto the People, he would bring in a new tumultuary Conduct, and full of Confusions [' confusion populaire ' —Aymon and ms.], upon it, from whence would follow many great and dangerous Inconveniencies." [1]

By this time Morély had had his fill of signing recantations. Further remonstrance and debate failed to shake him, and the synodical minutes report that Morély " persists in his Assertions, saying, That he is perswaded those his Opinions are built upon God's Holy Word." In spite of this unusually open obstinacy, the Synod decided to proceed with unusually great circumspection. One suspects that anxiety about the Cardinal's reactions weighed rather heavily with the synodical delegates. The final decision of the Synod was that since Morély accepted all " the fundamental principal Articles of our Faith " he should continue to " be received to the Peace and Communion of the Church." Two strings were attached to this final decision, however. One was that Morély was to cease spreading his opinions, and specifically was not to reply to a " Treatise in confirmation of " the received discipline " which may shortly be printed," presumably a reference to the tract which Chandieu

[1] J. Quick, *Synodicon*, I, 56-57, Cf. J. Aymon, *Synodes*, I, 2nd pagination, pp. 58-59, and the slightly but not significantly different contemporary ms. text in Geneva, BPU, Ms. fr. 446, fols. 69-69v. For a more detailed report on the discussion, see Geneva, BPU, Ms. fr. 446, fols. 13-13v.

was preparing. The other was that he was to reconcile himself with the Genevan authorities.[1]

In spite of the relative circumspection of the Paris National Synod, the Morély affair was still far from settled. Indeed, if anything, the crisis deepened. Morély's complaints about the way he had been treated were widely circulated among the Protestant aristocrats, and again reached the ears of the Cardinal of Châtillon. What was worse, to the orthodox, was that this time local churches and pastors began to show sympathy for Morély. Two letters addressed to Chandieu, in the spring of 1566, make this clear and provide interesting details.

One of these letters was written from La Charité, on behalf of a Synod of the local province which met in March, by a man named Rouviere.[2] It reported the vehement written protest submitted to the Synod by the brothers of the Church of Châtillon-sur-Loing. The geographical source of this protest was ominous enough, for Châtillon-sur-Loing was the ancestral home of the Coligny brothers. But its content was even more ominous. The Church of Châtillon-sur-Loing asked the members of the local Synod to join it in opposition to the decisions of the national Synod. It argued that these decisions were illegitimate both in matter and in form. And it warned darkly that a "tyrannical ambition" might "slip into the Church" if something were not done.[3] This protest was followed by a more explicit message to the provincial Synod from Pastor de la Haye, a personal pastor of the Cardinal of Châtillon. De la Haye warned that if the commissioned response to Morély was indeed published, as scheduled, an answer to it would be distributed within five or six days. This particular threat particularly worried the provincial Synod, and led Rouviere to propose an elaborate scheme for advance distribution of copies of the book to local colloquies, before its general release, so that the faithful would be sure to receive it before the retort in defense of Morély appeared. Both de la Haye and the Church of Châtillon-sur-Loing seem to have hinted strongly that they were supported by the Cardinal of Châtillon himself in these protests.[4]

The second letter to Chandieu gives even more direct evidence of the Cardinal's interest in the affair. It was from Pastor Merlin of the Paris Church, writing on behalf of the local Consistory. Its purpose was to urge Chandieu, then in Lyon, to publish his book either under his own name alone or anonymously, rather than in the name of any of the French synods. It reported that even that loyal friend of Geneva, Pastor des Gallars of Orleans, was now opposed to the printing of the book. And the reason for this growing dissatisfaction was, bluntly, the opposition of the Cardinal of Châtillon. The Cardinal had written to the Paris Church, urging it to take steps to prevent the printing of the book in that city. The reasons he gave for this

---

[1] J. Quick, *Synodicon*, I, 56-57.

[2] Rouviere [spelling uncertain] to Chandieu, 11 March 1566, in Geneva, BPU, Ms. fr. 446, fols. 72-73, original with address and signature partially mutilated.

[3] *Ibid.*: "il se failloit bien garder qu'une ambition tyrannique soubs laquelle nous avons esté ne glisçast en l'eglise."

[4] Châtillon is referred to as the "Comte de Beauvais" throughout this letter. For evidence that de la Haye was his pastor, see letter cited in n. 1 to p. 75.

request at last reveal something of his own thinking on the problem of ecclesiastical discipline. He is reported to have written that,

" it is not reasonable that two or three or a few people give the law to others, and that it is necessary that the discipline which one would want to have observed by all the churches should first be seen and approved by all the churches, indeed after long and mature deliberation."

He furthermore warned the Parisians that the whole Morély case revealed that unilateral statements of doctrine were likely to provoke continued protests. And he suggested that it would be wise for the Reformed movement to wait until it had more liberty of action before establishing a system of discipline that might well have to be changed soon afterwards, with considerable difficulty.[1]

This summary of the Cardinal of Châtillon's views suggests that his interest in Morély transcended a simple desire to protect a man who complained of unjust persecution. He seems also to have had doubts about the entire system of synodical and consistorial discipline which the men of Geneva were so strenuously seeking to construct in all of France. There is no hard evidence, however, that he had been converted to Morély's program of democracy in the Church, or that he was even aware that such a proposal was at issue.

Châtillon's support for Morély, if it had continued, could well have forced profound modifications of the entire structure of the French Reformed Church. At least the alarm of Chandieu's correspondents, and the defections which they report either to the side of Morély or to a policy of prudent neutrality, suggest that this was a real possibility. The Cardinal's support, however, seems to have been relatively short-lived. It was undercut by the visit to his court of two ministers of the Paris Church. They explained to the Cardinal at length the reasons for the decisions of the recent national Synod. They also engaged Morély in an open debate on both the procedures of the Synod and the substance of his ecclesiastical opinions. They apparently persuaded the Cardinal that he had been poorly informed about the whole affair.[2]

The loss of such powerful and promising support, must have persuaded Morély to seek reconciliation again. It was probably just after the debate at Châtillon's court that he wrote again to both the Consistory and Council of Geneva, explicitly in pursuance of the last national Synod's directive, to beg for their forgiveness and to ask for reconciliation.[3]

If the Genevan pastors had ever been afraid of the threat which the Cardinal of Châtillon posed to their system of discipline, they showed no sign

---

[1] Merlin to Chandieu, 2 April 1566, in Geneva, BPU, Ms. fr. 406, fols. 17-18v., published in E. Droz, " Autour de l'affaire Morély : La Roche Chandieu et Barth. Berton," BHR, XXII (1960), pp. 572-574. The quoted passage : " qu'il n'estoit pas raisonnable que deux ou trois ou peu de gens baillassent la loy aux autres, et qu'il falloit que la discipline qu'on vouloit estre observée par toutes les eglises, eut esté premierement veue et approuvée par toutes les eglises, voire apres longue et meure deliberation."

[2] This interview is described in Geneva, BPU, Ms. fr. 446, fol. 13v. It was probably held early in April, since it is not mentioned in either of the letters to Chandieu, yet it probably occasioned Morély's renewed plea for reconciliation with the Genevan Consistory and Council cited below and in n. 3.

[3] Morély to the Geneva Council, 12 April 1566, in *ibid.*, fols. 22-23 ; to the Geneva Consistory, same date, *ibid.*, fols. 24-25 ; signed originals.

now. Morély's retraction was again rejected as insufficient.[1] The Paris Church was again informed of this rejection.[2] And a few days later the famous printer Henri Estienne appeared before the Geneva Council to make formal application for permission to print a manuscript which had just been reviewed by Theodore Beza.[3] This manuscript was almost certainly the long-awaited official response to Morély.

3. *The Official Reply to Morély*

The official response to Morély bears the title, *La confirmation de la discipline ecclesiastique observee es eglises reformees du royaume de France; avec la response aux objections proposees alencontre*, or *The Confirmation of the Ecclesiastical Discipline Observed in the Reformed Churches of the Kingdom of France; with the Answer to the Objections Proposed Against It.* For a number of reasons it deserves an extended analysis at this point: it constitutes the fullest and most formal defense of Reformed polity against Morély's attack; it had become a subject of controversy even before its publication and affected the future course of the quarrel; it seems to have become a main source of information about the quarrel in later centuries.

There were two early editions of the *Confirmation.* Both of them appeared in 1566. The edition which must have come first and which had a more official character, came from the press of that great Calvinist printer of classical texts and works of erudition, Henri Estienne of Geneva.[4] The other edition came from the press of an obscure but fascinating printer specializing in works of popular Calvinist propaganda, Barthélemy Berton of La Rochelle.[5]

Both editions of the *Confirmation* were anonymous. But there can be little doubt that the author of the treatise was Antoine de la Roche Chandieu. The content of the book strongly suggests that the author was someone like Chandieu. It is obviously the work either of a clergyman or of someone strongly pro-clerical. It is obviously the work of a man more interested in French than in Genevan ecclesiastical practice. And there are other bits of internal evidence that point toward Chandieu. But the external evidence is even stronger. The two letters addressed to Chandieu early in 1566, to which we have just referred,[6] make it clear that he was preparing such a

---

[1] Pastors of Geneva to Morély, 17 May 1566, *ibid.*, fols. 75-76, contemporary copy.

[2] Pastors of Geneva to Paris Church, 17 May 1566, *ibid.*, fols. 77-78, contemporary copy.

[3] Geneva, Arch., RC, LXI, fol. 43v., 23 May 1566: " Henry Estienne. A presente requeste pour avoir permission d'imprimer une copie de la Reformation des eglises de France reveue par Monsieur de Beze. Arreste quon en aye advis." Permission was apparently granted on May 28, *ibid.*, fol. 45v., " Henry Estienne, [and other printers]. Les livres par eux presentes estans veus. Arreste quon leur permet de les imprimer." Chandieu's ms. may have been brought from Lyon to Geneva by the prominent printer Antoine Vincent. He appeared before the Council with a request from the Lyon Church just before Estienne appeared on May 23.

[4] Its title page does not indicate place or printer, but does bear the famous olive-tree mark of the Estiennes. See also Henri Estienne's application for permission to publish in Geneva, above, n. 3.

[5] Demonstrated by E. Droz, " Autour de l'affaire Morély: La Roche Chandieu et Barth. Berton," BHR, XXII (1960), pp. 570-577.

[6] Above, n. 2 to p. 74; n. 1 to p. 75.

LA CONFIR-
mation de la diſcipline ec-
cleſiaſtique, obſeruee es e-
gliſes reformees du royau-
me de France.

Auec la reſponſe aux obiectiõs propoſees alencontre.

M. D. LXVI.

book. And the minutes of the national Synod of 1578, designate Chandieu as the author of a book with almost exactly this title.[1]

The *Confirmation* is organized in a much more tight and formal fashion than Morély's book. In fact its organization is really scholastic: it states a number of general propositions, and lines up several categories of evidence for each; it states a number of objections to each of these propositions; then it methodically presents one or several refutations to each of these objections. The *Confirmation* purports to be a general defense of Reformed polity against all criticisms. These criticisms are divided into four sorts: from people who do not want any discipline; from people who support the Roman Church in its insistence on apostolic succession of clergy; from people who appoint themselves to the ministry; from people who claim that the Reformed polity is not that instituted by Christ and His Apostles. Even a quick glance at the book, however, makes it clear that the author is really interested only in refuting the last type of criticism. While he does present answers to the other criticisms, they are short and, to some extent, contradictory. He counters the Roman argument, for example, by claiming Biblical foundation for the necessity of "extraordinary" vocation of clergy when the Church is in need of reform.[2] And yet later he denies the right of anyone to claim "extraordinary" vocation for himself, and insists on the necessity of the Reformed procedure for election of clergy.[3] Chandieu shows awareness of the logical difficulties created by this stand, but does not work hard at eliminating them. His reluctance to do so is understandable. For at this point he faced a dilemma which confronted all the founders of "magisterial" Protestantism. They had to carve a path between, on the one hand, the appeals to tradition of the Roman Catholic communion with all the stability and rigidity which such a stance entails, and, on the other hand, the appeals to individual conscience of the sectarians with all the freedom and dangers of anarchy which that stance entails.

In any case, however, the attack which obviously most concerned Chandieu at this point was from another quarter, from those who argued that the polity of the French Reformed did not conform to Scripture. Chandieu's refutation of this charge was clearly aimed at Morély. He does not, to be sure, ever mention Morély's name, no doubt because of the pressures upon him to keep his book anonymous. But he does initiate this part of his argument by saying that it is cast in the form of a refutation of a book titled, "On the Discipline and Police of the Church, which was published four or five years

---

[1] J. Quick, *Synodicon*, I, 121, in the acts of the Synod of St. Foy, February 1578: "These same Commissioners deputed (as in the immediately foregoing Article) unto the Conference in Germany, are ordered to peruse that Treatise of Monsieur de Chandieu, Intituled *La Confirmation de la Discipline des Eglises Françoises*, and to prefix their manual Approbation of it, and to dedicate it with a Preface unto the Church of Christ, and to hasten, with as much Expedition as they can, its Publication."

Cf. J. Aymon, *Synodes*, I, 2nd pagination, p. 132. No doubt the reference to publication is to publication in Germany.

[2] A. Chandieu, *Confirmation*, pp. 18-33, especially pp. 28, ff., re "les vocations extraordinaires." The copy of the *Confirmation* which I have used throughout is the one of the Estienne ed. in Geneva, BPU, Bd 865.

[3] *Ibid.*, pp. 47-52, developing argument, "Que l'ordre establi du Seigneur, ayant lieu, il n'est point question de se fonder sur quelque vocation extraordinaire."

ago,"[1] which he feels to be the chief arsenal of ammunition used by people holding this point of view. While this title is not exactly the same as Morély's, it is close enough, and further reading in the argument of the *Confirmation*, with its continual references to the book it is trying to demolish, makes it obvious that this is, indeed, an answer to Morély.

Right at the beginning of his debate with Morély, the author of the *Confirmation* seeks to shift its grounds somewhat. He makes it clear that what he is defending is the polity of the French Reformed churches, as first adopted in the National Synod of 1559.[2] He is not trying to defend Calvinist polity generally. This is, therefore, a more nationalistic argument than one might have expected from Calvin himself, or from one of his colleagues in Geneva. It is also more explicitly nationalistic than Morély's *Treatise*. Not that Chandieu rejects or ignores completely other Reformed disciplines. At one point he speaks with explicit favor of one of the practices of the Church of Geneva, " the most flourishing in Europe." [3] And in another place he refers with approval to another specific practice of " some of the Christian churches outside of France, of which there are a good number." [4] But these references are rare. His chief interest obviously is in French practice.

This shift in grounds makes one important difference. It means that the chief institution being defended is the consistory, of pastors and elders. There is no mention in the *Confirmation* of a formally organized Company of Pastors independent from the consistory, with its own powers and functions. The nearest approach to mention of such an institution comes in certain passages on responsibilities of the pastors, apparently alone. But there is no explicit defense of the Company of Pastors on the Genevan model. In abandoning this institution, the *Confirmation* simplifies the problem of reply to Morély. It also tacitly concedes, by default, a part of his argument.

Chandieu's argument is further narrowed by his tactics. He concentrates the greatest part of his fire on Morély's Biblical exegesis. Time and again he picks out particular Biblical verses cited rather casually by Morély, and examines them at length in order to demonstrate that Morély misinterpreted them. These rebuttals are cast in the scholastic form to which I have already alluded. Typically, the *Confirmation* briefly states one of Morély's contentions and then develops a number of answers to it. The first is often a flat denial of Morély's interpretation of a given passage in Scripture. Later answers often argue that even if Morély's interpretation is correct, different conclusions would have to be drawn from it. Only an expert in Biblical exegesis could

[1] *Ibid.*, p. 69 : " un livre intitulé, De la discipline & police de l'Eglise, qui a esté publié depuis quatre ou cinq ans en ça."

[2] *Ibid.*, pp. 70-71 : " La discipline observee es Eglises de ce royaume a esté dressee, non à l'appetit d'un homme ou de deux : mais par le meur advis & jugement d'une grande & notable assemblee des Ministres de ce royaume en l'an 13 du feu roy Henry, l'an de grace 1559. Lesquels Ministres n'ayans autre but que la gloire de Dieu, & l'edification de son Eglise, fonderent ladicte discipline sur la parole de Dieu, l'examinans selon icelle au mieux qu'il leur fut possible. Et parapres layans presentee aux Eglises de ce royaume, elle fut receue & approuvee par leur consentement : & y a esté jusques à present soigneusement & religieusement prattiquee."

[3] *Ibid.*, p. 142 : " Elle a esté aussi remise en usage en l'Eglise la plus fleurissante de l'Europe " ; marginal gloss : " Cela fut ainsi prattiqué à Geneve l'an 1536."

[4] *Ibid.*, p. 225 : " quelques Eglises Chrestiennes hors de France, esquelles il y en a bon nombre."

judge the objective validity of many of these arguments. But even an amateur can be impressed by the concision, the rigor, and the authoritative tone of their statement.

The *Confirmation* often bolsters these arguments by appeal to the Fathers of the Church, especially certain Greek Fathers like St. John Chrysostom. For the rest, it uses a few simple common-sense arguments, most of them reiterated assertions that Morély's proposals are obviously impractical. But there is, in general, less range and less variety in the *Confirmation* than in Morély's book. An argument which is based primarily on the Bible is thus refuted by one which is based almost wholly on the Bible.

The main thrust of argument in the *Confirmation* is against popular government in the Church, and in particular against the use of the majority vote as an instrument of popular government. The generality of the population, particularly in France, is simply too corrupt and too ignorant, too sinful and too fickle, to make this a workable form of church government. Furthermore, Chandieu insists that this is not the sort of church government decreed by God in Scripture. That sort of government is one directed by properly chosen leaders, grouped into consistories. And these consistories were not intended to be simple moderating bodies, but to have actual powers of decision.[1] All questions of doctrine are supposed to be decided "not by all the people of the Church but properly by those whom God has ordained pastors and conductors of it."[2] Questions of moral discipline are explicitly granted to "pastors assisted by elders, according to the Word of God, and not to all the multitude."[3] Elections and depositions of clergy "belong to consistories well ordered, and not to all the body of the Church."[4] It becomes clear in the development of these arguments, that the consistories are not only disciplinary bodies but also possess full powers of appointment, powers which in Geneva were vested, as we have seen, in the Company of Pastors. However it never becomes really clear whether consistories also possess power to make doctrinal decisions, since the *Confirmation* speaks of the pastors alone making such decisions. This vagueness would, of course, justify the creation of a Company of Pastors on the Genevan model, perhaps with more limited powers, but the *Confirmation* nowhere calls for such an institution. Perhaps this vagueness is a tactical one, designed to sidestep that difference in practice among the Reformed.

---

[1] *Ibid.*, p. 77: "Si nos adversaires respondent qu'ils n'ostent pas aussi les Consistoires, mais veulent qu'ils soyent moderateurs de l'assemblee du peuple, laquelle neantmoins se gouvernera soy-mesme par la pluralité des voix: ceste response est assez combatue & deffaicte par les paroles de l'Apostre, quand il les assigne tellement conducteurs, qu'il commande qu'on leur obeisse, & qu'on s'y soubmette, avec ceste raison qu'ils veillent sur l'Eglise, & en ont à rendre comte à Dieu."

[2] *Ibid.*, p. 149: "que la decision de la doctrine appartient non à tout le peuple de l'Eglise. mais proprement à ceux-la que Dieu a ordonnez Pasteurs & conducteurs d'icelle."

[3] *Ibid.*, p. 155: "Que la charge mesme d'excommunier est commise aux Pasteurs assistez des Anciens selon la parole de Dieu, & non à toute la multitude." See also p. 150: "Que la censure des scandales appartient aux conducteurs de l'Eglise, & non à toute la multitude d'icelle."

[4] *Ibid.*, p. 205: "Que les elections & depositions appartiennent aux Consistoires bien reglez, & non à tout le corps de l'Eglise."

Not all popular participation in church government is rejected by the *Confirmation.* It leaves open to the general membership of the churches rights to certain kinds of information, about projected decisions and accomplished decisions. In certain exceptional cases, it would even permit some popular initiative. For example, in a community where a church was being formed for the first time, the general membership may choose those who will make up the consistory. From then on, however, the consistory perpetuates itself by co-optation.

The *Confirmation*, likewise, does not reject lay participation in church government. Indeed much is made of the continuing role of the elders [1] in much of the government of the Church, particularly in its discipline of its members. And the role of the deacons is also mentioned often, although not discussed at great length. However it is clear that in general the pastors will provide most of the leadership, particularly in dogmatic decisions.

In spite of the vehemence of the *Confirmation*'s attack on popular church government, the word " democratic " is never used. Chandieu never rises to the bait offered by Morély when he suggested that analogy so widely unpalatable to his contemporaries. The reasons for this omission, however, probably can be traced to an important secondary theme which runs through the entire *Confirmation*, including some of the sections not devoted to refuting Morély. This is a reiterated insistence that matters of civil government and matters of ecclesiastical government must be kept entirely separate. In that part of the book devoted to refuting Morély, this insistence takes the form of an attack, not so much upon his suggestions that " remonstrances " be addressed to civil authorities, as upon his continued use of analogies between civil and ecclesiastical government. This line of attack is summed up succinctly at the end of the book, when Chandieu says that one of the three principal errors of his adversaries is to " disguise the ecclesiastical discipline in a civil authority." [2] He goes on to accuse them, specifically, of trying to make pastors and elders into " masters and conductors of a city hall." [3] In conclusion, he charges them with seeking to substitute, " in the place of a spiritual and Apostolic rule, an Athenian or Roman police." [4]

The virulence of Chandieu's attack on Morély's political activism may well stem from his own earlier career. As I suggested above, he had definitely been involved, if only in a minor way, in the disastrous Conspiracy of Amboise, and he had learned of the rumor spread by Morély that Calvin and certain of his clerical colleagues were also involved. As we shall see later, Chandieu had

[1] Chandieu reverts to normal French Reformed usage, in calling them " anciens," rather than adopting Morély's term, " senieurs." See W. Richard, *Kirchenterminologie*, pp. 127-131, on this normal usage.

[2] A. Chandieu, *Confirmation*, p. 237 : " ils desguisent la discipline ecclesiastique en une autorité civile."

[3] *Ibid.*, pp. 237-238 : " quand ils veulent que les Consistoires ayent puissance de commander aux marchands d'ouvrir leurs greniers en temps & lieu, & par ainsi des Pasteurs & Anciens font des maistres & conducteurs d'un hostel de ville."

[4] *Ibid.*, pp. 238-239 : " considerons la discipline de nos adversaires, confuse, pleine de brigues, de seditions, de partialitez, meslant sans distinction les choses civiles avec les ecclesiastiques, & produisant au lieu d'un reglement spirituel & Apostolique, une police Athenienne ou Romaine." This may be an allusion to Morély's appeal for democracy on the Athenian or Roman model, in his *Traicté*, p. 183, a passage analyzed above, p. 58, and n. 1.

also been charged with involvement in certain other plans to resist the French crown. Perhaps these experiences had taught him of the dangers involved when pastors enter politics, particularly conspiratorial politics. Certainly they had taught him that political activities of this sort must never be given publicity. And they must have made him bitter about those, like Morély, who gave them publicity, even if only of an informal and casual sort.

Thus runs the official reply to Morély. Its author hoped that it would end the quarrel. But if it did not, he was prepared to answer again in writing, "those who know as little about keeping quiet as about speaking well."[1] However the controversy did not end. It flared up again in a yet more virulent form before the year was over.

4. *Morély at the Court of Navarre*

Early in May of 1566, the royal Court of France returned to Paris, after an unusually extended tour of the provinces to the south. Its arrival brought back to the capital that supreme direction of French legislation, diplomacy, and military affairs which always traveled with the Court. It also brought back to Paris that intense intrigue over religious policy which was a constant feature of French high politics in this period. Among those who returned with the Court was Jeanne d'Albret, Queen of Navarre. For several years this indomitable woman had been one of the most powerful and resolute defenders of the Protestant cause in France. She had become a particularly outspoken champion of that cause after the death, in 1562, of her vacillating husband, Antoine de Bourbon. With the Queen was her twelve-year-old son Henri, immediate heir to the throne of Navarre, and, more important, next in line to the throne of France, if the present King and his brothers should die without sons. Eventually, of course, Henri was to win both of those thrones and was to make a lasting mark in history as Henri IV, perhaps the most popular king ever to reign in France. It was of great concern to Jeanne that her son be properly trained to take his place as leader of the Protestant religious and political movement to which she was devoted. The tutor who had been charged with providing this training, however, had recently died. Consequently, soon after settling her household in temporary quarters in Paris,[2] the Queen hired a new tutor to supervise the education of her son.

It was Jeanne d'Albret's choice of a tutor which provoked the next great crisis in the Morély controversy. For the man she chose for this critically important post was Morély himself. I have not been able to discover precisely how she came to choose him. Probably one of his friends in the aristocracy, perhaps even the Cardinal of Châtillon or one of his brothers, recommended Morély to her. The fact that Morély was of noble birth must have appealed to the Queen, for she complained that later tutors had bad manners and did not know how to behave at a court. Morély's education and his strong interest in Reformed religion must also have appealed to the Queen.

---

[1] *Ibid.*, p. 246: " comme nous ne nous lasserons jamais de maintenir par escrit une si bonne & juste cause, aussi n'avons-nous pas deliberé ni entrepris d'imposer silence à ceux qui sçavent aussi peu se taire que bien parler."

[2] See de Ruble, ed., *Mémoires et Poésies de Jeanne d'Albret* (Paris, 1893), p. 38 and n. 4, re her arrival in Paris.

From the beginning, Morély proved to be a great success as the tutor of a prince. At least that was the opinion of Jeanne d'Albret. She later reported to Theodore Beza that Morély had been marvelously successful, particularly in teaching her son grammar. In the three or four months of Morély's tutorship, young Henri had learned more than in the previous seven years.[1]

News of this appointment soon reached the leaders of the Reformed clerical party. By August 4, it was being relayed to Geneva.[2] These leaders were naturally greatly alarmed. It was bad enough that their great enemy had been appointed to such an important and sensitive job. It was worse that he was handling it so well that he could reasonably hope to win a position of real influence at the political headquarters of French Protestantism. A number of French pastors soon protested, both in person and in writing, to the Queen of Navarre, to the Cardinal of Châtillon, to the Admiral Coligny, and to other influential leaders.[3] The immediate aim of these protests seems to have been to gain some kind of assurance that Morély's appointment did not mean adoption of his ecclesiastical ideas. These protests were apparently seconded by a volley of letters from Geneva, almost all of which seem to have been lost, which peppered both the spiritual and temporal leaders of French Protestantism about the matter.

In this campaign to discredit Morély, his enemies suddenly and unexpectedly gained some powerful new ammunition. They gained it by the discovery of a cache of very compromising letters, in Morély's own hand, among the private papers of a pastor of the Reformed Church in Orleans, a man named Hugues Sureau, dit du Rosier. As we shall shortly see, these letters turned out to be a decisive weapon in the clergy's struggle to force Morély's dismissal from the Court of Navarre. We should stop at this point, however, to examine the paradoxical fact that they were found among the private papers of a Reformed clergyman. This introduces into our story one of the more complex and fascinating minor figures of the French Reformation.

Hugues Sureau, dit du Rosier, is best known to students of the French Reformation for his spectacular double apostasy following the St. Bartholomew's massacre in 1572. Within one year he abandoned his ministry in the Reformed Church to accept a royal appointment as an official charged with the task of converting back to Catholicism a number of Huguenot nobles, and then abandoned that post to flee to Protestant Germany. Each of these

---

[1] In Jeanne d'Albret to Beza, 6 December [1566], BSHPF, XVI (1867), 64-67: " je le souhete d'afection de cestuy cy [Morély] pour la grasse que Dieu avoit mise en lui de bien et doctement instruire mon filz en sa gramaire ; car je feray isy une parenthayse pour vous dire que les sept ans que feu monsieur de La Gaucherie a tenu mon filz, il les a perdus, n'ayant rien appris que par certaynes regles mal assurées, en sorte que n'ayant nuls fondements aux rudiments, le bastiment qui se montroit aparant, parce qu'il lui avoit fort aprins par cueur, sans art, est tombé en ruine, de fasson que en troys ou quatre moys que Morelly l'avoit entre mains, il avoit plus profité qu'en ces sept ans."

[2] La Fonteine to Beza, 4 August 1566, in Geneva, BPU, Ms. fr. 446, fols. 81-82, signed original, reports that Morély had recently acquired, " le gouvernment de de M. le Prince de Navarre comme nous a faict entendre Monsieur Du Falsne retournant de la cour."

[3] Des Gallars to Beza, early September 1566, in *ibid.*, fols. 88-89, signed original in poor condition, reports on these protests and the initial answers to them.

dramatic switches he justified by a published confession of faith with abjuration of his previous errors. To this part of his career we shall return later.[1]

In the period which interests us now, Sureau was best known as an able and effective Protestant polemicist. He had shown talent for this sort of activity almost since his arrival in Orleans, probably in 1561, to serve as pastor of that city's key reformed Church. He seems to have prepared himself for this role by a period of informal study in Geneva, preceded by a period as corrector for the early Protestant printer Pierre de Vingle of Neuchatel.[2] Perhaps he had developed a taste for theological polemic even earlier, before his first conversion to Protestantism, when he was apparently for a time a Roman Catholic canon.

Sureau's polemical abilities were most widely displayed in a running controversy with Gentian Hervet. Hervet was a well-known clerical scholar with a particular interest in Greek, who had recently become a protégé of the Cardinal of Lorraine. He was one of the earliest and the most resourceful of a generation of Roman Catholic polemicists who were responsible, on the intellectual level at least, for stemming the rapid advance of Protestantism among thinking people and paving the way for Catholicism's reconquest of France. It was Hervet who initiated this controversy, in 1561, with an open letter to the Reformed ministers of Orleans. Of the several talented Reformed ministers in that city, Sureau was the one who took up the challenge by writing a response. Their debate soon broke into print. Both Hervet and Sureau openly published a number of treatises of attack and response, continuing until 1567 at least, well after Hervet's journey to the final session of the Council of Trent and his translation to the new post of canon of Reims. The chief subject of this controversy, as it was so often in the sixteenth century, was sacramental theology. Sureau, for his part, showed himself a skillful and orthodox defender of the Calvinist sacramental position, and particularly of the Calvinist doctrine of the Eucharist.[3]

An interesting by-product of this controversy may well have been Hervet's turn to arguments drawn from the skeptics of antiquity. Perhaps the first realization that these arguments could be used for Catholic polemic,

---

[1] See below, pp. 113-120. For biographical information on Sureau, see P. Beuzart, " H. Sureau du Rosier (1530?-1575?)," BSHPF, LXXXVIII (1939), 249-268, supplemented and corrected by Robert M. Kingdon, " Genève et les réformés français : le cas d'Hugues Sureau, dit du Rosier (1565-1574)," BSHAG, XII (1962), 77-87. Both articles also list titles of Sureau's books.

[2] Suggested by E. Droz, in " Pierre de Vingle, l'imprimeur de Farel," E. Droz, ed., *Aspects de la propagande religieuse* (Geneva : Droz, 1957), pp. 73-74.

[3] Hugues Sureau, *Sommaire resolution de quelques points de la religion chrestienne, en forme d'epistre responsive aux escrits publiez par M. Gentian Hervet contre les fideles de l'Eglise d'Orleans* (1564) ; fols. 2-6, an introductory letter to Hervet, recounts the controversy to date. For the substance of the arguments, see Sureau's text, as well as those of Gentian Hervet, *Trois epistres, l'une à Maistre Hugues Sureau, ministre des calvinistes à Orleans, l'autre à Messeigneurs les gouverneurs, lieutenant, bailliff, prevost, eschevins, & autres magistrats de ladite cité d'Orleans, la troisiesme, aux princes, seigneurs, dames & damoiselles de ce royaume, tendans à ce que les ministres acceptent l'offre qu'on leur fait de gager, sur le fait de prouver la verité du corps & du sang de Jesus Christ en l'eucharistie*, ... (Reims, 1565), and *L'Antihugues, c'est à dire, responce aux escrits & blasphemes de Hugues Sureau, soy disant ministre calviniste à Orleans, contre les principaux points de la foy & religion catholique* (Reims, 1567). I consulted copies in Geneva, BPU, Bc 3393 (Sureau), and Paris, BiblSHPF, R 15872 and 1079 (Hervet). For biographical information on Hervet, see *Dictionnaire de théologie catholique*, art. " Hervet."

is found in Hervet's preface to a translation of Sextus Empiricus, written in March of 1567, just as the controversy with Sureau was drawing to a close, and published in 1569.[1] These arguments, of course, in particular the skeptics' claim that no criterion can be found to distinguish true faith from false faith, came to enjoy a great vogue among Catholic polemicists, and probably found their most powerful expression in the writings of Montaigne.[2]

Sureau's rise to prominence as a polemicist, however, may well explain some of the troubles he ran into thereafter. It was not healthy in sixteenth-century France to be known to the general public as a Reformed pastor. The fact that Sureau was, may well explain a bit of serious trouble that he ran into in 1566. He was thrown into jail, in the dread Bastille, and then brought to trial before the Parlement of Paris, one of the most powerful judicial bodies in the kingdom.[3] The charge: that he was author of an anonymous treatise reportedly titled, *La deffense civile & militaire des innocens & de l'Eglise de Christ*, or *The Civil and Military Defense of the Innocents and of the Church of Christ.* This mysterious book, no copy of which seems to have survived to the present day, was regarded by royal authorities as a particularly seditious work. It apparently argued for continuation of the war undertaken by the Huguenots against the royal government, and may have been a particularly virulent example of the books justifying armed revolt which appeared every now and then during the wars of religion. It was apparently published in Lyon, in 1563, just after the end of the first war of religion. It had already provoked one trial, of the famous jurisconsult Charles du Moulin. The charge against du Moulin was patently ridiculous, and he did not have much trouble in exonerating himself.[4]

Sureau also succeeded in exonerating himself, without much trouble. The treatise, after all, had been published in Lyon. It seemed to have dealt particularly with political control of that key city. And Sureau, at the time of its publication, was in Orleans, and did not, as one chronicle puts it, have any more notion of what was going on in the government of Lyon than in that of the Indies.[5]

His skill as a pamphleteer and his ability in defending himself before the highest regular court of the land, probably explain why Sureau, shortly after release from prison, was thrown into yet another polemical adventure. He was asked to serve as one of two Protestants who would debate in public two Catholic doctors of the Sorbonne. This debate was organized under high auspices, by the devoutly Catholic Duke of Montpensier, with help from people at the royal Court, and ran from 9 July 1566 until August 7. Its object was

[1] Pointed out by Richard H. Popkin, in " Skepticism and the Counter-Reformation in France," ARG, LI (1960), 60-61. See also Popkin's *The History of Scepticism from Erasmus to Descartes* (Assen: van Gorcum, 1960), pp. 35-36, 67-68.

[2] See Popkin article cited in n. 1, pp. 58-86, especially 62-63; also Popkin book cited in n. 1, especially ch. 3; Donald M. Frame, *Montaigne, a biography* (New York: Harcourt, Brace, & World, 1965), pp. 170, 178, and *passim.*

[3] See BSHPF, L (1901), 582, for text of the order, 13 June 1566, for his release from the Bastille on bail, in order to appear before the Parlement for trial.

[4] See below, pp. 153-156, on the probable contents of this book and the attempt to attribute it to du Moulin.

[5] *Hist. eccl.*, III, 247: " du Rosier, ministre d'Orleans, qui n'estoit lors à Lyon, ains à Orleans, ne sachant non plus ce qui se faisant lors à Lyon, que le gouvernement des Indes."

to persuade the Duke's Protestant daughter, the Duchess of Bouillon, to return to the Roman fold. It failed in this object, as did most of the many sixteenth-century debates of this sort. Credit for this failure must go in part to Sureau, who, with his colleague, skillfully defended Protestant doctrines of the authority of the Scriptures, the almighty power of God, and the nature of the Eucharist.[1]

This description of Sureau's polemical career may seem tangential to a history of the disciplinary quarrel within the French Reformed Church. To some extent it is. And yet there are direct connections of a surprising and striking sort.

It should be noted, first, that the dates of Sureau's imprisonment and of his debate before the Duchess of Bouillon, coincide exactly with the dates of the crisis created by Morély's appointment to the Court of Navarre. A letter to Geneva from one of Morély's opponents among the French clergy reveals, further, that Sureau had been suspected for some time of sympathy for the ideas of Morély. So had one of his colleagues in the Orleans pastoral corps, a man named Baron about whom we know little. So had the chaplain of Admiral Coligny, a pastor named Mallot.[2] Mallot may have come under suspicion because of the relative impartiality with which he had presided over the provincial Synod of the Ile-de-France in July of 1566, the Synod which had received the Cardinal of Châtillon's letter defending Morély.[3] But he had already taken steps to clear his name, in a letter he wrote to Beza in June of 1566.[4]

Sureau, however, was in no position to clear his name. And the fact of his prolonged absence created a golden opportunity for his enemies in Orleans. They simply entered his home, rummaged around among his private papers, and came upon a stack of personal letters sent to him by Morély. These letters not only provided definite proof of the link between the two men. They also provided precisely the sort of hard evidence which the orthodox Calvinists needed to discredit Morély before the great political leaders of the Protestant party. For in these letters Morély had fully and freely given vent to all his most personal feelings about the people with whom he was embroiled in the disciplinary quarrel. No wonder that Beza and his friends in France hailed discovery of these letters as a singular act of divine providence.[5]

This cache of letters from Morély seems to have been discovered toward the end of Sureau's absence from Orleans, or perhaps even after his return.

---

[1] There is a published Protestant account of this debate, *Actes de la dispute & conference tenue à Paris, és mois de Juillet, & Aoust, 1566, entre deux docteurs de Sorbonne, & deux ministres de l'eglise reformee* (Strasbourg, 1566), copy in Geneva, BPU, Ba 4385; also a Catholic account, with a title only slightly different (Verdun, 1568), copy in Paris, Bibliothèque Mazarine, 12726. See also *Hist. eccl.*, III, 475, re choice of Sureau to participate in this debate.

[2] Suspicions reported by La Fonteine to Beza, 4 August 1566, in Geneva, BPU, Ms. fr. 446, fols. 81-82, signed original.

[3] See Mallot to Beza, 10 July 1565, in *ibid.*, fols. 47-50, signed original, a report of this Synod's actions, and two drafts of Beza's reply, 6 September 1565, fols. 51-52, 53-54. Mallot is also identified as presiding officer of this Synod by the ms. account in *ibid.*, fol. 12v.

[4] Mallot to Beza, 27 June 1566, in *ibid.*, fols. 79-80, signed original.

[5] Beza to Hesperien, 15 January 1567, in *ibid.*, fols. 121-122, draft, and letters to Beza cited below. Sureau had been ordered released from prison in June, according to the letter cited in n. 4, but apparently did not return to Orleans immediately.

The first word of them which arrived in Geneva seems to have been a letter to Beza written in late September of 1566, by a man named La Mare.[1] About a month later, Nicolas des Gallars, the leading figure in the Orleans Church, sent more information to his old friends and former colleagues in the Geneva Church, in a letter largely devoted to quoting for them some of Morély's choicer remarks about the Geneva community and about Beza.[2] Des Gallars, because of his prominence and experience, would seem to have been the logical person for the job of exploiting these letters. However the fact that some of Morély's insults were directed against him personally may have made such an assignment seem tactically unwise. In any case, the job of using this new ammunition against Morély was turned over to a figure new to the controversy : François Bérauld (also Beroald), a close friend of Geneva who had been officially sent by that city's Company of Pastors to teach in the newly established Reformed Academy of Orleans, and who was now Professor of Hebrew Letters there.[3] Bérauld was one of the leading lights of a faculty whose most distinguished and popular member was probably des Gallars, in an institution subsidized in part by the Cardinal of Châtillon. This faculty may well have found itself in a rather delicate position, caught between its leader and its patron. But if this was so, one finds little reflection of it in Bérauld's behavior. He played a role as prosecutor with a tenacity and thoroughness which could not have failed to please Morély's most determined enemies.[4]

Bérauld's first assignment was to prepare a translation of the Morély letters, from their original Latin into French, so that the lay elders and deacons of the Orleans Consistory could understand them. The Consistory then studied the letters, discussed what action should be taken, and decided to give Bérauld a second assignment. He was commissioned to prepare a set of extracts of the most notable points made in these letters, for the express purpose of presenting them to the Queen of Navarre in order to persuade her to dismiss Morély from his post as royal tutor. It was then arranged that Bérauld should be received by the Queen. In their first interview, on 17 November 1566, the Queen, hearing the gravity of the charges, asked that a full examination of them be postponed until she could assemble a more substantial group of people concerned in the affair.

That group assembled nearly a week later, in what amounted to a formal hearing on the charges against Morély. It was held at St. Maur, near Paris, where the Queen had installed her court for the time being. It was attended

[1] La Mare to Beza, 25 September 1566, in *ibid.*, fols. 93-94, signed original.

[2] Des Gallars to the Pastors and Professors of Geneva, 24 October 1566, in *ibid.*, fols. 97-98, signed original in bad condition. See also des Gallars to Beza, same date, in *ibid.*, fols. 95-96, signed original in bad condition.

[3] On the Orleans Academy, see below, p. 100. For more on Bérauld, see *France protestante*, 2nd ed., art. " Bérauld," which omits his career as a teacher in Orleans, and R. M. Kingdon, *Geneva & Coming, passim.* He is identified as " professeur des lettres hebraiques en l'eglise reformee d'Orleans," on fol. 99 of the ms. account described in n. 4.

[4] A detailed manuscript account, dated 4 December 1566, of Bérauld's preparation and presentation of a case against Morély can be found in Geneva, BPU, Ms. fr. 446, fols. 99-108. See also fols. 8-11, what appears to be a set of excerpts, in the original Latin, from many of the letters from Morély to Sureau which Bérauld used in his arguments.

by two of the Châtillon brothers: the Cardinal, Morély's sometime protector, and the Admiral, Gaspard de Coligny. It was also attended by a number of Reformed pastors, most of them attached either to the Paris Church or to various aristocratic courts. And the usual group of courtiers was also there.

The hearing opened with Bérauld taking the floor. He began his attack with a rhetorical flourish. By God's favor, the true nature of the prince's new tutor, who had impressed so many people so favorably, had been revealed. This revelation had been made possible by "an extraordinary miracle" and manifestation of the "singular providence of God," the discovery by the Church of Orleans of a series of his writings.[1] These writings revealed that Morély was "infected with heresies," that he encouraged heretics, that he mocked and blackened the names of Reformed ministers whose fidelity was universally recognized. They revealed further that he was a villainous mocker and detractor of the Church and Seigneury of Geneva, that he was guilty of contempt of the Church of Paris which he had mocked and menaced and in which he had committed perjury, that he was a self-confessed schismatic. Finally they revealed that he had never abandoned his doctrine of ecclesiastical discipline, which was contrary to the pure and express Word of God.[2]

Bérauld then proceeded to particulars. Each of his initial charges was documented, mostly by quotations from Morély's letters, with Bérauld's conclusions therefrom and his comments. Bérauld refers to these letters by number. Apparently they had been neatly arranged in categories and numbered for this hearing. No doubt copies of them were available for the inspection of those in attendance.

The most serious charge, of course, was the one of heresy. It was based on Morély's expressions of sympathy for a man named Costanus, who had been convicted of heresy and deposed from the pastorate in the Church of Paris. The charges against Costanus seem to have centered largely around his ideas on divine providence, on predestination, and on the reprobation of the damned, doctrines about which the Calvinists generally were peculiarly sensitive. Costanus was also charged with a variety of moral aberrations. As Bérauld himself noted, however, there was one key difficulty in holding Morély to this charge of heresy. In one of the same letters in which he sympathized with Costanus, Morély also expressed as his own a view of predestination which was unquestionably an orthodox Calvinist one.[3]

---

[1] *Ibid.*, fol. 100: "dun miracle extraordinaire & dune providence singuliere de Dieu des escritz de Morely estoyent venus en la congnoissance de l'Eglise d'Orleans."

[2] *Ibid.*: "Car par tels escrits M. Morely estoit congneu infecté d'heresies, fauteur d'heretiques, moqueur & blasonneur des ministres de l'eglise reformée desquels la fidelité estoit assez congneu en lœuvre du Seigneur. Item estoit recogneu mocqueur vilain & detracteur de l'Eglise & Seigneurie de Geneve, plus contempteur de l'eglise de Paris, delaquelle non seullement sestoit mocqué, mais aussy avoit menacé & luy avoit violé sa foy par perjure notable. En apres que par sa propre confession estoit schismatique. Or pour conclusion que la doctrine de la discipline ecclesiastique, qu'il mettoit en avant, estoit contre la pure & expresse parolle de Dieu, des quels crimes le moindre estoit assez suffisant pour le retrancher non point seulement d'une si honorable maison, mais aussy de l'Eglise."

[3] *Ibid.*, fol. 100v., on Costanus, deposition of him and reasons for it, and his correspondence with Morély. A striking demonstration of contemporary Calvinist sensitivity about predestination, can be found in Beza's later comment on this charge, in a letter to Hesperien, 15 January 1567, fols. 121-122, draft, that "cest article de la predestination... est le fondement de toute notre foy." Would Calvin himself have gone this far?

With the charge of slander, Bérauld was on much stronger ground. Morély had clearly defamed a number of the most prominent Reformed pastors. He had called Nicolas des Gallars a liar and a fake, particularly skilled at feigning modesty and honesty, both in expression and in word.[1] He had called Theodore Beza " this Jupiter of the lake of Geneva," and " this new Antichrist " who had established from Geneva a " cruel and insupportable, even impious tyranny " over the Church as a whole.[2] He had accused François de Morel of being the " bellows and firebrand " of all the actions taken against him.[3] Monsieur de Blezy, pastor of the Paris Church, and one of those in attendance at this hearing, had been called a compiler of decrees, a new Gratian, a chameleon who changed his color from one moment to the next.[4] Morély had even criticized his friends among the pastors. He had made fun of the poor Latin and flowery rhetoric of de la Haye.[5] He had complained of the villainous behavior of François Perrocelli, the chaplain to the Prince of Condé, who had long been reputedly opposed to the rigor and rigidity of Calvinist discipline, in fleeing a session of a synod when he had learned that Morély's case was to be treated there.[6] Decidedly there was enough in these letters to infuriate Morély's enemies and embarrass his friends.

Bérauld's next charge was the somewhat parallel contention that Morély had attacked and mocked the Church and Seigneury of Geneva. This could also be documented, although Morély's language in dealing with the Genevans was decidedly more sober than that which he used to describe individual clergymen. Many of his complaints about Geneva were legal ones, as to whether the Genevan Council had jurisdiction over a man who had always remained a subject of the King of France, and the like.[7]

There followed a charge that Morély had scorned and menaced the Church of Paris. The charge of menace was particularly serious. Morély said he had prepared for the Cardinal of Châtillon a written treatise on synods, designed to persuade the cardinal to abandon his attempts to secure a modification of that clause of the Edict of Roussillon which had forbidden all

---

[1] *Ibid.*, fol. 101 : " ' O le mensonger & faux visage de votre de Saule, les yeux trompeurs, la langue & le parler contrefaisant bien la modestie & honnesteté.' " Des Gallars was the sire de Saules.

[2] *Ibid.*, fols. 101-101v. : " ' ce Juppiter du lac de Geneve... Dieu veuille delivrer son Eglise de la felonne tyrannie de ce nouvel Antichrist... O cruelle & insupportable tyrannie mais plustost impieté. Qu'est ce cela sinon estre assis au temple de Dieu, & regner comme Dieu ? Mais le Seigneur veuille regarder de son sainct habitacle, & delivrer son Eglise laquelle il a racheptée de son sang de la tyrannie de Geneve, comme il l'ha retiree de la tyrannie de l'Antichrist Romain.' "

[3] *Ibid.*, fol. 101v. : " soufflet & bouttefeu des procedures faictes contre luy."

[4] *Ibid.*: " ' le compilateur & rabobolineur de vos decrets & ordonnances, un Gratian tout nouveau, ... changeans de moment, de temps a autre de couleur comme un chameleon.' "

[5] *Ibid.*: " ' son langage est assez mauvais, & non trop bien semme a un theologien. De quoy on se peut appercevoir de ce qu'en une sienne lettre Latine il baille deux soufflets a Priscian... il faut mettre a part ses fleurs & phrases eloquentes, affin que lon n'appreste a rire pour les autres.' "

[6] *Ibid.*: " ' Parrocely sen est enfuy villainement du Synode, voyant qu'on vouloit traicter de mon fait.' " The name is also spelled Pérussel. For more on him, see *France protestante*, 1st ed., art. " Pérussel," and below, pp. 157-159.

[7] *Ibid.*, fols. 102-103.

synodical meetings.[1] This maneuver was, of course, a logical application of the criticisms of synods as not being sanctioned by Scripture which can be found in his book, and about which he no doubt felt increasingly strongly because of his own unhappy experiences with a number of synods. But if the maneuver had succeeded, it would have had serious consequences from the orthodox Calvinist point of view, menacing the French Reformed Church with decapitation by withdrawing from its governing bodies important aristocratic protection. It is no wonder that this particular charge was regarded with special seriousness by some of the orthodox commentators on the hearing.[2]

Bérauld then charged that Morély had acknowledged that he was a schismatic. This was bolstered with quotations in which Morély admitted that his ideas had upset relations between a number of pastors and consistories, and between several consistories and congregations, and had also created tensions between the Genevans and the French.[3] And his final charge, that Morély had never fully accepted the received discipline of the Reformed Church, was bolstered with a number of quotations indicating that Morély, in spite of his public retractions, had never entirely abandoned some of his characteristic ideas on church discipline. This concluding charge was documented at some length. As one might expect, it had considerable substance.[4]

All this part of the hearing at the Court of Navarre had taken place in Morély's absence. When Bérauld was finally finished with his bill of accusations, Morély was invited to appear for questioning. He seems not to have known in advance that his letters to Sureau had been discovered. His first reaction was of indignation that personal letters were being used against him. He noted that the greatest rulers of antiquity had never stooped this low, even when faced with opportunities to do so. The argument from antiquity did not impress the Queen of Navarre, however. She cut him short by observing that he was talking of matters "prophane" while the matter at hand concerned "the honor of God." [5] Morély then tried to respond to the substantive charges based on these letters, but was obviously handicapped in doing so. Finally the entire bill of charges was read to him and he was given a day to prepare his answers. The answers were then turned over to an elder of the Paris Church, who, with four ministers, was deputed to study them. After two days of study, these deputies made a formal report to the Queen of Navarre. They found Morély more or less guilty as charged, and seem to have reported that his responses to the charges only compounded their seriousness.

These findings more or less dictated the action that Jeanne d'Albret had to take. In another formal session of her court, on November 27, 1566, in

---

[1] *Ibid.*, fol. 103v.: "'Jay entre mains une epistre en laquelle je traitte amplement des Synodes, pour envoyer a mon Seigneur le Cardinal de Chastillon, affin qu'il soit muny & garny des responses, quand les ministres le presseront de poursuivre labolition de ce point de l'Edit de Rossilon, par lequel sont deffenduz les Synodes.'" On the Edict of Roussillon, and attempts to modify it, see below, p. 160.

[2] See marginal comment on passage quoted in n. 1: "Parjure de Morely car un peu auparavant avoit promis a l'Eglise de Paris ne faire ne dire rien contre lordre estably." See also La Mare to Beza, 25 Septembre 1566, *ibid.*, fols. 93-94.

[3] *Ibid.*, fols. 103v.-104.

[4] *Ibid.*, fols. 104-106v.

[5] *Ibid.*, fol. 106v.: "la Royne luy disant qu'il alleguoit choses prophanes & qu'il estoit question de l'honneur de Dieu."

the presence of Bérauld, the Admiral, the Cardinal of Châtillon, and the deputies assigned to investigate the case, the Queen of Navarre summoned Morély to announce her decision. While she had great respect for his qualities and was completely satisfied with his services as her son's tutor, and while she realized that his family responsibilities were heavy and accordingly did not want to cut him off without resources, she nevertheless felt obliged to dismiss him.[1]

The Queen's decision, naturally, delighted the orthodox. Bérauld returned to Orleans triumphant. Excited letters relayed the good news to Geneva.[2] Morély had finally been disgraced, where it mattered most, and the threat posed by his ideas was at last ended.

This delight proved to be somewhat premature. The Queen had apparently agreed to dismiss Morély only when a suitable replacement had been found for him as tutor to the prince. Although she had sent Beza, shortly after the hearing, a very personal letter, signed " your good mistress and friend," in which she announced that she had decided to dismiss Morély, she made it clear that it had been a difficult decision. She told Beza in some detail that Morély had been a remarkably fine teacher.[3] Obviously her first concern was for her son's education. While she was sorry that her Protestant advisers could not agree with each other, the substance of this quarrel does not seem to have disturbed her greatly.

Bérauld, when he returned to Orleans, apparently thought that a satisfactory substitute tutor had already been chosen to take Morély's place, a young man named Martinius, from Navarre.[4] But substitution did not turn out to be that easy. Five weeks later, Beza received a report from a friend at the court, that the Queen had found Martinius " too simple and uncivil," that she still felt that Morély was the best teacher she had ever seen, and that her son had profited more in three months of study with him than in eight years with his predecessor. And Morély was still at her court, instructing the prince.[5]

Morély himself had taken immediate steps to mend his fences in hopes that he could keep his choice post. Before his hearing had ended, he had already purged himself of the charge of heresy. He had prepared a written statement of his notion of predestination for the study of the men assigned to examine him. They had certified in writing that it was thoroughly orthodox,

---

[1] *Ibid.*, fol. 107v. This gives the date of the session as November 28, but the letter written on the day which is cited in n. 2, makes it the 27th.

[2] Hesperien to Beza, 26 November 1566, with postscript of 27th, in *ibid.*, fols. 109-110, signed original, was the earliest of these letters.

[3] Jeanne d'Albret to Beza, 6 December [1566], BSHPF, XVI (1867), 64-67, signed " vostre bonne maîtresse et amie, Jehanne." On Morély's competence as a teacher, see passage quoted above, in n. 1 to p. 83.

[4] In Geneva, BPU, Ms. fr. 446, fol. 107v. : " En la place dudit Morely a esté substitué, Martinius qui est Navarrois homme craignant Dieu & docte es langues."

[5] In de l'Esperandiere, dit Merlin, to Beza, 10 January 1567, in *ibid.*, fols. 119-120, signed original : " elle [the Queen] me respondit qu'elle avoit este contrainte de retenir Morelly pour ne laisser perdre le temps a Monsieur le Prince son fils, et qu'elle n'en avoit encore peut recouvrer un autre qui fut propre pour l'enseigner. 'Car,' disoit-elle, 'Martinius qu'on luy avoit presenté estoit trop simple et incivil '... Adjoustant qu'elle estoit fort fachee qu'il [Morély] n'estoit bien d'accord avec les Eglises, et qu'au demeurant il est le plus propre et le mieux adroit a bien enseigner qu'homme qu'elle ait jamais veu et que son fils avoit plus profité en trois mois avec luy qu'il n'avoit fait en huit [cf. ' sept ' in her own letter] ans avec feu Monsieur de la Gaucherie."

as indeed it was.[1] As soon as the hearing ended, Morély took a second step. He wrote a letter of abject apology to Nicolas des Gallars for the personal insults to him, which Bérauld was to take back to Orleans.[2] Several days later he wrote to Theodore Beza in Geneva.[3] He begged for forgiveness of the insults which a loss of temper had led him to include in his letters to Sureau. He declared himself ready again to abandon his campaign for changes in church government, and to abide by the terms of reconciliation stipulated by the synods. He said that he had never meant to question the value and the Scriptural foundation of present Reformed church government, but had only wanted to suggest a way of improving it and making it more Scriptural in the future. This letter was accompanied by one to Laurent de Normandie, the wealthy French emigré who was now a leading publisher in Geneva.[4] To de Normandie, Morély confided in a more personal way his hopes of maintaining his position as tutor to the prince, partly in order to support his own seven children. He pled for de Normandie's help in securing a reconciliation with Beza. At almost the same time, Morély's brother-in-law, a man named Du Mesnil, wrote to de Normandie, also begging him to try to reconcile the two men.[5] These pleas, as usual, failed. A month later Beza wrote to Morély, forgiving him for the personal insults, but insisting that he purge himself of his insults to the Geneva Consistory and Council, and expressing pointed doubts about the orthodoxy of his beliefs.[6]

By the end of 1566, warfare by letter was becoming increasingly unsatisfactory to all parties involved in this controversy. At one point the Genevan Consistory decided to send one of the city's pastors to the Court of Navarre to present the Genevan point of view. In December they had selected as their delegate one of the most prominent of the Genevan pastors, Nicolas Colladon. He had been instructed to inform the Queen of the actions taken in Geneva against Morély, and to warn her of the true nature of the "instrument of Satan who had slithered into her house." [7] The Council had agreed to finance his trip, and he was ready to go, when word of the discovery of the letters to Sureau and the subsequent hearing persuaded the Consistory that this trip was unnecessary.[8] The trip was made doubly unnecessary by the Queen of Navarre's decision to send a personal representative to Geneva.

---

[1] For a copy of this statement and the certification that it was orthodox, dated 27 November 1566, see *ibid.*, fol. 35.

[2] Morély to des Gallars, 29 November 1566, in *ibid.*, fol. 26, contemporary copy.

[3] Morély to Beza, 7 December 1566, in *ibid.*, fol. 27, signed original.

[4] Morély to de Normandie, 4 December [1566], in *ibid.*, fol. 37, signed original. For more on de Normandie, see Heidi-Lucie Schlaepfer, "Laurent de Normandie," in E. Droz, ed., *Aspects de la propagande religieuse* (Geneva : Droz, 1957), pp. 176-230.

[5] Du Mesnil to de Normandie, 8 December 1566, in *ibid.*, fol. 111, signed original. The fact that this letter and the one cited in n. 4 are in this dossier, suggests that de Normandie turned them over to the pastors of Geneva.

[6] Beza to Morély, 15 January 1567, in *ibid.*, fols. 113-114, draft.

[7] According to Beza to Hesperien, 15 January 1567, in *ibid.*, fols. 121-122, draft: "quel instrument de Satan s'estoit glissé en sa maison." For the authoritative yet drier account of these deliberations, see Geneva, Arch., RConsistoire, XXIII, fols. 134, 28 November 1566; 138v., 5 December 1566. See also the vaguer account in RCP, B1, [December] 1566. Colladon is named as the envoy in RC, LXI, fol. 121, 9 December 1566.

[8] Geneva, Arch., RC, LXI, fols. 117, 2 December 1566; 121, 6 and 9 December 1566, re arrangements for the trip; 123v., 16 December 1566, re cancellation of trip. See also Beza to Hesperien, 15 January 1567, cited in n. 7.

That representative was the Queen's own chaplain, a man named Brodeau. He arrived in Geneva in the middle of February, 1567. Representatives of royal courts did not arrive in Geneva every day. The city's authorities were clearly impressed by this visit, and were careful to render special honors to the Queen's delegate. He was courteously received before the governing Council, and invited to dinner with two of its most distinguished members. At Beza's suggestion, these two councillors were instructed to speak to Brodeau of the Morély problem.[1]

Brodeau brought with him at least one letter from Morély to Beza, and probably others from Morély to the city's Syndics and Council, to Beza, and to the members of the Consistory.[2] He also may have been the porter of a letter to Beza from Admiral Coligny, written at about the same time.[3] In any case it must have been the letter from Coligny which carried the greatest weight. It revealed that Coligny had definitely turned against the protégé of his brother. He did confess that he had once been "deceived" about Morély's true character. But his sense of chivalric honor had apparently been touched by the bitterness of Morély's attacks upon the pastors. And he did not share the Queen of Navarre's compunctions about losing a good teacher. He announced himself to be fully in agreement with Beza, that Morély and his supporters should be punished harshly, with "the strongest medicines and rigorous reprimands," and that "gentleness, as you wrote me, only makes the evil worse."[4] This letter also contained a touching postscript in Coligny's own hand, protesting his high personal regard for Beza.

With such strong political support behind their point of view, it is not surprising that the Genevans did not budge at all. Brodeau was sent back to his royal mistress with an official letter from the Geneva Council, again rejecting Morély's apologies, and insisting that he could not be forgiven until he did a better job of "recognizing so many faults and so many horrible scandals by him committed."[5] The Genevans, however, were also careful not to lose sight of the Queen of Navarre's continuing need for a teacher. A couple of weeks later, Beza wrote to offer her the services of a young man named Massaillan, of good family, well educated, acquainted in "good"

---

[1] Geneva, Arch., RC, LXII, fol. 3, 11 February 1567.

[2] Morély to Beza, 20 January 1567, in Geneva BPU, Ms. fr. 446, fols. 28-29, signed original, specifies it is to be carried by the Queen's chaplain; Morély to Syndics and Small Council of Geneva, fols. 30-31, to Beza, fols. 32-33, to Pastors and Elders of Geneva, fols. 34-35, all signed originals dated 4 February 1567, about the time Brodeau must have left Paris, presumably also carried by him.

[3] Coligny to Beza, 21 January [1567], in *ibid.*, fols. 123-124, signed original.

[4] In *ibid.*: "Quant a Morelly, je confesse certainement que j'ay esté deceu ayant maintenant fort bonne cognoissance de son humeur et complexion et estant bien au demeurant de cest advis qu'on doit, a l'endroit de ceux qui le ressemblent et qui sont touchés de mesme maladie, user de medicamens des plus forts et reprimendes rigoreuses et que la douceur comme vous m'escrivés ne fait que empirer le mal."

[5] In Geneva to the Queen of Navarre, 25 February 1567, in Geneva, Arch., Copies de Lettres, VIII, fols. 88-88v.: "que ledit Morelli faire meilleur debvoir de recognoistre tant de faultes & tant d'horribles scandales par luy q[com]mise." For the rather uninformative order to draft this letter, see RC, LXII, fol. 9v., 17 February 1567.

circles in Lyon, who was willing to take on the job of tutoring the prince if she would have him.[1]

At about the same time, Beza wrote some other letters designed to tuck in certain loose ends remaining from the controversy. One was to Viret, who was soon to assume a position of great importance in the crown territories of the Queen of Navarre. From the beginning, as we have noticed, Morély had expressed a special admiration for Viret and had even dedicated his book to him. Apparently Viret had done little to disavow this admiration, and his authority was still being used in support of Morély's views. This, at least, is suggested in a letter written to Beza from the Paris Church, asking that he write Viret to get him to take an open stand.[2] Beza did so, in a letter which suggests, with what might be a subtle kind of tact, that Viret had not followed the controversy at all.[3] It outlines Morély's basic ideas, attacks them bitterly, and urges that Viret disassociate himself more openly from Morély and his party.

A second letter of this sort went from Beza to the Orleans Church.[4] It was intended particularly for pastors Sureau and Baron. It reproached them in general terms for not having accepted the decisions of synods and of the Genevan Church in regard to Morély. And it reproached Sureau in particularly personal and bitter terms for his close friendship with Morély, reminding him of his personal debt to the city, church, and school of Geneva, pointing out to him the evident wickedness of Morély's machinations, his calumnies, and his hypocrisy, and accusing Sureau of rank ingratitude.

We have no record of the reactions of these prominent French pastors to the messages from Geneva. But perhaps we can guess what they were from their later actions. Viret may well have serenely ignored his letter, as he did a good deal of what happened in Geneva. He continued to work himself to the bone for the Reformed faith, in his own exceedingly effective and rather independent way, now in Béarn, a territory which the Queen of Navarre controlled directly and was determined to make completely Protestant.[5]

---

[1] In Beza to Jeanne d'Albret, 1 March 1567, in Geneva, BPU, Ms. fr. 446, fols. 129-130, draft: " Celuy auquel nous nous sommes adressés est nommé Massaillan, d'une bonne maison d'Avignon, de l'aage d'environ 34 ans, de face honneste et bonne contenance. Sa nourriture a esté en plusieurs universites où il a fort bien estudié es langues grecque et latine, et depuis aussi, en hebrieu quelque temps en ceste ville, combien que son but principal ait esté l'estude des loix. Cependant il a conversé en toutes bonnes compaignies à Lion et ailleurs, et a mesmes esté employé pour bons affaires, tellement que, graces à Dieu, il n'est desgarny de toute bonne civilité, et ne se trouvera estrange à mon advis en quelque compagnie que ce soit."

[2] In Du Croissant [to Beza], enclosed with Church of Paris to Church of Geneva, 1 March 1567, in *ibid.*, fols. 127-128, signed originals: " Je vous prie de confermer par vos lettres ladicte dame [Queen of Navarre], et est besoing d'executer le mesme a l'endroict de Monsieur Viret affin que Morely nabuse plus du nom et autorité d'un si excellent serviteur du Seigneur."

[3] Beza to Viret, in *ibid.*, fols. 6-7, undated draft. Its contents suggest it was written at the same time as Beza's letter to Jeanne d'Albret, cited in n. 1, of March 1. Yet it was also apparently written at the suggestion of the letter from Paris cited in n. 2, also of March 1. Perhaps one of these dates, more probably the one on the draft to Jeanne d'Albret, is in error.

[4] Beza to the Church of Orleans, without date, but apparently soon after discovery of the Morély-Sureau letters, BSHPF, XXI (1872), 313-318.

[5] See R. D. Linder, *Viret*, pp. 50-51, for a brief summary of this phase of Viret's career, and further bibliography on it.

Sureau, on the other hand, may well have reacted with bitterness. As we shall see, he became more and more critical of Genevan discipline in the years that were to follow, and finally scandalized all his fellow Protestants by apostasizing. Perhaps an important source of his disenchantment can be traced to this episode. After all, he had just returned to his normal pastoral duties, from months of grueling imprisonment and trial, and from an exhausting public debate, all undertaken in defense of the Reformed faith. But rather than receiving compliments and praise for his constancy and skill, he found his personal papers ransacked by his colleagues, his friend Morély in public disgrace, and a letter bitterly critical of him personally, addressed to his congregation by the ecclesiastical leader of the movement to which he was dedicated. All of which might be enough to make any man waver.

In a final and really venomous letter, to Morély, Beza gave full vent to all his own bitterness at the attacks upon him. He complained at length of the inadequacies of Morély's apologies in the letters which Brodeau had brought to Geneva. He throws back in Morély's face many of the statements found in the letters to Sureau. And he coins some rather choice new insults of his own. For example he accuses Morély of having "raped the virginity of the French churches." [1] It would be charitable to hope that Beza never actually posted this letter, and was simply blowing off steam by writing a draft. But it seems more probable that he had gotten word of Morély's definitive dismissal from the Court of Navarre, and consequently no longer felt it necessary to be even relatively circumspect.

At about this point a curtain of war falls to conclude this act in the Morély controversy. Even before these last letters had been written, hostilities were clearly in the offing. The Queen of Navarre's open encouragement of Protestant worship in Paris, so very near to the royal Court, had made King Charles IX furious. He had even ordered that the pastors attached to Jeanne d'Albret's Court be seized. The uproar created by this order had delayed Brodeau's departure for Geneva.[2] Furthermore the outbreaks of mob violence and the hardenings of Court factions which preceded every resumption of religious war in France, were again beginning to appear. And in any case, Jeanne d'Albret had long been planning to return to Béarn, to put into effect some drastic new plans for the establishment of the Reformed Church as the only church in the domains under her personal control. Within a few days her court left Paris for the south.[3] A few months later open war broke out on a newly bitter scale. I do not know for certain what happened to Morély, his friends, and his opponents in the Paris area during this critical period. Probably they had to scatter or lay low. It seems likely that Morély himself was left behind at the time the Court of Navarre moved south, and that his dismissal was thus accomplished. Soon after Jeanne d'Albret's arrival in Béarn, she was making new arrangements for the education of her

[1] In Beza to Morély, 25 March 1567, in Geneva, BPU, Ms. fr. 446, fols. 133-135, draft, fol. 133v.: "Car c'est vous qui aves violé la virginité des Eglises francoyses."

[2] Reported by La Mare to Beza, 5 January 1567, in *ibid.*, fols. 117-118, signed original.

[3] It had arrived in Pau, her usual capital, by 1 February 1567, according to de Ruble, ed., *Mémoires et Poésies de Jeanne d'Albret* (Paris, 1893), p. 45, n. 2, based on unpublished correspondence. This would have required an unusually hurried trip.

son. She hired a man named Florent Chrestien as his tutor and worked out herself his course of study.[1]

If Morély himself was now in eclipse, however, his ideas certainly were not dead. They were to return to bedevil the French Reformed Church in another virulent form, as soon as peace returned to the realm.

5. *Ramus Enters the Quarrel*

By 1567, Morély's program for modification of the structure of the Reformed Church seems to have won the support of a definable faction within the French branch of that church. This faction drew most of its support from the area around Paris and apparently included entire congregations in that area. It seems to have grown in strength and developed in organization during the years following Morély's disgrace at the Court of Navarre. And before long it won the services of an eloquent new spokesman, that great stormy petrel of the sixteenth-century French academic scene, Peter Ramus. For a period of several years, however, this faction seems to have devoted itself to quiet consolidation, avoiding open conflict with the titular leaders of the Reformed movement. At least there is little record in print or in Geneva of further conflict during this period. The National Synod which met in Vertueil, in September of 1567, did, to be sure, restate in general but emphatic terms its support of the received discipline of the Reformed churches.[2] It also insisted that all churches be governed by consistories alone, rather than by other types of councils,[3] and that consistory members continue to be chosen by co-optation rather than by general election.[4] But it did not deal with any more specific protests of relevance. Soon after the Vertueil Synod, the renewal of religious war in France forced upon the Reformed a necessary pre-occupation with the rude task of survival. No more national synods were held during the next four years.

When the next national synod did assemble, however, it was on a scale of unprecedented grandeur and significance. This Synod, which met in La Rochelle in April of 1571, was probably the most important single synod of the century, perhaps of the entire history of French Protestantism. This importance stems, to begin with, from the fact that this Synod could be held openly. It was the first national synod of the French Reformed Church whose assembling was authorized by the royal government,[5] which was not illegal and thus necessarily secret. This importance stems, also, from the

[1] Described by Martha Walker Freer, *The Life of Jeanne d'Albret, Queen of Navarre* (London, n.d.), pp. 263-264.

[2] J. Quick, *Synodicon*, I, 71, art. XI. Cf. J. Aymon, *Synodes*, I, 2nd pagination, pp. 75-76, art. XXII.

[3] J. Quick, *Synodicon*, I, 73, art. VIII. Cf. J. Aymon, *Synodes*, I, 2nd pagination, 79, art. IV.

[4] J. Quick, *Synodicon*, I, 76, art. XIII, attacks unnamed churches that "thought good to leave the Election of the new Consistory unto the body of the people," and insists that they conform "with the other Churches of this Kingdom unto that Canon of the Discipline, *viz.* That Elders and Deacons shall be chosen by the Consistory, and then presented unto the people." Cf. J. Aymon, *Synodes*, I, 2nd pagination, 80, art. VIII.

[5] By special *lettres patentes* according to G. de Félice, *Histoire des synodes nationaux des églises réformées de France* (Paris, 1864), p. 83, who provides no details or source, however.

locality in which it was held. La Rochelle had become entirely Protestant early in 1568, as a result of a local coup. It had subsequently become the most important military and diplomatic headquarters for the Huguenot forces. And it had also become an important center for the diffusion of printed Protestant propaganda.[1] By meeting in La Rochelle, therefore, the Synod could be assured of local sympathy, protection, and publicity of a sort enjoyed by no earlier synod. Its meetings could be more public and more fully attended. Its decisions could be made known more quickly and more widely.

A revealing index to the importance attached to the La Rochelle Synod is provided by the names of those in attendance. The clerical representatives were headed by Theodore Beza himself. He had come all the way from Geneva to attend the Synod,[2] and he was elected its Moderator. The records suggest that he made a vigorous and partisan Moderator : many of his express suggestions were adopted as acts of the Synod. In this task of direction, Beza was assisted by his old friend and former Geneva colleague, Nicolas des Gallars, who was elected one of the Synod's two scribes.[3] Beza was no doubt also assisted by such other loyal Geneva-trained clergymen among the delegates in attendance as Guy Moranges and Arnaud Banc.[4] Beza's pre-eminence at La Rochelle was probably also fortified by his friends and allies, the pastors of the Reformed Church of Zurich. They sent a message of warm fraternal greetings to the Synod.[5]

The lay representatives who attended the La Rochelle Synod were no less distinguished. Among them were the Admiral Coligny and the Queen of Navarre, the two most important political leaders of the Huguenot movement, since the assassination of Louis I de Bourbon, Prince of Condé, following the battle of Jarnac in 1569. Among them were also the young princes of Navarre and Condé, the titular leaders of French Protestantism and the movement's greatest hopes for its political future, and Louis of Nassau, younger brother to William of Orange, the most militantly Protestant member of the house which was to lead the Dutch revolt against Spain.[6]

Consolidation was the essential task to which the La Rochelle Synod devoted itself. Its delegates made a thorough study of the Confession of Faith and the Discipline adopted by the first national Synod in 1559, and modified by succeeding synods. They tried to iron out certain confusions that had resulted from the circulation of variant copies of the key documents which recorded these acts. They modified both Confession and Discipline in numerous minor ways. And they ordered that three definitive texts of the Confession be prepared on parchment, for deposit in Geneva, La Rochelle, and some place in Béarn.[7] These La Rochelle texts have ever since provided French Protestantism with its most fundamental statements of faith.

---

[1] See below, pp. 172-173, for a more extended analysis of these developments.

[2] Although he had some difficulty in getting permission to leave Geneva. See below, pp. 194-195, for more on this.

[3] J. Quick, *Synodicon*, I, 91 ; J. Aymon, *Synodes*, I, 2nd pagination, p. 98.

[4] Their signatures can be found on the parchment copy of the Confession adopted at La Rochelle, in Geneva, Arch., PH No. 1905. For more on these two men, see R. M. Kingdon, *Geneva & Coming*, *passim*.

[5] A. Bouvier, *Bullinger*, pp. 389-390.

[6] See below, pp. 195-196, for more on the participation of these aristocrats.

[7] J. Quick, *Synodicon*, I, 92-93, art. VIII ; J. Aymon, *Synodes*, I, 2nd pagination, p. 100, art. VIII. The Geneva copy is preserved in Arch., PH No. 1905. On its original receipt, see below, p. 196, n. 4.

It must have been in its survey of Reformed discipline, that the Synod stirred up the Morély faction again. As we shall see, its members were obviously agitated following this Synod. While the parchment copy of the Confession adopted does not make clear the reasons for this agitation, some of the glosses and supplements to it do. These supplementary documents do not contain any explicit repudiation of Morély, as had the synodical acts of Orleans and Paris. But many of their strictures were obviously directed against his program of reform. Of these strictures, subsequent controversy suggests that the most important was a fairly general one, announcing, in language reminiscent of Chandieu's refutation of Morély, that the assembly " rejected and rejects the error of those who wish to abolish the discipline of the Church, confounding it with the civil and political government of the magistrates." [1] Some texts suggest that this stricture was actually only a part of a specific condemnation of a certain unnamed " Physitian," who was accused of having " maintained the Supremacy of the Magistrate as Head of the Church, and had published certain Writings under his own Hand and Name containing the Reasons of his Opinion." [2] This specific condemnation was furthermore implemented, according to these same texts, by a directive to Beza, to gather more information about this physician's criticisms from another pastor, and to take this information back to Geneva for the preparation of a formal answer.[3] Contemporaries and scholars since, on reading this version, jumped to the erroneous conclusion that it was aimed at Thomas Erastus, the great doctor-theologian of Heidelberg, and at his blunt criticisms of Calvinist use of consistorial excommunication as a disciplinary weapon.[4]

Another disciplinary decision, which also became a matter of controversy, involved the composition of the consistory. It tightened clerical power yet further, by ruling that " Ministers and Elders compose the Consistory, in which Ministers shall always preside, and the Deacons may be present, if so be the Consistory do judge it fitting." [5]

Other decisions at La Rochelle, which may well have provoked the Morély faction further, dealt with specific churches in certain areas. One concerned the Church of Meaux near Paris. Its elders and people had complained " that they be deprived of their Freedom and Priviledge in Elections " by existing disciplinary regulations, and this complaint was presented to the Synod by the deputy from Brie. The Synod refused to consider this petition,

---

[1] This is the wording found in the manuscript excerpt from the Synod's acts, sent by Beza to Bullinger, as an appendix to his letter of 13 November 1571, in Zürich, Staatsarchiv, E II 381, fol. 1310, original: " la dicte assemblée ratifiant l'Article trente deuxiesme de la dicte Confession a rejetté & rejettent l'erreur de ceux qui veulent abolir la discipline de l'Eglise la confondans avec le gouvernement civil et Politicque des Magistrats."

[2] J. Quick, *Synodicon*, I, 92, art. V. Cf. J. Aymon, *Synodes*, I, 2nd pagination, 99, art. V, which adds, following the claim for magisterial supremacy: " & que ce que les Ministres entreprennent n'est que tirannie."

[3] *Ibid.*, art. VI.

[4] Apparently including Bullinger: Beza to Bullinger, 13 November 1571, cited in n. 1 above, fol. 1307v., and below, p. 213, makes a considerable point of denying that condemnation of Erastus was intended. Also J. Quick, in table to ed. in *Synodicon*, I, 90; and Ruth Wesel-Roth, *Thomas Erastus* (Lahr/Baden: Schauenburg, 1954), p. 112.

[5] J. Quick, *Synodicon*, I, 96, art. III. Cf. J. Aymon, *Synodes*, I, 2nd pagination, p. 104, art. XII.

and suggested that the Church of Meaux apply to a synod of its own province if its members wanted further discussion of the matter.[1] This suggestion, as we shall see, may well have led to further trouble.

Another La Rochelle decision which may have provoked the Morély faction, concerned the churches of Languedoc. Apparently a measure of ecclesiastical democracy had also taken root in that part of France, for the Synod was informed,

" that certain Churches in Languedoc do practise divers things contrary to our Discipline, as that in the Election of Elders, and in the Mission and Loan of Ministers they gather the Peoples Votes one after another."

The Synod announced that,

" it doth disapprove and condemn all those Usages and Customs, and admonisheth the said Churches to conform themselves unto that Order established and observed by us, according to the Discipline, and in case of default those Churches shall be censured." [2]

There is also one further decision of the La Rochelle Synod which we need to note at this point. Although it did not relate directly to Morély's reform program, it nevertheless became intimately involved in the next stage of the quarrel over that program. It was on eucharistic theology. The Synod explicitly rejected the opinion of those who would not accept use of the word " substance " in the official description of the way in which the faithful communicate with Christ in the Lord's Supper.[3]

Although one has the impression that some of these decisions were preceded by some debate, the Synod agreed, in a fairly short period of time, upon the flat and unequivocal formulae recorded in the reports of its deliberations. Then the Synod adjourned in a blaze of glory. Jubilant announcements of its accomplishments were quickly relayed all over Reformed Christendom.[4]

The glory of La Rochelle's accomplishments was soon tarnished, however. It was tarnished by an attack from a new, somewhat surprising, and very dangerous quarter. For the faction seeking structural reform of the Reformed Church at this point produced a new spokesman, Peter Ramus. Ramus, of course, was one of the most colorful and remains one of the best-known intellectuals of the sixteenth century. He is particularly well known for his contributions to the study of logic, his tempestuous career as a professor in Paris, and his gory death during the Saint Bartholomew's massacres.[5] But it should not be forgotten that this death cut short a meteoric and stormy rise

---

[1] J. Quick, *Synodicon*, I, 95, art. VIII. Cf. J. Aymon, *Synodes*, I, 2nd pagination, p. 103, art. VII.

[2] J. Quick, *Synodicon*, I, 101, art. II (2nd). Cf. J. Aymon, *Synodes*, I, 2nd pagination, p. 111, art. VII.

[3] J. Quick, *Synodicon*, I, 92, art. VII. Cf. J. Aymon, *Synodes*, I, 2nd pagination, pp. 99-100, art. VII.

[4] E.g. the letters of the Synod to the Church of Zurich, April 1571, and of Beza to Bullinger, 8 April [1571], published in A. Bouvier, *Bullinger*, pp. 544-549.

[5] The best biography remains C. Waddington, *Ramus*. It has been superseded for study of his thought and bibliography of his writings by Walter J. Ong, *Ramus, Method, and the Decay of Dialogue*, and *Ramus and Talon Inventory* (Cambridge, Mass. : Harvard, 1958).

to prominence within international Protestant circles, a rise in which the quarrel over church discipline played a key part.

Ramus had first become interested in Protestantism at the time of the Colloquy of Poissy, in 1561, when Calvinist doctrines had reached their height in popularity, and when it seems to have been fashionable for courtiers to join the movement. This, at least, is the time he fixes for his conversion in a later letter to his long-time protector, the Cardinal of Lorraine, and this chronology is corroborated by the hostile testimony of Beza.[1] For a long time, however, Ramus apparently did not take a very active part in Protestant ecclesiastical affairs. He no doubt did make important contributions to the movement through his teaching. And he seems to have helped Protestant education substantially in indirect ways. One chronicler reports, for example, that it was Ramus who persuaded the Cardinal of Châtillon to help underwrite the new Reformed Academy in Orleans, by providing in 1565, scholarship funds for some hundred worthy young students.[2] It is ironic, in view of later developments, that Ramus and Châtillon were responsible for such an important element in the support of an institution whose program was dominated by one of Morély's bitterest enemies—Nicholas des Gallars.

When Ramus finally did enter directly the arena of Protestant internal politics, it was in part as a result of mounting pressures put on intellectuals of Protestant tendencies in Paris, by Roman Catholic church authorities, university officials, and governmental authorities. These pressures resulted in a series of royal edicts in 1568, designed to remove all Protestants from teaching posts. The edicts were followed by court actions aimed at specific people, most prominent among whom was Ramus.[3] When civil war broke out again later that year, Ramus left Paris and joined the Huguenot army assembling near the German borders of France. While with that army, he reportedly rendered the cause a signal service. An important part of the army was composed of German mercenaries who had been promised substantial advance payments. At the time of mobilization, however, funds had not yet arrived for these payments. The Germans threatened to return home, and the situation was saved only by the raising of a part of the funds through the levying of a collection among the Huguenot troops present, particularly the nobles, and by the impassioned oration of Ramus, who helped persuade them to proceed with the campaign in France.[4]

After giving the Huguenot military cause this assist, however, Ramus left the army and proceeded to visit Protestant Germany and Switzerland. For more than two years he toured leading centers of Protestantism. Among other places, he visited Strasbourg and its intellectual leader, his old friend and teacher, Johannes Sturm; he visited Basel, and spent more than a year

---

[1] C. Waddington, *Ramus*, Part I, ch. V, esp. pp. 135-136, re letter to Lorraine; Beza to Bullinger, 14 January 1572, excerpt quoted in translation by C. Borgeaud, *Université*, I, 114.

[2] Claude de la Grange, quoted by N. Weiss, in " Une des premières écoles de théologie protestantes en France (Orléans 1561-1568)," BSHPF, LX (1911), 223.

[3] C. Waddington, *Ramus*, p. 219, re 29 January 1568 dismissal of Ramus as Principal of the Collège de Presles. BSHPF, LXXX (1931), 503, quotes text of 28 June 1568 Parlement order that Ramus appear at hearing on request from the University Rector that he be forbidden to teach.

[4] C. Waddington, *Ramus*, pp. 186-187, based on de Thou and Brantôme.

there studying theology and writing; he was invited to Zurich, and received royally there; he visited Calvinist Heidelberg, and, at the Prince Elector's request, briefly taught in the university there; he went to Geneva and taught a short course there; he then moved on to Lausanne with some of his Genevan students and continued teaching there.[1] In Lausanne, in September of 1570, he received word from Paris of the return of peace and decided to return home.[2] Nearly everywhere Ramus went on these travels, he made the same dramatic and disturbing impression that he made in Paris. Nearly everywhere he aroused the enthusiasm of students and the anger of colleagues. In Heidelberg, he quarreled with Erastus and the local theologians.[3] In Basel, he quarreled with Sulzer and other local theologians.[4] In Geneva, the pastors, at the beginning of May, 1570, had begged the city Council to permit Ramus to lecture, "to help the university's reputation."[5] By the end of that month, some of these same pastors were formally reprimanding Ramus for his method of teaching. He abruptly stopped his course of lectures. Angry students protested by posting verses in praise of Ramus and in condemnation of those who they felt had forbidden him to teach.[6]

In one city, however, Ramus made friendships with the prominent which remained close and important. This city was Zurich. Heinrich Bullinger, Zurich's 'Antistes,' or principal preacher, and the chosen successor of Zwingli, and Bullinger's colleagues in the Zurich pastoral corps, were most impressed by Ramus' intellectual qualities. And Ramus responded by becoming more and more attached to Zwinglian theology. This attachment and his concurrent quarrels gave direction to several of Ramus' later outbursts of bad temper.

A first outburst occurred in 1569, even before Ramus' return to France, when he urged the Church of Zurich to break with that of Basel, on a point of eucharistic theology.[7] A second and more serious outburst followed the La Rochelle national Synod in France. The appeal to Zurich, or to the churches of Germany, was not a new one for French Christians who disliked Geneva's direction. It had been tried by French Catholics, who saw in the existence of Protestant disunity a way of blunting the edge of Protestant growth and, perhaps, of winning Protestants back to the Roman Church.[8] It had also reportedly been tried by Morély, in an earlier stage of the disci-

[1] *Ibid.*, Part I, ch. VII.

[2] BSHPF, XXI, (1872), 472, text of permission granted by Lausanne Council, 5 September 1570, to Ramus and others to return to France.

[3] C. Waddington, *Ramus*, pp. 199-208; Ruth Wesel-Roth, *Thomas Erastus*, p. 70 and n. 237 on p. 141.

[4] See letter cited in n. 7.

[5] Geneva, Arch., RC, LXV, fol. 76, 8 May 1570: "Ramus Docteur. Les seigneurs ministres... ont declare quilz ont prie ledit Sr Ramus de faire quelques lecons pour donner bruit a luniversite ce quil a accorde."

[6] Geneva, Arch., RCP, Bl, [fol. 39 v.], 31 May 1570, published in C. Borgeaud, *Université*, I, 112. Beza and the Rector were the pastors who had reprimanded Ramus.

[7] Ramus to Gwalter and Lavater of Zurich, 22 [or 31] July 1569, full text published in BSHPF, XXXIX (1890), 524-530.

[8] Most notably by the Cardinal of Lorraine, who appealed to sections of certain Lutheran confessions at the Colloquy of Poissy in 1561, ostensibly as a basis for compromise. See H. Outram Evennett, *The Cardinal of Lorraine and the Council of Trent* (Cambridge, 1930), ch. X, *passim.*

plinary quarrel. According to one account of his hearing at the Court of Navarre, he had at one point suggested that the whole controversy be submitted to the Church of Zurich for adjudication, and at another claimed certain of his views to be identical to those of the " churches of Germany." [1]

Ramus was in a much better position to play this game, however, once he had become acquainted personally with the Reformed theologians of Germany and Switzerland. And play it he did. In September of 1571, he sent to Bullinger a long report on the actions of the national Synod of La Rochelle, which could not have been better calculated to make Bullinger angry with the Genevans.[2] The immediate purpose of this letter was to elicit from Bullinger an opinion that could aid a provincial Synod of the Ile-de-France in its forthcoming deliberations. Ramus raised three objections to the decisions of the La Rochelle Synod. One was that its disciplinary decisions were concentrating too much power in the hands of the pastors. Ramus reported that deacons were being excluded from the consistories, that elders were being limited to disciplinary work, and that the pastors alone retained the power to make decisions on matters of doctrine, just as in Geneva. His second objection was that the Synod had voted to damn as heretics those who rejected ecclesiastical discipline and confounded ecclesiastical matters with civil and political affairs. His third was that the Synod attacked those who refused to accept the word " substance " in explanations of what takes place in holy communion, a move which he suggested was a direct slap at Zurich and the Swiss. He bolstered these objections by quotations from the relevant parts of the synodical acts.

Of these three objections, the first seems to have bothered Ramus most. He elaborated on it at the greatest length. He made it clear that he did not want to destroy altogether the power of consistories, and that he was perfectly willing to leave them the supervision of the routine and ordinary business of the local church. But he did suggest that in cases involving decisions of doctrine or discipline, election or deposition, excommunication or absolution, the whole church should be consulted at the beginning, rather than merely being called in at the end either to accept or reject a consistorial decision, without any guarantee that a rejection would be honored since final authority remained with the consistory. In this suggestion, Ramus summarized an important part of Morély's entire reform program, albeit in a rather tentative way.

This report really upset Bullinger. In a letter full of alarm and distress, the Zurich Antistes wrote to Beza.[3] He was particularly upset by the French condemnation of those who failed to use the word " substance," and he rather pointedly reminded Beza that Calvin himself had agreed to leave the word out of their joint Helvetic Confession. He was also upset by the French condemnation of those who refused to accept " discipline," which he took to

---

[1] In De Lesperandière dit Merlin to Beza, 10 January 1567, in Geneva, BPU, Ms. fr. 446, fols. 119-120, signed original : " que si on vouloit, il [Morély] deferoit le jugement de toute ceste controverse à l'Eglise de Zuric." It is also Merlin who reports that at another point Morély claimed one of his views to be that of " les Eglises d'Alemaigne."

[2] Ramus to Bullinger, 1 September 1571, text, with a few apparently inadvertent omissions, in C. Waddington, *Ramus*, pp. 433-435.

[3] Bullinger to Beza, 24 October 1571, relevant passages published in A. Bouvier, *Bullinger*, pp. 549-551.

mean those who rejected use of excommunication by the Church. This was precisely the practice which Erastus had insisted was the great weakness of Genevan ecclesiastical polity, and on this point the Zurich Church had long been inclined to agree. Bullinger felt that the whole Zurich Church might well be compromised by being associated with these decisions through the minor role it had played in the La Rochelle Synod. He begged for an explanation.

Beza took Bullinger's complaints very seriously. The Zurich Church and its leader probably had an even greater international reputation among the Reformed communities than did the Genevans. At least the volume of Bullinger's correspondence with the Reformed in England, Germany, and central Europe, certainly suggests that.[1] And the Zurich Church was of considerable political importance to Geneva. The city of Geneva was still very dependent on the powerful but uncertain military protection of Berne and her Swiss allies. And Berne was Zwinglian in her theology and looked to Zurich for spiritual leadership. These practical considerations, combined with a proper consideration for Christian unity, help explain the reply Beza prepared for Bullinger. It was more than a simple letter. It was practically a small book, accompanied with lengthy extracts both in the original French and in Latin translation of the acts of the La Rochelle Synod, all elegantly re-copied by a professional scribe.[2] Anyone who looks at the originals can see at a glance that this was not another one of the hasty notes which Beza normally dashed off for Bullinger in his own handwriting.

Beza's letter to Bullinger is one of the most complete reports available of his whole attitude toward the Morély reform program. It is also an exceedingly skillful brief, showing full knowledge of precisely the problems that were most likely to bother Bullinger. The letter begins with a long sketch of ecclesiastical organization and disciplinary practice, as it had been developed in Geneva and spread to France, with particular attention to the institution of the consistory, which must have been the least known to the men of Zurich.[3] It proceeds to a detailed account of the whole quarrel with Morély, which roundly damns the man and accuses him repeatedly of calling the Reformed Church an "oligarchy" or "tyranny," and of trying to introduce within it "the most troublesome and most seditious democracy."[4] While Beza concedes that in the beginning, when churches were first being created in France, relatively "democratic" procedures were sometimes used, he insists that this was merely a temporary expedient, and that in principle the churches of France "have always had and still have in common with us the aristocratic principle of the consistory."[5] This letter even adds some new details about

---

[1] This argument is developed by Joachim Staedtke, "Bullingers Bedeutung für die protestantische Welt," *Zwingliana*, XI (1959-1963), 372-388. N.B. the estimate on p. 376 that Bullinger's correspondence, much of which remains unpublished, totals some 12,000 letters, about three times as many as in the correspondence of either Luther or Calvin. Staedtke also documents the wide dispersal of Bullinger's published works.

[2] Beza to Bullinger, with annexes, 13 November 1571, in Zürich, Staatsarchiv, E II 381, fols. 1304-1311v., signed original. See Appendix II, for text of the letter alone.

[3] For summary and comment, see above, pp. 38-42.

[4] E.g., in letter described in n. 2, fol. 1306v., and below, p. 212, re charges of Morély, Ramus, and supporters: "quasi Oligarchiam aut Tyrannidem in Ecclesiam invehant, qui perturbatissimam & seditiosissimam Democratiam stabilire in Ecclesia recusarint."

[5] In *ibid.*, re the French churches: "Habuerunt autem semper, et adhuc nunc habent in genere aristocratiam Consistorii nobiscum communem."

the Morély affair. Beza says that he was informed at La Rochelle that Morély had failed to reconcile himself with the churches of his own province, and during the last war had tried to win the favor of the local Catholics by presenting a child for Catholic baptism. All this part of the letter is accompanied with blasts at Ramus for having revived and revivified the whole matter. In passing, he even criticizes Ramus' teaching, claiming that he had never lectured on any noble writer of antiquity without attacking in an outrageous fashion the writer's ignorance.[1]

Only after he has fully described and blackened the Morély reform program, does Beza proceed to the matters which worried Bullinger most. Here he becomes very conciliatory. He begins by denying any intention of wanting to attack Erastus and his doctrines. He insists that the references to "discipline" in the synodical minutes referred to the program of church organization generally, not to the single practice of excommunication. He denies that the condemnation of a "physician" was intended for Erastus, and explains it was rather meant for a doctor in the Bordeaux area, who wanted to give civil governmental authorities sole power to select and depose pastors, and to promulgate and abrogate ecclesiastical laws. And he notes that Ramus is in no position to reproach the French Reformed for criticizing Erastus, since he had a nasty personal row with Erastus himself over the disciplinary question, during his stay in Heidelberg.

On the matter of the use of the word "substance" in definitions of what takes place in the sacrament of holy communion, Beza goes to even greater lengths to be conciliatory. He insists that its use was required only to undercut the wild doctrines of a group of Italian troublemakers in Lyon. He declares himself personally willing to forego use of the word, if the description of what takes place in the sacrament is expressed with the care which the Zurichers normally use.

Finally Beza pleads with Bullinger not to allow his own great authority to be used by those who would disturb the order of the French Church.

There seems to be no real reason to doubt the factual accuracy of this long letter of Beza's. At points where he can be checked by reference to other witnesses, his account stands. It is a matter of record, for example, that Ramus got into one of his famous rows with Erastus while in Heidelberg.[2] And a good deal is known about Lodoico Alamanni and the other Italian troublemakers in Lyon, and of Beza's concern for checking the spread of their ideas.[3]

Beza's letter seems to have had the desired effect on Bullinger. The Antistes of Zurich immediately reverted to a role which he frequently assumed,

---

[1] In *ibid.* This criticism is substantially expanded in Beza to Bullinger, 14 January 1572: see the short excerpt in Borgeaud, *Université*, I, 114, or the original in Zürich, Staatsarchiv, E II 381, fols. 1322-1323. This habit of Ramus no doubt explains much of his popularity with students and his friction with colleagues.

[2] Ruth Wesel-Roth, *Thomas Erastus*, p. 70 and n. 237 on p. 141. The latter note quotes from Erastus' bitter comments about Ramus in a letter to Gwalter, and refers to letters from Erastus to Bullinger which contain equally bitter comments. Originals are preserved in the Zürich Staatsarchiv.

[3] Henri Meylan, "Bèze et les Italiens de Lyon (1566)," BHR, XIV (1952), 235-249. Note particularly the summary, on p. 244, of Alamanni's denial of Christ's material presence in the sacrament of communion, a denial reminiscent of Zwingli's, but more extreme.

of mediator. This is revealed in two letters which he wrote almost at the same time, to Ramus and Beza. One of the more interesting techniques of conciliation he adopted was to discover a common scapegoat. The one he discovered was an old favorite with him—the Anabaptists. In his letter to Beza, Bullinger wrote that he and his colleagues in Zurich had never heard of Morély before, but that if Beza's description was accurate the man was clearly mad and they suspected him of belonging to the Anabaptists.[1] On the other hand, he defended Ramus' intelligence and piety at length, and urged Beza to be gentle with him so that such a great and useful ornament to the cause would not be lost. The letter to Ramus was largely a warning to watch out for Anabaptists.[2] Bullinger did not take Ramus' suggestions for ecclesiastical reform very seriously. He noted that most of the practices to which Ramus had objected, particularly those relating to the choice of ministers, were either similar to those in use in Zurich or ones which the Zurichers were willing to allow other churches to use. To both Ramus and Beza, however, he made it very clear that Zurich was not going to change its eucharistic formulae to include such an unScriptural word as "substance."

Ramus took this as a cue. In his subsequent letters to Bullinger he devoted much more space to the eucharistic problem than to the disciplinary problem.

This did not mean that Ramus had abandoned ecclesiastical reform, however. Indeed he pushed it with such ardor and with such skill that he scored a success which Morély had never been able to achieve. He persuaded an entire provincial Synod to consider compromise with the Morély program. This Synod, furthermore, was a successor to the ones which had already spent the most time investigating Morély and his ideas. It was a provincial Synod of the Ile-de-France.

The Synod at which Ramus appeared met at Lumigny-en-Brie in March of 1572. Unfortunately its acts seem to have been destroyed, there is reason to believe deliberately. Our knowledge of its discussions, therefore, must come from contemporary reports. I have found two of these. One, from Ramus himself to Bullinger, is not particularly revealing.[3] It slights the discussions of disciplinary problems and concentrates upon those on eucharistic theology, a pattern to which I have already alluded. The revealing report is one to Beza, from a pastor named De Lestre de Beaulieu, who was also in attendance. Like Ramus' letter to Bullinger, it was written on March 19, shortly after the Synod had adjourned.[4] According to De Lestre, ecclesiastical reform was the main item on an agenda for a session which lasted several days. If his account can be trusted, and I see no reason why it cannot,

---

[1] In Bullinger to Beza, 4 December 1571, full text in A. Bouvier, *Bullinger*, pp. 557-565, on p. 558. On Bullinger's general attitude toward the Anabaptists, see Heinold Fast, *Heinrich Bullinger und die Täufer* (Weierhof, Pfalz: Mennonitischer Geschichtsverein, 1959), including brief comment on these two letters, pp. 87, 156.

[2] Bullinger to Ramus, 2 December 1571, full text in A. Bouvier, *Bullinger*, pp. 551-557.

[3] Ramus to Bullinger, 19 March 1572, full text in C. Waddington, *Ramus*, pp. 438-440.

[4] De Lestre de Beaulieu to Beza, 19 March [1572], copy in Geneva, MHR, Beza Correspondence, based on signed original in Paris, Bibliothèque Nationale, f. Dupuy 268, fols. 237-238, excerpted in *France protestante*, 1st ed., VII, 45-46, art. "de Lestre." For more on de Lestre, see also Beza, *Corr.*, II, 208, n. 9.

it provides the fullest account available of Ramus' actual ideas on ecclesiastical organization.

Morély had apparently planned to come to Lumigny himself. When he did not get there, his views were nevertheless sustained by Ramus and a man named Bergeron. They were only sustained in part, however. As De Lestre put it:

" Morély insisted that all important affairs should be considered by everyone. Ramus and the others, although they condemned on several points the disorderly spirit of Morély, nevertheless approached it closely. They only wished that the advice of some would weigh more than of others, according to geometrical proportions." [1]

Ramus, therefore, was apparently not willing to go as far as full ecclesiastical democracy with Morély. Rather he wanted to increase lay participation in decision making, in a way which would be weighted, no doubt socially, much as secular government in his day was often weighted, both in city governments and in provincial and national Estates. Unfortunately the details of the system of weighting which he advocated are never spelled out.

These proposals were carefully and seriously studied at Lumigny. The Synod concluded with a set of decisions involving a series of delicately balanced compromises, according to De Lestre's report, all of them the result of careful study and discussion of relevant Scriptural passages. The main decision was that local churches be permitted to hold conferences apart from regular services, similar to the " congregations " which Calvin had established in Geneva for Bible study.[2] At these conferences, laymen would be permitted to speak on prophecy and other " holy things." These conferences were to be presided over and controlled by regularly ordained pastors, and lay speakers were to be screened in advance by the local pastors and elders. These conferences were also not to be established without the permission of the provincial synod of the locality. Special conferences of a similar sort were also recommended to resolve dogmatic controversies. They would again be presided over by pastors, but laymen would be permitted to attend. Their decisions would be made and announced by the pastors, but in the presence and with the silent assent of the laymen. It was hoped that such conferences could " moderate both the license of the people desired by some, and the tyranny of the pastors." [3]

The Lumigny Synod also recommended increased lay participation in other ecclesiastical procedures. In the selection of pastors, for example,

---

[1] In *ibid.*: " Moreli pressoit que toutes les affaires principales devoient passer par les advis de tous. Ramus et les autres, combien qu'ilz condamnassent en quelques points l'ataxie [disorderly spirit] de Morely, toutesfois en approchoient bien fort. Seulement vouloient que les advis des uns poissassent plus que des autres, selon les proportions geometriques."

[2] Eugène Choisy, *La Théocratie à Genève au temps de Calvin* (Geneva, 1897), pp. 227-228, describes the Genevan " congregation," but gives the impression that only the pastors spoke in it. However his own references to single " congregations," pp. 67, 69, 113, make it clear that laymen often participated, and a passage in Geneva, RCP, Kingdon & Bergier, eds., II, 70, suggests that laymen sometimes led them, at least from 1557 on.

[3] In *ibid.*: " modérer et la licence des peuples desirée par aucuns, et la tyrannie des Pasteurs."

nomination by the people as well as the normal nomination by the pastors and elders, was to be permitted. And when new pastors were presented to their congregations, members were to be permitted to register their consent by voice-vote, by vote of hands, or by silence. Further, each decision by a consistory to punish a sinner was to be announced publicly, in the hope that publicity would induce repentance and make excommunication unnecessary. Decisions to absolve sinners were also to be announced in public. All of these suggestions, of course, would have increased congregational participation in the operations of Reformed church government. But they would have left intact such existing institutions as the consistory and the synods. Furthermore certain of the powers traditionally reserved to the clergy, for example the powers to ordain and depose pastors, were not to be modified.

Altogether, therefore, the Lumigny decisions represented only modest concessions to the Morély-Ramus program for reform. Yet according to De Lestre, these were concessions enough to satisfy Ramus. De Lestre felt that a satisfactory compromise had at last been reached, and urged Beza to accept it too. He supported this request with reflections on the great utility to the cause of a man of Ramus' learning and reputation. In this he was following a line of argument which Bullinger also used repeatedly in his letters to Beza. De Lestre also reported that Ramus and his friends had promised to try persuade Morély himself to accept the compromise

If De Lestre and the other delegates to Lumigny really expected Beza to accept a compromise, however, they were naive. Some hint of Beza's reaction can be guessed from the violence with which he had already castigated Ramus as well as Morély in his long December letter to Bullinger. Beza was never the man to surrender a polemical position, no matter how extreme, once he was publicly committed to it.

A real showdown between the factions led by Beza and the supporters of Morély took place at the next national Synod of the French Reformed Church, which met in the southeastern Protestant stronghold of Nîmes, in early May of 1572. Indeed this Synod seems to have been called primarily to deal with the growing chorus of protest provoked by Ramus and his allies. This is suggested by the terms in which the Protestants of Nîmes begged the Small Council of Geneva to permit Beza to attend. Their petition offered this primary explanation of the Synod's need for Beza:

" For as much for the very rare graces with which the Lord has endowed him, as for the almost irreconcilable differences raised in the kingdom against the ecclesiastical discipline since the last Synod, we have such a need for his person in the next assembly that we simply cannot do without him." [1]

The Genevan authorities, after some hesitation and with some reluctance, finally granted Beza permission to go.[2] Again, as we shall see, he was to play a central role in the Synod's deliberations.

---

[1] In Church of Nîmes to Syndics and Council of Geneva, 14 January 1572, in Geneva, Arch., PH No. 1918, signed original: " Car tant pour les graces tres rares dont le Seigneur l'a doue que pour les differens presque irreconciliables esmeuz en royaume contre la discipline ecclesiastique depuis le dernier synode, Nous avons tel besoin de sa personne en la prochaine assemblee que ne nous en pouvons aucunement passer."

[2] E. Choisy, *Genève au temps de Bèze*, pp. 76-78. See below, p. 197, for more on this negotiation.

In further preparations for the Nîmes Synod, the French Reformed took careful steps to disarm the suspicions sown by Ramus among the German Reformed. Bullinger and his colleagues in Zurich were informed in detail of the plans for the Synod. Beza wrote Bullinger that it would concern itself primarily with " democratic propositions and other questions which were not resolved at La Rochelle." [1] The Church of Nîmes also sent the Zurichers a formal notice of the coming Synod and invited them to submit a statement for the Synod's consideration.[2] They, in turn, took the rather unusual step of informing the Reformed Church in Berne about the approaching Synod and its agenda, with the suggestion that the Bernese pastors might want to follow its deliberations with care.[3] This maneuver forced further caution on Beza and his associates. While Johannes Haller and the other pastors of Berne may not have been among the most highly respected intellectual leaders of the Reformed movement, they were in a position of great strategic importance from a political point of view, advising as they did, the leaders of one of contemporary Europe's major military powers. The benevolence and, hopefully, the military assistance of Berne were likely to continue to be essential to the city of Geneva, in her struggles to maintain her independence as a Protestant republic. They were also important to the Huguenot aristocrats who would have to organize the resistance if religious war again broke out in France.

Yet another preparation for the Nîmes Synod may have been the meeting in Lumigny of the provincial Synod of the Ile-de-France to which we have referred. Its compromise formulae were almost certainly intended for transmittal to the national Synod by the province's delegates. In any case, it was the delegates from the Ile-de-France who dictated the direction of discussion at Nîmes. They presented to the Synod a whole battery of papers supporting a program of structural reform. These papers included an abridged set of recommendations for reform adapted by their province (perhaps at the Lumigny Synod) from a recent " book " prepared by Morély. They also included this " book," most probably still in manuscript, which was an extended refutation of Chandieu's *Confirmation* of the French discipline. They also included " books " in defense of this position by Ramus and Sureau.[4] These latter pieces, of course, made explicit and open the support of these two intellectuals for the Morély program. Unfortunately these papers apparently were not preserved, at least in print or in Geneva, so there does not seem to be any detailed record of the substance of Morély's new arguments or of those of his supporters. However hints of their nature are provided by the records of the Synod's deliberations.

---

[1] In Beza to Bullinger, 3 February 1572, Zürich, Staatsarchiv, E II 381, fols. 1349-1350, signed original : " in qua democratici audientur, et quibus altera Synodus Rupellana non satisfecit."

[2] Church of Nîmes to Church of Zurich, 15 January [1572], full text in A. Bouvier, *Bullinger*, pp. 408-409.

[3] Bullinger for all the Pastors of Zurich to Haller, 9 March 1572, cover letter to be accompanied by a dossier of copies of nine relevant documents, in Zürich, Staatsarchiv, E II 381, fol. 1329, contemporary copy. For the signed answer of Haller and his colleagues, 17 March 1572, see *ibid.*, fols. 1332-1333.

[4] J. Quick, *Synodicon*, I, 111-112, art. III. Cf. J. Aymon, *Synodes*, I, 2nd pagination, pp. 122-123, art. III.

These deliberations began with the assignment of all these papers to Pastor Cappel, for examination and report. This assignment may have raised the hopes of the supporters of Morély, for Louis Cappel was from the Ile-de-France himself and had participated actively in the Lumigny Synod. Consequently he knew the partisans of structural reform personally and was even suspected by some of favoring their program.[1] Their hopes may also have been raised by the Synod's unusual decision to permit open debate on this matter, in sessions open to observers as well as official delegates. These hopes would soon have been dashed, however, by the selection of a committee of three to prepare formal answers to the arguments contained in these papers, particularly those not advanced by Morély earlier. For the members selected for this committee were Beza, Chandieu, and a man named de Beaulieu—perhaps De Lestre de Beaulieu.

The Synod then received the report that the reformers' recommendations covered four matters:

"1. About the Decision of Points of Doctrine.
2. About the Election and Deposal of Ministers.
3. About Excommunication out of the church, and Reconciliation with, and Re-admission into it.
4. And lastly about Prophesying."

The first three of these problems had been at issue for years, since the initial writing of Morély's book; the fourth had assumed considerable importance at the Lumigny Synod. Presumably the reformers still took a basically democratic line in their recommendations, perhaps modified along the lines suggested at Lumigny. In any event, the Nîmes Synod ruled against them on every single issue:

" None of these shall be received among us, because they have no Foundation in the Word of God, and are of very dangerous consequence unto the Church, as the whole hath been verified and made appear in the presence of this Synod."[2]

This decision was followed up immediately by a number of retaliatory measures. Antoine de la Roche Chandieu was asked again, this time openly, to prepare the official response. It was to take the form of an account of the synodical debates and decisions. It was to omit the names of the men concerned in the quarrel. And its manuscript was to be delivered to the Lyon Colloquy for publication.

But a general reply was not enough to satisfy the brothers at Nîmes. They were in a mood for vengeance. The Lumigny Colloquy was ordered to raze the memoirs of the Synod which had met there, its members were sternly warned that it was not legitimate for them to adopt any " Canons of their own," and they were admonished to see to it that henceforth they abided " by those of our Discipline."[3] Furthermore action was taken against the reformers as individuals. Ramus, Morély, Sureau, and Bergeron were to be notified

---

[1] Ramus to Bullinger, described in n. 3 to p. 105 reports favorably on Cappel's role in the Lumigny Synod. For more on Cappel, see *France protestante*, 2nd ed., art. "Cappel."

[2] J. Quick, *Synodicon*, I, 112, art. IV. Cf. J. Aymon, *Synodes*, I, 2nd pagination, p. 123, art. IV.

[3] J. Quick, *Synodicon*, I, 112, art. V. Cf. J. Aymon, *Synodes*, I, 2nd pagination, p. 123, art. V.

individually of the Synod's rulings against their suggestions. To give teeth to this notification, the provincial synod of the Ile-de-France was ordered to summon them before the Colloquy of Beauvoisin, " and remonstrate to them their Offences, but to deal gently and sweetly with them: And in case upon their appearance they should reject their Admonitions, they shall be proceeded against as Rebels and Schismaticks, according to the Canons of our Discipline." [1] So determined were the brethren at Nîmes to prevail, that they were quite prepared to drive right out of the French Reformed Church its most distinguished intellectual and one of its most devoted polemicists, along with the most troublesome thorn in its flesh.

The only issue upon which the Synod of Nîmes showed the least disposition to be conciliatory, was the sacramental one. Bullinger's dismay at the La Rochelle statements on the eucharist had clearly disturbed the French. Accordingly, the Nîmes delegates withdrew the earlier blanket condemnation of all who fail to use the word " substance " in describing what takes place in the Lord's Supper. They did not abandon its use for the French Reformed, but conceded the right of " Forreign Churches " to do so. And they adopted further modifications of their statement on eucharistic theology, designed to bring it more nearly into line with the Zwinglian position. For example, the phrase, " That by Mystical and Spiritual Communication with him, we may derive that true eternal life," [2] was substituted for a phrase which had a more substantial ring and thus approached more nearly the Lutheran position on the matter.

Ramus, in a report to one of the Zurich pastors about the Synod of Nîmes, claimed this concession as a victory for Sureau.[3] It is certainly possible that Sureau's brief for the Synod may have contained comments on sacramental formulae, for this was a matter upon which he was quite expert.

But I have found no independent evidence for this claim. And it is likely that Beza and other leaders of the Synod would have made concessions of this sort in any event, to mollify the Zurichers and their powerful allies.

Beza himself was clearly the driving force behind these decisions. That is a conclusion one can easily draw from the synodical acts alone. And it is reinforced by the reports to Geneva of the role he played. A letter from the Nîmes Church reported that he had "closed the mouth of certain troublemakers who wanted to disturb our churches, to whom he so greatly and so learnedly opposed himself that we all have a great opportunity to praise God." [4] The Synod itself reported that he had headed off the most serious internal threat

---

[1] J. Quick, *Synodicon*, I, 113, art. XII. Cf. J. Aymon, *Synodes*, I, 2nd pagination, p. 124, art. XII.

[2] J. Quick, *Synodicon*, I, 104, art. II. Cf. J. Aymon, *Synodes*, I, 2nd pagination, p. 112, art. II.

[3] Ramus to Gwalter, 1 July 1572, Zürich, Staatsarchiv, E II 368, fols. 316-317, signed original. See also Ramus to Gwalter, 17 July 1572, *ibid.*, fol. 320, signed original, accusing Beza of misrepresenting Bullinger's views at Nîmes.

[4] In Church of Nîmes to Syndics and Council of Geneva, 19 May [1572], in Geneva, Arch., PH No. 1918: "a fermer la bouche a certains brouillons que veulent troubler noz eglises a quoy il s'est tellement et si doctement opposé que nous tous avons grande occasion de louer Dieu."

that had ever been posed to the French Reformed Church at one of her synods, and praised the unique erudition and dexterity that made this possible.[1]

Again Beza had triumphed. But the triumph turned out to be a bitter one. For French Protestantism, without any of the customary danger-signals or warnings, was about to face its most traumatic experience : the St. Bartholomew's massacres.

6. *The St. Bartholomew's Massacres End the Quarrel*

The massacres of French Protestants which began when King Charles IX ordered assassination of their political leaders of the eve of St. Bartholomew's day, August 24, in 1572, and which quickly spread all over France as fanatic mobs of Catholics indiscriminately murdered all the Protestants and Protestant sympathizers they could find, constitute one of history's great atrocities.[2] It may be that only in our own century, when the Nazis applied modern technology to the mass slaughter of human beings, has the Western world seen them substantially surpassed in scale. They had a traumatic impact upon the whole French Protestant movement, from which it has never really completely recovered. And they brought to an abrupt halt, for a time at least, practically every activity in which French Protestants were engaged, including their quarrel over the appropriate structure and discipline for their Church.

This quarrel was halted partly because of the general paralysis among French Protestants induced by the massacres. But it was halted also because the massacres were particularly severe in the very area, around Paris, where the faction seeking structural reform of the Church had won its strongest support. In fact many of the leaders of that faction seem themselves to have been victims, in one way or another, of the massacres. The fates of two of them can be documented in some detail. They were Peter Ramus and Hugues Sureau, two of the four whose leadership of this faction had provoked the Synod of Nîmes to threaten them with punishment as "rebels and schismatics." The stories of their fates are most instructive.

Ramus was murdered during the massacres. At the time they began, he was living again in Paris, in his old quarters at the Collège de Presles, although he had still not regained permission to lecture. As the mobs began their bloodthirsty search for victims, Ramus became a particularly desired target. His very prominence probably explains this. But it may also be that some of his students or some of his colleagues spurred on the search. No one well acquainted with academic communities would find this beyond the realm of possibility. For whatever reason, assassins got to him. The first would-be assassins were turned away by bribes. But finally a gang of cutthroats forced its way into his college, smashed through his apartments, and pounced on Ramus, praying. They shot and stabbed him on the spot, and pitched him out an upper-story window. His still-palpitating body was

---

[1] Synod of Nîmes to Syndics and Council of Geneva, 18 May 1572, in *ibid.*

[2] The bibliography on these massacres is large. See, for a recent example, Philippe Erlanger, *Le Massacre de la Saint-Barthélemy* (Paris : Gallimard, 1960), and its bibliography, available in English translation (New York : Pantheon, 1962).

further mutilated by fanatics in the courtyard below. And then what remained of the mortal Ramus was tossed into the Seine, to deepen the crimson with which the blood of hundreds of his fellow Protestants had already stained that river.[1]

For leaders of orthodox French Protestantism, however, Ramus' death was decidedly awkward. To be sure, it ridded them of their most annoying and dangerous internal opponent. But it also made a martyr of a man whom they were thinking of expelling from their Church. In the sixteenth century the crown of martyrdom was a precious prize. Everyone recognized that " the blood of the martyrs is the seed of the Church." [2] And every Church, without exception, did its best to publicize as fully as possible and to take full credit for the feats of its martyrs. For the French Reformed, however, Ramus made an embarrassing martyr.

Some notion of the shape of this embarrassment is provided by an exchange of published polemics which followed the massacres. This exchange was between Pierre Charpentier and Francesco Porto. Charpentier was a lawyer and former Protestant, who had taught law briefly in Geneva and then seems to have become a government spy on the Protestant community in Paris.[3] Porto had been one of Charpentier's colleagues on the Geneva Academy's faculty, and continued to teach Greek there.[4] Before the massacres were decently over, Charpentier rushed into print with a defense of the royal government's decision to launch them, which took the form of an open letter to Porto.[5] In it, Charpentier developed the claim that the French Reformed had brought the massacres on themselves by continual seditious and disloyal intrigues against a king who, until then, had conscientiously protected them against Roman Catholic fanaticism. He claimed further that these intrigues had been systematically sponsored by Church leaders, most prominently by Beza,[6] and had been an important function of certain synodical meetings. Against these intrigues, said Charpentier, a small number of loyal Protestants had fought. This group would probably have included the Prince of Condé,

[1] See C. Waddington, *Ramus*, pp. 254-255, for a description of Ramus' assassination, based on contemporary accounts of Banosius and Nancel; also A. Bouvier, *Bullinger*, p. 412, for another, based on contemporary account of Geizkofler. Waddington, Part I, ch. IX, tries to pin direct responsibility for this assassination on Ramus' bitter academic rival, Jacques Charpentier, an argument effectively refuted by Walter J. Ong, *Ramus, Method, and the Decay of Dialogue* (Cambridge, Mass.: Harvard, 1958), p. 29, n. 68 on p. 327, and others there cited.

[2] The common English adaptation of Tertullian's " semen est sanguis Christianorum," *Apologeticus*, 50.

[3] *France protestante*, 2nd ed., art. " Charpentier (Pierre)."

[4] C. Borgeaud, *Université*, I, 75-77, and *passim*. See also works there cited.

[5] *Lettre de Pierre Charpentier, Jurisconsulte, addressée à François Portes, Candiois, par laquelle il monstre que les persecutions des Eglises de France sont advenues, non par la faulte de ceux qui faisoient profession de la Religion, mais de ceux qui nourrissoient les factions & conspirations qu'on appelle la Cause* (1572). Copy in Geneva, BPU, Rés. Gg 2651. Dated, fol. 36v., Strasbourg, 15 September. Further bibliographical information on this exchange can be found in the biographical notice on Porto in Emile Legrand, *Bibliographie hellénique des XVe et XVIe siècles* (Paris: G. P. Maisonneuve & Larose, 1962, reprint), II, xiv-xvii.

[6] He never mentions Beza by name, but describes his activities in recognizable detail, and on *ibid.*, fol. 36, gives " Sebe " as an anagram of his name.

if he had lived longer.[1] It definitely had included Charpentier himself, Ramus, and several pastors, one of whom was Sureau.[2]

Even though Porto had seldom, if ever, become involved in polemical controversy before, he felt obliged to publish a reply to Charpentier. He took some time to prepare it, but by March of 1573 it was ready.[3] In this tract, Porto advanced a refutation for every specific charge that Charpentier had made. This meant, of course, that Porto could not avoid an assessment of Ramus' career. And this faced Porto with the dilemma to which I have already alluded. The way he took to resolve it, may well have been suggested by Beza. In one of his letters to Bullinger reporting on the massacres, Beza had mentioned certain disgusting apostates. One of them was Sureau, who, said Beza for the first time, " aided and even incited Ramus to trouble the churches." [4] Shifting the blame for Ramus' activities to Sureau was particularly attractive then, because Sureau's apostasy had made him a villain among Protestants generally. Unfortunately this solution could not work for long, since Sureau soon returned to the Protestant fold. In Porto's published reply, however, the blame for Ramus' activities is still shifted to others. He says of Ramus, that since " the Lord honored him with the martyr's crown, the memory of this personage is certainly dear and precious to us." [5] He does not hide the fact of the quarrel over discipline and of Ramus' part in it. But he argues that Ramus had " been bewitched by one or two personages, the errors and dreams of whom had been refuted and condemned many times." [6]

Even more instructive, however, is the case of Sureau. It seems most unlikely that Ramus deliberately sought martyrdom or could in any way control his fate. Sureau, on the other hand, did have the opportunity to claim the martyr's crown, and rejected it.

At the time the massacres began, Sureau was on duty in a small church near Paris.[7] As soon as he learned of the magnitude of the threat, he assumed

---

[1] *Ibid.*, fols. 24-24v.

[2] *Ibid.*, fols. 13-14, re a joint protest of Charpentier and Ramus against a seditious sermon ; fols. 17v.-18, re Ramus' unpublished " book " attacking Beza's faction prepared for a synod [no doubt of Nîmes] ; fol. 14, re six dissenting pastors, including Sureau ; fol. 24v., re sympathy of Condé's chaplain, Perrocelli.

[3] *Response de Francois Portus, Candiot, aux lettres diffamatoires de Pierre Carpentier, Advocat, pour l'innocence des fideles serviteurs de Dieu, & obeissans subjects du Roy, massacrez le 24 jour d'Aoust 1572, appellez factieux par ce plaidereau. Traduite nouvellement de Latin en François* (1574). Copy in Geneva, BPU, Gg 1313. Dated, p. 75, Geneva, 1 March 1573.

[4] Beza to Bullinger, 12 November 1572, in Zürich, Zentralbibliothek, Ms. A 44, pp. 613-616, signed original, re apostate pastors : " quorum unus Roserius [Sureau] nomine, author et adiutor fuit Ramo ad turbandas Ecclesias."

[5] F. Porto, *op. cit.*, p. 68 : " Et puis que le Seigneur l'a honnoré de la couronne de martyre, certainement, la memoire de ce personnage nous est chere & precieuse."

[6] In *ibid.* : " ayant esté ensorcelé par un ou deux personnages, les erreurs & resveries desquels avoyent esté refutees & condamnees beaucoup de fois : en lieu d'acquiescer aux articles du Synode de la Rochelle, il les rejetta, & en abolissant la discipline ancienne, entreprint d'en establir une nouvelle."

[7] This account is largely taken from Sureau's own, in his *Confession et recognoissance de Hugues Sureau dit du Rosier, touchant sa cheute en la Papauté, & les horribles scandales par lui commis...* (Heidelberg : Mayer, 1573), copy in Geneva, BPU, Ba 4363, sigs. Aiiiv and ff. Hereafter cited as Sureau, *Protestant*. There are several later editions of this work described in E. Droz, *L'imprimerie à La Rochelle*, III, *La veuve Berton et Jean Portau*, 1573-1589 (Geneva : Droz, 1960, vol. XXXIV*** in THR), 13-15.

CONFESSION
DE FOY FAICTE PAR
H. S. DV ROSIER AVEC ABIV-
ration & deteſtation de la profeſſion
Huguenotique : faicte tant par deuant
Prelats de l'Egliſe Catholique & Ro-
maine, que Princes du ſang Royal de
France & autres, enſemble la refutatiõ
de pluſieus poincts, mis en auant par
Caluin & Beze, contre la Foy & Egliſe
Apoſtolique.

*Le tout que deſſus confirmé & ſigné
d'iceluy, ainſi qu'il appert par la copie qu'il a baillee.*

Confession de Durosier

A PARIS,

Chez Sebaſtien Niuelle aux Cicognes,
rue ſainct Iaques.

1573.

AVEC PRIVILEGE.

a disguise and tried to make his way to safety in Basel.[1] Before he had gone far, however, he was seized for questioning, identified as a Protestant pastor, and jailed. It was the second time he had been jailed for his faith, but this time circumstances were infinitely more dangerous. If he had shown the constancy which he had displayed in 1566, he would very probably have died a martyr for his faith. Instead, he announced to his jailer a desire to return to the Roman Catholic Church. His announcement created a sensation. An apostate Calvinist pastor was still a rare and valuable bird at this period. Sureau's decision was immediately communicated to the royal Court. And the Court, at once realizing the utility of this conversion, hired Sureau for the task of winning back to the Catholic faith and catechizing a number of Protestant lay leaders who had been taken into custody. He was particularly charged with the job of converting the young King of Navarre and his cousin, the young Prince of Condé. He was also asked to work over the Duchess of Bouillon, whose Protestant faith he had worked so hard to preserve in 1566. And he was also ordered to try to convert and catechize a number of other eminent Protestants who were in custody and had avoided execution so far. In this campaign for conversion or reconversion to Catholicism, Sureau had to work closely with several leading Roman preachers. Probably the most famous of them was Juan Maldonado.[2] This eloquent Jesuit had created a sensation upon his arrival in Paris in the 1560's, and had joined Hervet as one of the most effective Roman Catholic opponents to Protestant propaganda in France. Maldonado and Sureau together toured the northeast area of France, making special efforts to reduce to Catholicism such Protestant strongholds as Sedan.

Sureau's greatest success as a converter came with the young King of Navarre. As his later career was to show, Henri of Navarre never did take his religion very seriously. Whenever one religious connection proved to be too awkward, he switched to another. This first conversion to Catholicism did not last long. It may well have been induced primarily by fear. But it is interesting to speculate about other possible reasons. Henri cannot have forgotten Jean Morély, his favorite boyhood teacher (if his mother's report is to be believed). And he may well have harbored resentment at the rather brutal way in which Calvinist leaders had chased Morély away from the Court. All this could have easily come back to him, as he talked to Sureau, Morély's old friend, about which religion was the true one. One wonders if the Morély affair does not help explain Henri's rather shallow and temporary 1572 conversion. In any case, it may well have weakened the loyalty to the Reformed cause which his devout mother had tried to instill in him since childhood.

Henri of Navarre's 1572 conversion to Roman Catholicism was not the only one which proved temporary, however. Before the next year was out, Sureau himself had returned to the Protestant fold. It was during his conversion tour of northeast France with Maldonado that he saw his chance

[1] *Confession de foy faicte par H. S. du Rosier avec abjuration & detestation de la profession Huguenotique...* (Paris: Nivelle, 1573), but dated 16 September 1572 on fol. 37. Copy in Geneva, BPU, Bc 3299. Fol. 30 identifies Basel as his destination. Hereafter cited as Sureau, *Catholic.*

[2] *Dictionnaire de théologie catholique,* art. "Maldonat, Jean."

CONFESSION

ET RECO-

GNOISSANCE DE HVGVES SVREAV DIT DV ROSIER TOVCHANT SA CHEVTE

en la Papauté, & les horribles ſcandales par lui commis,

SERVANT D'EXEMPLE A tout le monde, de la fragilité, & peruerſité de l'homme abandonné a ſoi, & de l'infinie miſericorde, & ferme verité de Dieu enuers ſes esleuz.

A HEIDELBERG,
Par Ian Mayer.
M. D. LXXIII.

to make a break. He made his escape good, to Protestant Germany, first to Strasbourg, then to Heidelberg, finally to Frankfurt. He never again became a pastor. Instead he returned to his earlier trade as a printer's corrector, taking a job with André Wechel of Frankfurt.[1] Several years later Sureau and his entire family died of the plague.

Sureau's spectacular double apostasy raises a number of extremely interesting psychological problems. In any time of savage ideological conflict apostasy must at once pose peculiarly strong temptations and yet excite peculiarly strong revulsions. It was a phenomenon that was to become relatively frequent and important in the France of the late sixteenth and early seventeenth centuries. The most important examples, of course, are found in the cluster which includes Henri of Navarre's second conversion to Catholicism in 1593, the conversion which won for him the crown of France.[2]

Fortunately more can be known about the apostasies of Sureau than about most. For he was an intelligent and articulate man, and his explanations of his religious decisions were rushed into print and widely circulated, first, of course, by the Catholics, then, naturally, by the Protestants.[3] His own explanations of his apostasies do reveal traces of the external pressures which quite naturally must have loomed large in many apostasies. To begin with, he turned Catholic during the St. Bartholomew's massacres of thousands of his fellow Protestants. This was partly, no doubt, in the hope that an emergency conversion would save his own life, as, in fact, it did. But it was also a decision influenced by the fleeting but understandable fear that the massacres themselves were a sign of God's displeasure with the Protestant cause and His determination to establish the Church of Rome as His only true one.[4] Such a fear could come easily to any Christian as committed to a view of the power and constant activity of divine providence as the average Calvinist. Similarly, Sureau returned to the Protestant fold, at the urging of a number of his old friends, only after he had received certain word that his family had been smuggled out of France and was safely in Protestant territory. The natural fear of death and of divine judgment in the first instance, the natural desire to return to his family in the second—these were clearly factors in his decisions.

But he insisted that they were not the only factors. And his explanations of both his decisions cohere well enough so that I, for one, think we can take

[1] On this later career, see Robert M. Kingdon, "Genève et les réformés français : le cas d'Hugues Sureau, dit du Rosier," BSHAG, XII (1961), 79, and the sources there cited.

[2] Studied in great detail by Ernst Staehelin, in his *Der Uebertritt König Heinrichs des Vierten von Frankreich zur römisch-katholischen Kirche*, ... (Basel, 1856).

[3] Described above in n. 7 to p. 113 (Protestant) and n. 1 to p. 115 (Catholic). For a more detailed analysis of these apostasies, see Robert M. Kingdon, "Problems of Religious Choice for Sixteenth-Century Frenchmen," *The Journal of Religious History*, IV (1966), 105-112.

[4] Sureau, *Protestant*, sig. Aiiii, says he saw in the massacres, " une ruine entiere de l'Eglise, sans y avoir apparence, par laquelle on peust esperer restablissement aucun, je commencay a l'estimer estre un tesmoignage de l'indignation de Dieu : comme s'il eust declaré par ce moyen qu'il avoit en detestation & qu'il condannoit la profession & exercice de nostre Religion : veu qu'il estoit retourné par tant de fois a nous fraper, & finalement ainsi nous renverser, comme voulant entierement ruiner ceste Eglise, & favoriser la Romaine."

his word. Sureau was honestly tormented by doubts on the correctness of theological doctrines, both Protestant and Catholic, which he, in common with most thinking men of his century, thought were of absolutely crucial importance. Some of these doctrines concerned matters which, as he himself admitted, involved fine points upon which differences of opinion were not of great moment. Thus, in his Roman Catholic *Confession of Faith,* Sureau attacked with considerable finesse certain details of the doctrines of Calvin and of Beza on the second person of the Trinity, the precise accomplishment of the Incarnation, the time of Christ's descent into hell, the decrees of predestination and the workings of free will, and the operation of justification. On all of these matters, he was able, in his subsequent Protestant *Confession,* to work himself without much difficulty back to a position which was essentially Calvinist.

On two key doctrines, however, Sureau could never make full recantation. He never did completely adopt the Catholic theology of the mass, which he had attacked so thoroughly and bitterly in his own earlier polemics. He could not persuade himself that this theology had an adequate foundation.[1] And, if his own later account is to be believed, he told the prominent laymen he converted back to Roman Catholicism that they should indeed attend mass and even communicate, but that their understanding of what happens in this central sacrament should take a form which we can recognize as clearly Calvinist.[2] On the other hand, Sureau never did completely abandon a belief in Apostolic Succession. He insisted that his decision to convert to Roman Catholicism was one which he had been considering for months before the St. Bartholomew's massacres, because of his growing doubts about the legitimacy of his vocation to the Protestant pastorate and about the legitimacy of the Protestant pastorate generally. Had not the Fathers of the Church, most notably Augustine and Tertullian, insisted on lineal succession from the Apostles themselves as one of the marks of the True Church? And had not the Roman Pontiffs the clearest title to such an Apostolic Succession among all the claimants to the leadership of Christianity in sixteenth-century Europe? Farel, who established the Reformed Church in Geneva, which in turn had established the Reformed churches of France, obviously had not had any legitimate connection with any previous ecclesiastical authorities in that city.

---

[1] Sureau, *Catholic,* fol. 27, lists as Protestant doctrines he found it difficult to abandon, " de confesser que le corps & sang de Jesus Christ n'estoit à la saincte Messe offert & sacrifié, & que pareillement n'estoit rien la veneration des sainctes reliques, ny les prieres des saincts, non plus que les prieres pour les morts " ; fols. 27-27v., " Que si nous n'eussions esté en different d'avec elle [Eglise Catholique] que pour la Messe, &c. l'eusse esté deliberé de demeurer tousiours en ma vacation estant persuadé que nous avions du meilleur." ; fols. 36-36v., in contrast to rationalism of most of his argument, finally recommends acceptance of transubstantiation simply because Church teaches it : " Quant à la conversion de la substance des choses materielles au corps & sang de Jesus Christ, quittons nos subtilitez, demandes, repliques & objections : submettons nous au sens qui est enseigné en la saincte Eglise."

[2] Sureau, *Protestant,* sigs. [Avii-Aviiv], " puis que c'est là [la Messe] un tel quel reste & trace du vray Sacrement de ce precieux cors : & qu'en regardant le sacrement, (encor qu'il soit grandement different & esloigné de l'institution de Jesus Christ, & de l'administration de l'Eglise ancienne) il suffit que nous levions le cueur au ciel, auquel lieu est seulement ce vray cors vivant, auquel nostre Seigneur regne & se sied a la dextre de Dieu son Pere."

Indeed he had been instrumental in chasing them all away.[1] In his Protestant *Confession*, and even more in his *Treatise on the Marks of the True Church*, which succeeded and amplified it, Sureau, did, to be sure, abandon the Roman doctrine of Apostolic Succession, and announced adherence to a doctrine of succession from the Apostles in true doctrines rather than in persons, which is typically Protestant.[2] But even at this stage, he could not forego lengthy expositions of the Roman doctrine of Apostolic Succession and of the patristic authorities for this view—with the announced purpose of explaining to his readers how it was that he could have entertained doubts about the Protestant doctrine.[3] These arguments in defense of Apostolic Succession, significantly, also appear in a letter which Sureau wrote apparently to Beza shortly after his flight from France and at the time he must have been drafting his Protestant *Confession*.[4]

The conclusion suggested to me by these arguments is that Sureau was a man who was honestly torn between a settled belief in Calvinist sacramental theology, and a persistent respect for the Roman Pontiffs' claim to Apostolic Succession. In such a situation, it was quite simple for him to be pushed from side to side by arguments which he regarded as relatively trivial or by external events.

There remains the problem of the connections between Sureau's apostasies and his earlier career, and this is not an easy one. For Sureau's personal expressions of his views on ecclesiastical discipline seem to have disappeared. In the books defending his apostasies, he practically never refers directly to the problems of church discipline and church organization. In his Protestant *Confession*, for example, he contents himself with an exceedingly brief declaration of his complete acceptance of the published Reformed " ecclesiastical discipline, for the conduct and government of the people of God." [5]

But it seems to me significant that the very months during which Sureau, by his own account, was discovering increasingly strong arguments for the Roman doctrine of Apostolic Succession, were also months in which he personally was under bitter attack for questioning the ecclesiastical organization imposed upon Reformed France by Geneva and the national synods.

[1] Sureau, *Catholic*, fol. 29: " Farel quand il occupa la chaire de Geneve, il n'eut point de predecesseur. Car celuy qui estoit l'Evesque ordinaire fut dechassé. Et par ainsi fut establi un ordre sans origine, comme dit sainct Augustin."

[2] Sureau, *Protestant*, sig. Cv, confesses he now is " advouant pour vrayes marques de l'Eglise la succession non des personnes, mais en la doctrine des Prophetes & Apostres." Cf. H. S[ureau] Du Rosier, *Traitte des certaines et inseparables marques de la vraye Eglise de Dieu* (Heidelberg: Mayer, 1574), copy in Geneva, BPU, Bb 1207, pp. 17-18: " nos disons que ce qui rend l'Eglise vraye Eglise, est la verité de la doctrine qui y est annoncee, & la pure administration des Sacremens: & que par ceste marque se doit discerner d'avec la fausse."

[3] Sureau, *Traitte*, pp. 7-13.

[4] In H. S[ureau]. Roserius [apparently to Beza], 12 March 1573, in Geneva, BPU, Archives Tronchin, V, fol. 236v., signed original: " Haeret animus in perplexa admodum quaestione de vera Ecclesia, deque genuinis ipsius notis... Ecclesiae Catholicae initium ab ipsis Apostolis repetitur, continuatio autem successione nunquam intermissa Episcoporum ac Sacerdotum agnoscitur."

[5] Sureau, *Protestant*, sigs. Cv-Cii[sic]: " j'embrasse la confession de foy publiee au nom des Eglises Reformees de France, la reconnoissant & advouant confession Chrestienne, par la confirmité qu'elle a avec lesdittes Escritures saintes, jointe aussi la discipline Ecclesiastique, pour la conduitte & gouvernement du peuple de Dieu."

It would, I should think, take really unusual constancy to persuade any man to die willingly for a Church which several months earlier had threatened to expel him as a "rebel and schismatic." It is hard to avoid the conclusion that Sureau was pushed to apostasy, in part at least, by Beza's open and harsh hostility and by synodical condemnations. If this be true, Calvinist leaders had only themselves to blame for some of the defections and some of the cooling enthusiasm which plagued their movement.

No doubt others in the group campaigning for ecclesiastical change of the Reformed Church suffered the same fate as Ramus or Sureau. Perhaps Morély himself met one or the other. In any event, he seems simply to disappear from history at this point, leaving no obvious trace. One scholar believes he went to La Rochelle.[1] Others have advanced a rather tenuous theory that he fled to England.[2] But he seems never again to have assumed a prominent role in French Reformed internal politics.

Even though the St. Bartholomew's massacres destroyed or dispersed the leaders of the faction seeking structural changes in the French Reformed Church, the fear of their program lingered on. This fear remained particularly strong in their greatest enemy, Theodore Beza. Two pieces of evidence make this clear.

One can be found in Beza's publication of a selection from his own correspondence, which appeared in two editions, in 1573 and in 1575.[3] The introductory letter to both editions is dated August 15, 1573, almost a full year after the St. Bartholomew's massacres. By this time the shock and horror which that event had induced in Beza had worn off a little, and he was busy again at the work of directing the international Reformed community.

The letters contained in these volumes cover a wide variety of subjects. But among these subjects is the disciplinary problem and the relation of Peter Ramus to the Reformed Church. Beza's own letters to Ramus are included, apparently to clarify his personal relations with the Protestant cause's most prominent new martyr. One of them explains in courteous but firm terms why Ramus could not be given a regular position at the Academy of Geneva. The basic reason was philosophical. Aristotle provided the foundation for Calvinist education in logic and in other fields, and Beza was determined not to depart from his teaching in any respect.[4] Ramus' notorious open

---

[1] Carl Weiner, a Ph. D. candidate in history at the University of Wisconsin, tells me that he has discovered evidence of this.

[2] *France protestante*, 1st ed., art. "Morély." See below, pp. 130-131, for further discussion of this possibility.

[3] Frédéric Gardy and Alain Dufour, *Bibliographie des œuvres théologiques, littéraires, historiques et juridiques de Théodore de Bèze* (Geneva : Droz, 1960), Nos. 296, 297. There was also a 1597 edition, No. 298, from which my references are taken.

[4] In Beza to Ramus, 1 December 1570, No. 36, p. 156 in 1597 ed. : "quod nobis certum ac constitutum sit & in ipsis tradendis Logicis, & in caeteris explicandis disciplinis ab Aristotelis sententia ne tantillum quidem deflectere." There are French translations and comments in C. Waddington, *Ramus*, pp. 229-230, and C. Borgeaud, *Université*, I, 113-114. See also Beza to Ramus, 30 September 1569, No. 34, pp. 153-154 in 1597 ed., which objects more explicitly to Ramus' view of Aristotle : "Miror autem a me requiri quod tam multi doctissimi viri tam accurate & verbis & scriptis praestiterunt, quibus summo consensu tuas in Aristotelem animadversiones prorsus displicuisse non ignoras." Beza also objected to Ramus' method of teaching. See above, p. 101 and n. 6.

contempt for Aristotle, and many other masters of antiquity, obviously made it impossible for Geneva to find a useful place for him on its teaching staff.

Beza's letters on the disciplinary problem are a little harder to interpret. The most interesting of them, particularly letter number 83,[1] were deliberately left anonymous. Beza published them without any indication of the recipient, the date of writing, or the place to which they were sent.[2] The arguments which they contain are not new. In letter 83, for example, Beza begins by denying that the Church should be " democratic," and insisting that it should rather be a " monarchy," with Jesus Christ as its ruler.[3] He then discusses the role of different orders of clergy, the possibility of " tyranny " arising within an ecclesiastical organization, and relations between clerical and civil authorities. He also refutes a number of arguments from Scripture advanced by the proponents of more democratic church government, and notes that one of these refutations was earlier worked out and stated by a French Synod, in answer to an argument advanced by Morély and others.[4]

What is new, is that Beza should want to give this controversy further general publicity, by putting these letters into print. It is also interesting that he should publish them in Latin, thus making them available to the European-wide scholarly public rather than solely to the lay public in France where Morély himself had most of his supporters. Perhaps he feared continued strength of the Morély program among French intellectuals of the sort who had admired Ramus. Perhaps he was trying to justify his position further to such friends as Bullinger and to avoid the possibility of fresh misunderstandings of the sort which had plagued them in 1571 and 1572.

A second piece of evidence that Beza continued to fear the Morély reform program, can be found in his letter of advice to the next national Synod of the French Reformed churches.[5] This Synod was held in 1578, in Ste. Foy. The dislocations caused by the massacres and the resulting renewed religious war had made it impossible to hold a synod for the better part of six years. Finally in 1577, it seemed possible to call one again, and the Synod actually assembled in February of 1578. Beza could not attend this Synod in person, and his letter expresses regrets, although it does not explain what made his attendance impossible. His letter then proceeds to give the Synod some general pieces of advice. The first and most prominent is that the Synod take care to preserve the single confession of faith with which God had blessed the French Reformed. He reminds the delegates that some had tried to

---

[1] Pp. 303-307 in 1597 ed.; pp. 398-403 in 1573 ed. For an incisive comment on this letter, see in Charles Mercier, " Les théories politiques des calvinistes en France au cours des guerres de religion," BSHPF, LXXXIII (1934), 235.

[2] In a hasty check in Geneva, MHR, Beza Correspondence, I could not find manuscript copies of these letters. I suspect they will have to be identified and explained on the basis of internal evidence.

[3] On p. 303 in 1597 ed.: " Statum Ecclesiasticae gubernationis in terris nusquam lego esse Democraticum, sed vere Monarchicum, quanvis & suos optimates Ecclesia, & coetus ipse in communi suum quoque ius quoddam habeat, sub uno videlicet capite nostro Iesu Christo, qui tum positis a se legibus, tum suo Spiritu per eos quos administratores constituit, Ecclesiam suam gubernat."

[4] On p. 306 in 1597 ed.: " sicut adversus Morellium & alios deinceps eius sectatores, in Synodis Gallicis est abunde probatum."

[5] Beza to Synod of Ste. Foy, 15 January 1578, published in BSHPF, XIV (1865), 135-139.

change the very foundations of that discipline. Becoming more specific, he reminds them that at Nîmes the views of the late Sureau, of the late Ramus, and of Morély had been examined carefully and refuted. And he begs their followers to give the battered Church time to recover and become consolidated before raising these problems again.[1] His phrasing, it is interesting to note, suggests that Morély was still alive.

Proponents of democratic reform within the French Reformed Church did not, in fact, disturb the Synod of Ste. Foy. The threat to Protestant unity with which it was most concerned came from quite a different quarter. It came from Germany. Rows between Lutherans and Calvinists in parts of Germany had become so fierce, that this Synod decided to do something to try to secure conciliation. Among the measures its delegates resolved upon was the sending to Germany of an embassy of three pastors, including Antoine de la Roche Chandieu.[2] With these envoys were to be sent several documents, including Chandieu's *Confirmation of Ecclesiastical Discipline*,[3] probably the one originally prepared to refute Morély. The disciplinary quarrel was perhaps not yet dead, but if still alive, it had taken a new form and found a new locale. It was no longer a serious internal problem for the Reformed Church of France.

7. *Epilogue*

If the quarrel over the structure of the Reformed Church was over in France by the end of 1572, it was far from over in those other parts of Christendom where Calvinist influence was strong. In some of them, in fact, it was really only beginning. It would be instructive to study the effect of the quarrel between the factions led by Morély and by Beza on other countries and at later periods. A thorough study of this sort would take us beyond the bounds of this book, of course, and the research upon which it would have to be based still has not been done, at least to my knowledge. But I would nevertheless like to present at this point certain pieces of evidence which any study of this sort will have to consider. They should help to set this quarrel within a wider context. And in doing this, they should help us to evaluate more accurately its significance.

There are two tantalizing paths along which these pieces of evidence lead. One is to later quarrels over ecclesiastical government, particularly in England. The other is to later quarrels over secular government, particularly in France. Since the first of these paths is by far the widest and best marked, it is down it that I would first like to venture.

The decade during which the quarrel provoked by Morély raged, from 1562 to 1572, was a period of rapid advance of Calvinism in other countries.

[1] In *ibid.*, pp. 136-137 : " Que s'il y en a encores de reste de ceulx du passé, ou qui soyent survenus depuis, qui ne se contentent de ce qui en fut résolu au synode général tenu à Nismes, là ou toutes les opinions de feu du Rosier, de feu Ramus, de Morelli et de leurs adhérens, furent tout au long déduictes, examinées et résolues, je les prie que s'il y a quelque charité à eux, ils ayent pour le moins pitié de ceste paovre mère, à savoir l'Eglise, pour luy donner quelque loisir de respirer, ..."

[2] J. Quick, *Synodicon*, I, 120-121, art. XXXI ; J. Aymon, *Synodes*, I, 2nd pagination, pp. 131-132. For an account of Geneva's role in these German rows, see E. Choisy, *Genève au temps de Bèze*, Part I, ch. XIV.

[3] J. Quick, *Synodicon*, I, 121, art. XXXII ; J. Aymon, *Synodes*, I, 2nd pagination, p. 132.

This advance did not occur without opposition, however, and some of the opposition was directed toward Calvinist organizational and disciplinary practices.

Probably the area in which Calvinist advance was most rapid during this period was Germany. And within Germany it was most rapid in the Rhenish Palatinate, centering on the old university town of Heidelberg. This, at least, was the area which, after France, attracted the most attention from Beza and his colleagues in Geneva, judging by his correspondence and by the Registers of the Company of Pastors. And it was also the area in which Calvinism scored the greatest overt successes. These successes were made possible by the accession of Frederick III, the Pious, as Elector of the Palatinate in 1559. He quickly appointed, as his ecclesiastical advisers, a number of theologians of distinctly Calvinist leanings. The most prominent of them were Caspar Olevianus and Zacharias Ursinus. Before another year had ended, Olevianus was writing to Calvin for advice on how to go about organizing a truly Reformed Church.[1] Calvin responded by sending Olevianus a letter describing the basic structure of the Genevan Church.[2]

The changes in the Church of the Palatinate sponsored by Olevianus were not enacted without opposition, however. This opposition came from theologians of both Lutheran and Zwinglian persuasions. And it flared up into a particularly bitter controversy between 1568 and 1570. The central figure in this controversy was Thomas Erastus, a doctor with strongly developed side interests in theology.[3] His theology was basically Zwinglian, and he was in frequent touch with Heinrich Bullinger and other leaders of the Zurich Church. He had co-operated closely with Olevianus in sharp debates with certain Lutheran theologians over eucharistic theology, which had taken place as the Calvinist regime was getting established in Heidelberg. But he was provoked to open opposition by arguments advanced by a wild English visitor, George Withers. Withers, who had previously visited Geneva and Zurich, had come to Heidelberg seeking support for the Puritans' campaign against the use in England of certain " papal " vestments and ceremonies.[4] He had enrolled in

---

[1] Olevianus to Calvin, *Calvini Opera*, XVIII, 191-196, 22 September 1560, especially pp. 194-195. Cf. Olevianus to Calvin, XIX, 538-540, 24 September 1562, a report on progress, with request for further advice. The standard accounts of the Calvinist Reformation of the Palatinate are August Kluckhohn, *Friedrich der Fromme, Kurfürst von der Pfalz: der Schützer der reformirten Kirche, 1559-1576* (Nördlingen, 1879), and Karl Sudhoff, *C. Olevianus und Z. Ursinus: Leben und ausgewählte Schriften* (Elberfeld, 1857). For a useful recent partial survey, see Bard Thompson, et al., *Essays on the Heidelberg Catechism* (Philadelphia & Boston : United Church, 1963).

[2] Calvin to Olevianus, *Calvini Opera*, XVIII, 235-237, 5 November 1560.

[3] See Ruth Wesel-Roth, *Thomas Erastus* (Lahr/Baden : Schauenburg, 1954), especially Part I, ch. III, for a recent study of Erastus and his role in this controversy. Cf. G. V. Lechler, *Verfassung*, Book II, ch. VI, for an account which sets the controversy more fully in context. Erastus' attack on Calvinist discipline and a defense of it which Beza prepared in retort, circulated only in manuscript and were not published until the controversy flared up again in 1589-1590. See P.-F. Geisendorf, *Beza*, pp. 382-385, re this later episode. Wesel-Roth suggests, pp. 59-60, that Ursinus also was not overly enthusiastic about Calvinist church polity and would have preferred a system which assigned a greater role both to the general church membership and to the state than was the case in either Zurich or Geneva.

[4] See Adrien Chopard, " Genève et les anglais (XVIe-XVIIIe siècles)," BSHAG, VII, 234, for a useful summary of Withers' activities on this visit to the continent.

the university there, and had engaged in its usual academic exercises. In one of them he strenuously defended the Genevan system of ecclesiastical discipline, with its liberal use of excommunication as a weapon for punishing sinners, and its vesting of that weapon in an ecclesiastical body, the Consistory. And he bitterly attacked those unwilling to adopt these means of enforcing discipline.

Erastus prepared a lengthy retort to Withers, which denied that the Church had the right, let alone the obligation, to assume these disciplinary functions. He insisted that the control of human behavior belonged to the secular state alone. And he argued that the establishment of consistories on the Genevan model would undermine in a crucial way the state and the administration of justice which was its primary function. In doing this, Erastus was attacking many of the same practices and institutions which Morély had attacked. In particular, Erastus joined Morély in attacking the Consistory, as it operated in Geneva, under the effective control of the clergy, wielding exclusive powers of excommunication and absolution. But Erastus attacked this institution from a somewhat different standpoint. Rather than seeking to transfer its functions to the entire membership of the local congregation, he sought to transfer them to the existing apparatus of secular courts. In doing this, he was recommending the system which had been adopted in Zurich, with the Zwinglian Reformation. And he must have become aware of the distance between his position and that of Morély when he met Ramus in Heidelberg. At least it was Beza's impression that their disagreement was over these questions of ecclesiastical discipline.[1]

The Erastian controversy ended in partial victory for the Calvinists in Heidelberg, for the time being, as Olevianus broke with his colleague to side with his Genevan mentors, and persuaded the Elector to enact in 1570 a set of disciplinary ordinances which were substantially Calvinist. But the issues raised in this controversy were to bedevil Reformed Christendom for decades to come, and the very adjective "Erastian" came to be applied to all who wished to allocate to the secular state responsibility for the temporal organization and temporal functions of the Church.

Another area in which Calvinist advance was rapid during this period was the Low Countries. In fact it was during this decade that militant Calvinism provoked the Spanish government to the brutal repressive measures which touched off the Eighty Years' War for Dutch independence, ending ultimately in the creation of a northern Netherlands largely controlled by Calvinists and a southern Belgium controlled by Catholics. This ultimate alignment can cause one to overlook the geographic pattern of the earliest Calvinist expansion into the area, however. For Calvinism entered the Low Countries from the south, coming down the many trade routes which led from northern France, through the French-speaking Walloon provinces, to the great industrial and commercial centers of Flanders and Brabant. And it was in these great centers, in such cities as Valenciennes, Ghent, and Antwerp, that Calvinism won its greatest numbers of early converts.

In all of this area, Calvinism was operating illegally, against the laws and the administrative measures of the Spanish regency. It was operating, to use its own term, "under the cross." But its leaders nevertheless moved quickly to establish the synods and other institutions typical of Calvinism

[1] See above, p. 104.

generally. And since so many of them came from France, it was natural that they patterned their new institutions on the ones developed in France or Geneva. Some evidence of this respect for the French and Genevan models can be found in the correspondence of these men with Geneva. In particular, pastors Jean Taffin and Thomas van Til, who quickly succeeded pioneers like Guy de Brès and who, with Peter Dathenus, were especially important as builders of the Dutch discipline, were in frequent touch with Beza, asking for his advice on a whole range of ecclesiastical and theological problems.[1] But even more significant evidence of this respect for French or Genevan models can be found in the earliest acts of the synods held in the Netherlands.[2] For example, the 1563 provincial Synod held in Tournai, voted to follow the advice of "those of Geneva" on the problem of baptizing the children of those who were not yet active members of a Reformed church.[3] And the 1571 national Synod held in Emden, ordered that the Genevan Catechism, which had originally been drafted by Calvin himself, be used in all French-speaking churches in the Netherlands.[4] It also resolved another question about baptism by appeal to the authority of the "Brothers of Geneva."[5]

This same Emden Synod, which, although it met outside the Netherlands, was the first significant national synod held by its Reformed churches and was consequently particularly normative for later practice, went to even greater lengths to establish solidarity with the Calvinists of France. Its delegates not only subscribed to their own Confession of Faith but they also subscribed to the French Confession as a gesture of solidarity.[6] They also commissioned their two most prominent clerical leaders, Dathenus and Taffin, to attend the next national synod in France in order to inform the French of this action and to suggest that they subscribe to the Belgic Confession as a reciprocal gesture of solidarity.[7]

That this solidarity was not complete, however, is suggested by other acts of these same synods. It is suggested, for example, by the Emden Synod's instruction to Dathenus and Taffin that they inquire, when they reached France, about one of the decisions reached at the La Rochelle Synod

---

[1] See Herman de Vries de Heekelingen, *Genève, pépinière du calvinisme hollandais*, I (Fribourg : Fragnière, 1918), and II (the Hague : Nijhoff, 1924), *passim*, including texts and summaries of several letters.

[2] Texts of these synodical acts can be found in N. C. Kist, ed., "De Synoden der Nederlandsche Hervormde Kerken onder het kruis, gedurende de jaren 1563-1577, gehouden in Braband, Vlaanderen enz.," *Nederlandsch Archief voor Kerkelijke Geschiedenis*, IX (*Archief voor Kerkelijke Geschiedenis*, XX), (1849), pp. 113-210, and F. L. Rutgers, ed., *Acta van de Nederlandsche Synoden der zestiende eeuw*, in *Werken der Marnix-Vereeniging*, ser. II, deel III (1889). I have also consulted in the Archief der Gemeente Rotterdam, Archief van de Waalsche Kerk, No. 41 (1563-1644), variant manuscript copies of most of the texts printed by Kist and French translations of some of the texts printed by Rutgers. However the variant wordings in them are practically all trivial.

[3] In N. C. Kist ed., p. 131, art. 2 : "Qu'on suivra le conseil de ceux de Geneve, ..."

[4] In F. L. Rutgers ed., p. 57, art. 5 : "Catechismi formulam in Ecclesiis quidem Gallicanis Genevensem, in Teutonicis vero Heydelbergensem sequendam duxerunt fratres."

[5] *Ibid.*, p. 92, art. 9 : "Qui sibi satisfieri cupiunt, exemplar sumant articuli a fratribus Genevensibus ea de re conscripti."

[6] *Ibid.*, p. 56, art. 2.

[7] *Ibid.*, p. 57, art. 3.

of 1571, apparently the one condemning the Bordeaux physician whose opinions resembled those of Erastus.[1] It is suggested further by certain provisions for the election of the various orders of ministers, some of which have a distinctly "Morellist" sound. The provincial Synod held at Armentières in 1563, provided that in areas where churches were being organized for the first time, elders and deacons could be elected "by the common voice of all the people with their pastors," but that once churches were organized election should be by the "Senate of the Church with the ministers and the deacons."[2] This procedure, of course, was almost identical with the one which had first been adopted in France, with the main departure being the greater role allowed by the Dutch to deacons. But in a provincial Synod held in Teurs, also in 1563, it was decreed that in the election of elders and deacons, the local consistory should present two names for each vacancy to "the company," which would then make the final choice of the single officer.[3] And in the normative national Synod of Emden, two methods for selecting pastors were permitted. The normal one was to be election by consistory, in consultation with the local "classe" (colloquy) and the neighboring ministers. But "if nevertheless some church has the custom of popular election which she does not find good to change, it shall be allowed until otherwise ordered by a general synod."[4] This clause stands in surprising contrast to the flat condemnations of popular election adopted in the French synods of La Rochelle, which immediately preceded the Emden Synod and of which its delegates must have been aware, and of Nîmes, which quickly followed Emden. It suggests the existence in the Netherlands of a party favoring a more democratic form of church government, which was either stronger or more easily tolerated than the Morély faction in France. Such a party might provide a remote source or at least an analogue for the Remonstrants of the seventeenth century, whose new Church adopted in 1633, a basically congregational polity.[5]

In the sixteenth century, other internal objections to the establishment of Calvinist institutions and discipline in the Reformed Netherlands, came from those who would have preferred to take their models from the Lutherans

---

[1] *Ibid.*, p. 91, art. 5. The decision they were to inquire about is identified only as "Quintae quaestioni de Actis Synodi Rupellensis in Galliis," but both Quick and Aymon list as article five, the controversial condemnation of the Bordeaux physician discussed further above, p. 98. The request for this inquiry suggests some sympathy for the Erastian point of view among the delegates at Emden, which would not be surprising, given their many connections to Heidelberg.

[2] In N. C. Kist ed., p. 135, art. 1: "Es lieux où l'ordre de l'Eglise n'est point encore dressé, tant les Diacres que les Anciens seront esleus par la voix commune de tout le peuple avec leurs Pasteurs, mais où la discipline sera desja dressée seront esleus au Senat de l'Eglise avec les Ministres et les Diacres."

[3] *Ibid.*, p. 127, art. 11: "Quant à l'election des Anciens ou Diacres, s'il en faut un, on en eslira deux au consistoire, lesquels seront presentez à la compagnie, laquelle après l'invocation du nom de Dieu en eslira un pour soy."

[4] In F. L. Rutgers ed., p. 61, art. 13: "Ministri eligentur a Consistorio, cum iudicio Conventus Classici, aut duorum triumve ministrorum vicinorum. Electi autem sistentur coram Ecclesia, ut vel tacitis suffragiis comprobentur, vel si quid sit, cur in electionem minus consentire velit Ecclesia, infra dies plus minus quindecim obiiciatur. Si quae tamen Ecclesiae consuetudinem electionis popularis, quae apud eas est, mutandam non esse censerent, ferentur, donec Synodo Generali sit aliter constitutum."

[5] See *Theologisch Woordenboek*, art. "Remonstranten," and works there cited.

or Zwinglians. The more prominent of these were attached to the House of Orange, which provided the nucleus for the organization of successful military resistance to the Spanish crown, and which possessed traditional connections to certain of the Lutheran noble houses of Germany. These objectors opposed the establishment of synods and consistories, on the grounds that such institutions usurped powers properly belonging to secular governments. They provoked quarrels resembling the Erastian controversy in the Palatinate.[1] But most of these quarrels became bitter only after the period upon which this book concentrates. In that period, Dutch Calvinists were naturally pre-occupied with the elemental problems of survival, in the face of the brutal program of systematic repression directed from 1567 on by the Duke of Alva.

Yet another area which witnessed a significant Calvinist advance during this period was Britain. In both Scotland and England, changes in government had permitted the establishment of Protestant churches in 1558. And in both realms those churches had been partially staffed by exiles returning from the continent, some of whom had become personally well acquainted with Calvin and Beza, with their theology, and with the ecclesiastical institutions they had created. Much of this theology was integrated, without too much difficulty, into the official statements of belief adopted by the Church of Scotland and the Church of England. But there was an important body of Protestant opinion in each country which objected to the replacement of traditional ecclesiastical institutions, capped by the historic episcopate, with new institutions modeled on those of Geneva or France. In each country this conservative opinion won support of the reigning monarch and of his government. It was against this conservatism that the Puritan party formed, and its formation became newly significant in the period upon which this book concentrates.[2] It became particularly significant and open in Cambridge University. There several brilliant young academics who came to be led by Thomas Cartwright, moved from criticisms of traditional vestments and ceremonies to frontal attacks upon the whole system of episcopal government of the Church of England. Their attacks were vigorously opposed by other academics, notably John Whitgift, who was ultimately to become Archbishop of Canterbury and hence primate of England. This controversy reached a peak between 1569 and 1571. It ended with the dismissal of Cartwright from most of his academic appointments and his flight to Geneva.[3]

One significant connection tied all these variegated controversies together. At issue in every case was the Calvinist discipline, developed by Calvin in Geneva, applied by his disciples in France, and explained and defended by Beza and Chandieu. And in every case this discipline was defended by members of the same closely knit group, each of whom possessed close personal

[1] For a useful survey of these quarrels, see G. V. Lechler, *Verfassung*, Book II, ch. VII; also L. Knappert, *Geschiedenis der Nederlandsche Hervormde Kerk gedurende de 16e en 17e eeuw* (Amsterdam: Meulenhoff, 1911), Book I, ch. III, "De strijd om de Kerkorde."

[2] On this formation, see M. M. Knappen, *Tudor Puritanism* (Chicago: University, 1939), especially ch. XI.

[3] See A. F. Scott Pearson, *Thomas Cartwright and Elizabethan Puritanism, 1535-1603* (Cambridge, 1925), ch. I, especially pp. 25-54, for an extended description of Cartwright's role in this controversy and his flight to Geneva.

links to each other and to Geneva. Olevianus, for example, had studied in Geneva shortly before he was invited to the Palatinate,[1] and kept in close touch with Calvin and Beza during the years he was superintending its reformation. Taffin and van Til also kept in close touch with Beza and his colleagues. In 1572, when persecution made their work in the Netherlands dangerous, they both took refuge in Geneva and organized a Dutch Church there, of which van Til became the pastor.[2] Philippe Marnix van St. Aldegonde, the noble layman who provided an indispensable liaison between these pastors and the House of Orange, had also studied in Geneva and kept in occasional touch with Beza.[3] Cartwright fled to Geneva after he had been stripped of his academic positions at Cambridge, and taught theology in the Academy there.[4] In Geneva he must have met Andrew Melville, who was to be more responsible than anyone else for the establishment of Presbyterian polity in the Church of Scotland, then an instructor in the Genevan secondary Collège.[5] He must also have met Walter Travers who visited Geneva at about the same time and who was probably then working on the book which was to become the great manifesto for all English Presbyterianism, the *Ecclesiasticae Disciplinae et Anglicanae Ecclesiae ab illa Aberrationis plena e verbo Dei & dilucida explicatio*, a book which Cartwright himself was to translate into English, under the title, *A Full and Plaine Declaration of Ecclesiasticall Discipline.*[6] The very fact that these men knew and respected each other so much, and kept in such constant contact with each other, meant that their ideas became quite uniform. A kind of " party line " developed which all their followers were expected to accept. And this " party line " developed in the area of thought on church organization and discipline, as it did in many other areas. As the ideas of Beza and Chandieu concerning these problems became increasingly rigid and complex, in response to the repeated challenges from Morély, Ramus, and their supporters, so did the ideas of the entire international Calvinist leadership. The result of this development was that the entire Calvinist movement became increasingly, even irretrievably, committed to synodical polity and consistorial discipline. It became far more committed than it ever had been in Calvin's own day. To institutions and practices which he had improvised quite casually to meet the needs of the moment, were now ascribed the character of institutions and practices willed by God. This is probably the really important historic result of the Morély quarrel.

No similar unity can be found in the opponents to Calvinist discipline. They attacked it from so many different angles that this should not surprise us. It is obvious that there could not be much in common among men like

---

[1] Karl Sudhoff, *C. Olevianus und Z. Ursinus: Leben und ausgewählte Schriften* (Elberfeld, 1857), p. 15.

[2] de Vries de Heekelingen, *op. cit.* in n. 1 to p. 125 above, I, 295-297, re van Til's selection; p. 293, re Taffin's participation. They both also used Heidelberg as a foreign base of operations.

[3] Geneva, LR, Stelling-Michaud ed., p. 83, No. 94; de Vries de Heekelingen, *op. cit.*, II, 7, 9, and *passim.*

[4] C. Borgeaud, *Université*, I, 107-108.

[5] *Ibid.*, pp. 108-110.

[6] DNB, art. " Travers, Walter." Editions of the translations described in STC, Nos. 24184, 24185, 24186.

Erastus, who attacked Calvinist discipline in the name of the secular state, Whitgift, who also attacked it in the name of the historic episcopacy, and Morély, who attacked it in the name of the body of individual believers. Except, of course, their common enemy. It is consequently not surprising that they knew relatively little of each other, and often did not seem to have great use for each other's ideas.

There are, however, a few random connections which did tie some of these opponents of Calvinist discipline together. Most of the ones which so far I have discovered existed in England. It is upon certain of them that I would now like to concentrate.

The idea that the faction created by Morély and Ramus had influence in England is a particularly intriguing one. For the quarrel between advocates of presbyterial and congregational church polity became particularly bitter and significant in that country. And it bears many analogies to the earlier quarrel in France. English Presbyterians consciously modeled their arguments on church organization and discipline on those of such continental Calvinists as Beza. The argument from consensus became quite important to them. And English Congregationalists developed arguments quite similar to those of Morély and his faction. They, too, wanted to increase congregational autonomy, lay leadership, and democracy within the local congregation. They, too, were suspicious of the clergy and of any synodical apparatus. They, too, found considerable value in " prophesyings " within local congregations, as did, for that matter, a number of other English non-conformists. They were also concerned in somewhat similar ways with relations between Church and State. A few of them even considered the possibility, hinted at by Morély, that the arguments for democracy in the Church might justify democracy in the State, although more of the political radicals among them seem to have favored a dictatorship of the saints.[1]

Furthermore the quarrel among the English first began to take shape in the years right after the collapse of the Morély faction in France. Robert Browne, who is often held to be the founder of English Congregationalism, took his academic degree from the same Cambridge which had just expelled Cartwright, in 1572. He soon began to criticize with increasing bitterness both the established Church of England and the reforms in its structure proposed by the Presbyterian Puritans. He finally denounced not only all forms of hierarchical authority and discipline imposed from above, but also formal ordination of clergymen. These criticisms of his became particularly sharp between 1578 and 1584. He led a few disciples out of the Church of England into a separating sect, first in the Norwich area, then in Middelburg in the Low Countries, then briefly in Scotland. He finally returned to the Church of England himself, but his ideas lived on.[2] They grew to dominance for a season in seventeenth-century England, when they won the allegiance of Oliver Cromwell and the Puritan armies which overthrew first government by king and then government by Parliament. And they also controlled the

---

[1] For a lengthy discussion of this problem, see Leo F. Solt, *Saints in Arms: Puritanism and Democracy in Cromwell's Army* (Stanford, 1959).

[2] On Browne, see Albert Peel and Leland H. Carlson, eds., *The Writings of Robert Harrison and Robert Browne*, vol. II, *Elizabethan Nonconformist Texts* (London: Allen & Unwin, 1953), especially in Introduction, pp. 4-8, and other works there cited.

ecclesiastical development of the English colonies then being established in New England.

A number of scholars have advanced the theory that Morély himself fled to England some time after the St. Bartholomew's massacres.[1] This would have brought him to that country at the very time Browne and his successors were developing their congregational ideas. It could establish him as an important source of those ideas.

There is really only one piece of evidence so far uncovered in support of this theory.[2] It is a book published in London, and titled *De ecclesia ab Antichristo per eius excidium liberanda.* It was first published in 1589, by the prominent London printer George Bishop.[3] A second Latin edition of it was published by Bishop in 1594,[4] and a German edition was also published in 1594.[5] The author of this book was a certain Joannes Morelius. Its preface reveals that he was an elderly man, who had been obliged by religious persecution to leave his native France.[6] All of these facts support the theory that the book was by Jean Morély, sire de Villiers, that he had in fact fled to England following the St. Bartholomew's massacres.

Other facts, however, complicate this identification. The content of the book, to begin with, has very little to do with the problems of church discipline and organization. It is basically a lengthy exposition of prophesies contained in the Biblical book of the Revelation recorded by John. It develops the basic identification of the Antichrist predicted in that book with the Pope, which was a commonplace in much sixteenth-century Protestant polemic. The introduction to the book, furthermore, creates more problems for this identification. It is a fervent dedicatory letter to Queen Elizabeth, full of jubilation at her recent victory over the Spanish Armada.[7] No doubt any English Puritan would have shared in this jubilation. But a Congregationalist Puritan's fervor would surely have been tempered by the knowledge that the Queen's ministers had recently seduced Robert Browne back to the established Church, and that they were then prosecuting and would soon order death sentences for such remaining leaders of the movement as Henry Barrow and John Greenwood.[8] Finally, the circumstances under which this book was published create problems for this identification. The Registers of

---

[1] Eug. and Em. Haag, in *France protestante*, 1st ed., art. " Morély (Jean-Baptiste) " ; F. de Schickler, *Les Eglises du Refuge en Angleterre* (Paris, 1892), I, 247 ; Drouot Toureille, *Etude historique sur le système d'organisation ecclésiastique de Jean Morély* (Strasbourg, 1850), p. 10.

[2] Drouot Toureille tries to bolster the theory further with a rather forced interpretation of one of Beza's published letters.

[3] STC, No. 18099. Cf. n. 1 to p. 131. There is typographical evidence that the copy of this work in the Folger Shakespeare Library was printed not by Bishop but by the clandestine Eliot's Court press. I assume, pending study of further copies, that the Folger copy is from a pirated edition.

[4] STC, No. 18100.

[5] A copy of which I have examined in Paris, Bibliothèque Mazarine, cote 23619.

[6] " Ego senex pene decrepitus, e Gallia religionis causa profugus...," on fol. 1 of the 1589 ed.

[7] Fols. 1-3 of the 1589 ed., dated 1 January 1589.

[8] DNB, arts. " Barrow, Henry " ; " Greenwood, John." Cf. Leland H. Carlson, ed., *The Writings of Henry Barrow, 1587-1590; The Writings of John Greenwood, 1587-1590*, vols. III and IV, *Elizabethan Nonconformist Texts* (London : Allen & Unwin, 1962).

the Company of Stationers of London reveal that George Bishop was authorized to publish it by the Archbishop of Canterbury himself.[1] But that Archbishop was then none other than Whitgift, the archenemy of all Puritans, Presbyterian and Congregational alike.

It may be that the opposition of Jean Morély, sire de Villiers, to synodical church government had led him to abandon the congregational alternative and embrace an Erastian dependence on the guidance of the secular state in all ecclesiastical matters. There are occasional hints of such an Erastianism in some of his earlier attacks on Calvinist church polity. But unless he did have such a change of heart, it seems most unlikely that he is the Morelius who wrote the *De ecclesia... liberanda*. And if he did have such a change of heart, he would obviously have had little to do with Browne and the other founders of English Congregationalism.

Firm evidence that certain British ecclesiastical leaders knew of the debate upon Calvinist church polity provoked by Jean Morély, sire de Villiers, does survive. But almost all the examples of such knowledge that I have discovered or that have been called to my attention by friends, date from a much later period. Specifically they date from the 1640's, when the Anglican Establishment had been overthrown, and when Parliament called the Westminster Assembly of Divines to determine the new shape which English theology and church organization should take. That Assembly was composed largely of Presbyterians, and its commitment to Calvinist church polity was further strengthened by the presence at its deliberations of a delegation of Scottish commissioners, who represented a Church in which that polity had triumphed. But the Assembly was under considerable pressure to consider the methods of church organization and discipline favored by the Congregationalists. For the real power in the land was then the army fashioned by Cromwell. And the prevailing sentiment within the army was Independent, or Congregational.[2]

In developing the arguments for and against Presbyterian and Congregational forms of church polity, there was a wide search by seventeenth-century polemicists for earlier works that would develop one or the other of these sets of arguments. This search led naturally to French writings. For the history through which the seventeenth-century Puritan Revolution led England contained so many parallels to the history of France during the sixteenth-century wars of religion, that the French polemics of the earlier period contained an arsenal of arguments useful to the later English pamphleteers.[3] And in this search, some of the English polemicists naturally discovered

---

[1] Edward Arber, ed., *A Transcript of the Registers of the Company of Stationers of London, 1554-1640 A. D.*, II (London, 1875) : "Master Georg[e] Bysshop. Alowed unto him under the Archbishop of Canterburies hand, a booke entitled, *De ecclesia ab Antechristo liberanda...*"

[2] The classic study is W. M. Hetherington, *History of the Westminster Assembly of Divines*, several eds., e.g. the 4th, ed. by Robert Williamson (Edinburgh, 1874).

[3] A connection analyzed at length by J. H. M. Salmon, *The French Religious Wars in English Political Thought* (Oxford : Clarendon, 1959). Salmon demonstrates that many of the writings provoked by the French wars of religion became known and appreciated in England only decades later, during the Puritan Revolution. The apparently late discovery of books produced by the Morély controversy would seem to provide another example of this generalization.

the books written in the course of the Morély controversy. I do not find any evidence that any of them actually read Morély himself. But a number were aware of the main argument of his book. They do seem to have known the attacks upon him written by Chandieu and Beza. And some of them were aware of Ramus' support of the Morély position.

Some of the ways in which this search for polemical ammunition operated are revealed by the letters of Robert Baillie. Baillie was one of the more prominent commissioners representing the Church of Scotland at the Westminster Assembly. He was strongly committed to the presbyterial organization and discipline of his own Church and eager to win acceptance of them in England. In his campaign for presbyterianism, he became very sensitive to the volume and strength of attack upon this system of church order then being launched by English Independents. He felt it very important that arguments to counter those of the Independents be prepared and published. And for preparing these counter-arguments, he felt a great need for the books in which the arguments for and against presbyterian polity had been presented in the past. In consequence, he sent a number of appeals for specific books to a cousin named William Spang, then pastor to a Scottish congregation in the Netherlands, hence in a good position to obtain books published on the continent.

Among the books Baillie asked for most frequently, were the treatises on church discipline by Morély and Chandieu.[1] He clearly knew the main line of argument in each, but he does not seem to have seen either. The fact that his requests were repeated, suggests that copies of both were rare. A copy of what purported to be the book by Chandieu was finally supplied to him, but he was skeptical that it was in fact that treatise.[2] I have not found evidence that he ever obtained a copy of Morély. Accompanying these requests were ones for other related books. One was for the writings of Robert Browne, which Baillie obtained with less difficulty.[3] Another was for a book by the emphatically Calvinist Dutch theologian Voetius, which Baillie titled *De episcopis et presbyteris*.[4]

In a memorandum he sent to Scotland at this time, Baillie also asked that statements in defense of presbyterial polity be solicited from continental Calvinists. He asked David Buchanan, who had lived in France for a time, to:

" write to some of the ministers of Paris, Geneva, and Berne, the true estate of our affairs, how that a mighty faction is arisen, to press liberty of conscience for all sects, at least a freedom for Morellius's popular government of the Church ; that the Scotts, and most of the Synod [at Westminster] and Parliament, are for the establishing of the Government by synods and classes. It would encourage them much, if the Divines of Geneva and Switzerland would, in their answers to the synod's

---

[1] Baillie to Spang, in David Laing, ed., *The Letters and Journals of Robert Baillie...* 3 vols. (Edinburgh, 1841-1842), II, 115, 165, 184, 193 (for Morély alone), 7 December [1643]—9 June [1644]. I am indebted to the Rev. Dr. Douglas Horton for calling my attention to this correspondence.

[2] Baillie to Spang, 31 May [1644], in *ibid.*, II, 188.

[3] Baillie to Spang, 17 May [1644], in *ibid.*, II, 184, requesting Browne's writings ; 9 June [1644], in *ibid.*, II, 193, announcing he had acquired them.

[4] Baillie to Spang, 7 December [1643], in *ibid.*, II, 115.

letter, as the Divines of Zeland hes done in their letter, and the Divines of Hessia also, exhort the synod at some length, and in earnest, to beware of that pernicious liberty of all sects, and in particular of these who are enemies to the discipline of all the Reformed." [1]

The reference to Morély suggests that his name now supplied one of the current epithets applied to those advocating Congregational polity.[2]

In response to such requests, and even more official ones,[3] a number of defenses of Calvinist church polity were prepared. One of particular interest was prepared by Wilhelmus Apollonius, a friend of Spang and pastor of the Dutch Reformed Church in Middelburg. As an ecclesiastical leader of a community in which both English Presbyterians and English Independents had been particularly active, Apollonius was very well informed on their quarrels. And as the representative of the most devotedly Calvinist of all the Reformed churches, he could speak with authority on the orthodox position. His defense was written in Latin, formally presented to the Assembly, and published in 1644 in London.[4] It was also soon published there in English translation.[5] In the course of his argument, Apollonius refers to the Morély controversy, in terms reminiscent of Baillie:

" Hence also have the Reformed Churches alwayes rejected a popular Church-Government; See Sadeel's [pseudonym for Chandieu] treatise in French, concerning Ecclesiasticall Discipline, against Morellius: Of whom Reverend Beza, (*libro de Ministrorum gradibus*, cap. 25) when he had described the manner of Election in the Church, saith thus, which order by the goodnesse of God religiously and prudently observed hitherto in this City, when one democraticall fanaticall Morellius of Paris was bold by word and writing to find fault with, that his writing was both in this Church and in France in many Synods worthily condemned." [6]

---

[1] *Ibid.*, II, 179-180, attached to a letter dated 9 May [1644].

[2] For other such usages, see in W[illiam] R[athband], *A briefe narration of some church courses* (London, 1644), Wing No. R-298, p. 26, a slighting reference to "Morellian and popular Government," which, he says, the Independents " professe to condemne "; also in Samuel Rutherford, *The Due right of Presbyteries...* (London, 1644), Wing No. R-2378, p. 21, a condemnation of the Independents for seeking " meere popular government, such as our writers condemne in Morellius," and again on p. 22. I am indebted to Dr. Horton and the Reverend F. Benjamin Carr, Jr., for calling my attention to these passages.

[3] One of which, from the Westminster Assembly, was published in 1644 under the title *Literae a conventu theologorum in Anglia*, Wing, No. W-1444.

[4] Wing, No. A-3534. For a brief discussion of its composition, see Douglas Horton's introduction to his ed. of Norton's *Answer*, described in n. 2 to p. 134, below, pp. ix-xiii; *Biographisch Woordenboek van Protestantsche Godgeleerden in Nederland*, in art. " Apollonius," I, 203-205.

[5] Wing, No. A-3535.

[6] *Ibid.*, p. 56. I am indebted to the Rev. Dr. Geoffrey Nuttall of London, for calling this passage to my attention. The original Latin, pp. 66-67 of Wing, No. A-3534 reads: " Hinc etiam Ecclesiae Reformatae populare Ecclesiarum regimen semper rejecerunt,vide Sadaelis tractatum Gallice editum de Disciplina Ecclesiastica, contra Morellium: De quo Cl. Beza cum ordinem Electionis in Ecclesia descripsisset, sic inquit, Libro de Ministrorum gradibus, cap. 25 quem ordinem Dei beneficio, religiose simul, & prudenter adhuc in hac Civitate observatum, cum Democraticus quidam fanaticus Morellius Parisiensis ausus esset voce & scriptis reprehendere, merito fuit ipsius scriptum, & in hac Ecclesia & in Gallia plurimis Synodis damnatum."

It must be doubted, on the strength of this passage, that Apollonius knew Morély's own argument. But he was obviously acquainted with the refutations of Morély advanced by Chandieu and Beza.[1]

Apollonius' book provoked, as so many polemics of this period did, a published retort. And this retort provided a classic defense of Congregational polity as it was being worked out in the English-speaking world. This defense was by John Norton, pastor of the Church in Ipswich, in New England. It was published in London, in 1648.[2] Norton, however, does not seem to have been acquainted with the history of the French quarrel over church discipline. In refuting this particular charge of Apollonius, he simply denies quite flatly that the English Congregationalists have any connection at all with Morély.[3]

This did not prevent the English Presbyterians from continuing to blast their Congregational rivals with the charge that they were resurrecting the errors spawned by Morély's faction. Probably the most widely circulated such charge is contained in that best-seller of the period, Richard Baxter's *The Saints Everlasting Rest,* first published in 1650.[4] In a passage in which he rather restlessly inveighs against the Independents, Baxter rhetorically asks,

" Is it not strange that so learned a man as Pet. Ramus should be advocate for the multitude's authority in church-government? But that God must use so sharp a cure for those contentions, as that bloody French massacre, methinks should make England tremble to consider it, lest the same disease here must have the like cure." [5]

His statement that Ramus held this view, Baxter documents with copious quotations from Latin lives of Bullinger, Chandieu, and Beza. His rather novel explanation for the St. Bartholomew's massacres, Baxter does not document.

It is important to notice that all of these English references to Morély and his associates are negative. There is no evidence that has come to my attention that anyone knew his ideas well and was prepared to acknowledge

---

[1] The French Reformed Church took official notice during this same period of the argument between Presbyterians and Congregationalists, and sided quite emphatically against the Congregationalists. In the Synod of Charenton of 1645, all the French Reformed, and particularly those in the maritime provinces, were warned to beware of " some Persons going by the Name of Independents," who were arriving " from other Countries." The Synod informed its constituents that these Independents refused to " own or acknowledge the authority of Colloquies or Synods in matters of Discipline and Order," and concluded that they would be both " prejudicial to the Church of God " and " dangerous unto the Civil State." (J. Quick, *Synodicon*, II, 467, art. IX ; J. Aymon, *Synodes*, II, 678-679, art. IX.) Nowhere did the Synod acknowledge that these wicked foreigners might have had French ancestors or sympathizers. This condemnation was quickly adapted for polemical purposes in England, by being incorporated in editions of Ephraim Pagitt's slashing attack on the Independents, titled *Heresiography*, e.g. in the 4th ed. of 1647 (Wing No. P-178), p. 90, and in the 5th ed. of 1654 (Wing No. P-180), pp. 79-80.

[2] Not in Wing. Translated and edited, with commentary, by Douglas Horton, as John Norton, *The Answer to the Whole Set of Questions of the Celebrated Mr. William Apollonius*,... (Cambridge, Mass. : Harvard, 1958).

[3] P. 6 in the Horton ed.

[4] Wing, No. B-1383.

[5] Richard Baxter, *The Saints Everlasting Rest*, Part III, ch. XIV, section X, 5. In vol. XXIII, p. 135, of the William Orme ed. of Baxter's *The Practical Works* (London, 1830). I am indebted to Dr. Nuttall for calling this passage to my attention.

a debt to them. This fact reinforces my earlier conclusion, that the main importance of the entire Morély controversy was that it hardened the orthodox Calvinists in their commitment to presbyterian polity and consistorial discipline.[1] It seems clear that the resurrection of the controversy by these seventeenth-century Englishmen served precisely the same purpose. Again it was used to make more rigid the position held by orthodox Calvinists.

The second path which leads from the Morély controversy to later developments is even more tangled and obscure. But it may nevertheless be interesting to glance down it. This is the path which leads to later quarrels over secular government. A hypothesis which has intrigued a number of students of the development of secular democracy, is that it grew from ecclesiastical congregationalism, as the theories Congregationalists had advanced to justify operation of their own churches came to be adapted to arguments about the proper operation of secular political institutions.[2] There is a hint of such a connection of ecclesiastical and political theory in the thought of Morély himself, as we have already noted.[3] And the connection is developed and expanded in the thought of such seventeenth-century English Independent splinter groups as the Levellers.[4] It would be intriguing if the arguments by analogy between state and church, suggested by both Morély and Beza, could be connected to later thought on secular politics.

It can be demonstrated that such arguments by analogy did not disappear altogether from later Calvinist controversy. This is revealed in the records of an argument which broke forth within the city of Geneva, in 1578, only a few years after the Morély controversy had subsided.[5] In that year a citizen named Jaques Boutilier, at the sessions of the Council of Two Hundred which at the beginning of every year helped allocate a number of governmental responsibilities, proposed a series of changes in the constitution of the Genevan state. He argued that since Geneva is " by the grace of God constituted in a state of democracy," [6] its governmental procedures should allow more voice to the general population. And he proceeded to make a number of specific suggestions for change in the methods of initiating proposals for laws, of electing city officials, of staffing the governing Small Council and the judicial benches. All of these suggestions were designed to permit more participation in government by the average citizen. Boutilier bolstered his argument with analogies to other city-states, notably Venice and Lucca.[7] He did not draw analogies to the government of the Church.

---

[1] Above, p. 128.

[2] A theory developed by A. S. P. Woodhouse, in introduction to his *Puritanism and Liberty, Being the Army Debates (1647-1649)*... (2nd ed., London: Dent, 1951), pp. 60 and ff. Cf. the critical evaluation by Leo F. Solt, in " Puritanism and Democracy in the New Model Army," ARG, L (1959), 234-252.

[3] See above, pp. 57-58.

[4] On the Levellers, see Perez Zagorin, *A History of Political Thought in the English Revolution* (London: Routledge & Kegan Paul, 1954), chs. II and III, and other works there cited.

[5] This argument is described, with copious quotation from the relevant documents, in A. Roget, " Les propositions de Jaques Boutilier, ou discussion constitutionnelle à Genève en 1578," MDG, XVII (1872), 58-76. I am indebted to Professor E. William Monter of Northwestern University for calling this article to my attention.

[6] " par la grâce de Dieu constituée en état de démocratie," *ibid.*, p. 62.

[7] *Ibid.*, p. 63.

One such analogy is contained, however, in the official reply to Boutilier, prepared at the command of the Small Council. This is not surprising, given its authors. One of them was Beza, another was one of his fellow pastors, the third was the devotedly Calvinist lawyer Germain Colladon. In general, their report rejected the notion that Geneva was in fact democratic and vigorously attacked the ideal of "pure democracy." In its place, the report held up the classical ideal of a mixed government, made of democratic, aristocratic, and monarchic elements, and argued that Geneva was controlled by such a mixture, with the aristocratic element predominating.[1] The report also argued that any change in constitutional arrangements was risky, particularly in times as unstable as at present. And at this point, it introduced an argument based on an analogy with the Church. The primitive Church had obviously been directed by a mixed government, "under one chief, Jesus Christ, with the administration which was partly democratic, that is conducted by the church, and partly aristocratic, that is governed by the pastors and elders." But because this primitive government had been changed into "a papal monarchy," everything had been ruined.[2] It was clearly implied that similar disasters might overtake Geneva if it changed its mixed government.

This reply was taken to be a sufficient refutation of Boutilier's suggestions, and he was thrown in jail for his temerity. In the records of this tiff there is no explicit link to the earlier controversy sparked by Morély. But the language of the rebuttal to Boutilier which Beza helped to draft, is reminiscent of Beza's published rebuttals of the Morély-Ramus program. And there is a hint that some of Boutilier's supporters shared the resentment of clerical leadership which Morély had articulated. Shortly before Boutilier had submitted his proposals, an anonymous placard clandestinely posted in the city had charged, along with a number of criticisms of the city government, that "miserable Beza is flattered too much." [3]

The Boutilier flare-up was quickly squelched and there was little further agitation of the issues he raised for more than a century in Geneva. Only in the eighteenth century, in the decades preceding the French Revolution, when agitation for more democratic government cropped up here and there all over Europe, did Genevans of the less privileged classes again demand a greater share in the city's government. These demands were sporadic, and quickly suppressed by the city's Small Council. But they probably had an effect

[1] *Ibid.*, pp. 68-69: "D'ailleurs jamais homme prudent n'approuva une pure démocratie, c'est-à-dire un gouvernement du tout attribué à la multitude populaire, puisque jamais il n'y en a eu de telle nature qui ait esté de longue durée... Voilà pourquoi les sages et renommés législateurs ont jugé d'un commun accord, qu'un Estat, pour estre bien dressé doit être meslé et attrempé de trois espèces de gouvernement, à savoir de celui du peuple, de celui des principaux et de celui du monarque... Ce tempérament de ces trois différens estats existe dans une très-exacte proportion dans Genève, dont on peut dire que le gouvernement participe plus du démocratique, moins du monarchique, et que l'aristocratique tient comme le milieu."

[2] *Ibid.*, p. 67: "Ains a aussi esté l'église chrétienne mise en désolation, lorsqu'au lieu de l'estat establi sous un chef Jésus-Christ avec l'administration, laquelle estoit en partie démocratique, c'est-à-dire conduite par l'église en partie aristocratique, c'est-à-dire gouvernée par les pasteurs et anciens, on avoit voulu faire une monarchie papale." Cf. the even more detailed analysis of the Church as a mixed government developed by Peter Martyr Vermigli, in Appendix III, below.

[3] *Ibid.*, p. 60: "Bèze misérable est trop flatté."

on one young citizen of Geneva. This was Jean-Jacques Rousseau, whose spectacular reputation in France as an apostle of more democratic government needs no elaboration.[1] It is curious and fitting, that in Rousseau one once again finds reference to Jean Morély and the quarrel which he had provoked.

In his *Lettres écrites de la montagne,* Rousseau discussed the 1563 trial of Morély at some length.[2] He even reproduced the entire text of the judgment condemning Morély, just as it has been printed at the time.[3] But the point of Rousseau's reference was quite particular and quite limited. He was at that time tremendously upset that the government of his native city had ordered the public burning of his master-work, the *Social Contract,* after legal proceedings which seemed to him arbitrary and unfair. There was little certain information upon which Rousseau could base such a complaint, however, in a day when the Genevan state archives, in common with most, were closed to the general public. Rousseau consequently seized upon the published record of Morély's trial because it did provide information about legal proceedings of this sort. For Morély had also been the author of a book which the Genevan magistrates had ordered burned, and the published trial record contained full information on the charges brought against Morély and the way in which they had been judged. Rousseau used this information largely to argue in his own defense, that his case was radically different. He pointed out that the Consistory had not examined him and his book as it had Morély and his. He pointed out that his book did not deal with ecclesiastical matters as had that of Morély. But he showed no consciousness of the substance of Morély's argument. There is no evidence that he read Morély himself. Hence it cannot be concluded that Morély's arguments for ecclesiastical democracy helped shape Rousseau's arguments for secular democracy, even by analogy. At most, one can only claim that the persecution of Morély helped Rousseau, in a rather backhanded way, to develop his own arguments for greater freedom of expression.

Even if Morély did not in fact have any influence on English Congregationalists or French democrats, the story of the controversy which he provoked is still not without significance. It constitutes an important and revealing strand in the internal history of French Protestantism during the sixteenth century. It provides yet another demonstration of the increasing rigidity and narrowness and clericalism which closed in upon Calvinism in the years following its founder's death. And this changed character of the movement helps to explain why it increasingly lost the appeal which it had possessed in its infancy for free spirits, why they increasingly turned elsewhere for intellectual nourishment, in directions which were sectarian, secular, or Reformed Catholic.

---

[1] See Patrick F. O'Mara, " L'affaire des lettres anonymes et l'agitation politique à Saint-Gervais en 1718," BSHAG, X (1951-1955), 241-279, for a detailed analysis of one such set of demands. N.B. pp. 263, ff., re the Rousseau family, who did not participate in this particular affair, but were neighbors to some who did.

[2] J. J. Rousseau, *Lettres écrites de la montagne* (Amsterdam, 1764), I, 190-197, alluded to again in II, 14.

[3] Pp. 193-196. For description and analysis of the original publication, see above, ch. 3-C-1, esp. n. 3 to p. 64.

D. The External Attack: Charles du Moulin

Calvinist institutions were subject to attack in France during this period not only from within but also from without. Most of the external attacks came from orthodox Roman Catholic sources, and could be flatly rejected by Calvinists as part of their general rejection of all things Roman. Some of these external attacks, however, came from quarters which Calvinists could not afford to defy, since it was from them that they enlisted important support. Specifically these attacks came from members of a group which may be labeled Gallican. This group possessed enormous influence in sixteenth-century France. From its ranks were recruited the "politiques" who rose to power with Kings Henri III and Henri IV, and who had a decisive voice in the religious settlement finally reached toward the end of the century. The general discontent of these men with the Church of Rome made of them a most important and promising source of allies and supporters for the Calvinist movement. A few of them were actually persuaded to join Reformed churches, but most of them did not. Of those who did, most joined before Calvin died. It is an important symptom of the decreasing momentum of the Geneva-directed missionary campaign that there were fewer converts to Calvinism from this group in the years that followed. An explanation of Calvinism's failure to maintain its appeal to these men would help substantially in explaining Calvinism's general failure to win France. One ingredient in any such explanation is a Gallican reaction against certain Calvinist institutions and practices. Striking evidence of the existence and shape of this reaction can be found in certain of the writings of Charles du Moulin.

Du Moulin was probably the best known and most articulate spokesman for the Gallican view in the 1550's and 1560's. As one of France's most distinguished jurisconsults, in a period when France was famous for its jurisconsults, du Moulin won an international reputation in some ways comparable to that of Ramus. This reputation was based largely on du Moulin's monumental studies of French common law, particularly in the area around Paris. These studies had gone far to codify that law and from their first publication had won for their author enthusiastic acclaim in French legal circles. They expressed a legal point of view of particular use to the French crown, since they documented in enormous detail the claims of the monarchy itself, of such institutions especially useful to the monarchy as the Parlements, and of the traditional legal system which the king and his courts interpreted and enforced.[1]

The utility of du Moulin's views to the rising monarchs of Renaissance France, probably also helps explain the spread of his reputation to other countries. Those foreign countries in which his reputation was greatest seem to have been certain of the German principalities, in which the rulers faced similar problems of asserting and maintaining their power.

One institution with which a person of du Moulin's legal views was bound to come into conflict, was obviously the Roman Catholic Church. And conflict did in fact develop. It developed over du Moulin's famous treatise

[1] For a useful summary of du Moulin's contribution to French legal thought, see William Farr Church, *Constitutional Thought in Sixteenth-Century France* (Cambridge, Mass.: Harvard, 1941), pp. 180-194.

on small dates, which attacked certain procedures established by the papal curia to regulate the granting of benefices in France, procedures to which the government of Henri II objected strongly. The ideas which this treatise contained and the violent polemical tone in which they were expressed won for du Moulin the applause of his fellow Gallicans but the bitter enmity of the clergy and its friends, particularly those among them most devoted to Rome.[1]

In the middle of the sixteenth century it would be surprising if du Moulin's Gallicanism had not led him to explore Protestant ideas. And this in fact did happen. In 1542 he became a Protestant. His Protestantism soon took a Calvinist turn, as was natural at that date. In 1552, and again in 1553, he made the standard pilgrimage to French Switzerland, to the headquarters of the new faith. If we can trust his own later account, however, his visits to French Switzerland dampened his ardor somewhat. He reported that he had had violent arguments with young Beza in Lausanne, that his relations with Calvin in Geneva had been correct enough but cool, and that he had openly challenged certain points of Calvinist doctrine in a Synod and in other meetings in Neuchâtel.[2] The focus of these challenges allegedly was the Calvinist doctrine of predestination. It seems likely, however, that du Moulin's later account exaggerates the extent of these quarrels, and may be colored by later bitterness. The letters which he and Calvin exchanged at the time seen cordial enough. And Calvin even recommended him warmly for a teaching position in Strasbourg, shortly after the Neuchâtel Synod.[3]

In any event, du Moulin decided to shift his field of operations to Germany. His legal reputation was spreading there. He was in particular demand among the Protestant principalities of the Empire. After voyaging about and considering several tempting offers, he finally accepted a professorship at Tübingen. His lectures there seem to have attracted considerable public interest. They also seem to have revealed his own ever greater interest in theology. More and more he commented upon Scripture and upon theological matters, less and less upon pure law. The two, of course, were not, and in that period could not, be totally disconnected. Nevertheless du Moulin got deep enough into theology to anger his colleagues in the chairs of theology. Their anger led to controversy and finally to du Moulin's departure. It is hard to determine the precise nature of this controversy. Du Moulin's biographer suggests that the jurisconsult was attacked for being a ubiquitarian, one of those orthodox Lutherans, then led primarily by Brenz, who insisted that the body of Christ was in many places at once during the celebration of the Lord's Supper.[4] But this explanation certainly does not square with du Moulin's own rather bitter later attacks on ubiquitarians, in his most impor-

---

[1] See C. du Moulin, *Opera*, IV, 299-515, for Latin and French texts of this treatise; I, 1st pagination, pp. 19-25, for account of its composition and reception by his biographer, Julien Brodeau.

[2] In Simon Challudre [reputedly an anagram for du Moulin himself], "La defense de Messire Charles du Moulin...," in *ibid.*, V, 610-612. Cf. account of Brodeau in I, 1st pagination, p. 26.

[3] Calvin to Jac. Sturm, 10 July 1553, in *Calvini Opera*, XIV, 564-565. See vols. XIV, XV, XX, *passim* as indicated by indexes, April [1552]—September 1555, for the letters between Calvin and du Moulin, most of them written after du Moulin's move to Germany.

[4] In C. du Moulin, *Opera*, I, 1st pagination, p. 29.

tant theological work, the *Collation and Union of the Four Gospels*.[1] Nor does it square with letters he wrote at the time. He reported to Bullinger, for example, that he was under attack by partisans of Brenz for adherence to doctrines of a Zwinglian kind.[2] It seems likely, indeed, that du Moulin's biographer has inverted his explanation, and that the jurisconsult got into trouble for attacking rather than maintaining ubiquitarianism.

In any case, du Moulin left Germany and returned to France and eventually to Paris, scene of his greatest triumphs and of his violent early legal controversies. And he returned determined to become even more of a theologian. When the first war of religion broke out, he moved to Orleans, the headquarters of the Protestant armies. There he began giving lectures on theology and began an intensive personal study of New Testament exegesis. His studies led the very next year to his publication in Lyon of a new Protestant catechism, which seems to have departed at several significant points from the catechism of Geneva which was then received generally among the French Reformed.[3] It also led to the writing of his massive and scholarly *Collation and Union of the Four Gospels*.[4] For two years, however, he could not find a printer for the *Collation*. His own explanation of this difficulty is that the hostility of Calvinist pastors blocked every attempt he made. The explanation may well be true. The pastors were reportedly furious when his catechism appeared in Lyon, and proscribed its use among the Reformed faithful.[5] Some of them were also involved in legal proceedings against du Moulin, in Lyon, in 1563. These proceedings stemmed from a charge that du Moulin was author of an anonymous and seditious pamphlet, *The Civil and Military Defense of the Innocents and of the Church of Christ*.[6] Du Moulin purged himself without much difficulty of this charge, and published a thorough and violent refutation of the pamphlet. To his published refutation was joined the city governor's official order that the pamphlet be burned in public and a formal condemnation of its contents signed by all the leading pastors of Lyon, headed by Pierre Viret.[7]

Agreement between du Moulin and the pastors of Lyon in condemning resistance theories, however, did not presage a general reconciliation, and was probably forced by governmental authorities. The warfare between du Moulin and the clergy broke out all over again, in an even more violent form, when he finally found a publisher for his *Collation*, sometime in 1565. The publisher he found was a man named Nicholas Laurent, a native of Tournai,

---

[1] E.g. in *ibid.*, V, 597, vs. " novi Ubiquistae impie "; 605, vs. " novae illi & schismaticae Ubiquitati."

[2] Du Moulin to Bullinger, 4 September 1554, in *Calvini Opera*, XV, 225-226. Cf. the somewhat similar report in his slightly later letters to Calvin, pp. 466-469, 474-477.

[3] Published in Latin and French in 1563, according to *France protestante*, 1st and 2nd eds., art. " Du Moulin," No. 30 on his list of Charles' publications, but not included in du Moulin's *Opera*.

[4] *Collatio et unio quatuor Evangelistarum Domini nostri Jesu Christi...* (1565). Included in C. du Moulin, *Opera*, V, 447-606.

[5] According to du Moulin himself, *Opera*, V, 617-618, and to Brodeau, I, 1st pagination, p. 41.

[6] *La deffense civile & militaire des innocens & de l'Eglise de Christ*, a wording taken from du Moulin's attack on it—cf. n. 7.

[7] See C. du Moulin, *Opera*, V, [xv]-xxii, for a complete text of this refutation and the accompanying condemnations. For more on this episode, see below, pp. 153-156.

at that time operating in a Paris suburb. He was a Protestant. He seems to have been a fairly small operator even by sixteenth-century standards.

One does not have to read very far in the *Collation*, to comprehend the fury of the orthodox Calvinist reaction to the book. It is intended to be a systematic supplement and correction to Calvin's famous collation of the Gospels.[1] It attacks Calvin's exegesis in general[2] and in detail at many specific points. In its critical apparatus it also attacks Beza's exegesis at many specific points. It also includes a number of comments on such other contemporary exegetes as Erasmus, Bullinger, Bucer, Brenz, and Melanchthon. Its tone, nonetheless, is thoroughly Protestant. Other exegetes are most commonly attacked for not sticking to the literal sense of some Scripture text. And it is clearly a work of considerable erudition and authority. Such a distinguished and relatively independent commentator on Scriptural exegesis as Richard Simon, the great seventeenth-century liberal Catholic exegete, found much to praise in du Moulin. Simon found du Moulin's knowledge of Greek far superior to Calvin's, and du Moulin's faithfulness to the exact Scripture text somewhat superior to Beza's.[3]

Scholarly considerations of this sort, however, did not mean much to the leaders of the contemporary Calvinist movement. They were much more conscious of du Moulin's intemperate attacks upon their beloved leaders and upon doctrines of whose verity they were absolutely convinced. The *Collation* was consequently condemned almost as soon as it appeared. Action against the book was taken almost simultaneously, in Geneva and in Paris, toward the end of 1565. The action in Geneva was provoked by the imprudent appearance in that city of the printer Laurent. He had personally brought in copies for sale. He was jailed for a long period of time, and finally sentenced to a humiliating public penance. As a climax to his penance, Laurent was required to attend a public burning of du Moulin's book between the gates of the Geneva City Hall. The draft sentence makes it clear that the contents of du Moulin's book were the main reason for this judgment. The draft also suggests that Genevan authorities realized that legal warrant for their action was somewhat slim. It acknowledges that the book was not published in Geneva, and most Genevan censorship laws were aimed only at books printed in the city. And it stipulates expressly that the final copy of the sentence, which apparently has not survived, should omit the name of the printer being punished.[4]

It is clear that the proceedings against Laurent in Geneva were the work of the clergy. The Council records of the case reveal that Beza was consulted several times, and that the final sentence was drafted by him. Furthermore,

---

[1] The *Commentarius in Harmoniam Evangelicam*, many eds. See bibliographical information and text in *Calvini Opera*, XLV.

[2] In his introductory letter to the *Collation*, C. du Moulin, *Opera*, V, 452, du Moulin attacks Calvin for having only covered the first three Gospels in his *Harmony*.

[3] Richard Simon, *Histoire critique des principaux commentateurs du Nouveau Testament*... (Rotterdam, 1693), pp. 772-774, re du Moulin, including comparison to Beza; pp. 745 and ff., re Calvin, including, p. 745, comparison to du Moulin, and, p. 746, reflections on Calvin's Greek; pp. 751 and ff., re Beza, generally rather flattering.

[4] Geneva, Arch., Jur. Pen. A-4 (Livre des Criminelz, 1565-1566), fols. 76v., 77, 77v., 22-26 November 1565. Cf. Laurent's corroborative account in C. du Moulin, *Opera*, V, 629-630.

the Consistory entered the case, after the Council's judgment had been executed and before Laurent could leave town. It summoned Laurent to one of its sessions, to answer not only the charge of having printed du Moulin's book, but also a heresy charge that he claimed to have exorcised devils and spread ideas labeled "Anabaptist." [1] Laurent later reported that he also had to listen to a good deal of thundering clerical invective against du Moulin at this session of the Consistory, as individual pastors called du Moulin "a beast," "a masked dog, worse than a beast," and other things.[2] No further temporal action was taken against Laurent. He had already been punished for his publication, and there does not seem to have been much ground for the heresy charges. He was, to be sure, excommunicated, but he was permitted to return to Paris with the order that he purge himself before the Church there.

Meanwhile the *Collation* had also been roundly condemned in Paris, by the national Synod of the Reformed churches which met in that city at the end of 1565. One of the "general advertisements unto the churches" included in the acts of that Synod specifically warned the Reformed of France "to beware of a Book written by Mr. Charles du Moulin, Entituled *Unio quatuor Evangelistarum.*" [3]

These violent reactions by orthodox Calvinist leaders to du Moulin's most substantial contribution to theological studies, were paralleled by equally violent reactions in du Moulin. He prepared a general denunciation of the Calvinist churches in the form of a legal complaint submitted to royal courts in Paris, apparently to clear his own name, perhaps to collect damages. This complaint was bolstered by notarized affidavits of a number of witnesses, including the unlucky printer Laurent.[4] These legal proceedings did not lead to anything, however. Perhaps du Moulin did not really intend that they should. It is hard to see upon whom among the many Calvinist leaders operating clandestinely in France any judgments could be executed. In any event, the publicity given to these complaints was quite enough to upset Calvinist leaders further. Several of the same letters to Beza which report on developments in the controversy surrounding Morély at the Court of Navarre, also report on du Moulin's charges and publications. In two of them La Mare urged Beza that an open reply to du Moulin be prepared and published, to stanch the flow of venom which du Moulin was vomiting and the wicked calumnies which he was sowing.[5] But the Calvinists' concern

[1] Geneva, Arch., Jur. Pen. A-4 (Livre des Criminelz, 1565-1566), fol. 79, 30 November 1565, the initial accusation: "ledit Laurent avoit proferer certains propos par lesquelles il dict avoir jeter hors les diables de quelquez corps & aultres propos dAnabaptistes"; RConsistoire, XXII, fols. 181-181v., 191, 6 and 20 December 1565, reports of the Consistory's investigation and action.

[2] In deposition published in C. du Moulin, *Opera*, V, 629, one pastor said "ledit du Molin n'estoit qu'une beste"; another said "ledit du Molin n'estoit qu'un chien masqué, pire qu'une beste."

[3] J. Quick, *Synodicon*, I, 67, art. XXXII. Cf. J. Aymon, *Synodes*, 2nd pagination, p. 70, art. IX.

[4] See texts in C. du Moulin, *Opera*, V, 621-625, 625-632.

[5] La Mare to Beza, 25 September 1566, in Geneva, BPU, Ms. fr. 446, fols. 93-94: "nous voions que ce malheureux du Moulin continue a desgorger son venein et ne tache qu'a semer ses meschantes calomnies par tout"; La Mare to Beza, 5 January 1567, in *ibid.*, fols. 117-118, reporting du Moulin's death but again suggesting a reply.

about du Moulin's attacks was soon cut short by an event which seemed to them providential. Very soon after these documents were drafted, du Moulin died. His death was reportedly preceded by a last-minute conversion back to the Roman Catholic faith.[1] If this conversion upset Beza's correspondents, however, they did not reveal it. Perhaps they did not even know of it. In any case, their principal reaction was one of relief.

It is in these polemical documents written at the end of his life, that one must look for the fullest expression of du Moulin's critique of the Calvinist system of ecclesiastical organization.[2] Traces of this attack, however, can also be found in the *Collation*. The 1565 Paris Synod's article of condemnation lists that book's main errors as " about Limbus, Free-Will, and the Sin against the Holy Ghost, and the Lord's Supper, and in particular about the Calling of Ministers, and Church-Discipline, which he treats with scorn, and would totally subvert." [3] As if to justify this emphasis, du Moulin then turned to yet more systematic attack on the Calvinist disciplinary system.

One source of du Moulin's dislike of the Calvinist ecclesiastical system, was the fact that he himself was continually treated as an amateur by the ordained Calvinist clergy. Like Ramus after him, du Moulin seems to have been considerably annoyed by this treatment. Again and again Calvinist leaders attacked his teaching, his publication, his catechizing, and his other churchly activities, on grounds that he had never been properly trained or ordained to the ministry. This attack reached a climax in the Paris Synod's warning, " The Faithful also are warned not to assist at any of his [du Moulin's] Sermons or Sacraments, it being against the Discipline of our Church." [4] And du Moulin reacted bitterly against these attacks, comparing his own erudition to the ignorance of the average Calvinist pastor, insisting on the religious validity of his status as a doctor, and denying the Scriptural foundations claimed for the Calvinist system of ordination.[5]

But du Moulin's dislike of the Calvinist ecclesiastical system was also profoundly influenced by his Gallicanism, and this gave his criticism its peculiar flavor. Even his resentment against criticism of his religious, semi-clerical activities, seems to have been justified partly by a Gallican argument. He felt that a doctoral degree from an established institution like one of the French universities, should take precedence as a certificate of quality over the rite of ordination practiced by an upstart foreign institution like the Calvinist Church.

This line of argument was quickly expanded to cover a whole range of Calvinist ecclesiastical institutions. Again and again he made parallel and

---

[1] Reported by Brodeau in C. du Moulin, *Opera*, I, 1st pagination, p. 51. The compilers of *France protestante*, 1st ed., art. " Du Moulin," IV, 414, are dubious about this report.

[2] See Michel Reulos, " Le jurisconsulte Charles du Moulin en conflit avec les Eglises Réformées de France," BSHPF, C (1954), 1-12, for a skillful analysis, emphasizing, perhaps too much, the extent to which even du Moulin's early criticisms of Calvinism were directed against its discipline.

[3] J. Quick, *Synodicon*, I, 67, art. XXXII. Cf. J. Aymon, *Synodes*, 2nd pagination, p. 70, art. IX.

[4] *Ibid.*

[5] E.g. in du Moulin, *Opera*, V, 615, he says " quil estoit ancien Docteur, & qu'il avoit vocation plus qu'un simple nouveau Ministre : & que le Docteur est pardessus un simple Ministre."

allied charges that they were "foreign" and subversive of the French way of life. He found them foreign because they were of Genevan or Swiss origin. He found them subversive because they sought to upset or replace existing French institutions. Both complaints can be seen entwined in the following characteristic passage:

"The said pretended ministers, true evil-doers, seditious and usurpers, are foreign people, or sent and appointed by those of Geneva, on whom they are entirely dependent, and to whom they have taken an oath, and send there each day a messenger, to have their advice and counsel to follow in every way and always, at the expense of the French people, and the subjects of the king, to reduce all this kingdom to the subjection and popular estate of Geneva, to change and overthrow the police of the kingdom of France, even at the expense of the people of France." [1]

This particular complaint, like most of these later complaints of du Moulin, was clearly overstated. Very few of the Calvinist pastors then active in France were in fact foreign to the country. Most of them had been born and had received their earliest training there. It seems unlikely that the Reformed ever had the means to maintain a daily messenger service of the extent and efficiency suggested by du Moulin. And anyone very familiar with sixteenth-century Genevan institutions would hesitate to call them "popular." Still there remains an important kernel of truth in these charges. As both this book and its predecessor have demonstrated, Geneva did assume a commanding role in the formation and the direction of the Reformed ministry in France. And even if Genevan institutions can more precisely be labeled "aristocratic" (to use Beza's word) than "popular," they were still sufficiently different from the web of institutions superintended by the French monarchy to upset anyone really devoted to monarchic government.

The Calvinist institution to which du Moulin objected with the most vehemence was the consistory. He charged that consistories were usurping a whole range of functions that properly belonged to established branches of civil government. They were usurping tax powers by raising money to maintain their churches and to help the poor. They were usurping judicial functions by acting as courts in all sorts of cases involving morals and doctrine. In their judgments they were insinuating foreign laws and traditions into France. To provide an example of a specific charge, he claimed that they were trying to undermine French primogeniture and to replace it with the Genevan principle of "popular equality among all the children" in the division of estates.[2] And he even contended that the consistories were going so far as to urge the faithful to avoid the established courts.

Du Moulin's attack on the consistory was partly a religious one. He insisted that the institution had no basis in Scripture and was therefore not Christian. But the main reasons for his attack seem to have been political, and Gallican. This impression is strengthened by the comparisons which

[1] In *ibid.*, V, 621: "lesdits pretendus Ministres vrais mal-faicteurs, seditieux & usurpateurs, sont gens étrangers, ou envoyez & instituez par ceux de Geneve, dont ils dépendent entierement, & ausquels ils ont le serment, & y envoyent chacun jour Messager, pour avoir leur advis & conseil pour le suivre en tout, & par tout, aux dêpens de peuple François, & des sujets du Roy, reduire tout ce Royaume à la subjettion & estat populaire de Geneve, changer & renverser toute la police du Royaume de France, aux dépens mesme du peuple de France."

[2] *Ibid.*, V, 624, re Calvinist attack on "le droit d'aisnesse des fiefs, & entre les Nobles, pour mettre égalité populaire entre tous les enfans, comme l'on fait à Geneve."

du Moulin made between the "Consistorial Calvinists" and other contemporary religious groups, in the course of these attacks. He found the Calvinists much like Roman Catholics in trying to subvert the French monarchy and introduce foreign tyranny. Indeed he found them worse than Roman Catholics, in that they had nearly accomplished in three years what it had taken the Catholics three hundred years and more to accomplish.[1] This, of course, recalls the attacks on papal legal practices which began du Moulin's public career. Both Calvinists and Catholics, in du Moulin's eyes, now were inferior to the followers of the Confession of Augsburg in Germany, or Lutherans. They were also both inferior to those Swiss who followed Zwingli, particularly in Zurich. Clearly du Moulin preferred the "cuius regio eius religio" principle of the Lutherans, and the Erastianism of the Zwinglians, to the political activism of the Christians doing battle for France. And this should not surprise in a Gallican. In du Moulin's case, the preference for Lutherans and Zwinglians was reinforced by an ostensible admiration for their theology. This admiration, however, was no longer overly troubled by attention to the sharp differences between the two groups of which most of their contemporary members were increasingly aware.[2]

To gain a more precise appreciation of the nature and impact of du Moulin's attack on Calvinist ecclesiastical organization, it would be well to turn now to a comparison of his attack with Morély's. In both the realms of events and ideas there are striking parallels. But in both there are also significant differences.

If one considers events, one notes first certain parallels in chronology. Both Morély and du Moulin worked out their criticisms of Calvinist institutions at about the time of the first war of religion in France. Their criticisms may well have reflected a dampening of Calvinist enthusiasm and a growing uncertainty about the total rightness of the Calvinist cause induced by the very fact of war. Further, the controversies provoked by their criticisms reached a climax of sorts in the last months of 1565 and in 1566, when enough peace had returned to the kingdom to give Protestants the opportunity and leisure to quarrel among themselves. Morély's criticism was published first, of course, and the controversy it provoked accordingly began earlier. Both Morély and du Moulin, furthermore, had connections to the secular leaders of French Protestantism. The nature of Morély's connections we have already examined. The nature of du Moulin's I cannot describe in equal detail, because of lack of information. But it is nevertheless interesting to note that du Moulin at one time styled himself "counsellor and master of requests to the Queen of Navarre," [3] which meant that at one time at least he

[1] *Ibid.*, V, 614, addressing Calvinists: "Vostre but estoit... establir un nouveau regne en France, pire que le Papal... dés la tierce année cela fut tout commun, on commença ne parler plus que de Consistoire... le Clergé Romain n'acquist pas si grande autorité trois cent ans."

[2] For examples of praise of Lutherans, see *ibid.*, V, 557 (in the *Collation*), 620, 624; of praise of Zwinglians, 557. See also du Moulin's complimentary letters to Bullinger in *Calvini Opera*, XIV, 387-392, 511; XV, 224-226.

[3] On the title page of the *Collation*, reproduced in C. du Moulin, *Opera*, V, 447, du Moulin is styled: "Jurium Doctorem Sacrarumque Literarum Professorem, Consiliarium, Libellorumque supplicum Magistrum Illustrissimae Reginae Navarrae." Brodeau, in I, 1st pagination, p. 39, notes that du Moulin was "Conseiller & Maistre des Requestes" to both the King and Queen of Navarre.

apparently served as a consultant to the court at which French Protestantism's political power was centered. It is also interesting to note that du Moulin apparently benefited at one point from the protection of Odet de Coligny, the Cardinal of Châtillon. According to one contemporary witness, the Cardinal saved du Moulin from hanging during the troubles in Lyon.[1]

Those troubles suggest yet another parallel, this one quite mysterious. Both du Moulin and one of Morély's leading supporters, Sureau, were charged with authorship of the same seditious pamphlet, *The Civil and Military Defense of the Innocents*. In each case they were imprisoned on the charge, and in each case exonerated without much difficulty. This peculiar coincidence has led some scholars to conclude that the charges were the work of common enemies within the Calvinist clergy.[2]

In the maneuvers of those common enemies about which we have surer information, there are again interesting parallels. Orthodox Calvinist leaders in both Geneva and France took remarkably similar measures to counter both attacks. The Genevan city government and Consistory both took action against the books in which these criticisms were expressed, and action in both cases led ultimately to the public burning of the books, an unusual procedure for which there does not seem to be much warrant in contemporary Genevan law, since neither book had been printed in the city. Both burnings were well publicized. Within France, both attacks were considered at national synods of the Reformed Church, and both were explicitly condemned by the Paris Synod of 1565. Furthermore, both kinds of criticism were refuted in print, in the official defense of Calvinist ecclesiastical organization prepared by Antoine de la Roche Chandieu.

A closer look at these reactions from the leaders of orthodox Calvinism, however, reveals that they were clearly much more worried by Morély's attacks. Not one, but several synods, both provincial and national, considered his criticisms. The sentence condemning his book to burning in Geneva was printed for widest possible distribution. Chandieu's official refutation was devoted largely to a direct reply to his book, with only incidental replies to other kinds of criticism.

One reason for taking Morély more seriously, of course, is that his attack was a more sustained one, and disturbed the churches in one way or another for an entire decade. But this in turn is partly explained by the differences in character between the men. Morély remained eager to be a member of the Reformed Church, continually begged for reconciliation, and remained in contact with certain spiritual and secular leaders of the movement. His criticisms consequently had a more upsetting effect internally, within the Reformed churches. Du Moulin, on the other hand, was always the rugged individualist, and most of his life did not seem to care much whether he was in the good graces of any church.

While this reaction on the part of Calvinist leaders is understandable, it may have been a mistake. Du Moulin, after all, was a man of much greater prominence. His ideas, furthermore, seem to have been much better calculated to appeal to the leaders of sixteenth-century French society, particularly to that all-important group dependent upon the royal court.

---

[1] Deposition of Robert Trehet, in *ibid.*, V, 626.

[2] Compilers of *France protestante*, art. "Du Moulin," both 1st and 2nd eds.

The Calvinist leaders might well have been better advised to have taken his attacks more seriously and to have prepared a more thorough refutation of them, even after their author had died.

When one turns to the parallels in ideas, one has the advantage of du Moulin's express opinions on the subject. Among his specific charges against the leaders of contemporary Calvinism, were two that mentioned Morély. One complained that " Jean Morély, native of Paris, who was of their sect, for having written that their consistories are illicit usurpations, was by them excommunicated and thrown out, and his book burned in Geneva." It then went on to acknowledge that the Calvinists were not as yet burning books in France, but charged that they " are waiting until they are as great Lords there as they are in Geneva to do as much and more." [1] This charge, of course, provided an ideal complement to du Moulin's complaints about the way in which his own book had been treated. It was followed by another charge, that " they have done the same against a de Villiers whom they have thrown out and excommunicated, because he had said that they are taking over police functions." [2] Apparently du Moulin did not realize that Jean Morély was also the sire de Villiers.

This particular charge of du Moulin's was considerably amplified by witnesses whose affidavits supported his complaint. One witness, a certain Robert Trehet who was one of du Moulin's students and also a good Protestant, had actually read Morély's book. He reported that it was " against the consistories and illicit usurpations of the police and republic " characteristic of the Calvinist movement. He reported further that he had read a Lyon printing of the Genevan sentence against Morély, ordering his excommunication and condemning his book to the flames. His additional report, that he had heard certain pastors say that a certain de Villiers had been excommunicated for having " attacked their vocation and found fault with their police," is probably the source of du Moulin's confusion of the two cases.[3]

It should be noted, however, that both du Moulin and his witnesses spoke only of the negative side of Morély's argument. They knew about and heartily approved of his attacks on Calvinist consistories. They did not, however, reveal knowledge of his positive recommendations for more democratic government of the Church. And, indeed, it is difficult to see how

[1] In C. du Moulin, *Opera*, V, 623 : " Un Jean Morelli natif de Paris, qui estoit de leur secte, pour avoir écrit que les Ministres entreprenoient sur la police, & que leurs Consistoires estoient usurpations illicites, a esté par eux excommunié & retranché, & son Livre brûlé à Geneve : ils ne brûlent pas encore les livres en France, ils attendent qu'ils y soient aussi grands Seigneurs qu'ils sont à Geneve pour en executer autant & davantage."

[2] In *ibid.* : " Ils ont fait le pareil, contre un de Villiers qu'ils ont retranché & excommunié, parce qu'il avoit dit qu'ils entreprenoient sur la police."

[3] In *ibid.*, p. 628 : " Plus dit ledit deposant [Trehet], qu'il a veu & leu le Livre de Morelli natif de Paris, escrit & composé, comme appert par la lecture d'iceluy, contre les Consistoires & usurpations illicites sur la police & republique ; Ensemble dit ledit deposant, qu'il a veu avec ledit Livre la Sentence d'excommunication, par laquelle lesdits Ministres avoient excommunié ledit Morelli, & condamné son Livre à estre bruslé : ce qui fut fait à Geneve, ainsi que ledit deposant auroit veu par la Sentence d'excommunication imprimée à Lyon. Dit outre ledit deposant qu'il a oüy dire ausdits Ministres qu'un nommé de Villiers estoit retranché & excommunié de leur Eglise, pour ce qu'il oppugnoit leur vocation, & reprenoit leur police." See also p. 630, report of witness Laurent that he had seen the printed condemnation of Morély ; p. 632, report of witness de Villereau that he had heard of the Morély controversy.

du Moulin himself could ever have accepted this part of Morély's program. For the institutions which Morély wanted were even more "popular" than those which du Moulin condemned, partly because they were already too "popular." They were united in their dislike of the central Calvinist institution of the consistory. But the basic grounds of their opposition were really quite different. Du Moulin was against consistories primarily because they were not French and threatened monarchic institutions. Morély was against them because they were not Scriptural and were not sufficiently responsive to popular pressure.

This basic difference in the criticisms which Calvinist leaders faced from two directions, makes clear, I think, the fact that they faced a serious dilemma. Any concession which they might have made to Morély and his supporters, would have angered powerful Gallicans of du Moulin's persuasion, and opened the Reformed Church to yet more sweeping charges that it was attempting to introduce Swiss democracy into France. And such charges could have compromised the Church yet more seriously in the eyes of the royal government and before many of the leaders of French society among whom they hoped to win converts. But any concession to Gallican opinion could have angered further those sympathetic to Morély. And these men were of more actual importance to the internal operation of the Church as it then existed. If they had been pushed too far, the Church might well have split into congregational and presbyterian wings, as Puritan non-conformity later did in England. That would have imposed upon French Protestantism the scandal of further division and the tactical weakness which must accompany such scandal. Such considerations make more understandable the harsh decision taken by Beza and his French disciples: to maintain "discipline" precisely as Calvin had left it, and to wipe out as completely as possible any criticism of it, no matter from what direction. They thus help to explain further the growing rigidity in which Calvinism found itself encased.

CHAPTER IV

Geneva and the French Wars of Religion, 1563-1572

A. The Peace of Amboise

1. *Immediate Protestant Reactions*

Transcending the internal problems of appropriate ecclesiastical organization, were certain external problems which the Reformed churches in France had to face during this period. These were the rude problems of survival, with which they had been faced from the beginning, and with which they had to grapple for decades in increasingly dangerous forms. For Protestant survival in France was repeatedly threatened by the massed powers of Roman Catholicism, led on the intellectual level by the increasingly alert and effective theologians clustered around the university in Paris, led on the political and military level by the increasingly well-organized Catholic nobility clustered around the Guise family, supported more often than not by the crown itself. The existence and character of opposition on the political and military level, goaded or tempted the Protestant party time and again to armed resistance. But armed resistance posed, as it must in any relatively civilized society, formidable problems of both moral and practical kinds. It is upon Geneva's continuing role in the resolution of these problems, that this chapter focuses.

At the very beginning of this period, two sharply different official Protestant responses to the problem of resistance became evident. They were quickly complicated by a clandestine response. The official responses became differentiated during the negotiations preceding the treaty of Amboise, which ended the first war of religion in 1563. These negotiations saw a sharp disagreement develop among Protestants over minimum acceptable terms for a peace settlement. This disagreement was quickly solidified by the formation of two factions. One was led by the Prince of Condé, then the principal leader of the Huguenot armies. It included most of the nobility. The other was headed by the Protestant pastors attached to the army headquarters in Orleans. Among them were many of the most distinguished religious leaders in the Reformed movement, many of them trained in Geneva, most notably Theodore Beza. It also included certain of the nobility, most prominently Gaspard de Coligny, the Admiral of France.

Briefly, the party of Condé was willing to make substantial concessions in return for peace. The party of the pastors pleaded for better terms, even at the risk of continued fighting. The argument centered on retention of the Edict of January, whose promulgation early in 1562 had touched off the first war of religion, and to whose maintenance the Protestants were pledged as a party. This edict had granted them legal toleration for the first time, permitting them freedom of worship in the suburbs to every municipality in France and in the private homes of every nobleman who supported their party. Protestant exercise of these rights had provoked the Duke of Guise into the massacre which had touched off the first war. The principle remaining military leader of the Catholic party, the Constable Montmorency, in preliminary negotiations with Condé, insisted that he would never accept a peace that required reinstatement of this edict.

At this point negotiations were broken off, and each leader retired for consultation with his advisers. Condé returned to his headquarters in Orleans and asked for the advice of both his military and ecclesiastical advisers. His request seems to have been in part a formality, since he was apparently already pretty well determined on peace, for military and political reasons. Still, since any settlement would affect the state of the churches so directly, he did feel obliged to ask for the advice of their spiritual leaders. In his request, Condé seems to have asked only that his advisers comment on a two-step plan of action: (1) he would ask for reinstatement of the Edict of January, since violation of it had caused him to take arms in the beginning; (2) if that failed (as he must have sensed it would), he would ask the Queen Regent to suggest other possible terms of peace to serve as a basis for further negotiation. Most of the nobility supported this tactical plan.[1]

The pastors reacted sharply against this plan, however. The three of their leaders with whom Condé first consulted urged that he insist on maintenance of the Edict. Condé then asked for a more extended and considered opinion from the pastors. Seventy-two of them accordingly gathered together and prepared a formal written proposal which was even more extreme. It asked that Condé not only insist on the confirmation and enforcement of the Edict of January. It also asked that he request full toleration of the Protestant administrative apparatus of consistories and synods, legal recognition of baptisms and marriages which Protestant pastors had performed, return of offices and property to Protestants who had been deprived of them for religious reasons, and punishment of those responsible for the massacre of Vassy and all other crimes in violation of the Edict. This last suggestion was a particularly daring one, since it could have involved punishment of men as prominent in the government as members of the Guise family. On top of all this, the pastors asked that Condé request legislation which would make it clear that Calvinism was the only tolerated form of Protestantism in France, and that would bring the full penalties of the heresy laws to bear against Atheists, Libertines, Anabaptists, and the followers of Servetus.[2]

This set of demands only served to anger Condé. Not only did he refuse to introduce them into his negotiations with the royal government. He also announced that he would no longer consult anyone but the nobility in matters of high policy. And he apparently kept his word. At least one chronicler reports that from then on no pastors were called to Condé's Council, and he

[1] See *Hist. eccl.*, II, 279, for Condé's proposal; p. 282 for advice of the nobility. See also J. A. de Thou, *Hist. univ.* (1740 ed.), III, 404-406.

[2] See *Hist. eccl.*, II, 279-282, for report of Condé's preliminary meeting with pastors Channorrier, Perez, and Chandieu, and for complete text of the proposal of the seventy-two pastors.

refused even to listen to their advice on problems of this sort.[1] He immediately plunged into final peace negotiations. They were quickly successful, and on March 19, 1563, the treaty of Amboise was signed. It permitted free Protestant worship in the country homes of Protestant noblemen, in one city to be assigned to Protestants in each "bailliage," and in the cities which they held on March 7. It also contained a pardon to Condé and his commanders for extraordinary financial and judicial measures which they had taken during the war. The treaty's list of areas in which Protestant worship was to be permitted was obviously somewhat more restrictive than the more general permission contained in the Edict of January. Furthermore the treaty made no mention of the other clauses proposed by the Protestant pastors.[2]

One Protestant nobleman reacted sharply against this agreement. He was the Admiral Coligny, second in rank only to Condé in the Huguenot armies. Coligny had not been present during the negotiations, and arrived in the Orleans camp only after the peace treaty had actually been signed, a few days before its official promulgation. He protested vigorously against the treaty's sharp reduction in the number of places where Protestant worship was tolerated, pointed out the considerable inconvenience even to the nobility of limiting services to their country homes and to a single town per "bailliage." He insisted that the Protestants at the moment actually possessed a military advantage, with two of the triumvirate who had commanded the opposing armies now dead, and he begged for exploitation of this advantage.[3] However Coligny arrived too late. Condé was not minded to reverse the course of events. Only four days after Coligny's appeal, the treaty was officially published and registered in Paris, and then immediately forwarded to other parts of the kingdom for registration in the courts which controlled the French provinces. The party led by the pastors was forced to accept peace. They did not do so with grace, however. Mobs in the Huguenot headquarters city of Orleans destroyed most of the church buildings which the treaty required be returned to Catholic authorities.[4] In a giant communion service, Beza, who had acted as one of Condé's principal advisers throughout the war, offered somewhat tepid thanks to God for the return of peace.[5] A few days later he left for Geneva, with bitter parting comments to the English ambassador on the behavior of the military leaders of the movement.[6] Perhaps it was partly to mollify Beza that Condé sent a letter to the Genevan Council, full of praise for Beza's help and regret at his departure.[7]

The Protestant split over the terms to be sought in these peace negotiations, had a number of important and continuing effects. For one, it revealed

---

[1] J. A. de Thou, *Hist. univ.* (1740 ed.), III, 405. Cf. the similar but less explicit statement in *Hist. eccl.*, II, 282.

[2] Full text in *Hist. eccl.*, II, 283-290.

[3] On Coligny's reactions, see *ibid.*, II, 335-336. Cf. Delaborde, *Coligny*, II, 250-252.

[4] *Hist. eccl.*, II, 290.

[5] Described in Smith to Elizabeth I, 31 March 1563, text in d'Aumale, *Condé*, I, 423-424.

[6] Reported by Myddlemore to Cecil, 30 March 1563, text in d'Aumale, *Condé*, I, 421. Cf. Beza's own report to Calvin, 29 March [1563], in Beza, *Corr.*, IV, 138-140.

[7] Condé to the Small Council of Geneva, 28 March 1563, text in d'Aumale, *Condé*, I, 402-403.

a rift between the religious and military leaders of the movement, in particular between the pastors and Condé, which was to grow. Condé continued to keep a chaplain at his court to provide himself, his family, and his retinue with religious consolation. But the man he had picked for this position, François Perrocelli or Pérussel, also called La Rivière, had not gained any particular prominence among the Calvinist pastors and had long played a role relatively independent of direction from Geneva or the synodical apparatus. And even Perrocelli had trouble handling Condé, particularly when, after the return of peace, he got involved in some rather spectacular love affairs at the royal court. Direct communication between Condé and the other pastors did not cease altogether. What there was of it, however, was not always calculated to narrow the breach. Calvin and Beza, for example, wrote Condé a rather petulant letter which, among other things, scolded him for the bad reputation he was gaining in circles influenced by doings at the court, for "making love to women." [1] While Condé liked this meddling in his personal life even less than ministerial meddling in his political decisions, he was not prepared to break with Geneva. A year after he had been scolded from Geneva for his amours, he sent a formal request to Geneva for assignment of a chaplain to his powerful colleague, the Marshall d'Estrées, who, in spite of Protestant sympathies, had fought on the royal side during the first war of religion. It was important that d'Estrées be lured further into the Protestant camp, since he had a position of pivotal military importance. He had commanded the royal artillery, for more than a century probably the best in Europe, and a key factor in anti-Protestant strength throughout most of the French religious wars. Geneva, of course, saw the importance of Condé's request, and promptly sent d'Estrées one of their very best young pastors, Jean Hellin.[2] Communications of this sort, however, were by no means frequent, and Condé obviously reached most of his decisions in the years that followed, without bothering to secure the pastors' advice. There is not even much record in Geneva of what those decisions were.

On the other hand, the link between the pastors and Coligny became tighter. Before long Jeanne d'Albret, the Queen of Navarre, acting on her own initiative now that her vacillating husband had died in the course of the first war, joined this circle. She was of crucial importance to the entire movement not only because of her not inconsiderable personal leadership, particularly in her domain lands in southwest France, but also because of her tutelage of young Henri of Navarre, the titular leader of the entire movement because of his blood relationship to the royal family. We have already observed how the resolution of the Morély affair strengthened the bonds among Beza, Coligny, and Jeanne. Those bonds were to become ever tighter in the course of the second and third wars of religion. They were to receive a final tightening at the Synod of La Rochelle, when the three actually met in person to cooperate at this key step toward consolidation of the entire French Reformed Church. And they meant that the connections between pastors

---

[1] In Calvin and Beza to Condé, 13 September 1563, in Beza, *Corr.*, IV, 201-202: "quant on orra dire que vous faites l'amour aux dames, cela est pour deroger beaucoup à vostre authorité et reputation."

[2] See Geneva, RCP, Kingdon & Bergier, eds., II, 111, on the receipt and fulfillment of this request.

and political leaders were important again on the eve of the disastrous St. Bartholomew's massacres.

The actual issues which divided nobility and ministry in the negotiations preceding Amboise also merit attention. They cast grave doubts on the facile generalization that the nobles wanted wars, the pastors peace. In this particular instance, the exact reverse was true. A generalization that comes nearer to the mark is that the nobles wanted change, the pastors maintenance of the *status quo*. While it was almost always groups of nobles who provoked actual fighting, either by plot or by mustering or both, it was also groups of nobles who were usually the first to demand peace when military considerations made that desirable. While the pastors often opposed the beginning of war, particularly if its beginnings lay in a foolhardy plot of some sort, once war was underway they generally wanted it to continue until some tangible advantages had been secured for the Protestant cause.

It was, of course, impossible for the Calvinist pastors in France to continue war without substantial noble support. So there was no course open to them and their remaining noble supporters but to accept the terms of the Peace of Amboise, and make the best of it. That this eminently sensible decision was not satisfactory to all Protestants, however, is revealed by one curious incident which occurred in Lyon, only weeks after the return of peace.

This was the publication of a curious pamphlet titled *La defense civile & militaire des innocens & de l'Eglise de Christ*, or *The Civil and Military Defense of the Innocents and of the Church of Christ*. It was published anonymously, without any indication of place of publication, although presumably one of the many Lyon's presses was responsible. Not a single copy of it seems to have survived the period of its publication. Fortunately we do have, however, an extended refutation of its argument, together with several comments on the circumstances of its publication and its suppression.

Briefly, this pamphlet seems to have argued for a right of popular armed resistance to established authorities, in a religious cause.[1] It was apparently more radical than almost all other early Protestant pleas for resistance, both the sketchy ones of earlier date and the fuller ones following the St. Bartholomew's massacres, in one important respect. It seems to have vested the right of resistance in the population as a whole, rather than in such constituted authorities as princes of the blood, the Estates of the realm, or the magistrates governing provinces and municipalities. This argument was apparently supported largely by an extended exegesis of certain passages in the Old Testament, describing Jewish revolts upon which God had looked with favor. Its author had also dipped into the Scriptural Apocrypha, for approving accounts of the Macchabean revolts. And he had ornamented his case with reference to the works of certain eminent contemporary thinkers. One of these was a book called the *Courtier*, probably the influential best seller of

[1] The summary which follows is based on the *Apologie de M. Charles du Moulin, contre un Livret, intitulé, La deffense civile & militaire des innocens & de l'Eglise de Christ* (1565), fully described and analyzed by Alfred Cartier, *Bibliographie des éditions des de Tournes, imprimeurs lyonnais* (Paris: Editions des bibliothèques nationales, 1937-1938), II, 530-535, and republished in C. du Moulin, *Opera*, V, xv-xxii. Cf. the analysis in Vittorio de Caprariis, *Propaganda e pensiero politico in Francia durante le guerre di religione*, I (1559-1572) (Naples: Edizioni Scientifiche Italiane, 1959), pp. 113-114.

that title by Baldassare Castiglione, the great Italian specialist on courtly etiquette, which contains several passages on the obedience due a prince. Others were certain of the works of Charles du Moulin, the great jurisconsult and sometime Calvinist. It was no doubt some of the more sharply anti-clerical and anti-papal passages in du Moulin's writings which attracted the anonymous writer. His attitude toward the *Courtier* was mixed. He seems to have cited with approval Castiglione's insistence that a courtier is not bound to obey treacherous or immoral commands of his prince, but criticized sharply the *Courtier's* claim that princes possessed a semi-divine status.[1]

Such an argument was bound to embarrass the leaders of French Protestantism. It gave color to Catholic charges that they had signed the treaty merely to gain time, and had no intention of keeping the peace any longer than necessary. And it gave fuel to the suspicions of men in established positions all over France, but particularly around the royal court, that there were elements within the Reformed movement which meant to subvert the entire institutional fabric of the country, elements of the same temper as the more violent Anabaptists of Germany.

The most prominent to react to this publication was the Seigneur de Soubize, the Governor of Lyon. He had been installed in that position by Condé, in July of 1562, shortly after the first war of religion had begun. But he had been confirmed in the office by the royal government, and was still in ultimate authority over the metropolis which then ranked second only to Paris in importance within France. Soubize must have been personally embarrassed by this publication, since his tenure in his important office depended upon the swift and efficient enforcement of royal commands, including those regulating religion. He must have been joined in embarrassment by the pastoral corps of the city of Lyon, then headed by the eloquent Pierre Viret. Viret's conviction that free preaching of the Protestant view could convert everyone, was apparently about to be offered an opportunity for demonstration, since in Lyon Protestant services were permitted by the Treaty of Amboise, thanks to the military seizure of the city by Huguenot troops during the war.[2]

Both Soubize and the pastors issued sharp public denunciations of the booklet. That by Soubize simply denounced it as seditious, prohibited its sale or shipment on pain of summary hanging, and ordered that all available

---

[1] See C. du Moulin, *Opera*, V, xxi-xxii, arts. 35, 36, 37, for discussion of references to the "Cortisan," not identified further; xviii, art. 1, for discussion of references to du Moulin's works, which he says were cited without naming their author. The anonymous writer of the *Defense* could have used one of several editions of the *Courtier* published in French since 1537, or one published in Italian in Lyon itself in 1562, just before his pamphlet appeared (see printed catalogue of Paris, Bibliothèque Nationale). His references to the *Courtier* would probably be to book II, arts. 23 and 24, on the limits of obedience due a prince, particularly if he commands something "disoneste e vituperose"; book IV, arts. 22 and 23, on the semi-religious status of a prince, "più presto semideo che omo mortale," in the Vittorio Cian annotated ed., *Il Cortegiano di Baldesar Castiglione*, 2nd ed. (Florence: Sansoni, 1910), pp. 171-174, 432-434.

[2] On Viret's ministry in Lyon, see R. D. Linder, *Viret*, pp. 45-50, and *passim*; on Viret's belief in conversion by peaceful means, see pp. 153 and ff. A later modification of the Treaty of Amboise stipulating that foreign-born Protestant pastors could not serve churches in France, forced Viret to leave Lyon in 1565.

copies of it be turned over to an official for public burning.[1] That by the pastors denounced its content, as " full of false and bad doctrine, conforming on several points to that of the Anabaptists, inducing men to sedition, rebellion, and disobedience of kings and princes," [2] and, after raising this Anabaptist bugaboo, denounced it particularly for having supported its contentions by perverting many passages of the Holy Scriptures.

Even these extreme statements and the apparently effective destruction of the entire press run of the book, were not enough to rescue the Protestant leaders of Lyon from their embarrassment. They immediately began a search for a scapegoat, the anonymous author of the pamphlet. That search led them in some interesting directions.

The first scapegoat pounced upon was none other than Charles du Moulin. That great legal authority happened to be in Lyon right then, and he had recently annoyed orthodox Calvinists considerably by publishing there his unauthorized catechism. Perhaps this annoyance led the Lyon pastors to accuse du Moulin of writing the seditious pamphlet. At least he himself charged that it did.[3] Or perhaps they were guided to this suspicion by the citations of du Moulin's writings in the pamphlet. At any rate, du Moulin was charged, jailed, and forced to exonerate himself.

Exoneration did not prove difficult. The charge was farfetched, as anyone familiar with du Moulin's career and writings must have known. If there is any one thread which runs through them all it is absolute loyalty to the French crown. He had fought with vigor and consistency against all attempts by papal agents to diminish the crown's powers in ecclesiastical matters. And in doing so he had made such a strong case for the prerogatives of the crown and the loyalty due it by subjects, that it is extremely improbable that he would have entertained even mild forms of a resistance theory. All this du Moulin was able to make clear quickly to Soubize and the others responsible for the administration of justice in Lyon. And he was soon released.[4]

To demonstrate his innocence fully and publicly, however, du Moulin published a detailed refutation of the seditious pamphlet. This refutation was given wide circulation and is, indeed, our only record of the precise contents of the pamphlet. Most of du Moulin's tract was devoted to a refutation of the anonymous author's exegesis of Scripture. He examined it verse by verse and illustration by illustration, with the general purpose of demonstrating that all the revolts sanctioned by the Bible were led by duly constituted agents of the government of Israel, by " inferior magistrates " to use the terminology of the sixteenth century, and that they were generally aimed against " tyrants " rather than against legitimately selected kings. He cited several of his own important early works, both to bolster his argument and to demonstrate his record of loyalty to the crown. He refuted in detail three of the pamphlet's references to the *Courtier*. At one point, he accused

---

[1] Text published in C. du Moulin, *Opera*, V, xxii.

[2] In text published in *ibid.* : " plein de fausse & mauvaise doctrine, conforme en aucuns poincts à celle des Anabaptistes, induisant les hommes à sedition, rebellion & desobeissance des Rois & Princes."

[3] In *ibid.*, V, 619.

[4] See account of his biographer, Julien Brodeau, in *ibid.*, I, 41.

the author of wanting to " turn this kingdom over into a popular Swiss state,"[1] a rather gratuitous swipe at the institutions of the country in which the Protestantism he professed to support had its deepest roots. His general opinion was that Christians had never had any proper recourse from tyranny but prayer for the conversion of their oppressors. And he felt that even this might not at present be necessary, since France was governed by a young prince who had offended no one and of whom much might be hoped.[2] With that typically obsequious assertion of loyalty to the crown, he concluded his argument.

The second scapegoat pounced upon as author of *The Civil and Military Defense* was Hugues Sureau, dit du Rosier. Reasons for the filing of charges against him are even more obscure than for those against du Moulin. He had not even been in Lyon at the time of the pamphlet's publication, but rather was on duty as a pastor in Orleans. In any event, he was seized and jailed shortly after one of his public debates with Roman Catholic controversialists, in 1566, and was held for several months of examination before finally being released as innocent.[3] It was during or just after this imprisonment that his correspondence with Morély was discovered and seized by the Calvinist leaders in Orleans, and used to discredit Morély decisively with the Queen of Navarre and Admiral Coligny. In the circumstances, the charges against Sureau might have originated on either side. Perhaps they were lodged by his Catholic opponents, seizing upon something he had said in the debates. Or perhaps they were suggested by his fellow Protestant clergymen, remembering something he had said at the time of the discussion among the pastors in Orleans over the treaty of Amboise, and irritated by his lack of sympathy for the Reformed system of church government. It is an interesting coincidence that both men accused before royal courts of writing this seditious pamphlet were prominent Protestants who happened at the moment to be at odds with the leaders of their Church. Perhaps it is no more than a coincidence.

While the author of this pamphlet was never identified, there is no question that it appeared. So did others with similar arguments.[4] And this fact is significant in itself. It reveals an undercurrent of hard-core Protestant determination to resist the royal government by force, which was to surface again and again in the succeeding years.

---

[1] In *ibid.*, V, xxi, art. 29: " Il semble que l'autheur dudit livret veuille renverser ce Royaume en un estat populaire de Suysse, à fin d'avoir occasion de pescher en eau trouble, & piller tout."

[2] In *ibid.*, V, xxii: " car nous avons un jeune Roy, qui n'offensa onques personne, & de qui l'on peut esperer autant de bien que de Prince qui fut jamais en ce Royaume."

[3] See above, p. 85, re this episode. De Caprariis, *op. cit.* in n. 1 to p. 153 above, p. 113, n. 127, argues that Sureau's later apostasy creates a presumption that he was indeed author of this tract. I do not understand this argument.

[4] E.g. *La juste et saincte defense de la ville de Lyon* (Lyon, 1563), reprinted in L. Cimber and F. Danjou, eds., *Archives curieuses de l'histoire de France*, 1er série, IV (Paris, 1835), 195-214, defending the Huguenot seizure of the city during the war, and denying that the Huguenots wanted to make of the city a " république " or a " canton " allied to the Swiss (p. 206). See also the lengthy refutation of this pamphlet, Gabriel de Saconay, *Discours des premiers troubles advenus a Lyon* (Lyon, 1569), reprinted in Cimber & Danjou, vol. cited, pp. 215-342.

2. *Continuing Rumors of Sedition*

Of more immediate importance than continuing Protestant resistance, was the Catholic fear of such resistance. Although based on only a kernel of reality, this fear was systematically fanned by the unscrupulous to proportions which on occasion approached hysteria. It provoked strident denials from the Protestants. Yet it also provoked reactions and events which made the open resumption of armed hostilities ever more inevitable. Another demonstration of these developments is provided by an incident which took place in 1564, the year following the return of peace, in the northern part of the kingdom.

At the end of April 1564, a provincial Synod of the Reformed churches of Picardy, Champagne, Brie, and the Ile-de-France, met in the town of La Ferté-sous-Jouarre. Antoine de la Roche Chandieu was elected president and the session of the Synod continued for the better part of a week. Its deliberations were carefully documented, and by chance those documents survive, giving us an almost unique view of the workings of a sixteenth-century French provincial Synod. Much of the Synod's time was occupied, as we have already noted, by consideration of Morély's plea to be reconciled with the Church.[1] That plea was considered gingerly but favorably and reconciliation was agreed upon, provided Morély fulfilled certain conditions. Most of the rest of the Synod's time was devoted to a wide variety of relatively routine matters. Assignments of pastors to particular parishes were accomplished or confirmed. Questions about the proper administration of sacraments and rites in certain unusual circumstances were settled. And one man was dismissed from the ministry.

That dismissal was to have fateful consequences. The man dismissed, Pierre Denise, promptly sent to someone with access to the royal Court what purported to be a full account of the Synod's deliberations.[2] And Denise's account was inflammatory. It claimed that the Synod was devoted almost entirely to discussion of political matters, and that it concluded with the preparation of plans for a monstrous conspiracy. Denise said that the Synod had begun with the reading of a letter from Beza, warning the churches that the Catholics were raising money to exterminate them and urging the churches to get in touch with Protestants across the northern border in Flanders. The Synod had then proceeded to a general discussion of the current state of events in France. Pastors Chandieu and Cappel had said, according to Denise, that the churches would never have peace as long as the Queen Mother Catherine de Medicis remained as regent, that the government of France was a tyranny, and that there was no legitimate magistrate in the entire realm. The Synod then turned to consideration of specific measures that could be taken in this situation. Perrocelli, Condé's chaplain, was asked to recommend the cause of the Church to his master. The Prince of

---

[1] See above, pp. 67-69.

[2] The summary which follows is based on a photocopy of the manuscript version in London, PRO (S.P. 70), vol. 73, No. 469-II, fols. 33-34, an extended summary of which can be found in *Calendar of State Papers, Foreign, 1564-1565*, No. 358. Cf. the slightly different copy sent to Cardinal Granvelle, published in Ch. Weiss, ed., *Papiers d'état du cardinal de Granvelle* (Paris, 1841-1852), VII, 528-531, No. CXVIII, and in BSHPF, IV (1856), 196-198.

Porcien allegedly sent a letter to the Synod through his pastor promising full support to their machinations. Certain gentlemen were deputized to begin raising money for the cause. Troops were to be raised in Flanders. An armed assembly was called for Pentecost, when it could meet disguised as a religious observance. Guards were to be posted along the frontier between Picardy and the north.

It is highly unlikely that there was much truth behind this lurid report. But it did seem plausible. A provincial Synod had met on the days specified. Denise had been in attendance. Practically all of the people he mentioned by name were in fact there, fulfilling the functions he said they fulfilled. There appear to be some obvious slips in vocabulary, however. No loyal Protestant scribe would have called his Church the "pretended Reformed religion" ("religion pretendue reformee"), as did one version of the report supplied by Denise, or his fellow churchmen "huguenots," as did another version.[1]

True or not, the Denise report was a godsend to the Catholic party at the royal Court. It provided what seemed like hard evidence for a contention which this party had insisted on for years: that Protestantism was seditious, a direct menace to the crown and the entire institutional fabric it headed. The Denise report was consequently immediately given wide publicity, not only in France but abroad. Manuscript copies of it were presented to ambassadors to the Court of France, and forwarded home by some of them.[2] Among the leading foreign statesmen we know to have received copies were William Cecil, Lord Burghley, then serving as principal minister in the government of Queen Elizabeth I of England, and Cardinal Granvelle, the trusted adviser to King Philip II of Spain, then serving as his principal minister in the Netherlands. A propaganda maneuver of this type was not unusual in the sixteenth century. Circulation of false charges of sedition was tried again by the French crown in 1572, to excuse its responsibility for the St. Bartholomew's massacres. And circulation of partially false charges of sedition was tried by the English crown in 1583, to justify its savage persecution of Jesuit and other Catholic missionaries sent into England from the continent.

French Protestants could obviously not let the 1564 challenge pass. An elaborate refutation of the Denise report coupled with a justification of the Protestant position was prepared by Chandieu and a few associates and quickly forwarded to the King.[3] The refutation began with a fairly elaborate explanation of the reasons for the meeting of the synods, and indeed for the entire synodical system. This introduction suggests bad consciences among the Protestant party. The royal government in its toleration edicts had

[1] For the former, London, PRO (S.P. 70), vol. 73, No. 469-II fol. 33v. For the latter, the Ch. Weiss ed. cited in n. 2 to p. 157, p. 529.

[2] A post-script to the letter which accompanied the batch of these manuscripts sent to England, noted that this document had been distributed to the ambassadors at the French court. Sir Thomas Smith, an English diplomat in France, to Cecil, 12 July 1564, in London, PRO (S.P. 70), vol. 73, No. 469, fol. 24, summarized in *Calendar of State Papers, Foreign, 1564-1565*, No. 553.

[3] The summary which follows is based on a photocopy of the manuscript version in London, PRO (S.P. 70), vol. 73, No. 469-III, fols. 35-40. Cf. the brief summary in *Calendar of State Papers, Foreign, 1564-1565*, No. 359.

never granted permission for the calling of synods. The request of the pastors at Orleans in 1563 for such permission had been pointedly ignored. Technically, the synods were probably illegal. Chandieu's claim that this one had been authorized by the Prince of Condé's wife,[1] seems rather lame. In any case, Chandieu insisted that synods were necessary. They fought the danger of heresy, which any policy of toleration aroused. They repressed vice. They maintained ecclesiastical discipline. Surely all of these laudable aims met the approval of His Majesty. Chandieu did not dwell on his belief that the use of synods was also commanded by Scripture.

The refutation then turned to a bitter personal denunciation of Denise. He was an apostate monk who had slyly insinuated himself into the Protestant ministry. From the beginning he had proved himself deceitful and untrustworthy. During the late war he had revealed even more dangerous tendencies, had actually entered the fighting, and had killed a man with his own hands, in cold blood. All these qualities had obviously made him an unsuitable pastor, and he had accordingly been deposed.

These rather lengthy preliminaries out of the way, the refutation settled on its business of demonstrating to the King the loyalty of his Protestant subjects. It listed all of Denise's more extreme statements and flatly denied that any such matters had even been discussed, much less decided upon. It denied, for example, that the Synod had discussed any letter from Beza. It pointed out that in its main item of business, the disciplining of Morély, Chandieu at one point had actually taxed Morély for tending to diminish the authority and power of the magistrate with one of his arguments for popular control of the machinery of church government. It reported that Chandieu had bolstered this argument by explanation of the Word of God, and that Morély had protested that he had never intended to suggest a limiting of secular power. This claim is substantially confirmed by the acts of the Synod.[2] The refutation also reported that all the pastors present at the Synod were instructed to admonish their flocks, and particularly the noblemen within them, to obey scrupulously all of the royal edicts. This claim, too, is confirmed by the acts.[3]

But the refutation did not rest its case on these matters of detail alone. It also insisted that as a matter of principle the French Reformed were devoted and obedient subjects of the King. It claimed that obedience to kings and princes, and avoidance of seditious activity, had been cardinal tenets of all their books and sermons, and was incorporated within their Confession of Faith, in every case firmly rooted in appropriate explanations of Holy Scripture. And it insisted that Protestant leaders had been among the first to attack recent pleas for revolt—specifically the "Epistle of Villegaignon," about one of the ringleaders in the abortive Conspiracy of Amboise back in 1560, and "a booklet made public in Lyon before the troubles,"[4] perhaps *The*

[1] London, PRO (S.P. 70), vol. 73, No. 469-III, fol. 36.

[2] *Ibid.*, fol. 38v., confirmed by *ibid.*, No. 469-I, fol. 28v., reporting on a synodical committee's findings of the defects in Morély's argument. See above, p. 68, for further comment.

[3] *Ibid.*, No. 469-III, fol. 39v., confirmed by *ibid.*, No. 469-I, fol. 29v. Perrocelli, Condé's chaplain, had suggested adoption of this resolution.

[4] *Ibid.*, No. 469-III, fols. 37v.-38 : "lepistre de Villegaignon et en ung livret divulgue a Lyon devant les troubles."

Civil and Military Defense, although this does not seem to have been published before the first war. All of this had a somewhat hollow ring from Chandieu, who had himself been implicated in the Conspiracy of Amboise.[1] It seems to have represented the official Protestant view at this period, however. Certainly it represented what Protestant leaders wanted the Court to think was their view.

This defense of the Synod also received wide circulation. Sir Thomas Smith, English ambassador to the French court, sent a copy of it to Cecil, along with Denise's damning report, and a copy of the authentic acts of the Synod. This last he thought would be of interest to the Archbishop of Canterbury and the Bishop of London, quite apart from its importance in the context of the present controversy, for what it revealed of the way in which a French Reformed synod operated.[2] It is perhaps not surprising that there seems to be no copy of the refutation among Granvelle's papers. It would be only natural for Catholic powers to value and keep the Denise attack, and for Protestant powers to value and keep the Chandieu refutation.

It is not easy to connect this polemical exchange directly with any turns in royal policy. But it is at least possible that it had something to do with the harsher line the royal government took in succeeding months. Violations of the Amboise Treaty's terms by Catholic officials or mobs became more common, partly because they were not punished systematically. And the royal government itself promulgated several interpretations of the treaty which tended to limit further the scope of the toleration it provided. The act among them which was most probably directly inspired by the reports of the La Ferté Synod was the Edict of Roussillon. It was promulgated on August 4, 1564, less than four months after the meeting of the Synod. Among its clauses was one flatly forbidding the meeting of any synods or similar groups, local or national.[3] We have already noted how this affected the Protestant quarrel over church organization, when Morély apparently attempted to dissuade the Cardinal of Châtillon from negotiating for permission to hold synods.[4] Most Protestants were in no mood to abandon them, however, and the Morély controversy only stiffened this mood. The Prince of Condé, the leading temporal spokesman for the Protestant party, issued strenuous protests against the Roussillon prohibition.[5] Synods continued to meet, both on the provincial and national levels, whenever they could be safely arranged. But it had become clearer than ever that they were illegal. And the tensions fed, among other things, by Catholic suspicions of Protestant synodical activities, continued to rise until they boiled over into renewed war.

---

[1] See H. Naef, *Conjuration d'Amboise*, p. 481, n. 3, and *passim*.

[2] Postscript from Smith to Cecil, 12 July 1564, in London, PRO (S.P. 70), vol. 73, No. 469, fol. 24.

[3] A paragraph outlining rules for Protestant pastors ends: " Leur defandans, & à tous ceulx de ladicte Religion sous pareilles peines, toutes assemblees en forme de Synode, & toute cotisation & levee de deniers." On fol. Biv of the text of the *Lettres patentes* announcing this edict, printed in 1564 by the royal printer Robert Estienne, copy in Geneva, BPU, cote: Ba 4326. The text of this edict is not included in such general collections of French laws as Isambert's.

[4] See above, pp. 89-90 and n. 1.

[5] See *Mémoires de Condé* (1743 ed.), V, in Condé to the Queen Mother, 31 August 1564, p. 203; in Condé's accompanying *Advertissement*, pp. 208-209.

Lettres patétes

DV ROY, POVR L'EN-
TRETENEMENT ET ENTIE-
re execution de l'Edict & declaration de la Pacificatió des troubles de só Royaume pour le faict de la Religion.

A PARIS,
Par *Robert Estienne Imprimeur du Roy*
M. D. LXIIII.
Auec priuilege dudict Seigneur.

B. The Renewal of War: Geneva and the Conspiracy of Meaux

The second French war of religion began in 1567, ending the uneasy truce which had prevailed since 1563. This time war was provoked directly by a Protestant plot, in which Condé, Coligny, and all the other great leaders of the Huguenot party were involved, the so-called Conspiracy of Meaux. The purpose of this chapter is to weigh Geneva's role in this event.

For several years, it had seemed clear to French Protestants that war was soon to begin again. Sporadic local violations of the toleration provisions of the Treaty of Amboise and repeated national limitations of their scope by succeeding edicts of interpretation, irritated Protestants generally and made them suspect that a concerted effort to stamp out their party was in the offing.[1] This suspicion deepened at the time of the Interview of Bayonne in 1565. The Interview itself was a spectacular formal meeting between the young King of France, Charles IX, and his sister, the new Queen of Spain, arranged and superintended by their mother, the Queen Regent of France, Catherine de Medicis, and attended by a number of ministers prominent in both governments. While much of the meeting was taken up with the pageantry and pomp with which sixteenth-century royalty clothed its official movements, the ministers took advantage of the opportunity for an extended exchange of views on matters of high policy. Everyone knew that among the matters discussed were the problems created by the patent inability of different religious groups to live together peacefully in the same state, problems which had already caused one bitter war in France and which were then provoking alarming riots in the Spanish Netherlands. And many suspected that the outcome of Bayonne was an understanding that the French and Spanish crowns would pool their tremendous resources in a joint effort to stamp out Protestantism in both realms.[2] Fresh color was given to this suspicion by the immediate steps taken by the Spanish crown to organize military repression of Protestantism in the Netherlands. The Duke of Alva, who had attended the Bayonne Interview and who was later reported, perhaps unjustly, to have advised the French there that in dealing with the religious problem they should go after the big salmon rather than the little frogs,[3] and eliminate the leaders of the Protestant party, was given a chance to try out this recipe himself. He was sent to Italy to organize a crack army of the best fighting men in Europe. It was arranged that this army should march north in 1567, through Savoy, Spanish-owned Franche Comté, and Lorraine, to the Netherlands. The Dukes of Savoy and Lorraine gave the Spanish formal permission to follow this route. A glance at a map will make it clear that this Spanish army would be marching along the French frontiers all the way, and that it had to pass close to the city of Geneva.

---

[1] See *Mémoires de Condé* (1743 ed.), V, 201-204, Condé's complaint to the Queen Mother, 31 August 1564, about the edicts of interpretation, particularly the Edict of Roussillon; 204-214, Condé's *Advertissement*, expanding this argument, and complaining of failure to enforce the Treaty of Amboise.

[2] For a study in depth of the Interview of Bayonne and the suspicions it engendered, see Erich Marcks, *Die Zusammenkunft von Bayonne* (Strassburg, 1889).

[3] Quoted from de la Noue in J.-A. de Thou, *Hist. univ.* (1740 ed.), III, 551, and from P. Matthieu in J. Delaborde, *Coligny*, II, 390.

This prospect alarmed the Protestants of Switzerland and France thoroughly. Their first fears were for Geneva itself.[1] Early warnings from Berne of the projected Spanish march led the Genevans to check their defenses and to borrow very large sums of money, from individuals in the city, from such financial centers as Basel, and from certain of the French Reformed churches.[2] They also seem to have made a number of discreet appeals for armed support. The responses to these appeals were prompt and substantial. Offers of aid were pressed upon Geneva by its powerful ally Berne, in turn supported by its allies, the Catholic and Protestant cantons of central Switzerland. These neighbors of Geneva, always wary of the entry of any really powerful military force onto the Swiss plateau or its approaches, wanted to station a large armed garrison in the city to protect it against surprise attack, with a further even larger force in reserve in case the city had to sustain an extended siege. Offers of aid were also received from certain of the French Reformed leaders most sympathetic to Geneva. They were prepared to loan Geneva large sums of money, which could be used to finance its defense, and were also willing to help in other ways.

The Genevan municipal authorities found these many offers of support somewhat embarrassing. While they were glad to have Bernese and Swiss forces as a reserve which they could fall back upon, they did not want to have any in the city itself, unless they were faced with a clear emergency. And their negotiations for loans seemed so promising, that they were not inclined to accept yet more money from the French, particularly since the French wanted to attach certain strings to their loan. They did ask the French to supply a small garrison, for the few months when the Spanish armies were actually passing through the vicinity. A troop of three hundred men, under the command of Paul de Richieu, sire de Mouvans, was accordingly quickly installed in the city, and funds were collected from the French Reformed churches to pay for the expenses of its maintenance.[3] However nominal command even of this unit was kept in the hands of a native Genevan.

Most of these negotiations were conducted by Geneva's secular magistrates. But the city's pastors were not unaware of them. Beza, at least, even participated actively in a number of them. That participation we shall examine in some detail in later chapters.[4]

Fears for Geneva soon faded. It became clear that Alva's armies had no intention of attacking the city. They skirted it miles to the west, and

---

[1] For accounts of the measures taken to warn and defend Geneva, see A. Roget, *Hist. de Genève*, VII, ch. IX ; J.-A. Gautier, *Hist. de Genève*, IV, 579-601. On the extent to which this threat to Geneva was real, see Lucien Cramer, *La seigneurie de Genève et la maison de Savoie de 1559 à 1603*, I (Geneva and Paris, 1912), 165-175.

[2] See, e.g., Geneva, Arch., Finances U, No. 1, Carnet de l'Arche, 1551-1568, especially fols. 232v.-233, re a loan from the Reformed Church of Lyon, installments of which were paid 25 February, 27 March, and 24 April 1567 ; fols. 234v.-235, re a loan from Basel ; fols. 235v.-236, re a loan from Claude Antoine de Vienne, sire de Clervans, a refugee noble, 18 June 1567. For more information on these and other loans and their consequences, see E. William Monter, *Studies in Genevan Government (1536-1605)* (Geneva : Droz, 1964), pp. 28 and ff. ; and " Le change public à Genève, 1568-1581," in *Mélanges Antony Babel* (Geneva, 1963), I, 266 and ff. See also above, pp. 24-26, re the Geneva pastors' reactions to the subsequent developments.

[3] See below, pp. 178-183, for more both on Mouvans and on the financing of this garrison.

[4] In chapters 4-C-2 and 4-C-3, below.

marched off through Franche-Comté, in the direction of the Netherlands. This did not allay the fears of the Protestants in France, however. It simply transferred them to France itself. This transfer was aided by the decision of the French crown to enroll within the royal armies a substantial body of Swiss mercenary infantry. In May of 1567, the ambassador accredited by the French government to the Swiss cantons, Pomponne de Bellièvre, was instructed to muster immediately a troop which had been promised to the French earlier in the year. He rammed through the final negotiations quickly, and by the end of July a Swiss army of about 6000 men was ready to head into France.[1] The official reason for recruiting the Swiss was that they were needed to guard against any attack by Alva, the northern frontier of France, especially the Picardy-Flanders frontier, near which were many of the Protestant strongholds Alva had been instructed to reduce.[2] And this may well have been the real reason, since sixteenth-century powers were always wary of each other. Even the Duke of Savoy had taken care to garrison the towns through which he had permitted Alva's armies to pass. But French Protestants had trouble accepting this explanation. With the French and Spanish crowns in apparent alliance, they could not believe the official explanation for the French recruiting of mercenaries. The move seemed to them to be another piece of a giant anti-Protestant plot. The Swiss would be used for a coup de grace, to destroy a movement already sapped by local harassment and royal indifference.

At this tense juncture, the military leaders of the French Protestant party held several secret meetings, in the fortified homes of Condé and the Colignys, at Valéry and Châtillon-sur-Loing.[3] The result of these meetings was the Conspiracy of Meaux. Some of these leaders at first opposed violent action. The Admiral Coligny may have been among them.[4] They seem to have feared that violence would anger unnecessarily the young King, who was about to reach his majority and was growing restive under his mother's tutelage, and would dangerously solidify opposition to the Protestant cause. But the day was carried by d'Andelot, the youngest of the Coligny brothers. He made an impassioned plea for action, arguing that it was the only way to avoid piecemeal extermination. His appeal won over the majority in attendance, including his brother, the Admiral. The group then prepared a plan of action. It was decided that an armed troop would be organized to approach the royal Court and to attempt forcibly to strip it of its Swiss guards and hostile advisers. This would amount to a capture of the Court, much like that by the Duke of Guise in 1562, which had precipitated the first war of religion. Simultaneously, Protestant forces would seize a number of widely scattered cities with strong Protestant factions in their populations. With the King and Regent cut off from such Catholic advisers as the Cardinal of Lorraine, and with positions of strength in many parts of the country, the Protestants would be in a position to demand more toleration for their form

[1] E. Rott, *Représentation*, II, 69-70.

[2] Reported, for example, by Norris to Elizabeth I, 29 August 1567, text in d'Aumale, *Condé*, I, 561.

[3] These meetings are described in detail by de la Noue, quoted in J. Delaborde, *Coligny*, 480-485, and by J.-A. de Thou, *Hist. univ.* (1740 ed.), IV, 2-6.

[4] So J. Delaborde, *Coligny*, I, 482, n. 1, ff. d'Aubigné.

of worship, and to make their demands stick. The Prince of Condé was again placed in charge of the entire enterprise.

In accordance with this decision, Protestant mobilization began. Orders went out from Valéry and from Châtillon-sur-Loing to Protestant fighting men all over France. The network of churches was again used to pass the word along. And troops of men began filtering through the countryside to Rosay-en-Brie, the point of rendezvous. All of this was supposed to be taking place in the highest secrecy. But as men discovered again and again during this century, it was hard to keep truly secret an operation of this size, requiring weeks to bring to fruition. Repeated rumors of a Protestant plot reached the royal Court, which was then traveling through northern France, approaching Paris. The rumors made the Court hurry to join forces with the Swiss mercenaries who were also marching into France along a northern route, toward Paris. A particularly explicit rumor persuaded the Court to take refuge in the fortified town of Meaux, on September 26. It joined forces there with a strong force of Swiss pikemen. On September 28, when the Prince of Condé and much of the small army he had gathered in secrecy approached the royal suite as it marched along the road from Meaux to Paris, he was not only refused audience, but kept away physically from the members of the royal family and the chief courtiers by hundreds of Swiss brandishing pikes.[1]

The critical first move of the Protestant plotters thus failed. Its only result was to infuriate the King and the Queen Regent. Once in Paris, with the military, popular, and logistic support which the capital could provide, there was no way to smoke the royal family out except by major military action. Condé, moving to Saint-Denis on the northern edge of the capital, resolved to do just that. The plans to seize provincial cities had already succeeded in a number of places, occasionally with flare-ups of savage violence. In Nîmes, for example, several dozen leading Catholics, many of them priests, were massacred and their bodies dumped into a huge public well.[2] So war began.

Of particular importance to this study, is the role of Geneva and its pastors in this war-producing plot. In brief, it seems minimal. In 1562, when the first war of religion began, Beza and most of the delegation of prominent pastors assembled for the Colloquy of Poissy, were still in France, advising Condé and his aides closely. This time Beza was in Geneva, at his pastoral post. Most of the other spiritual leaders of the French Reformed Church were similarly at their posts. The accounts of the meetings at Valéry and Châtillon-sur-Loing make no mention of any pastors being present. While it is at least possible that those who were chaplains to such leaders as Condé and Coligny were consulted, and even more likely that they knew what was going on, I have found no evidence that they played an important part in the decisions for war.

---

[1] For a description of these events, see d'Aumale, *Condé*, I, 290-296.

[2] Described in gory detail in Léon Ménard, *Histoire civile, ecclésiastique, et litteraire de la ville de Nismes*, V (Paris, 1754), 9-24. The Reformed Consistory met just as this massacre was ending and tried to punish its perpetrators, but without much success: pp. 22-23.

Furthermore, there is a distinct ambiguity in the public manifestos and formal demands which were issued from Saint-Denis in Condé's name, to justify the Protestant recourse to arms. One of the earliest blamed the war primarily on the wicked intrigues and usurpations of the Guise family. A later one added complaints about usurpation of the rightful place of the nobility, taxes, and Italians in public life, as well as about religious persecution. Only one of the latest made the religious issue central, devoting itself largely to demands that toleration of public Protestant services be extended by law and protected by government. The latter two also included appeals for the convocation of the Estates-General in order to resolve these problems peacefully.[1] Obviously Condé, in the beginning at least, did not want to rely solely on Protestant support in the approaching hostilities.

The Genevans do not seem even to have known that war had actually begun until about a week after the Conspiracy of Meaux had been exposed. Early in October the Company of Pastors received word that Lyon had been seized and that " the troubles of France " were starting again. The Company immediately ordered special prayers and repentance.[2] It also persuaded the city Council to order, on October 3, a special public fast.[3]

Condé's failure to seek the pastors' advice on what was, among other things, both a moral problem of considerable importance to his century and a practical problem of supreme importance to his Church, should not surprise. He had been cool to the pastors since 1563. But Coligny's failure to seek such advice is something of a surprise, since he had been moving closer to the pastors in the preceding months, and had been in particularly close touch with Beza. It may be, however, that he did seek some advice from Beza, albeit in a very guarded and highly general way. This is at least suggested by an extended letter which Beza wrote to him, apparently sometime either in 1566 or 1567.[4] This letter is not a *pièce de circonstance*, directed to the resolution of specific problems then facing French Protestants. It is rather a relatively abstract treatise on what should be the proper relations between Church and State, between the spiritual ministry and the secular magistrate. The letter from Coligny to which this was an answer has apparently been lost. But it is intriguing to suppose that scruples of conscience disturbing Coligny either before or after the Conspiracy of Meaux, may have occasioned it. At any rate, Beza's letter merits an extended analysis. Quite apart from its relevance to the events of 1567, it is one of the most considered and most important statements he ever made on relations between Church and State.

[1] For texts of these documents, taken from La Popelinière, see J. Delaborde, *Coligny*, II, 609-616, Nos. 31, 32, and 33. See below, pp. 170-171, re the diplomacy surrounding the issuance of these documents.

[2] Geneva, Arch., RCP, Bl, fols. [34-34v.] : "Au commencement d'Octobre vindrent nouvelles de la prinse de Lion et des troubles de France recommenceans. Pourtant fut signifié le jeusne publiq et toute l'eglise exhortée à prieres extraordinaires et repentance."

[3] A. Roget, *Hist. de Genève*, VII, 237-238.

[4] The analysis which follows is based on a photographic copy of Beza to Coligny, no date, in Amsterdam, Universiteits-Bibliotheek, III E 3, early unsigned copy, and upon a transcript of this Amsterdam copy prepared by Professor Henri Meylan of Lausanne. I am indebted to Professor Meylan, for calling this letter to my attention and for generously loaning me his transcript. And I am indebted to Jon C. Swan for ordering the photographic copy for me in Amsterdam. On the setting of the letter's date in 1566 or 1567, see below, n. 1 to p. 170.

In organization, Beza's letter to Coligny is divided into pairs of sharp dichotomies, a kind of organization which can easily be diagramed, which was very common in pedagogical works of this and immediately succeeding generations, and which Peter Ramus did so much to popularize.[1] Beza, of course, would doubtless have denied any debt to Ramus for his own use of the pattern, given his dislike for the man, although the years of their bitterest controversy were still to come.

Beza began by stating the general problem with which he was dealing. He knew that pastors had often been accused of usurping political power. He wanted so to delimit the realms of ecclesiastical and political power that in the future ambitious pastors would be restrained from attempting such usurpation, and those who calumniate the ministry would be silenced. He then proceeded to develop his first basic dichotomy. It was the classic one between the political and ecclesiastical powers that jointly rule man. He took it to be an axiom which all men of intelligence would accept, that God had created two governments—the political, to govern "the tranquillity of this world," and the ecclesiastical, to govern "the conscience, and the eternal life." And he argued that much of what appertains to each government is so obvious that it needs no discussion. Even Roman Catholic ecclesiastics, he noted, conceded that when they collected taxes and handled judicial proceedings, they were employing the "temporal sword," and not the spiritual. But he did concede that there were areas in which it was hard to draw the line between political and ecclesiastical authority. In fact he suggested that anyone involved in one domain was necessarily partially involved in the other. The areas of overlap which he examined first, stem from the ecclesiastical right to govern matters of conscience. Some people, Beza noted, while they would permit preachers to criticize private vice, objected to their attempts to keep public actions moral. To resolve this problem, Beza argued, one had to remember that a key function of ecclesiastical government was to maintain the "peace and tranquillity of the conscience of each," just as a key function of secular government was to maintain the "peace and tranquillity of the present life."

From this argument Beza drew two basic conclusions, which balanced each other and which provided the basic dichotomy around which the rest of his essay was structured. The first was that all action, either public or private, had to be done in good conscience, and that it was up to pastors to work toward this end. The second was that, since public tranquillity depended on the peaceful and orderly worship of God and this in turn depended on the relations among men in society, the secular government had an obligation to protect the Church from all "perturbators of the true religion, as the most dangerous enemies of the public." He then proceeded to discuss each conclusion in more detail.

The first conclusion Beza proved by an examination of passages in Scripture, particularly those recording the actions of the Old Testament prophets. The counter-argument that the age of prophecy has passed he brushed aside as irrelevant: the Word of God still existed and so did its ministers, even if special visions were no longer granted to them. He then

---

[1] As Walter J. Ong demonstrates in his *Ramus, Method, and the Decay of Dialogue* (Cambridge, Mass.: Harvard, 1958).

proceeded to examine what the pastors' power to govern consciences meant. To begin with, it obviously meant a right to condemn all criminals—not only those who blasphemed or lapsed into idolatry, but also those who murdered, robbed, counterfeited, or became involved in sedition. All such had violated God's Word, and in so doing had incurred spiritual as well as civil penalties. The types of penalties, of course, had to vary. The civil state might jail, examine, torture if necessary, and then punish, even with death. The Church should apply only spiritual penalties. And these could not be applied by one man alone, "for in the Church of God, there is no monarch but Jesus Christ." Rather they had to be applied by the regularly constituted body of elders, as Scripture requires. Here Beza was apparently defending the institution of the consistory. But he quickly moved on.

Cases of conscience of this type were not the only ones which it was the responsibility of the pastors to examine, however. Even matters of high policy had to be examined. Beza did not want to insist that pastors must sit regularly in the Council of Princes. But he did insist that no political decision should be taken except by a conscience "informed by the Word of God." And it was the duty of pastors to so inform consciences. This was not a duty he would institutionalize. Christian lords and magistrates should have the discretion to seek advice from their pastors when they needed it.

Beza then turned to examine the particular problems that faced the Church in an area which, like France and unlike Geneva, was largely ruled by magistrates who were still "contrary for the most part to the Gospel." He acknowledged the fact that many French Protestants felt it expedient in these circumstances to establish political assemblies, independent of regular ecclesiastical institutions, in which experienced laymen alone would handle, where possible, the secular affairs of the Protestant community.[1] He saw a number of plausible arguments for these assemblies, but he was inclined to side with Calvin, whom he quoted as having formally opposed such institutions as not provided for by Scripture. He also felt, perhaps mindful of the criticisms of men like du Moulin, that the establishment of such assemblies would expose the churches to charges of trying to usurp secular government. All in all, he concluded that if it was really necessary to set up these assemblies they should definitely be temporary and extraordinary, never permanent. These assemblies, as Beza described them, would be made up primarily of lay leaders, although they might invite in pastors as consultants. They would not be chosen by the regular machinery of the sort which chose members of consistories.

Next Beza argued for yet another role for the pastors. He felt that the great "Seigneurs and Gentlemen to whom God has given the heart and the power necessary to conserve his poor churches in the state to which they are now reduced," must consult their spiritual advisers. "I would pray and exhort them in the name of God not to conclude or undertake anything, without having been confirmed in their counsel (or council—"conseil") by those of the ministers of the kingdom they know to be the best versed in

[1] Political assemblies of this type became a regular French Reformed institution following the St. Bartholomew's massacres. For a history of them, see Léonce Anquez, *Histoire des assemblées politiques des réformés de France (1573-1622)* (Paris, 1859).

Scriptures." [1] This amounted to an emphatic plea for a pastoral voice in the high councils of the Huguenot party. It applied directly to meetings of the sort which preceded the Conspiracy of Meaux. One cannot help wonder if either Beza or Coligny thought of this. In this letter, however, Beza did not push the point further. He mentioned no names and pointed to no specific decisions. He simply laid this principle out as a basic guide line. And he turned to the second of his two main conclusions.

In some ways this second conclusion, which granted the civil authority certain powers in areas normally thought of as religious, can be regarded as a balance to Beza's first conclusion. In return for the rather strong demands of civil authority which he made under his first heading, he offered the substantial concession of power to regulate religious dissent. And his way of putting it, did give the entire argument a geometric sort of balance. But closer consideration makes it obvious that in this second area, too, Beza was trying to strengthen a basic principle of Calvinism.

Again he began with a proof. He cited a number of Old Testament kings who suppressed false religion by force, and added to them the Christian emperors from Constantine to Charlemagne. He insisted, however, that it was not for the secular ruler to make specific judgments of specific people in this area. All he had to do was to learn to recognize the only true Church. Then he had to support that Church with all his authority. The divinely ordained mechanism for suppressing false religion, the assembled pastors and elders within each church, would handle the specifics. It would ferret out the individual troublemakers who disturbed the discipline of the Church, and the heretics who spread false doctrine. Again Beza named no names. But he was no doubt thinking of some specific people. Morély would seem to be a particularly good example of the type he would regard as a troublemaker. Alamanni, the Italian sacramentarian who had upset the Lyon Church and whom Beza had helped to disgrace and drive away from Lyon in 1566,[2] would seem to be a good example of the type he would regard as a heretic.

Beza granted that some would urge modifications in the actual application of this principle in the current situation. He singled out for further consideration two concrete suggestions for modification. One was that greater moderation be used in the disciplining of church members who had strayed from the narrow path. The other was that disciplinary actions in important cases should only be taken after consultation with other churches, or in a synod. The plea for moderation he rejected in general, although he reluctantly conceded the possibility of minor modifications, provided they were uniform. But the primitive Church, he insisted, was so harsh that, in comparison, the discipline of the contemporary Church "is only sugar." And the law of God is absolute. Not even the angels can change it. The leniency which might be permitted by secular authorities in matters which

[1] In Beza to Coligny, described in n. 4 to p. 166, 6th page: "Et quant aux Seigneurs et Gentilshommes ausquels Dieu a donné le cœur et le pouvoir requis pour la conservation de ses pouvres Eglises en l'estat auquel elles sont maintenant reduictes, je les voudrois prier et exhorter au nom de Dieu de ne conclurre ny entreprendre rien sans avoir esté bien resolus de leur conseil par ceux des ministres du Royaume qu'ils sçauroyent les mieux verséz es Escritures."

[2] See Henri Meylan, "Bèze et les italiens de Lyon (1566)," BHR, XIV (1952), 235-249.

were merely human, could not be allowed in ecclesiastical discipline where the majesty of God was at stake. Even in human justice, however, Beza was inclined to believe that severity was good for society.

The plea for consultation Beza judged somewhat more sympathetically. In the present circumstances, however, he did not see that synods could be called with assured regularity. Furthermore the right answer in some cases was so obvious that consultation was not really necessary, and one could safely leave action to the local consistory. Such a case was the one which had recently developed in Lyon. With this apparent allusion to the Alamanni case,[1] Beza ended, abruptly. Or at least the surviving copy of his letter ends there. It is hard to believe that Beza did not at least add some sort of courteous conclusion.

From one of the points of view a historian can adopt, it is a pity that Beza did not spell his position out in more detail in this letter to Coligny. It would be fascinating to know more of the exact context in which it was written. But the brevity and sharp organization of this letter do have the advantages of clarity. They make very clear what Beza wanted of the great Huguenot lords: he wanted them to consult his pastors on matters of high policy; and he wanted them to suppress those elements within the French Reformed Church which challenged pastoral authority. We have already noted that some among the Huguenot leaders resisted these demands: Condé had resisted the first since the 1563 peace negotiations; the Cardinal of Châtillon had resisted the second for a time during the Morély controversy. But others among these leaders were normally willing to accede to Beza on these issues. First among them, of course, was the man to whom the letter was addressed—the Admiral Coligny.

C. Geneva's Support for War

1. *Diplomatic Background*

If Condé had hoped to make the second war of religion in France a national revolt for liberty rather than a crusade for Protestantism, he miscalculated badly. He did not take into account the attitude of his foreign allies. This was a slip which his opponents at the royal Court were quick to notice and exploit. The government immediately saw diplomatic value in the bitter complaints about the Guise family,[2] and the rather confused list of demands for lower taxes, political reforms, increased religious toleration, and a calling of the Estates-General,[3] which Condé and his advisers had formally presented to delegations from the royal Court that visited his camp shortly after the failure of the Conspiracy of Meaux. Two royal ambassadors, the Bishop of Rennes and the young sire de Lansac, were sent to Germany, with instructions to tour the German Protestant courts, explaining that the Huguenots this time were fighting against their lawful king for personal political reasons, not

[1] This apparent allusion to an event in mid-1566, permits us to suppose that this letter was probably written late in 1566 or in 1567.

[2] Text, taken from La Popelinière, in J. Delaborde, *Coligny*, II, 609-611.

[3] Text, again taken from La Popelinière, in *ibid.*, II, 612-614.

for religion. This explanation seemed plausible to many. It worried the Elector Palatine, Calvinism's most powerful friend in Germany, into sending a special ambassador named Zuleger back to France with de Lansac, to report directly on the importance of the religious issue in the new war.[1] And when Zuleger arrived at the royal court, he was pointedly shown copies of the demands presented by Condé.[2]

Even before Zuleger's arrival, however, leaders in the Huguenot camp had realized their error. They were helped to this by a dramatic event which took them somewhat aback : a royal herald in costume of fleur-de-lis appeared in the Saint-Denis camp, and, following three flourishes on the trumpet, announced that Condé, Coligny, and their associates were hereby summoned either to appear before the king or to admit openly that they were rebels.[3] This feudal ceremony had a sobering effect on the Huguenots. In the next set of negotiations, between the Châtillon brothers and their uncle, the Catholic military leader Montmorency, the Huguenots presented a much abbreviated and moderately stated list of grievances. This time they centered on a modest request that the Edict of Amboise be reinstated, without any of the restrictive interpretations which had been added to it, and with provisions for real enforcement.[4] Montmorency flatly refused to consider a settlement that would leave France divided into two religions. The issue thus became, again, the Calvinists' demand for toleration of their form of worship. By the time Zuleger arrived in France, he found plenty of evidence that the French were again taking this to be the real issue. He so reported to the Palatine.[5] As a result, the Elector permitted levy by the Huguenots of an army of some 6500 horse, 3000 infantry, and four field cannon, under the command of his brash young second son, Casimir. He rebuffed a last-minute attempt by the Bishop of Rennes to prevent the departure of this army into France. On January 11, 1568, it made junction with Condé's army on the banks of the Moselle.[6]

This meant a delay of several months, however. And the delay was critical. It meant that Condé had no support from foreign mercenaries in the first great battle of the war, that of Saint-Denis. And while he emerged from that battle with honor, and even with an important minor victory in the death on the battlefield of the Catholic commander Montmorency, he had

---

[1] For the text of Zuleger's account of his mission, with comment, see August Kluckhohn, " Zwei pfälzische Gesandtschaftsberichte über den französischen Hof und die Hugenotten, 1567 und 1574," *Abhandlungen der Historischen Classe der Königlich Bayerischen Akademie der Wissenschaften*, XI/2 (Munich, 1869), 182-205. Hereafter cited as A. Kluckhohn, " Zwei pfälzische Gesandtschaftsberichte." For a further description of these negotiations, see J.-A. de Thou, *Hist. univ.* (1740 ed.), IV, 14, 28-29.

[2] A. Kluckhohn, " Zwei pfälzische Gesandtschaftsberichte," p. 191.

[3] See J. Delaborde, *Coligny*, II, 490-493, for texts, based on mss., of this summons and accompanying instructions to the herald. Cf. more summary description in d'Aumale, *Condé*, I, 300.

[4] Text, taken from La Popelinière, in J. Delaborde, *Coligny*, II, 615-616. For description of these negotiations, see pp. 493-494.

[5] See A. Kluckhohn, " Zwei pfälzische Gesandtschaftsberichte," pp. 189-205. For a copy of Zuleger's report, addressed to the Prince, Joh. Casimir, 20 December 1567, see A. Kluckhohn, ed., *Briefe Friedrich des Frommen, Kurfürsten von der Pfalz*, 2 vols. in 3 (Brunswick, 1868-1872), II/1, 153-155.

[6] See d'Aumale, *Condé*, I, 319-323.

to make a basic change in strategy. The quick growth of the Catholic armies in Paris forced him to abandon his plan to encircle and starve out the capital. He had to make a quick march to Lorraine, to avoid annihilation and make juncture with the Palatine army. He then had to march quickly back to Orleans, to make juncture with the troops he had ordered mobilized in the south of France, which were now arriving along the line of the Loire. By the time he was again ready to go on the offensive, he was running short of money and supplies and already facing problems of desertion. At this point he decided to accept overtures for peace from the royal Court. The result was the peace of Longjumeau, which did little more than arrange for a return to the uneasy status quo preceding the Conspiracy.[1] Among these arrangements, the most complex were those for paying off the German mercenaries and securing their departure from France. Again there was a sharp difference of opinion among the Protestant leaders upon the terms of peace. Coligny again was bitterly opposed to peace at this price. But Condé and the majority of the Huguenot nobility again carried the day. The pastors do not seem to have been directly consulted this time.[2]

Everyone knew that the peace of Longjumeau was nothing but a flimsy truce, however. Within months, war had broken out again. This time it began with flight by Condé and the Châtillon brothers, flight provoked by royal troop movements which seemed clearly aimed at seizure of their persons. Condé, Coligny, and d'Andelot, first took refuge in a part of Burgundy where Condé and d'Andelot both owned well-fortified castles. Then, after collecting a small army to act as bodyguards for themselves and their families, and after sending to the Queen Mother a formal protest at the threats being made against them,[3] they made dashes across the whole width of France, highlighted by a particularly dramatic fording of the Loire just before a royal troop caught up with the detachment including Condé himself, to the city of La Rochelle.[4] At about the same time, the Cardinal of Châtillon had precipitately fled his episcopal see of Beauvais, complaining of similar threats upon his life, and had hurriedly crossed the Channel, to seek asylum in England.[5]

The third war of religion began, then, with the establishment of a Protestant military headquarters in La Rochelle, a city which was to become honored before all others in France as a center of Protestant resistance. La Rochelle was well suited to this role in several ways. It had become completely Protestant during the second war of religion, as a result of a sudden local coup. Protestant citizens, in January of 1568, with the support of their pastors, had jailed a number of locally prominent Catholics, had ransacked the city's church buildings, and had turned control of the city's government

[1] For text of the resulting edict of pacification, dated 23 March 1568, see J. Delaborde, *Coligny*, II, 624-628.

[2] For narrative accounts of these events, see *ibid.*, II, 494-539; d'Aumale, *Condé*, I, 301-325; A. W. Whitehead, *Coligny*, pp. 186-195.

[3] For text, taken from Serres, see J. Delaborde, *Coligny*, III, 496-516.

[4] Described in *ibid.*, III, 48-53; d'Aumale, *Condé*, II, 17-21.

[5] Described in Ernest G. Atkinson, " The Cardinal of Châtillon in England, 1568-1571," *Proceedings of the Huguenot Society of London*, III (1888-1891), 182-184; explained in Cardinal of Châtillon to Charles IX, 5 September 1568, text in *ibid.*, pp. 260-261. Hereafter cited as E. G. Atkinson, " Cardinal of Châtillon."

over to officers of Condé.[1] When peace came, La Rochelle refused to accept many of the provisions in the edict of pacification, and even succeeded in keeping out the royal troops sent to garrison the city and enforce observation of the edict.[2] When war returned, therefore, La Rochelle was entirely Protestant, and there could be no question of a portion of the local population sapping the Huguenot war effort.

La Rochelle also had the advantage of being closer to the great centers of Protestant strength in France. Its hinterland, the provinces of Aunis, Saintonge, and Angoumois, was an area in which Protestantism was growing. And these provinces bordered on Guyenne and Gascony, which from the beginning had been the areas in which Calvinist evangelization was most successful, in which the greatest numbers of Huguenot fighting men could be recruited, and in which the extensive sovereign rights of the house of Navarre could be used to advance the Protestant cause.

La Rochelle, finally, had certain obvious military advantages, particularly for defensive warfare. It could easily be defended from attack by land, because of the network of streams and marshes which surround the approaches to it. Condé and Coligny quickly took advantage of this fact, once established there, by sending out troops to take over and garrison a number of key towns in the neighboring provinces, thus establishing a sizable and easily defended perimeter around the city.[3] La Rochelle could also be easily supplied, from the Protestant sea, either by its own sizable fleets which regularly traded with the Gascon ports and with Britain, or by the even larger English and Dutch fleets which controlled much of the commerce along the French coast.

From La Rochelle, the Huguenots quickly mounted a campaign of propaganda and diplomacy, which far exceeded their efforts in those domains during the second war of religion, which in shape and size resembled more nearly their substantial efforts during the first war of religion. The propaganda was mostly in the form of public manifestos, generally issued in Condé's name, designed to justify the return to arms of the Huguenot lords, and to underline the religious reasons for their revolt. A small local press, run by Barthélemy Berton, was asked to print this material, and devoted most of its energies in the next few years to doing nothing much but that.[4] Other presses, mostly outside of France, in such places as Geneva, Heidelberg, and Frankfurt, provided some help in the distribution of these materials.[5]

The diplomacy was undertaken in the joint name of the great Huguenot lords. Many of the ambassadors sent out from La Rochelle were accredited by Condé. But some were accredited by Coligny or the Queen of Navarre, or were acting, less formally, on the instructions of one or more of the three. After Condé's death, at the battle of Jarnac, midway through the third war, letters of accreditation and instruction were generally issued in the names of the young princes of Navarre and Condé. But they were still so young

[1] Described in [Louis Etienne] Arcere, *Histoire de la ville de La Rochelle et du pays d'Aulnis* (La Rochelle, 1756-1757), I, 356-360.

[2] *Ibid.*, I, 362-368. See also d'Aumale, *Condé*, II, 12.

[3] D'Aumale, *Condé*, II, 28 and ff.; J. Delaborde, *Coligny*, III, 71 and ff.

[4] Described in detail in E. Droz, *Barthélemy Berton, 1563-1573*, vol. I of *L'Imprimerie à La Rochelle* (Geneva : Droz, 1960), pp. 71-106. Hereafter cited as E. Droz, *La Rochelle*, I.

[5] Some of these editions are mentioned in *ibid.*, *passim.*

that this was a fiction. Coligny was now clearly supreme military commander of the Protestant forces. And Jeanne d'Albret played an important part in this diplomacy, partly because of her influence on her son. Coligny and Jeanne, however, continued to work together very closely. The death of Condé, thus, helped unify the Protestant high command.

Two general purposes are revealed by the instructions given to the Huguenot ambassadors. One was positive, the other negative. On the positive side, they were to appeal to Protestant powers for mercenary troops and for money to pay both for the mercenaries and the other expenses of war. On the negative side, they were to do all within their power to block the diplomacy of the French royal Court, to interfere in all ways possible with the royal ambassadors' efforts—which were most commonly aimed at raising levies of mercenary troops.

This Huguenot diplomatic campaign was concentrated, as before, in three geographic areas—in England, at the Court of Elizabeth; in Rhenish Germany, at the courts of the Protestant princes; among the Swiss cantons, both Protestant and Catholic. The campaign in England was headed by the most distinguished of these diplomats—Odet de Coligny, the Cardinal of Châtillon, who took advantage of his formidable diplomatic experience and his temporary exile in England, to plead for the Protestant cause with Elizabeth I herself.[1] He was seconded by the sire de Cavaignes, sent direct from La Rochelle for this purpose.[2] And he quickly discovered that he could get powerful help within the English government from Cecil. From all reports, Odet proved to be an unusually successful ambassador. He captivated the Queen. He put on such a courtly show that he easily overshadowed the French royal ambassador, and provoked gossip among the courtiers about how much more impressive was the ambassador of the Prince of Condé than the representative of the King.[3] And he was successful. Elizabeth I, abandoning her normally stingy ways, agreed to pledge very substantial sums of money from her treasury to the Huguenot cause. These sums were offered as loans, at least one of which was secured by the crown jewels of Navarre, offered as collateral by Jeanne d'Albret.[4] Elizabeth also permitted Odet de Coligny to issue letters of marque, empowering privateers out of La Rochelle to seize and confiscate the contents of Catholic ships.[5] The use of English port facilities was granted to these legalized pirates.[6] The booty which they brought in, significantly increased the Huguenot treasury. And Elizabeth sent a token force of about a hundred men,[7] plus a few cannon,[8] to provide direct support to the Huguenot armies.

---

[1] These negotiations are described at length and heavily documented in E. G. Atkinson, " Cardinal of Châtillon." N. B. pp. 212-217, paraphrasing his letter of accreditation, 10 January 1569.

[2] *Ibid.*, p. 202; d'Aumale, *Condé*, II, 22-23, 368-369 (Cavaignes' credential letter).

[3] E. G. Atkinson, " Cardinal of Châtillon," p. 257, ff. Florimond de Raemond.

[4] *Ibid.*, pp. 226-227. See also p. 276, for text of the bond, dated 3 August 1569, for the loan covered by the jewels.

[5] *Ibid.*, pp. 221-223; J. Delaborde, *Coligny*, III, 82; d'Aumale, *Condé*, II, 44.

[6] Examples mentioned in E. G. Atkinson, " Cardinal of Châtillon," pp. 229, 231, and *passim*.

[7] D'Aumale, *Condé*, II, 44-45.

[8] E. G. Atkinson, " Cardinal of Châtillon," pp. 208-209.

These English negotiations were directly tied to the Huguenot diplomatic campaign in Germany. For much of the money supplied by Elizabeth I was earmarked directly for the hiring of German mercenaries. It helped make possible the assembly of a sizable mercenary army under the command of the Duke of Zweibrücken. Assemblage of this army was made possible also by the intensive efforts of a team of Huguenot ambassadors who were cultivating the Elector Palatine again, the Duke of Zweibrücken himself, Prince William of Orange and his brother Louis of Nassau, and certain other German princes and cities.[1] William, of course, had a material interest in France, by virtue of his holdings in Orange, as well as an interest in Germany by virtue of the family holdings around Nassau, in addition to the Dutch interests which helped encourage him to lead the revolt against Spain which was soon to make him the great hero of the Protestant Netherlands.

The Huguenot diplomatic campaign in Switzerland was of less importance to the total cause of French Protestantism than the campaigns in England and Germany. Yet to it we must look for the principal evidence of direct participation by the pastors of Geneva in these wars. Consequently it is worth a more extended examination. This campaign was primarily negative in character. For nearly a century, Switzerland had been probably the most important recruiting center for the mercenary infantry which constituted the largest and one of the most important parts of all French royal armies. To recruit these mercenaries, the French crown had long maintained in Switzerland one of its largest embassies, staffed with some of its ablest diplomats. It was important to the Huguenots that the work of this embassy be blocked. The Huguenots also nourished a strong but generally illusory secondary hope that those among the Swiss cantons which were Protestant might supply material help to their cause. These included Berne, the most powerful single canton militarily, but bound by profitable recruiting alliances to the French crown, despite its Protestantism. They also included Zurich, which was relatively weaker militarily but which exercised considerable moral influence over Berne and the other Protestant cantons, because of the prestige of its theologians. And they included peripheral Basel, and Geneva, which was the weakest of all, and technically not even in the Swiss confederation but only allied to certain of its members, although it, of course, had the strongest ties of sympathy to the Huguenots.

No official embassies had been sent to the Swiss by the Huguenots during the second war of religion, but no less than three were dispatched during the third war. On the eve of the war, as Condé was preparing to fly from his Burgundian stronghold of Noyers to La Rochelle, he and Coligny dispatched Félix de Bourjac, sénéchal of Valentinois, as their special ambassador to the Swiss leagues, the Grisons, and Geneva. Bourjac visited Geneva, Berne, and Zurich, was on hand when hostilities began again in France, persuaded the Zurich authorities to convoke the Swiss Diet, but could not block the royal ambassador's effort to recruit another 4000 mercenaries, and was not able even to enter the Swiss mountain cantons or the Grisons.[2] The other two Huguenot ambassadors to Switzerland were sent late in the war, after the death of Condé, with assignments largely secondary to ones in other

[1] J. Delaborde, *Coligny*, III, 83-91.

[2] See E. Rott, *Représentation*, II, 161-163, for an account of this mission.

countries. In November and December of 1569, Jacques du Broullat, sire de Lisy, representing the Prince of Orange and the young Prince of Condé, visited the Protestant cities of Basel, Berne, Zurich, and Geneva, in part simply to gain support for projects he had just launched in Germany. He also sought to encourage local opposition to further recruiting of mercenaries for the French crown. And he assured the Swiss Protestants that the Huguenots would fight on, in spite of the recent disastrous defeat of their armies at Moncontour. For du Broullat all this was simply an extension of a mission to Strasbourg.[1] In February of 1570, Guillaume Stuart, sire de Vézines, was sent on a somewhat more formal mission to the Swiss, accredited as ambassador to the Protestant cantons by the young King of Navarre, his mother Jeanne d'Albret, and the Admiral Coligny. He was on a general search for subsidy money and mercenary troops. The most important part of his job was already over, since most of the subsidy needed had been acquired in England and most of the troops in Germany. He arrived in Switzerland too late to block a new French royal levy of Swiss mercenaries, this time of 8000 men. But he nevertheless visited Basel, Berne, Zurich, and Neuchâtel, and, from the latter city, sent an appeal for negotiations to certain of the Protestant deputies at the Swiss diet in Baden, where decisions on levies of mercenaries were reached. The actual negotiations he turned over to the sire David Chalot, however.[2] By this time, it was becoming clear that Vézines' efforts would not be needed much longer. The factions in France were already corresponding about the peace negotiations which were to end the third war of religion only a few months later, in August of 1570.

In all this Huguenot diplomatic campaign, the contributions of the pastors of Geneva were largely limited to assisting negotiations in Switzerland. That this was so, is further evidence of their diminishing influence on the French scene. While Beza, in particular, was in frequent contact with the Queen of Navarre and the Admiral Coligny and remained on good terms with them, he was not this time in their actual entourage, in a position to offer them daily advice. Neither were any other prominent pastors. Pierre Viret, one of Geneva's ablest supporters and probably the most popular single preacher produced by the French Reformation, was now a client to the Queen of Navarre. But she had set him to work on the job of making her sovereign territory of Béarn entirely Protestant. When war came she left him there, in the stronghold of Pau, rather than taking him with her to La Rochelle, and he even spent part of the war as a prisoner of Catholic forces which seized Pau.[3] Geneva-trained Pastor Odet de Nort, to be sure, helped control the population within La Rochelle itself, and in his flamboyant way kept them devoted to the Protestant cause[4]. But his following was among the bourgeois and laborers of the port, not the high aristocrats, and it seems unlikely that he would have been admitted to the councils that determined policy. Only the aristocrats' chaplains would have been likely to gain that entrée and I have found no evidence that they did.

---

[1] *Ibid.*, II, 82, 163.

[2] *Ibid.*, II, 163-164.

[3] R. D. Linder, *Viret*, p. 50.

[4] E. Droz, *La Rochelle*, I, 118-126.

Furthermore, pastors were no longer being used as ambassadors. Both Beza and Spifame had been so employed during the first war of religion. During these later wars, practically all of the ambassadors were secular noblemen. Within Switzerland itself, Reformed pastors continued to make a contribution. Indeed it could be argued that they at least tried to make a greater contribution than before. Beza again, of course, was at the center of of these efforts. His work was aimed at two goals. He did what he could, within reason, to aid the official ambassadors of the Huguenot party. And he got involved deeply, in a special and highly secret private effort to recruit troops for the Huguenot armies.

2. *The Second War of Religion*

Beza's efforts to support the work of Protestant diplomats from France were in each case most intensive just before actual fighting began. And for that reason, they are particularly revealing. In 1567, when the second war of religion was in the offing, Beza became involved when a special ambassador, representing the French Huguenot leaders, sent by the Admiral Coligny and his brother d'Andelot, arrived in Geneva to offer the city special protection against any threat from the Duke of Alva's army. This ambassador was Guillaume Stuart, sire de Vézines, who was later to serve the Huguenots in even more important missions.[1] Vézines arrive in Geneva on April 2. He was received in the name of the city by a special "secret council." The very recourse to negotiation through this extraordinary committee of the governing Small Council reveals the great secrecy which surrounded the earliest negotiations. The composition of this "secret council" is also significant. It consisted of the four syndics, to whom were granted for the year the supreme executive and judicial powers within the city. And to this group was added Theodore Beza.[2] Since Beza, not having been born in Geneva, was never entitled to the full legal rights of a Genevan citizen, and since consequently he had no right to a position in the councils which regularly governed the city, his inclusion in this "secret council" was most extraordinary. It provides renewed testimony to the high regard which the Genevan governing class had for his diplomatic talents.

The proposals which Vézines laid before this "secret council" were complex and most revealing. He announced that the French Reformed churches had accumulated a war chest of some 240,000 ecus. They wanted to loan 50,000 of this sum to the city of Geneva, at a modest rate of interest. They proposed to loan another portion of this sum to the city of Berne. The bulk of it they wanted to loan to the Palatinate of the Rhine. This distribution of funds was to provide the material base for an informal alliance among the Huguenots and these three foreign governments who shared their religious point of view. Each party to the alliance was to stand ready to supply troops to any of its allies in case of need, or to permit its allies to levy troops in its territory.[3]

---

[1] E. Rott, *Représentation*, II, 160. For his later missions, see pp. 163-164.

[2] J. A. Gautier, *Hist. de Genève*, IV, 589. N.B. n. 2, re the membership of this "secret council."

[3] *Ibid.*, IV, 589.

It is extremely suggestive that the French Huguenots even made such an offer. Every clause in it suggests that they were already preparing for war, more than five months before their leaders' Conspiracy of Meaux actually provoked fighting. Even at that early date they had already accumulated a considerable sum of money. They were already lining up allies. And they were so making these arrangements that they could easily be used to hire and mobilize rapidly crack mercenary troops in the very parts of Europe from which the best such troops came—Bernese Switzerland and southern Germany.

The Genevans reacted to these propositions with great caution. After four days of deliberation, the "secret council" informed Vézines of its replies. With great politeness, Geneva declined the offer of a loan from the French churches. It was explained that, in case of any attack upon the city, any money on hand would have to be used to pay for its defense, and this could cause great embarrassment on both sides if the French wanted the money back, with interest, soon thereafter. Vézines was also informed that, while Geneva was sincerely concerned for the welfare of the French churches, it could not commit itself to any alliance before negotiations had been undertaken with all the parties concerned. Vézines was finally informed that the city would appreciate it very much if the French could supply a small temporary garrison of three hundred infantry and fifty cavalry, to provide protection until the present danger was past.[1]

It is impossible to tell in detail what may have been Beza's role in working out these Genevan replies. They do resemble in some ways those recommended to the city government by Calvin at one point during the first war of religion.[2] Perhaps Beza, like Calvin, anxious to spare the city's limited resources from the heavy drains that major war could bring, was responsible for some of the caution in the Genevan response. Or perhaps caution was the natural reaction of the Genevan syndics, preoccupied as they normally were with the more local diplomatic problems of dealing with Berne and Savoy. At any rate it is clear that Beza was consulted and had some share in the drafting of this response.

Even to this limited and cautious response, however, the French Huguenots replied with speed and generosity. In just eight days, on April 14, Paul de Richieu, sire de Mouvans appeared within the city to announce that Admiral Coligny had ordered him to raise the three hundred infantrymen in Dauphiné, all at the expense of the French Reformed, and that he was prepared to raise as many as 1000, still at the French churches' expense. The three hundred soldiers were quickly enlisted. Ten officers were brought in from the Metz area. Technical command of this garrison was vested in a Genevan magistrate, but it seems clear that Mouvans was in actual charge.[3]

In welcoming Mouvans within their walls, the Genevans were bringing in a man who was really a professional conspirator against the French crown. He had, to be sure, visited Geneva before, but had already embarrassed the city at least once by his presence. His visits to Geneva reveal one of the more concrete connections between the city of Calvin and the repeated attempts

---

[1] *Ibid.*, IV, 589-590.

[2] See R. M. Kingdon, *Geneva & Coming*, pp. 118-119.

[3] J.-A. Gautier, *Hist. de Genève*, IV, 590; A. Roget, *Hist. de Genève*, VII, 215-217. On the officers from Metz, see Geneva, Arch., RC, LXII, fol. 56, 9 May 1567.

to advance French Protestantism by bloody revolt. It should consequently be useful to backtrack a bit and examine his earlier career.

The first of the plots in which Mouvans had been involved was the Conspiracy of Amboise, back in 1560. This foolhardy attempt to seize the entire royal Court, at the Chateau d'Amboise, had failed disastrously, and had resulted in the mass execution of most of the young noble hotheads who planned it. Mouvans escaped their fate largely because his task had not required close approach to the royal Court in Amboise. He had been charged, rather, with raising rebellion in his home province, Provence. And he had been successful in a modest way.[1] When his fellow-conspirators near Amboise were put to death, he refused to admit defeat, kept the troops he had raised in the field, and joined with fellow-conspirator Montbrun who had been charged with raising revolt in the neighboring province of Dauphiné. Their forces began marauding expeditions which trailed through Provence, Dauphiné, the independent principality of Orange, and even brushed the papal enclave around Avignon.[2] When royal forces finally caught up with Mouvans and Montbrun, they disbanded their tropps, and, in disguise, fled separately to Geneva.[3] As soon as royal authorities relaxed their vigilance, however, Mouvans was back at his plotting in Provence. In 1561, when the royal Court was considering experimental toleration of Calvinism and had consequently relaxed persecution, Mouvans raised another band of soldiers, and had it on war footing a full three months before war began generally in France.[4] He served with distinction during the first war of religion, in the Huguenot armies organized for fighting in southeastern France under the general command of the Baron des Adrets. When des Adrets treacherously switched back to the Catholic side late in the war, Mouvans was one of several subordinate commanders who unmasked his plans, drove him out, and kept the bulk of the army loyal to the Protestant cause.[5]

With the return of peace, however, Mouvans found himself at loose ends. The Parlement of Aix, which controlled legislation in Provence, refused to register the pacificatory Edict of Amboise.[6] Even if it had, it is doubtful that Mouvans would have been welcomed home. His reputation for rebellion had become notorious, and much of his property was under attachment. In 1564, accordingly, he again retired to Geneva, and spent most of the years of peace in that city.

Even before he had settled in Geneva, however, he was back at his intrigues. In July of 1564, he sent to the Geneva Council an offer of "service," of type unspecified but almost certainly military, on behalf of a "great number" of "gentlemen" in Dauphiné.[7] And no sooner had he settled in Geneva, than he was off to Berne to seek support for a mysterious project of some kind which he hoped to mount. The Geneva Council supplied him with a

---

[1] E. Arnaud, *Histoire des protestants de Provence, du Comtat Venaissin, et de la principauté d'Orange* (Paris, 1884), I, 117-125. Hereafter cited as E. Arnaud, *Provence.*

[2] *Ibid.*, II, 14-20, 162-165.

[3] R. M. Kingdon, *Geneva & Coming*, pp. 74-75.

[4] *Ibid.*, p. 109; *Hist. eccl.*, I, 897 and ff.

[5] *Hist. eccl.*, III, 234 and ff.

[6] *Hist. eccl.*, III, 381.

[7] Geneva, Arch., RC, LIX, fol. 74v., 14 July 1564.

credential letter to help him begin this negotiation, but it does not specify the nature of the project.[1]

In 1565, the Genevan city government finally decided to find uses for Mouvans' military skill and devotion to the Protestant cause. He was formally hired to superintend the city's defenses, a job which in peacetime normally required the talents of a military engineer, who could keep the fortifications in a usable state.[2] While the Council felt that it could not afford to pay Mouvans a suitable salary for this important work, it was happy to grant him a number of rather generous tokens of its esteem. Over the years that followed, he was frequently awarded handsome amounts of cash, rations of grain for his family, oats and hay for his horses.[3] He was even honored with the assignment of a choice seat at religious services, so that he would not have to come early to be in a good position to hear the sermon.[4] When he was out of Geneva, on trips which he made with suspicious frequency shortly before the second war began, the city Council provided for the needs of his wife and family.[5] The Council continued to care for them in 1569, after Mouvans had died in battle.[6] His family was still living in Geneva in 1570, when two of his children died there.[7]

In return for this generous treatment, Mouvans could unquestionably provide the city with more professional military leadership than any of its own citizens. But his taste for conspiracy was really to embarrass its rulers. In May of 1566, another of the plots to which he was privy came to light when the Geneva Council received a furious letter from the Duke of Nemours, accusing it of plotting his assassination and that of the Cardinal of Lorraine, both of whom happened to be in Annecy, not far from Geneva. The Council, with reason, protested its innocence and expressed its dismay that such an outrageous charge should be brought against it. But it also launched an investigation to find out what ground there was for the charge. The investigation led straight to Mouvans. He told the Council quite openly that a soldier named " Pierre " had confided in him a plan to kill both Nemours and Lorraine. He admitted with disarming frankness that he told Pierre that he thought it would be a good idea to assassinate Lorraine, but that he would not encourage the murder of Nemours. He protested, however, that he had not formally commissioned the man to make an attempt on Lorraine's life. The Council sent off to Nemours a report of all this, and let Mouvans off with a warning that he had better be more discreet in the future.[8] That the Genevans normally took such matters with greater seriousness, however, is revealed by the trial later in the year of a professional spy named Boudier. He approached one of the governing

---

[1] Council of Geneva to MM. of Berne, 15 December 1564, contemporary minute in Geneva, Arch., Copies de Lettres, VII, fol. 224.

[2] Geneva, Arch., RC, LX, fol. 56v., 24 May 1565.

[3] E.g. *ibid.*, LX, fol. 64, 11 June 1565, a grant of cash plus oats and hay for his horses; LX, fol. 111v., 25 October 1565, another similar grant; LXI, fol. 39v., 13 May 1566, grant of cash and wheat.

[4] *Ibid.*, LXI, fol. 47v., 3 June 1566.

[5] *Ibid.*, LXII, fol. 32v., 31 March 1567, a grant of ca-h to his wife.

[6] *Ibid.*, LXIV, fol. 79, 26 May 1569, a grant of cash to his wife.

[7] Geneva, Arch., Registre des morts, X, 38, 39, 25 and 27 May 1570.

[8] A. Roget, *Hist. de Genève*, VII, 193-195.

syndics with a plan to seize the citadel of Lyon, a fortification which had been established in that city to give royal troops security in a community much of which was Protestant. It was suspected that the spy was a double agent, trying to trap the city into an extremely compromising situation. He was summarily tried, and condemned to be hanged.[1]

Not all of Mouvans' projects have left such open records. It would be interesting to know why, earlier in 1566, he applied for permission to have 500 arquebus " cannon " cast, for the use of a " certain personage. " Although this was a really sizable quantity of arms for that day, the Council simply authorized him to go ahead, without inquiring further.[2] One wonders if these guns were intended for Condé or Coligny. And at the beginning of 1567, Mouvans left Geneva abruptly.[3] He may have gone off to confer with Coligny. At any rate he returned as an envoy of the Admiral, to arrange for the garrison of which we have already taken notice.

Recruits for Mouvans' garrison soon began arriving in Geneva. The city immediately had to plunge into the chore of finding lodgings, military supplies, and food for the soldiers. It also had to make emergency provisions for summary justice within this little army, since its members, with nothing to do but wait for an Alva who never came, soon got involved in the brawls which usually divert any body of idle soldiers and annoy its civilian hosts. Furthermore Geneva had to arrange for the soldiers to be paid on schedule.[4] This garrison could have been expanded considerably, if Geneva had been willing to accept any of the other offers of support which it received in the succeeding months. Admiral Coligny offered to send a troop of 1200 men. The Bernese offered repeatedly, with considerable insistence, to supply a garrison of at least 1000 men. D'Andelot also offered the city troops, and sent with his envoy an immediate gift of 2000 ecus to cover military expenses. The Reformed Church of Montpellier even offered Geneva a boatman for its defense, an offer which the Council, with the warmest thanks, declined, since the threat the city faced was not by water.[5]

In fact all of these later generous offers were declined. Geneva simply could not afford to maintain a garrison of a much larger size for any length of time. Furthermore its governors did not welcome the prospect of so many foreign soldiers within their walls. While they were careful to couch their refusals in very tactful terms, they accepted no more gifts of troops. Among these refusals was one sent by Beza to Bullinger. There had been earlier correspondence about the possibility of securing for the defense of Geneva the services of a Swiss Protestant mercenary captain named Hohensax. Hohensax hesitated to come, and Beza then asked Bullinger that the captain be informed his services would not be needed after all.[6]

---

[1] *Ibid.*, VII, 197.

[2] Geneva, Arch., RC, LXI, fol. 25, 2 April 1566.

[3] Geneva, Arch., RC, LXII, fol. 32v., 31 March 1567, re an attempt to persuade him to return.

[4] A. Roget, *Hist. de Genève*, VII, 215-218.

[5] *Ibid.*, VII, 219, for the offers of the Admiral and the Church of Montpellier; 220, for a renewed offer from Berne and the offer from d'Andelot.

[6] Beza to Bullinger, 3 May [1567], in Zürich, Staatsarchiv, E II 350, pp. 55-58. For more on this episode, see below, p. 184.

These formal refusals did not stop all arrivals of soldiers in Geneva, however. Within two months the number in the French garrison had swelled to seven hundred, and the city had to stop the enrollment of any more. Although Mouvans was in actual command of this unit, nominal command was vested, as we have already noted, in the hands of a native Genevan. Furthermore a number of Genevans had been conscripted for the city's defense, and placed in a second unit. And all the able-bodied laborers and chambermaids of the city had been drafted for work on the fortifications, regulated by an elaborate timetable, which had the effect of requiring each to contribute at least one day's work to the job.[1]

From the beginning, it had been understood that the expenses of maintaining this garrison would be borne by the French Reformed churches. The actual sums which arrived, however, were never sufficient to cover the expenses of its maintenance. Not that the city ran short of cash. The substantial loans she had obtained when the threat from Alva seemed serious,[2] were more than sufficient to cover the expenses of the garrison and all the other expenses of preparing the city for defense. In fact they left a very substantial surplus. It was to put this surplus to use, that the city established for the first time the state bank, with its authorization to charge exceptionally high rates of interest, to which Pastor Colladon and his friends had objected with such violence.[3] But the loans would eventually have to be repaid. And the city kept hoping that gifts from the French Reformed churches would assist in this repayment. For years the city's books carried as assets, a series of debts payable by the French churches. One of these series was carried in the name of Mouvans himself.[4] At one point, the Council formally asked Mouvans to do what he could to collect the sum promised by the French.[5] The debt in his name was carried on these books even after the wars of religion began again, even after his death.[6] It was finally dropped from the books only after the St. Bartholomew's massacres had so prostrated the French churches that it had become obvious the debt could not be collected.

By July, it was clear that Alva was not going to attack Geneva. The Council began to take steps to demobilize. Mouvans was instructed to dismiss the French garrison.[7] These troops, of course, did not have to wait long for further employment. The Huguenot chiefs were soon to begin the meetings which culminated in the Conspiracy of Meaux. Mouvans was soon back in France again. When war began, he was one of a number charged with recruiting troops in southern France and bringing them up to the line of the Loire to help Condé.[8] As he passed near Geneva with one of these armies, he sent

[1] A. Roget, *Hist. de Genève*, VII, 217-218, 221.

[2] See above, p. 163, n. 2.

[3] See above, pp. 24-26.

[4] See Geneva, Arch., Finances U, No. 1, Carnet de l'Arche, 1551-1568, fols. 237v.-238, for an account of the expenses incurred by Mouvans for recruiting, maintaining, and supplying the French garrison, and of certain sums received to cover these expenses, leaving a net debit of about 12,000 livres.

[5] Geneva, Arch., RC, LXII, fol. 86, 21 July 1567.

[6] Geneva, Arch., Finances U, No. 1, Carnet de l'Arche, 1551-1568, fols. 244v. and ff.

[7] Geneva, Arch., RC, LXII, fol. 79v., 1 July 1567.

[8] J.-A. de Thou, *Hist. univ.* (1740 ed.), IV, 33.

his affectionate greetings to the city authorities.[1] Shortly after the third war began, he received another recruiting commission from Condé and Coligny. It was apparently then, while he was leading some troops to their support, that a Catholic band finally caught up with him. His detachment was cut to pieces, and Mouvans himself reportedly killed on the field of battle.[2]

It is interesting to speculate on the role of Mouvans and his garrison in the actual beginning of the second war of religion. The many offers of assistance which he and others brought to the reluctant city of Geneva early in 1567, are particularly curious. At least one historian has speculated that these troops were gathered for offensive purposes: that Coligny hoped to muster an army big enough to do battle with Alva, to block his march to the Low Countries, and thus to save his fellow Protestants in that area—both for the glory of true religion and the buildup of strong friendly forces on the northern frontiers of France. Such a plan would probably have required help from the French crown, for Alva's army was exceptionally well-trained and well-disciplined, and could only have been blocked by a much bigger and unusually well-equipped force. Since the French crown was not then interested in playing this game, Coligny abandoned the plan, and pressed no more troops on Geneva.[3] This speculation is plausible, particularly given Coligny's persistent attempts to unite France in war against Spain during the months preceding the St. Bartholomew's massacres, attempts which came close to succeeding. But there is little evidence in Geneva for such a plan in 1567, and it is doubtful that the Genevans would have been privy to it in any event.

It is undeniable, however, that these maneuvers did make of Geneva an important mustering point for the Huguenot armies which were so quickly assembled at the beginning of the second war of religion. Just as prewar mustering in Provence and Guyenne had made possible Condé's surprisingly rapid mobilization in the first war, so the muster to defend Geneva helped in the assembly of an army that could be used in the second war. By welcoming and maintaining a garrison, Geneva provided one of a number of cadres around which the armies of rebellion could gather. This contribution may have been inadvertent. But given Mouvans' well-known and repeatedly demonstrated penchant for conspiracy, it is hard to believe that the Genevans could have been entirely surprised at the eventual use of these troops for revolt in France. One can therefore hardly absolve Geneva of all responsibility for its coming.

In these developments, the Genevan pastors did not play a major role. Beza, however, helped in their initiation, was fully informed of them, passed much of his information on to Bullinger in Zurich, partly to secure what diplomatic support he could for Geneva's requests. So Beza, too, cannot be absolved of all responsibility.

3. *The Third War of Religion*

Beza must bear more direct responsibility for a fascinating though unsuccessful attempt to muster mercenary troops for the third war of religion.

---

[1] Geneva, Arch., RC, LXII, fol. 141, 18 December 1567.

[2] E. Arnaud, *Provence*, I, 197-199. Mouvans' body could not be discovered after this skirmish. H.-V. Aubert, in his Geneva, MHR, notes on Mouvans, claims that a letter of Beza's written early in 1569, indicates that Mouvans lived on for several months.

[3] A. Roget, *Hist. de Genève*, VII, 219.

In this instance, he acted more as a private citizen than as a consultant to the Genevan government. In concert with Bullinger, he engaged in a super-secret attempt to enlist a troop of Swiss soldiers for the French Reformed cause.

The initiative for this maneuver came from a group of noblemen in the German-speaking part of Switzerland who made a career of recruiting and commanding bands of the crack Swiss mercenary infantrymen which for decades had been among the most effective fighting men in Europe. Of these noblemen the most prominent was a Baron Ulrich Philip von Hohensax im Rheintal, a devoted Protestant who had sometimes worked for the city of Zurich, who knew Bullinger well, and who also had many friends among the mercenary captains in the cantons of Glarus and Grisons. He was occasionally mentioned in letters between Bullinger and the two leading pastors of Chur in the Grisons, Johannes Fabricius and Tobias Egli, as a source of news on political developments in other parts of Europe.[1]

Hohensax may have been led to propose this project by an overture which he had received a year earlier from Geneva. In a moment of panic, when first report of Alva's march near its borders had reached Geneva in 1567, the city Council had somehow sent a confidential appeal to Hohensax for help in defending the city. On April 8, 1567, Hohensax made a special trip to Zurich from his nearby castle, to ask Bullinger to send Beza an apologetic rejection of this appeal. Hohensax asked that Geneva be informed that his first allegiance was to Zurich, and he hesitated to take on a project of this sort without approval of the magistracy of that city. He also passed on the news, quite accurate as it turned out, that the Spanish ambassador to the Catholic cantons, Anguisciola, had formally promised the Bernese that Alva's army had no designs on them or their allies. If it turned out that this information was incorrect, and Geneva was indeed in danger, Hohensax would be happy to reconsider his decision, providing, of course, that local authorities would give him permission to help Geneva.[2] His decision, of course, did not have to be reconsidered. Beza's return letter to Bullinger asked that the thanks of the Geneva Council be conveyed to Hohensax, and reported that not only had the threat from the Spanish diminished, but also the arrival of French Reformed soldiers, the assurance of support from Berne, and the enrollment of local citizens, made any further military help quite unnecessary.[3]

Shortly over a year later, in the lull between the peace of Longjumeau which ended the second war of religion and the flight of Condé to La Rochelle which opened the third war, Hohensax and his friends took the intiative in suggesting a new plan. They took this initiative by speaking to Bullinger, urging that he write in extremely guarded language to Beza, who was then to pass their proposal along to Condé and Coligny. They did not make clear why they were offering their plan in this circuitous way, but there are several fairly obvious possible explanations for this approach. Because of the earlier correspondence, Hohensax at least knew that Beza and Bullinger were in

[1] See Traugott Schiess, ed., *Bullingers Korrespondenz mit den Graubündern*, II and III (vols. 24 and 25 in *Quellen zur Schweizer Geschichte* [Basel, 1905-1906]), *passim*. Hereafter cited as T. Schiess, *Bullingers Korrespondenz*.

[2] Bullinger to Beza, 8 April 1567, in Geneva, BPU, Ms. l. 120, fols. 71-72, signed original.

[3] Beza to Bullinger, 3 May [1567], in Zürich, Staatsarchiv, E II 350, pp. 55-58.

constant touch with each other and frequently exchanged political information of a privileged sort. He may also have wanted to use them to vault a language barrier, since they exchanged letters in Latin, while his language was German and that of Condé's suite French. He and his friends, furthermore, probably wanted to negotiate through private individuals in order to maintain a special secrecy. For their project was of a sort that could easily have angered the governing magistrates in Zurich and other cantons in German Switzerland, given their special claim on these mercenaries' services.

The first message from the Swiss captains to Beza was passed on by Bullinger in a letter of June 7, 1568.[1] It expressed regret that Swiss soldiers had been used by the French Court to destroy true churches. It asked that Condé and Coligny be informed that they had friends in Switzerland who might be able to give them substantial help, even if war should begin again. It asked that a time and place be set for formal but secret negotiations. All of this was couched in extremely guarded language, passed on by Bullinger with very little comment but with strict injunctions to maintain secrecy and destroy the letter. Beza's answers to this letter were still more guarded. The first of them were nothing but acknowledgments that he had received Bullinger's letters.[2] While this early exchange never even identified the Swiss captains or provided any details of what they proposed to do, it became quite clear from later letters that they meant to offer their services as recruiters and commanders of mercenary troops to the Huguenot leaders, even though France was technically still at peace. These later letters also make it clear that Beza quickly took steps to investigate their offer. He arranged to send for consultation with the Huguenot leaders, a French Protestant nobleman who had rendered important services to the cause before. His name was "Bernaud" or "Bernard." Most probably he was Nicolas Barnaud, one of the Protestant captains who had volunteered to defend Geneva in 1567.[3]

---

[1] [Bullinger] to Beza, 7 June 1568, in Geneva, BPU, Ms. l. 120, fols. 86-87, unsigned original, largely an extended quotation of a secret message from "an important personage." A later letter, 1st of 24 August 1568, in Zürich, Staatsarchiv, E II 441, pp. 600-603, incomplete contemporary copy, identifies him as Hohensax.

[2] Beza to Bullinger, 19 and 21 June 1568, in Geneva, BPU, Ms. l. 118A, fols. 71, 72-73, signed originals. (The first page of the second letter is in Ms. l. 118B, fol. 189.)

[3] Revealed by this passage in Geneva, Arch., RC, 1567: "Estant rapporté que Nicolas Barnaud est capitaine de bonne volonté qui désire faire service, aimant Dieu et cette ville, arrêté de le recevoir bourgeois gratis." Quoted in *France protestante*, 2nd ed., art. "Barnaud (Nicolas)," which goes on to identify him with the well-known author of works on hermetic philosophy, theology, and, perhaps, on politics. His entrance into the Geneva bourgeoisie is confirmed by an entry of 29 April 1567, in Geneva, LB, pp. 281-282. His role as a diplomat working for the Protestant cause is confirmed by a passage in Geneva, Arch., RC, LXII, fol. 143, 26 December 1567: "Ceux de Lyon voulant envoyer Barnaud à la cour pour leurs affaires, le Conseil décide de le licencier." Quoted in Beza, *Corr.*, IV, 43, n. 8, and called to my attention by M. Alain Dufour. The letters between Beza and Bullinger, when they refer to this envoy by name at all, call him only "Bernantii" (Beza to [Bullinger], 18 August 1568, in Geneva, BPU, Ms. l. 118A, fol. 81, signed original), or "Bernardum" or "Bernando" (Bullinger to [Beza], 3rd letter of 24 August 1568, in Zürich, Staatsarchiv, E II 342a, fol. 554, signed original). A little additional information is provided by this passage from Bullinger's diary for 1568: "Nicolaus Bernaudus venit 21 Iulii missus a Condeo principe propter scriptum, quod iussus a clariss. etc., miseram Bezae, sed frustra." Quoted in A. Bouvier, *Bullinger*, p. 300, who identifies the envoy as Godefroy Bernard, sire de Haumont, a special ambassador from Condé to the Swiss in 1562, an identification which seems to me less probable.

Barnaud found the Huguenot leaders, probably Condé, perhaps also Coligny and d'Andelot, enthusiastic about the prospect of support from the Swiss. They empowered him to negotiate further. Beza accordingly sent him along to Zurich, ostensibly to purchase two horses, a precaution taken to disguise the diplomatic purpose of the trip. With Barnaud went a letter from Beza to Bullinger, with word that he could report on the reactions of the Huguenot leaders, either directly or through some intermediary. Since time was of the essence, Barnaud had also been instructed to guide representatives of the Swiss directly to the Huguenot leaders' Court in France, for conclusive negotiations. This letter of Beza's was written on July 17, more than a month after the first overtures from the Hohensax group.[1] Barnaud's travels explain much of this delay, but one suspects that some rather deliberate consultations among the Huguenot leaders account for some of it.

Bullinger did what he could to get a quick response for Barnaud. But Hohensax begged for time to consult with his fellow captains and to permit return from another task of his son, whom he wanted to involve directly in these negotiations. Barnaud was accordingly sent back to Geneva, and told to await further instructions there. In the letter reporting this turn of events to Beza, Bullinger went on to express some cautions about the whole project. He noted that squabbles within the Grisons might well distract some of the people who proposed it. And he said quite frankly that he was pessimistic that these men could deliver the services they promised.[2] In reply, Beza urged Bullinger to continue the negotiations. He felt it obvious that the Lord had inspired these brave Swiss. He recommended complete trust in God's Providence, since it can produce unexpected miracles. And he reported that the Huguenot leaders had twice written to urge haste in the conclusion of this negotiation.[3] It was already August 6, at the time Beza wrote this last letter, just over two weeks before Condé and Coligny were to make their dash across France. On August 18, Beza wrote again for information of the Swiss intentions. He reported that the situation was becoming ever more tense in France, and that Huguenot troops were being mustered throughout the country, particularly in the southern provinces.[4]

Finally on August 24, Bullinger had to inform Beza that the whole project had collapsed. In no less than three substantial letters which he wrote to Geneva on that day, he explained in detail what its entire nature had been and offered Beza advice on what should be done next. Apparently the project's collapse made Bullinger feel free to abandon the extreme guardedness in which he had cast his earlier messages. He could now say openly that the men for whom he had been writing were not officials of any of the Swiss Protestant

[1] Beza to Bullinger, 17 July 1568, in Geneva, BPU, Ms. l. 118A, fols. 75-76, signed original, is the extremely guarded letter Barnaud took with him. Bullinger's reply (see n. 2), acknowledges Barnaud's arrival and reveals a bit more about his mission—it says he had been sent by the "prince," i.e. Condé. Only the later letters cited in n. 3 to p. 185, reveal Barnaud's name.

[2] Bullinger to [Beza], 24 July 1568, in Zürich, Staatsarchiv, E II 342a, fols. 540-541, signed original, mistakenly bound as a letter to Egli.

[3] Beza to Bullinger, 6 August 1568, in Geneva, BPU, Ms. l. 118A, fol. 77, signed original.

[4] Beza to Bullinger, 18 August 1568, in *ibid.*, fols. 81-82, signed original.

cities, but were rather mercenary captains, some from Glarus, some from the Grisons, including Hohensax. All of these men received pensions from the King of France, in part for past service, but even more to encourage them to recruit troops for his service whenever he had need of them. This was obviously a basic reason for the extreme secrecy in which the negotiations proceeded, since the King was unlikely to continue pensioning men who proposed to work for his enemies. It was also a reason for Bullinger's skepticism that anything would come of the project. While they were Protestant, and had refused to serve the King of France during the previous religious wars within that country, these captains had never gone so far as to join his enemies. If they had tried to do so, Bullinger thought it quite likely that they would have been subject to punitive action from the Catholic leaders who controlled most of the areas which supplied mercenary troops, and Bullinger suspected that realization of this prospect might well have dampened their ardor and made it difficult for them to recruit troops. He pointed out further that even if they had recruited troops, it would have been difficult to get them through Swiss Catholic territory into France; and even if they had arrived in France, they could have been recalled by the Catholic authorities who generally controlled the diet of the Swiss Confederation; and even if they had not been recalled, they would not have fought well unless Condé could have paid them handsomely. Each step in this lengthy argument Bullinger illustrated by references to actual difficulties experienced in recent years by Protestant powers in Germany and France who had tried to make use of Swiss mercenaries.[1]

This rather lengthy negative argument, revealing though it is of the ways in which the Swiss mercenaries operated, turned out at the moment to be quite superfluous. Later on in the same day, Bullinger received a message from the Hohensax group which he immediately forwarded to Beza. It was a long apology for their failure to enter into the negotiations which they had requested. They argued that the actual outbreak of hostilities (and by this they must have meant Condé's move to his Burgundian castle, since it is impossible that they could have had word of his flight, the day before, toward La Rochelle) made it too dangerous for them to proceed further with their plan. Furthermore the outbreak of plague in Geneva and the insecurity of the route from Geneva into France, made it unlikely that a negotiator could get through.[2]

Both Bullinger and the Hohensax group, however, did make an alternative suggestion. They urged that Condé send an ambassador to the Swiss Protestant cantons who could explain his case fully. Bullinger claimed that Condé had made a serious mistake in not doing so during the second war of religion. He said that none of the Swiss had received any information from

[1] Drawn from Bullinger to Beza, 1st letter of 24 August 1568, in Zürich, Staatsarchiv, E II 441, pp. 600-603, incomplete contemporary copy. The 2nd letter of 24 August 1568, in Geneva, BPU, Ms. l. 120, fols. 90-91, signed original, is largely an answer to Beza's letter of 18 August, about developments in France.

[2] Bullinger to [Beza], 3rd letter of 24 August 1568, in Zürich, Staatsarchiv, E II 342a, fol. 554, signed original. In spite of the collapse of this project, Hohensax in later years did try to renew relations with the French Huguenot leaders, again through Bullinger. In July of 1572, shortly before the St. Bartholomew's massacres, Bullinger wrote a letter of recommendation to the Admiral Coligny for the young Philip von Hohensax, probably a son of the man responsible for the 1568 intrigue, who planned to visit the French royal Court (A. Bouvier, *Bullinger*, p. 327 and n. 2).

Condé, and consequently could not defend his innocence. There was thus no one to stop the official French ambassador from persuading the Swiss that the French crown faced a simple rebellion and from enrolling all the troops he wanted. Both Bullinger and the Hohensax group felt that if Condé would send an ambassador this time, to counter the work of the French ambassador, he might well be able to prevent the enrollment of Swiss mercenaries for the Catholic cause, or at least to cut the size of the levy.[1]

Condé no longer needed this advice. He may have already realized the extent of his earlier error. In any event, he had already commissioned Félix de Bourjac, sénéchal of Valentinois, to go to Switzerland as his ambassador. Bourjac's formal instructions were drafted on August 13,[2] well before the collapse of the Hohensax group's intrigue, for that matter even before hostilities began in earnest. Bourjac had already passed through Geneva on his way to Berne,[3] when Beza acknowledged Bullinger's three letters on September 2. Beza urged Bullinger to see Bourjac and to help him in every possible way. Bourjac was to provide Bullinger with a printed copy of Condé's official explanation of the reasons he had been forced to arms again. Beza felt strongly that this document should be translated quickly into German and printed, although he thought it possible that arrangements for doing so had already been made in Heidelberg, where another copy was being sent.[4]

Bullinger immediately set to work, to do what he could to help Bourjac. He wrote to Hohensax and his friends, urging them to get in touch with the Huguenot ambassador.[5] The Zurich government, at Bourjac's request, took the initiative in calling a diet of the Swiss leagues, in order to decide on appropriate action, now that war had begun again in France. Bourjac also went to Schaffhausen and Basel, to state Condé's case to the authorities in those two Protestant municipalities. Bullinger felt it necessary to discourage Bourjac from entering the Catholic cantons, however, because of the dangers which such a trip would entail.[6]

Much of this hard work proved futile. The experienced royal ambassador, Pomponne de Bellièvre, in years of negotiation with the Swiss had proved himself extremely skillful at managing them. He adroitly persuaded the Catholic cantons' representatives to caucus three days before the opening of the Swiss diet, and they decided that they would not permit Condé's ambassador to address the diet. Bourjac, who Bullinger had to admit "does not know the first word of our affairs," was simply unable to counter these maneu-

---

[1] See 1st and 3rd letters of 24 August 1568, cited in ns. 1 and 2, to. p. 187.

[2] E. Rott, *Représentation*, II, 161.

[3] On his visit to Geneva, see J.-A. Gautier, *Hist. de Genève*, V, 18-19.

[4] Beza to Bullinger, 2 September 1568, in Geneva, BPU, Ms. l. 118A, fols. 85-86, signed original. The printed catalogue of the French Bibliothèque Nationale lists a *Lettres et requeste envoyez au roy, par Monseigneur le prince de Condé, contenant les causes et raisons de son despart de Noyers (23 août 1568)*, published in 1568, which may be the document to which Beza alludes. Or perhaps he alludes to a 1568 reprinting of the *Discours véritable des propos tenus par Monsieur le prince de Condé avec les seigneurs députez par le roy, contenant les causes qui ont contraint ledict seigneur prince et autres de sa compagnie à prendre les armes (Octobre 1567)*, which definitely was published in German in 1568, again according to the B. N. catalogue.

[5] Reported in Bullinger to Beza, 8 September 1568, in Geneva, BPU, Ms. l. 120, fol. 92, signed original.

[6] Reported in Bullinger to Beza, 18 September 1568, in *ibid.*, fol. 93, signed original.

vers. He could not even obtain a safe-conduct to Baden, where the diet was meeting, and had to settle for a written presentation of his case. Bellièvre, who was on the scene, had no trouble in countering that, and had little difficulty in persuading the diet to grant his master permission to enlist another 4000 mercenaries.

Bourjac's mission was not entirely without success, however. At his request, the Protestant cities, Zurich, Berne, Basel, and Schaffhausen, did decide to prohibit the enrollment of their own inhabitants in the new levy for the French King. And Bullinger expected that even the Catholic mercenary captains would run into trouble recruiting troops in certain areas, thanks to the widespread publicity which had been given to Condé's case. In reporting this, though, Bullinger again expressed regret that nothing had come of the overtures from Hohensax and his friends.[1]

Thus collapsed an intriguing attempt to enroll Swiss mercenaries for the defense of French Protestantism. The very considerable role which the Protestant spiritual leaders Beza and Bullinger played in these abortive negotiations is nonetheless extremely revealing. Neither betrayed any hesitation about becoming involved in political action, and furthermore action of an extremely suspect sort, which we might as well call conspiracy.[2] This in spite of their frequent public declarations of devotion to the governmental powers established by God. Their every step reveals implicit acceptance of the notion that resistance to these powers is indeed permissible, if undertaken in the name of the true religion by men who have responsible subordinate positions within a government. This doctrine of the right to resistance by " inferior magistrates " had, of course, been enunciated earlier by Calvin, and even earlier by certain of his predecessors. Beza himself had stated such a doctrine in passing.[3] But it was a doctrine which few except such rebellious Britons as Knox and Ponet were willing to develop in detail. Not until after the St. Bartholomew's massacres, were French Protestants, most prominently Beza himself, to develop this view in detail and with consistency.[4] It is therefore interesting to see them trying to put the doctrine into practice years before the massacres drove them to public avowal of it.

Of the two pastors, Bullinger was obviously the more cautious. Throughout his correspondence about the plot, he underlined the fact that he was only acting as an intermediary, and frequently expressed skepticism about its feasibility. His reservations were entirely prudential, however. He simply did not believe that such a project could succeed. At no point did he raise any objections to its morality. Yet practically any government and almost any objective observer would regard as subversive a plan such as this, to enroll foreign mercenary troops in the service of subordinate officers of a duly

[1] For a detailed report of this meeting of the diet and the aftermath, see Bullinger to Beza, 10 October 1568, in *ibid.*, fols. 94-95, unsigned original. See also E. Rott, *Représentation*, II, 74-77, a corroborrating but less detailed account, largely based on Bellièvre's dispatches.

[2] Cf. the curious claim of A. Bouvier, *Bullinger*, p. 256, that Zurich and Berne at this period were motivated only by " evangelical pacifism " (" pacifisme évangélique ").

[3] See Robert M. Kingdon, " The First Expression of Theodore Beza's Political Ideas," ARG, XLVI (1955), 88-100.

[4] Analyzed, *inter alia*, by Pierre Mesnard, *L'essor de la philosophie politique au XVIe siècle*, 2nd ed. (Paris: Vrin, 1952), pp. 315-363.

constituted legitimate government. Bullinger's prudence in dealing with this plot, is reminiscent of Calvin's at the time of the Conspiracy of Amboise, eight years earlier. Yet Calvin, as far as the leading modern expert can judge, had not permitted himself to be used to advance the conspiracy. Beza, on the other hand, apparently had helped its advance at that time, and so would have had few moral scruples to overcome in 1568.[1]

Perhaps another lesson can be drawn from this story. The 1568 conspiracy did not, after all, succeed. It did not even approach success, since the Huguenot leaders and the Swiss mercenary captains never actually entered into direct negotiations. For this failure, the Swiss must bear the primary blame, since the Huguenots, after a short delay, did press repeatedly for negotiation. But perhaps Bullinger and Beza also deserve a little of the blame. Maybe men more experienced in Swiss diplomacy or more skillful at intrigue would have been able either to advance the plot further or to see its futility earlier. It seems at least possible that the collapse of the plot embarrassed Condé seriously. He could have been counting on Swiss mercenary support when he decided to defy the royal Court and again resort to arms in August of 1568. Perhaps the pastors' ineffectiveness helps to explain why the great Huguenot leaders did not make more use of them in the political maneuvers to advance the common cause.

In any case, it seems clear that the great Huguenot leaders did not make much further use of the Genevan pastors during the further course of the third war of religion. Not only was there no attempt to use Beza as an ambassador, as he had been used during the first war. The two ambassadors who did arrive in Switzerland toward the end of the third war, do not seem to have bothered to work very closely with Beza. This may be due partly, however, to the fact that their missions were to some extent incidental to other more important ones in other areas. Both du Broullat and Vézines arrived in Switzerland from Germany, where they had been negotiating for the large levies of German Protestant mercenaries which were so important to the Huguenot military effort. Du Broullat arrived in Switzerland from Strasbourg, in November of 1569, and naturally visited Basel, Berne, and Zurich first. Only at the end of his stay, when he was about ready to return to France, did du Broullat even visit Geneva.[2] He did stay there for a while, probably largely just to rest. Vézines similarly arrived in Switzerland from Germany, on a diplomatic tour which had begun with a visit to London, aimed largely at raising subsidies and troops for the Huguenot cause. The most important part of his job was already over, since much of the subsidy had come from England and most of the troops from Germany. Furthermore, by the time he got to Switzerland, it was becoming clear that the war would not last much longer. Apparently neither of these ambassadors worked through the Protestant pastors. The continuing correspondence between Beza and Bullinger during these months says practically nothing of their missions.

Nevertheless, the pastors, in their own way, may have made contributions to Huguenot diplomacy more important than those of the ambassadors. Such

---

[1] See H. Naef, *Conjuration d'Amboise*, ch. VII, for a detailed judgment of the role of both Calvin and Beza. There is reason to believe that Calvin did consent to a later, similarly abortive, conspiracy, which was to be launched in Lyon : see Beza, *Corr.*, III, 63-64, and the work of Alain Dufour there cited.

[2] E. Rott, *Représentation*, II, 163.

an argument can be made particularly for Bullinger's activities. They included a very careful watch on the negotiations of Bellièvre, and particularly on the results of the meetings of the Swiss diets. Several times during the fall of 1569, these diets met, at Bellièvre's request, to consider the French King's renewed pleas for mercenary troops. In countering Bellièvre's maneuvers, Bullinger had several weapons. The one which involved Beza's cooperation most closely was simply dissemination of news from France. The uses to which he could put such reports, he reveals in a particularly explicit way in a letter of September 17, 1569. In it he reported that the diet was about to meet again, in Soleure, at Bellièvre's request. He noted that it was customary for the royal party to circulate rumors of victories by the royal armies in France, to encourage the Swiss to join an apparently winning cause. Some of these rumors were apparently enclosed in letters from the royal Court itself. In the present instance, the rumor which Bullinger had to counter was that Admiral Coligny had been killed in battle and his army torn to pieces. In countering it, he had found particularly useful Beza's report of September 14, that in fact a Protestant army under Coligny had invested the important city of Poitiers and was pressing its siege.[1] At other times, Bullinger begged Beza, often repeatedly, for confirmation of news of such events as the Huguenot defeats at Jarnac and at Moncontour and of Condé's death at the first of those two disasters.[2]

Beza, in return, tried to tailor his reports of news to meet Bullinger's needs. He was almost always optimistic. He denied rumors, some of which later turned out to be true, as the one of Mouvans' death in central France.[3] He minimized defeats, pointing out, for example, that the Huguenots had retired in good order from Jarnac, and in leaving the area had sucessfully raided Cognac,[4] or, again, that Coligny, in retreating after Moncontour, was rapidly retiring in good order to the south while the royal armies were disintegrating.[5] Beza made much of Huguenot victories. He also reported in detail on Catholic atrocities. Occasionally, he noted Protestant atrocities in passing, as, for example, a massacre of religious during the capture of Angoulême.[6] And occasionally, his optimism failed him and he would make some black remark about the dismal prospects for ultimate Protestant success.

It is not clear just what Bullinger did with these reports of French news from Geneva. He did mention passing some of them on to delegates at the Swiss diets. No doubt he simply turned them over to the magistrates charged with Zurich's diplomacy, for appropriate use.

Most of the rest of Bullinger's activities on behalf of the French did not depend on Beza's direct cooperation. Some were undertaken at Beza's request,

---

[1] Bullinger to Beza, 17 September 1569, Geneva, BPU, Ms. l. 120, fols. 116-117, signed original, and Beza to Bullinger, 14 September 1569, Zürich, Staatsarchiv, E I 25.8, signed original.

[2] E.g. letters of Bullinger to Beza, [10], 17, 24 April 1569, re Jarnac and Condé's death; 14 and 16 October 1569, re Moncontour; in Geneva, BPU, Ms. l. 120, fols. 102, 103-104, 105, 121-122, 123, signed originals.

[3] Beza to Bullinger, 20 November 1568, in Zürich, Zentralbibliothek, Ms. A 84, No. 533, signed original.

[4] Beza to Bullinger, 4 May 1569, in Zürich, Staatsarchiv, E I 25.8, signed original.

[5] Beza to Bullinger, 2 December 1569, in *ibid.*, signed original.

[6] Beza to Bullinger, 31 October 1568, in *ibid.*, signed original.

however, and on them Bullinger reported frequently, if rather vaguely. On August 11, 1569, when Beza knew that Bellièvre was going to ask for a new Swiss levy, he asked Bullinger's help in blocking this move, and, among other things, suggested that Bullinger do what he could to persuade the Protestant cantons both to renew their prohibitions on enlistment of their citizens in the mercenary bands being organized for service to the French crown, and to order their pastors to exhort the faithful in every parish to resist the enticements of the recruiters.[1] This request Bullinger worked actively to satisfy. It would take a detailed study of his correspondence to demonstrate precisely just what he did do. But even published samples from that mammoth treasury of unpublished letters, reveal much. On August 12, for example, even before Beza's request could possibly have reached him, Bullinger wrote to Egli at Chur in the Grisons, urging him to do what he could to stop French recruitment.[2] He repeated these urgings in subsequent letters to Egli. No doubt he sent similar appeals to many other pastors of Zwinglian persuasion in the Swiss German cantons. By September 17, he was able to inform Beza that he had worked hard to persuade those in Zurich, Glarus, and the Grisons to prevent recruitment, and, he felt, with some success.[3] Throughout the succeeding months his letters continue to report occasional success in the campaign to stop recruitment for the French crown at the local level. Even some of the Catholic cantons refused to support the royal levy, to Bullinger's delight, although he did not take credit for their decisions.

It is a little hard to estimate just how much credit Bullinger deserves for harassing the French ambassador's attempts to get mercenaries. In the end, after months of delay, Bellièvre did get most of the troops that his master wanted, and was commanded to lead them back into France in person. By that time, however, the critical stages of the war were past, and preliminary negotiations for peace were underway. Soon after Bellièvre got back to France, he had to begin negotiations with Swiss captains, both in the army he conducted and in detachments which had arrived earlier, for a general demobilization, negotiations which involved rather delicate matters of payment.[4] Perhaps Bullinger deserves considerable credit for the delay in this 1569-1570 levy which proved so opportune for the French Huguenots. It would be hard to prove it from Bellièvre's official report, however. He seems to have been much more aware of several other obstacles to the levy, some of which came from Catholic powers, both in and out of Switzerland. But Bullinger's influence, of course, would have been exercised behind the scenes, and might have come to Bellièvre's attention only as an increased stubbornness on the part of the Protestant delegates to the Swiss diet.

By dealing with mercenary captains, German Swiss governments, and Zwinglian pastors, Bullinger worked hard to advance the cause of French Protestantism. In many of these negotiations, he received useful support from Beza. That he did not receive more, is no doubt evidence of the Genevan

---

[1] Beza to Bullinger, 11 August 1569, in *ibid.*, signed original.

[2] Bullinger to Egli, 12 August 1569, in T. Schiess, *Bullingers Korrespondenz*, III, 157-158.

[3] Bullinger to Beza, 17 September 1569, in Geneva, BPU, Ms. l. 120, fols. 116-117, signed original.

[4] E. Rott, *Représentation*, II, 83-87.

republic's increasing weakness and isolation. Geneva's failure to contribute as much as she had in the first war of religion provides further evidence. Her main material contribution during this war, was a local relief program she organized for the substantial numbers of pastors and other refugees who flooded into the city, particularly in the fall of 1568.[1] Even this large relief program, however, was made possible, in part, by Bullinger. Working at Beza's request, he persuaded the governments of Zurich and St. Gall to send substantial gifts to Geneva, earmarked for relief.[2]

D. The return of Peace

The two years stretching from the Peace of St. Germain, signed in August of 1570, to the massacres of St. Bartholomew's, perpetrated in August of 1572, were probably the most halcyon in all of history for those French Protestants who looked to Geneva for guidance. From the edict of pacification which issued from the peace treaty, they received more than ever before. Not only were they granted, as before, right to hold worship services in the private homes of noblemen, in cities which their forces held as hostilities ended, and in certain other assigned communities—this time in the suburbs of an average of two cities per "gouvernement." They were also granted ways of escaping from the jurisdiction of certain notoriously hostile judges and courts—most notably the Parlement of Toulouse—which had harried them for years by stern application of anti-heresy laws. And they were, in addition, granted the use of four cities, in which armed Huguenot garrisons could be stationed for a period of two years, as places of refuge for those Protestants who were afraid to return home immediately. These four cities were La Rochelle, Cognac, Montauban, and La Charité.[3]

Furthermore, the course of events during the months following promulgation of the edict of pacification, promised much to the Huguenot cause. Admiral Coligny, their greatest remaining leader, returned to the royal Court and received an unexpectedly warm welcome. He rose to positions of ever greater prominence there, and seemed to be winning the favor and confidence of young King Charles IX himself. Coligny used this position to push ardently his anti-Spanish project.[4] It was designed to heal the wounds of civil war by uniting Frenchmen of all factions in battle against the nation's traditional foreign enemy, the Hapsburgs. The Hapsburgs were to be attacked in the Netherlands, an area uniquely open geographically to French invasion, and right then particularly ripe for assault, because of the Netherlanders' bitter reaction to Alva's campaign of suppression. This policy appealed to those Frenchmen moderate in religious controversy, who wanted to avoid further

---

[1] E. Choisy, *Genève au temps de Bèze*, pp. 68-73.

[2] Beza to Bullinger, 20 November 1568, with Bullinger's detailed notes on back, dated January 1569, re his successful appeals to authorities in Zürich and St. Gall; in Zürich, Zentralbibliothek, Ms. A 84, No. 533, signed original.

[3] For full text of the Edict of St. Germain, see J. Delaborde, *Coligny*, III, 569-578.

[4] Described in detail in A. W. Whitehead, *Coligny*, ch. XIV.

civil war at all costs. It appealed to the King's growing yearning for military glory. And it had a special appeal to French Calvinists, eager to rescue from Spanish persecution the growing number of their fellow Calvinists in the Low Countries.

Within the French Reformed Church, the mood was consequently one of growing confidence, and activity was concentrated on a national program of rebuilding and consolidation. This work of consolidation reached a formal climax at two national synods, one held in La Rochelle, in April of 1571, the other held in Nîmes, in May of 1572. We have already studied what those synods did to suppress the party of Morély, and maintain the authority of the synodical structure created under Calvin's direction.[1] There were other developments at these synods, however, which merit consideration from our present point of view.

The Synod held at La Rochelle in 1571, is sometimes called the " Synod of Princes." Practically all of the most prominent Huguenot military and political leaders actually attended its sessions and subscribed to its decisions. Their presence helped make this Synod probably the most important in French Protestant history. It also symbolized neatly the closeness of the cooperation then prevailing between the spiritual and political leaders of the movement. Among the aristocrats in attendance were : the young princes of Navarre and Condé, both of royal blood, in the line of succession to the national crown, hence the titular leaders of the Huguenot party ; Jeanne d'Albret and the Admiral Coligny, at that time the actual leaders of the party ; Louis of Nassau, better known today for his militant role in provoking the revolt of the Netherlands and in aiding his brother, William of Orange, in its prosecution, but honored then for his recent military achievements in France, as an army commander working with Coligny.

As we noted in an earlier chapter, the pastors at the La Rochelle Synod also included men of the greatest prominence.[2] They were furthermore men particularly devoted to the leadership of Geneva. This was demonstrated in the most direct possible way by the election of Theodore Beza as the Synod's Moderator. Beza came from Geneva expressly to attend the Synod. His departure, however, turned out to be unexpectedly difficult. In spite of the fact that the Geneva Council received a formal request that Beza be allowed to attend, from Jeanne d'Albret, her son, and the Admiral Coligny, its members hesitated to give Beza permission to make the trip.[3] Their hesitation was caused primarily by open and vigorous opposition to his departure from within the Company of Pastors. This opposition comes as something of a surprise, since Beza was, after all, the presiding officer of the Company. That it developed at all, is probably testimony to the growing strength of the faction led by Colladon and Le Gaigneux. The formal reasons advanced by the Company for its opposition, however, are quite revealing. Beza's colleagues were anxious, of course, about the risks involved in a trip, through hostile territory, by a man so well-known and so important to the cause. But they were also afraid that his participation in the Synod would give further plausi-

[1] See above, pp. 96-111.

[2] See above, p. 97.

[3] For a detailed account of its deliberations, see E. Choisy, *Genève au temps de Bèze*, pp. 74-75.

bility to the persistent charge, advanced first in Calvin's day, that Geneva wanted to assume a role of direction over the entire French Reformed Church.[1] And they were additionally afraid that the royal Court, on learning that Beza was at La Rochelle, would suspect that another political conspiracy was in the making. While these protests may be explained away, in part, as a result of internal jealousies within the Company, it is very interesting that Beza's closest associates should come close to accusing him of inordinate ambition and a taste for conspiracy. Finally, the pastors insisted that the admittedly important tasks facing this Synod could be handled competently by such other pastors formed by Geneva as Viret and des Gallars.

Weighty though these objections were, they were, in the end, rejected by the Council. In deciding to let Beza go regardless, the Council was swayed above all by political considerations. It did not want to irritate unnecessarily people as powerful and as useful to Geneva as the Queen of Navarre and Admiral Coligny. And it wanted very much to obtain certain items of information concerning the city, which Coligny said were important yet could not be put into writing, but which he would be happy to pass on to Beza in person. The fact the Huguenot aristocrats were sponsoring this Synod and planned to attend it themselves, was thus decisive in making possible Beza's attendance. With Council approval secure, Beza wasted no time in leaving Geneva, had soon crossed France, and took over the direction of the Synod.

The Huguenot aristocrats did more than simply sponsor this Synod. They also participated directly in its deliberations. This is made very clear in all the bewilderingly various versions of the official acts of the Synod. A concluding section in most of these versions proclaims the fact that the Queen of Navarre, the princes of Navarre and Condé, Louis of Nassau, and Coligny, as well as "divers other Lords and Gentlemen," were in attendance.[2] The Confession of Faith, which was the most important product of the Synod's deliberations, was furthermore formally signed by these aristocrats, as well as by the official delegates of the churches who made up most of the membership of the Synod. Signature by the aristocrats was provided for by an act of the Synod itself.[3] The official parchment copy of the Confession which has been on deposit in Geneva ever since 1572, accordingly still can be seen to bear the signatures, in order, of Jeanne d'Albret, Henri of Navarre, Henri of Condé, Louis of Nassau, Coligny, Beza, and the delegates, most of them pastors, deputed to represent each of the provincial synods in France.[4]

Participation of this sort, of course, is something of a formality and could be quite perfunctory. That it went further, however, is made clear by other articles in the official acts of the Synod. It is made particularly clear by an article noting that the Queen of Navarre had specifically asked the Synod, if she could, "with a good Conscience Receive and Establish Roman Catholick Officers in her Dominions, as also in her Court and Family." Her question is reminiscent of one she had earlier put to Beza, about the most effective way

[1] "entreprendre sur les aultres églises," in *ibid.*, p. 74, quoting from Geneva, Arch., RC.

[2] J. Quick, *Synodicon*, I, 101. Also J. Aymon, *Synodes*, I, 2nd pagination, p. 111.

[3] J. Quick, *Synodicon*, I, 92-93, art. VIII; J. Aymon, *Synodes*, I, 2nd pagination, p. 100, art. VIII.

[4] Geneva, Arch., PH No. 1905.

to persuade her people to abandon Roman Catholic "idolatry."[1] Both arose from her determined campaign to make entirely Protestant the principality of Béarn, which she controlled by sovereign right, without any accountability to the French crown. The Synod's answer to the Queen's question contains surprises, although it is somewhat less intolerant than one might expect in this period. She was advised:

"That her Majesty should take special heed about her Domestick Officers, and as much as possible only to imploy Persons fearing God, and of the Reformed Religion; And that she should cause the Papists that are peaceable, and of unblameable Lives to be instructed, and that she should utterly discard those Traytors, who forsook her in her Necessities, and cruelly persecuted God's Saints in these last Troubles." [2]

In other words, she was to be particularly careful in the choice of advisers as close to her royal family as Morély had been, she could continue to employ Catholics who were willing to endure Protestant catechizing (and, one suspects, who would seriously consider conversion, if they were at all ambitious), but she should not employ those who had actually fought in the Catholic armies during the preceding wars.

If there were discussions of a pointedly political sort at La Rochelle, of a kind that might have justified fears at Court of a new Protestant conspiracy, there is no official record of them. There is similarly practically no record of the precise nature of the political information concerning Geneva which that city's Council had been so eager to obtain, through Beza, from Coligny. Catholic observers of the Synod were convinced that some sort of intrigue was being mounted in the area around Geneva, largely because Coligny was taking as his second wife a Savoyard noblewoman, thus gaining a personal right to meddle in the politics of the area. Their marriage had actually been celebrated in La Rochelle, shortly before the Synod convened, in colorful ceremonies, including a strikingly feudal one in which Coligny pledged homage to the young prince of Navarre, was made "his" knight, and received a pair of golden spurs and a golden helmet.[3] However on Beza's return to Geneva, his main recorded preoccupation was that the parchment copy of the Confession which was from then on to be normative in matters of doctrine for the entire French Reformed Church, be put in a safe place. The city Council permitted it to be deposited in the "Ark of Seven Keys."[4] This was the most secure of the places in which the city kept its most important papers and supplies of cash, partly because the seven keys could be distributed to seven separate government officials, thus minimizing the chance that corruption of a few could lead to its being raided.

---

[1] Jeanne d'Albret to Beza, 6 December [1566], text published in BSHPF, XVI (1867), 64-67. This is the same letter in which she promised to dismiss Morély. Beza's answer, of about 15 January 1567, drafts of which can be found in Geneva, BPU, Ms. fr. 446, fols. 1-5, contains detailed advice on how to proceed with this effort at mass conversion.

[2] J. Quick, *Synodicon*, I, 99, art. VI; J. Aymon, *Synodes*, I, 2nd pagination, p. 108, art. XLVII. See also Quick, I, 94, art. I, and Aymon, I/2, 102, art. I, for an example of participation by several aristocrats; and Quick, I, 95, art. IX, and Aymon, I/2, 103, art. VIII [sic], for an example of participation by Coligny.

[3] A. W. Whitehead, *Coligny*, p. 233.

[4] Geneva, Arch., RC, LXVI, fol. 73v., 22 May 1571.

One of the aristocrats at La Rochelle whom Beza must have impressed particularly was Louis of Nassau. Almost immediately after Beza's return, he wrote the Geneva Council asking that Beza be permitted to visit his family's principality of Orange, in southeastern France, to superintend the establishment of a Reformed Church there. At the end of June, Louis repeated this request, stating that a visit of two months would suffice.[1] The Council seems to have turned a deaf ear on both requests.

The Synod held at Nîmes in 1572, was called basically to resolve problems created by the La Rochelle decisions. Those who called it, in consequence, wanted Beza to attend. Formal requests that he be permitted to do so, were accordingly sent by the Reformed Church of Nîmes, later seconded by that city's magistrates, to the Geneva Council.[2] However there was again strong opposition to his departure. Again most of it came from the Company of Pastors, which again contended that the trip would be dangerous and that Beza's participation would provide further ammunition for those who accused Geneva of seeking to dominate the French Reformed Church. This time the Council at first yielded to the protest, and suggested that Beza, instead of going, send a written brief of advice to the Synod. Beza appeared to acquiesce, but pointed out that it would be necessary to select someone to carry the brief to Nîmes. He also observed that it was particularly important that the brief arrive safely and be presented ably, since it would have to deal with the critical problems of church discipline and organization, again being agitated by the party of Morély. At this, the Council decided that it might as well let Beza go in person.[3] So Beza again attended the Synod, but this time as an ordinary delegate rather than as the presiding officer.

A great deal of the Synod of Nîmes' time and energy were devoted to the problems posed by Morély's party. Some of them were also devoted to appeasing Bullinger and the Zurichers, still irritated over the condemnations at La Rochelle of dogmatic positions very close to their own.[4] But at one point, at least, the Synod considered a basic political problem. It was the problem of the legitimacy of resistance, and it was brought to the Synod's attention by a letter from Admiral Coligny. At his request, "the Churches were all admonished of their Duty to his Majesty." Coligny was then formally notified that his message had been passed on.[5] He was then at the Court, working hard to win acceptance for his plan for war on Spain. Courtly suspicion of the continuing loyalty of the Protestants was certainly a hurdle he had to overcome in this intrigue. No doubt he asked for this statement as

---

[1] The original copies of these requests have been preserved in Geneva, Arch., PH No. 1906, and are dated 22 April and 30 June 1571. Louis' approach to Beza is not mentioned in the account of his arrangements to pacify and reform Orange, in E. Arnaud, *Provence*, II, 222 and ff.

[2] Geneva, Arch., PH No. 1918, letter of 14 January 1572, cited and quoted above, p. 107 and n. 1. The request was reiterated in letters from both the Church and Magistrates of Nîmes to the Syndics and Council of Geneva, 8 April 1572, originals also preserved in PH No. 1918.

[3] E. Choisy, *Genève au temps de Bèze*, pp. 76-78.

[4] See above, pp. 107-111.

[5] J. Quick, *Synodicon*, I, 112, art. VIII; J. Aymon, *Synodes*, I, 2nd pagination, p. 124, art. VIII.

concrete evidence to support his protestations that the Reformed would indeed remain loyal to the King.

The Synod also supported the request of another high aristocrat, the Queen of Navarre. This was on a matter more ecclesiastical than political, but it did directly concern Geneva. A year earlier, Nicolas des Gallars, who had been forced out of his strategic pulpit in Orleans during the recent wars and who had apparently agreed to return to Geneva, where he was wanted and needed both for the Church and the Academy, had instead been loaned to Jeanne d'Albret, to direct the reformation of Béarn for a year. Viret, who had begun this task, had recently died, and des Gallars had gone from the La Rochelle Synod directly to Béarn, to take his place. Now Jeanne wanted the Synod and Geneva to extend des Gallars' leave of absence, for another year. The Synod supported this request, by an official act of its own,[1] and by dispatching a letter to the Geneva Council.[2] Of course the request was granted. It would have been difficult, perhaps even futile, to refuse. This letter from the Synod, and another from the Church of Nîmes, also thanked the Geneva Council profusely for allowing Beza to attend.[3] As the letter from the Church forcefully put it, Beza, along with other services, had "shut the mouths of certain mischief makers who wanted to trouble our churches."[4]

These letters arrived in Geneva on June 10, less than three months before the St. Bartholomew's massacres. The preparations were already underway in Paris for the grand wedding between Henri of Navarre and Marguerite of Valois which was to symbolize and solidify Coligny's policy of religious reunion within France by uniting leaders from both Protestant and Catholic branches of the royal family. That wedding, of course, was to provide the occasion for the beginning of the massacres. Few Protestants seemed even to suspect this possibility. Beza and the other ecclesiastical leaders of French Protestantism seemed very much preoccupied with internal problems, and quite hopeful for the future of their cause. And at Nîmes they had just gone on public record as being devotedly loyal to the monarch who was soon to order that their secular leaders all be killed.

---

[1] *Ibid.*, art. IX.

[2] Geneva, Arch., PH No. 1918, Synod of Nîmes to Syndics and Council of Geneva, 18 May 1572, signed original.

[3] *Ibid.*, and Church of Nîmes to same, 19 May 1572, signed original, also in PH No. 1918.

[4] " a fermer la bouche a certains brouillons que veulent troubler noz eglises a quoy il s'est tellement et si doctement oppose que nous tous avons grande occasion de louer Dieu."

Conclusion

Early in the morning of August 24, St. Bartholomew's day, in 1572, Gaspard de Coligny died. His assassination touched off the chain of brutal murders known as the St. Bartholomew's massacres. Just as Calvin's death symbolized the beginning of the period upon which this book concentrates, so Coligny's symbolizes its end.

The murder of Coligny was one of the main purposes of the massacres. He was the ablest and the most respected among the lay leaders of French Protestantism. It was his growing personal influence on the King, which determined Catherine de Medicis and her relatively moderate supporters to seek destruction of the Huguenot party. It was his personal leadership of the Huguenot armies, which had lately frustrated attempts sponsored by Catholic extremists to wipe out the Calvinist heresy by military action. And it was his proposal of a war against Spain, which led many in both moderate and extremist factions to fear loss of political ends they valued more than military glory or territorial gain.

Not surprisingly, the young Duke of Guise was asked to superintend the actual assassination of Coligny. He headed the family which had provided leadership to that entire wing of French opinion which was both determined to preserve Roman Catholicism as the sole form of Christianity in France, and was also convinced that putting men to death by execution or in war were permissible and effective means to that end. Guise, furthermore, had personal reasons for hating Coligny. His own father had been assassinated, shortly before the end of the first war of religion, by a man who, under examination by torture, had implicated both Beza and Coligny in the planning of his deed. And while both Beza and Coligny protested their innocence, and most historians are inclined to accept their protestations, Coligny made no secret of his joy and relief at the death of the elder Guise. The Guise family repeatedly sought further judicial investigation of the charge that Coligny was an accessory to the assassination. As a boy, young Guise had sworn vengeance on the man he believed to be responsible for his father's death.[1]

---

[1] See A. W. Whitehead, *Coligny*, ch. IX, for a detailed examination of the question of Coligny's alleged guilt; pp. 169-177, re the further aftermath of the assassination of Guise.

Guise was dispatched to kill Coligny directly from the royal palace of the Louvre, by Catherine de Medicis and Charles IX themselves. He arrived at Coligny's nearby residence shortly before dawn on St. Bartholomew's day. A troop of royal soldiers placed on guard around the residence, after an earlier attempt to gun Coligny down on the street had wounded him seriously, actively aided Guise. Only the handful of servants, friends, and personal guards remaining within the house could provide Coligny with protection. For a time they barricaded the stairway to Coligny's bedroom. This delay permitted Coligny's chaplain and others who were then with him to escape, over the roof. But there was no possibility that the wounded Coligny could follow them. He dressed, said his last prayers, and resigned himself to death. When the assassins finally broke into his room they brutally chopped him down with swords and battle-axes. They shouted out the window to Guise and the Duke of Angoulême that Coligny was dead, but this report was not enough to satisfy those two blood-thirsty young fanatics. Coligny's body was consequently heaved out the window. One of the dukes wiped the blood from its face to make sure that it was indeed Coligny's. Then both rode off to direct the massacre of the other aristocratic leaders of the French Reformed movement who had been marked for destruction.

Meanwhile the Parisian mob, summoned to participate in the massacres by the tocsins pealing in the bell tower of St. Germain l'Auxerrois, swarmed around the bleeding corpse of Coligny. Its head was cut off, to be sent to the Pope or some Catholic ruler. Its other members were also chopped off, as insults to his memory, and as gory souvenirs. Its trunk was hauled to the river Seine, dumped in, pulled out again, finally hung up on the public gallows of Montfaucon. Only after the popular rage had abated, were some servants able to obtain the remains of Coligny, and arrange for decent burial.[1]

Such savagery, of course, was characteristic of the times. It was no monopoly of Catholics. We have alluded to examples of it practiced upon Catholics, even religious, as well as upon Protestants. But it was rare that it found a victim in a man of Coligny's eminence. And it was also rare that massacre reached the proportions that it was to reach in France in the days beginning with St. Bartholomew's. It seemed as if a whole nation had devoted itself to an orgy of killing. Rarely in all of modern French history were so many killed so brutally. Never were so many dispatched in the name of true Christianity.

The first effect upon Protestants of all this savagery, was, naturally, traumatic shock. This is strikingly evident, for example, in Beza's anguished letters to Bullinger. If his correspondence provides any index, he was never, in his entire tumultuous life, so near to real despair as in the first days after news of the massacres reached Geneva.[2] Many Protestants found their faith itself shaken by the massacres. They found it hard to believe that God could permit such savage treatment of their fellow believers, if their form of Christianity was really the only true one. Some, like Hugues Sureau, accordingly apostasized.[3]

---

[1] This account follows the detailed and judicious one found in *ibid.*, pp. 265-270.

[2] See the extensive quotations (in translation) from these letters in P.-F. Geisendorf, *Beza*, pp. 306-308

[3] See above, p. 117 and n. 4, where Sureau gives this as a reason for his apostasy.

Once this shock wore off, the will to live of French Protestantism reasserted itself. It now acquired, however, a sharper and more bitter edge. It was now willing to risk more and to go to greater extremes. Nowhere was this more evident than in La Rochelle. The leaders of that city refused to have anything further to do with the royal government. They refused even to accept the rule of a Protestant governor offered to them by the crown. When the city subsequently was placed under siege by royal troops, the citizens of La Rochelle defiantly fought back. And when an extreme shortage of food led some to begrudge the Catholic prisoners of war their rations, the Protestant pastors of the city actually sanctioned a proposal that the prisoners be put to death.[1]

Having decided to fight back, however, French Protestants faced the necessity of developing new tactics. To begin with, they had to find new military and political leaders. Along with Coligny, an entire generation of Reformed noblemen had been assassinated. Only a handful of the many who had gathered in Paris for the royal wedding which preceded the massacre, managed to fight their way to safety. To be sure, the titular leaders of the Huguenot party, the young princes of Navarre and Condé, had been spared by royal decision. In the long run, this was to prove a dangerous mistake from the point of view held by extremist Catholics. But for the first few months even these potential leaders were under house arrest, stripped of all armed support, pressured by force and cajolery into public conversion to Roman Catholicism. It was some time before it became clear that these forced conversions were going to be repudiated.

The accession of new political leaders, initially of a less exalted social station, required the development by Protestants of new political theories. Up until St. Bartholomew's, the position of French Protestant theorists had normally been one of professed loyalty to the French crown. They argued that the wars against that crown, undertaken to win toleration of Protestant worship, had always been aimed against the intolerant advisers of the king, never against the king himself. They pointed out that these wars had always been led by certain of the king's blood relatives, who, they claimed, had the only constitutional right to serve as close advisers to the crown.[2] Now, by ordering the St. Bartholomew's massacres and by publicly acknowledging their responsibility for them, the King and Queen Mother had revealed themselves to be personally opposed to Protestantism. Their religious policies could no longer be labeled the work of evil advisers. Furthermore, it was highly uncertain that princes of royal blood, with a constitutional right to advise the crown, could be obtained to lead a new revolt. The consequence was a flowering of Huguenot resistance theory. It began with crude pamphlets dashed off by anonymous writers in cities like La Rochelle.[3] It grew into the more sophisticated books of Beza, Francis Hotman, and others. These writings worked out in eloquent detail the case for religious revolt, in arguments based primarily on Scriptural exegesis in Beza's case, or based primarily on a reading

---

[1] E. Droz, *La Rochelle*, I, 109-110.

[2] For a recent detailed and judicious study of these early theories, see Vittorio de Caprariis, *Propaganda e pensiero politico in Francia durante le guerre di religione, I (1559-1572)* (Naples: Edizioni Scientifiche Italiane, 1959), especially ch. I.

[3] Analyzed by E. Droz, *La Rochelle*, I, 116-122.

of history in Hotman's case, or based largely on an analysis of the nature of government in the case of the anonymous *Vindiciae contra Tyrannos.*[1] Revolt still had to be in the name of religion, in these theories, and it still had to be led by constituted " inferior magistrates." But no longer did these inferior authorities have to be royal princes, and no longer was there any claim of fulfilling the crown's true wishes by liberating it from wicked advisers.

Most of this is already well known, in a general way, to scholars. What appears to be less known, is that there was a change in the Church that was to be defended, in the years following the St. Bartholomew's massacres. As we have already noticed, however, the massacres had the side effect of utterly destroying the " congregational " party led by Morély. The churches in the area around Paris, which had been especially sympathetic to his views, were largely wiped out and ceased functioning. Their leaders had been murdered, like Ramus, had apostasized, like Sureau, or had fled for refuge to such distant places as La Rochelle or Geneva. While Beza issued several warnings in later years, against recrudescence of these views, they proved to be unnecessary. Further controversies over the precise kind of ecclesiastical structure appropriate to a Reformed Church were to become bitter only in other countries.

Consequently the St. Bartholomew's massacres left Beza and his aides in a melancholy position not without an ironic side. They had more control over the French Reformed Church than ever before. Its synodical structure was never again as seriously challenged. But this newly unified and purified Church was now forced to fight desperately for its very existence. Increasingly it became clear that French Protestantism was doomed to a permanent minority status.

---

[1] For a useful general analysis of these writings, see, *inter alia*, Pierre Mesnard, *L'essor de la philosophie politique au XVIe siècle*, 2nd ed. (Paris : Vrin, 1952), pp. 315-347. On Beza, see also Klaus Sturm's critical ed. of his *De iure magistratuum*, heft 1 in Ernst Bizer and J. F. Gerhard Goeters, eds., *Texte zur Geschichte der Evangelischen Theologie* (Neukirchen—Vluyn : Erziehungsvereins, 1965). On Hotman, see the forthcoming critical ed. of his *Franco-Gallia*, by Professor Ralph Giesey of the University of Iowa.

This classification of arguments is quite rough, for there is a considerable amount of overlap. Beza's treatise, for example, contains many appeals to history and also some analysis of the nature of government.

APPENDIX I

Table 1: Names of Missionaries

Source: Geneva, Arch., RCP, B1 (1563-1571), fols. unnumbered, and B2 (1571-1572), fols. indicated. Texts for 1563 and 1564 are published in Geneva, RCP, Kingdon & Bergier, eds., II, 100-112. Bracketed names are added from other sources.

1. Arnaud, Jehan — B1, [fol. 26v.]
2. Baduel, Paul — B1, [fol. 43v.]
3. Bessoli, Jehan — B1, [fol. 29]
4. Bordes, [Jacques des] — B1, [fol. 31v.]
5. Cartwright, Thomas — B2, fol. 58v.
6. Chausse, Gilles — B1, [fol. 29v.]
7. Chevalier, Antoine — B1, [fols. 14-15v., 25]
8. Colliod, [Pierre], Sieur de Varendal — B1, [fol. 9]
9. Combes, Pierre — B1, [fol. 30v.]
10. D'Anduze, [Pierre d'Airebaudouze] — B1, [fol. 9)
11. De la Garde, Jehan — B1, [fol. 31]
12. De la Place, Aymé — B1, [fol. 25v.]
13. De Lery, Jehan — B1, [fol. 23]
14. De Louberan, François, [sieur de Montigny] — B1, [fol. 29]
15. De Valle, Grégoire — B1, [fol. 25v.]
16. Digne, Estienne, dict Bargemont — B1, [fol. 29]
17. Du Champ, Jehan, dict De la Boixière — B1, [fol. 25v.]
18. Enoch, Louis — B1, [fols. 33-33v.]
19. Férière, Jehan — B1, [fol. 29]
20. Godon, Raymond — B1, [fol. 29v.]
21. Helin, Jehan — B1, (fols. 22v.-23v.]
22. James (? spelling uncertain) — B1, [fol. 31]
23. Le Gaigneux, [Jean] — B1, [fol. 26v.]
24. Masson, Claude — B1, [fol. 29]
25. Monceau, Jacques — B2, fol. 72v.
26. Morel, Claude — B1, [fol. 29]
27. Parnasse, Philippe — B1, [fol. 27]
28. Rapine, [Jean] — B1, [fol. 26]
29. Salvard, [Jean-François] — B1, [fols. 22-23v.]
30. Tardieu, Arnauld — B1, [fol. 27]
31. Anonymous, chez Baron d'Aubeterre — B1, [fol. 42v.]

Table 2: DATES OF DISPATCH OF MISSIONARIES

Source: Geneva, Arch., RCP, as in table 1, with exceptions as noted.

1563 — COLLIOD, D'ANDUZE 2

1564 — DE LERY; HELIN; SALVARD (or early 1565 — see BSHPF, XXXVI, 499) 3

1565 — ARNAUD; DE LA PLACE; DE VALLE; DU CHAMP; LE GAIGNEUX; PARNASSE; RAPINE; TARDIEU 8

1566 — BESSOLI; BORDES; CHAUSSE; CHEVALIER (acc. to C. Borgeaud, *Université,* I, 102); COMBES; DE LA GARDE; DE LOUBERAN; DIGNE; FÉRIÈRE; GODON; JAMES; MASSON; C. MOREL 13

1567 — ENOCH 1

1568 — 0

1569 — 0

1570 — 0

1571 — P. BADUEL; ANONYMOUS minister sent to M. D'AUBETERRE 2

1572 — CARTWRIGHT; MONCEAU 2

Table 3: PLACES TO WHICH MISSIONARIES DISPATCHED

Source: Geneva, Arch., RCP, as in table 1, with exceptions as noted.
Place names identified more fully in Geneva, LH, I, tables, and *Stieler's Atlas of Modern Geography.*

France:

Picardy: HELIN (Cœuvres-et-Valsery, dép. Aisne, seat of M. d'Estrées, Baron de Dodenville)

Normandy: CHEVALIER (Caen)

Ile-de-France:

Champagne: JAMES (chez MM. de Briaille et Antoine de Croy, Prince de Porcien; seat of latter: Château-Porcien, dép. Ardennes)

Orléannais: DE LOUBERAN (Châteauneuf-en-Thimerais, dép. Eure-et-Loir); ENOCH (Montargis, seat of Mme de Ferrare, and Châtillon, both dép. Loiret); TARDIEU (apparently chez M. le Vidame de Chartres, who had supported him)

Poitou: DE LA PLACE (Talmont, dép. Vendée)

Touraine:

Berry:

Nivernais: DE LERY (Nevers); RAPINE (Nevers)

Burgundy:

Aunis, Saintonge, and Angoumois: COMBES (Cognac, dép. Charente); DE VALLE (Oléron, dép. Charente-Maritime, arr. Rochefort); PARNASSE (Pons, dép. Charente-Maritime, arr. Saintes; see BSHPF, VIII, 74); ANONYMOUS (chez M. d'Aubeterre, of Aubeterre, dép. Charente, arr. Angoulême)

Auvergne: P. BADUEL (Issoire, acc. to Geneva, Arch., RCP, B2, fols. 102v.-103, March, 1576)

Lyonnais: CHAUSSE (Lyon, temporarily); LE GAIGNEUX (Lyon, temporarily); SALVARD (Lyon—three churches asked for him: Geneva, Nevers, and Lyon [Geneva, RCP, Kingdon & Bergier, eds., II, 110-111]; Lyon finally got him [BSHPF, XXXVI, 499])

Dauphiné:

Guyenne and Gascony: BESSOLI ("Montauld-en Agenais," perhaps Montaut, dép. Gers); BORDES (Bordeaux); DE LA GARDE ("Allemans-en-Perigort," perhaps Allemans-du-Dropt, dép. Lot-et-Garonne); DIGNE (Périgueux, dép. Dordogne); FÉRIÈRE (Port-Sainte-Marie, dép. Lot-et-Garonne, arr. Agen)

Languedoc: ARNAUD ("Saint Michel-le-Ranse en Vivarais," probably dép. Ardèche); COLLIOD (Pézenas, dép. Hérault, arr. Béziers; see BSHPF, XLVIII, 79); D'ANDUZE (Montpellier); GODON (Lodève, dép. Hérault)

Comtat-Venaissin:

Provence: DU CHAMP (chez M. de Senas, whose seat was apparently Senez, dép. Basses-Alpes, arr. Castellane); C. MOREL ("Riers," probably Riez, dép. Basses-Alpes, arr. Digne)

Other Countries:

England: CARTWRIGHT (Cambridge, acc. to A. F. Scott Pearson, *Thomas Cartwright and Elizabethan Puritanism, 1535-1603* (Cambridge, 1925), p. 63 and *passim*)

Holy Roman Empire: MASSON (Ste. Marie-aux-Mines, Lorraine)

Low Countries: MONCEAU (Antwerp)

Table 4: PLACES OF ORIGIN OF MISSIONARIES

Source: Geneva, Arch., RCP, as in table 1, with exceptions as noted. Place names identified more fully in Geneva, LH, I, tables, and *Stieler's Atlas of Modern Geography*.

France:

Picardy: HELIN (no city indicated)

Normandy: CHAUSSE (Chanteloup, diocèse de Coutances, dép. Manche, acc. to Geneva, LB); CHEVALIER (Vire, dép. Calvados, acc. to Geneva, LB)

Ile-de-France:

Champagne: C. MOREL (Châlons; see BSHPF, XXXIII, 534)

Orléannais:

Poitou:

Touraine: LE GAIGNEUX (Tours, acc. to Geneva, LH, and Geneva, LB)

Berry: ENOCH (Issoudun, acc. to Geneva, LB)

Nivernais: RAPINE (Nevers)

Burgundy: DE LERY (Lamargelle, diocèse de Langres, dép. Côte d'Or, arr. Dijon, acc. to Geneva, LB)

Aunis, Saintonge, Angoumois:

Auvergne:

Lyonnais: COLLIOD ("Segusianus," acc. to Geneva, LR, Stelling-Michaud, ed., i.e. from area of Forez, dép. Loire; cf. BSHPF, XLVIII, 77-78, undocumented claim he came from Bourg-en-Bresse, Burgundy)

Dauphiné: DE LOUBERAN (Valence, acc. to Geneva, LR, Stelling-Michaud, ed.)

Guyenne and Gascony: BESSOLI (" Montauld-en-Agenais," as in table 3); BORDES (Bordeaux, acc. to Geneva, LB); DE LA PLACE (Bordeaux, acc. to *France protestante*, 1st ed., art. " Mazières "); FÉRIÈRE (Agen, acc. to Geneva, LR, Stelling-Michaud, ed.); TARDIEU (" Beseynac en l'evesche de Sarlat," probably dép. Dordogne)

Languedoc: ARNAUD (Vivarais or Nîmes, acc. to two entries in Geneva, LR, Stelling-Michaud, ed.); P. BADUEL (Nîmes, acc. to *ibid.*); D'ANDUZE (Anduze, dép. Gard, arr. Alès); GODON (Lodève, dép. Hérault)

Comtat-Venaissin: COMBES (Carpentras, acc. to Geneva, LR, Stelling-Michaud, ed.)

Provence: DIGNE (Bargemont, dép. Var, arr. Draguignan)

Other Countries:

England: CARTWRIGHT (Hertfordshire, acc. to Pearson, *op. cit.* in table 3, p. 1)

Holy Roman Empire: MASSON (Lorraine, immediately Ste. Marie-aux-Mines)

Low Countries: MONCEAU (Armentières, acc. to Geneva, LR, Stelling-Michaud, ed.)

Piedmont in Savoy: PARNASSE (" Avillianensis," acc. to Geneva, LR, Stelling-Michaud, ed., i.e. from Avigliana, Susa district); SALVARD (Valley of Aosta, acc. to *ibid.*)

Unknown:

DE LA GARDE; DE VALLE; DU CHAMP; JAMES; ANONYMOUS (chez M. d'Aubeterre)

Table 5: CLASS STATUS OF MISSIONARIES

Noble:

1. Pierre COLLIOD, sieur de Varandal, Lyonnais, dép. Loire (BSHPF, XLIV, 251).
2. Pierre d'Airebaudouze, sieur D'ANDUZE, Languedoc, dép. Gard, arr. Alès (Geneva, Arch., Mss. Protocoles du Notaire Jean Ragueau, V, 1017-1018, 1279-1280; VII, 558-562; cited and discussed in R. M. Kingdon, *Geneva & Coming*, p. 6).
3. François DE LOUBERAN, sieur de Montigny (dép. Seine-et-Marne, arr. Melun), d'Ablon-sur-Seine, d'Ablon-la-ville, de Mons-sur-Orge, et de Courcelles. These estates are mostly in the Ile-de-France, and he ministered in and near Paris (BSHPF, IX, 193-195); yet he may have been born in Valence, Dauphiné (Geneva, LR, Stelling-Michaud, ed., p. 89).

Bourgeois:

Source: Geneva, LB.

A. Bourgeois admitted free for services to the city, generally in teaching or preaching:

1. BORDES, Jaques des
2. CHAUSSE, Gilles
3. (Le) CHEVALIER, Antoine
4. ENOCH, Louis
5. LE GAIGNEUX, Jean

B. Bourgeois admitted on payment of fee, the common way:

6. De Lery, Jean

C. Of bourgeois family:

7. Baduel, Paul (father, Claude, professor, became bourgeois on payment of fee)
8. Digne, Estienne (an Antoine Digne, also of Bargemont in Provence, became bourgeois on payment of fee — father or brother?)

Table 6: Missionaries' Occupations at Time of Assignment

Students at Geneva Academy:

Source: Geneva, LR, Stelling-Michaud, ed., with exceptions as noted.

Arnaud (pp. 86, 88); Bessoli (p. 88, " Bessotus "; cf. Geneva, Arch., RCP); Colliod (p. 84); Combes (p. 88); De Louberan (p. 89, " Louberau "); Férière (p. 88); Godon (p. 88); Masson (Geneva, Arch., RCP); Monceau (p. 101); Parnasse (p. 87); Rapine (p. 85); Salvard (p. 84); Tardieu(p. 87). 13

Student at an earlier period: P. Baduel (p. 83).

Employees of Geneva:

A. *Educators:*

Source: C. Borgeaud, *Université*, I, with exceptions noted.

P. Baduel (" pedagogue des enfans en l'hospital "—Geneva, Arch., RCP); Bordes (Academy); Cartwrgiht (Academy); Chevalier (Academy); Enoch (Collège & Academy); Le Gaigneux (Academy); Anonymous, chez M. d'Aubeterre (" pedagogue chez M. Trembley "—Geneva, Arch., RCP). 7

Teacher elsewhere: Masson (" maître d'escole de Saincte Marie en Lorraine "—Geneva, Arch., RCP. i.e. Sainte-Marie-aux-Mines).

B. *Pastors:*

Source: H. Heyer, *L'Egl. de Genève*, with exceptions noted.

Bordes (and professor); Chausse (Vandœuvres & Geneva); D'Anduze (Geneva, frequently on leave to France); Enoch (and teacher); Helin (Céligny); Le Gaigneux (and professor); Monceau (substitute in country churches—e.g. Jussy—Geneva, Arch., RCP) 7

Total Employees of Geneva at time of assignment: 11

Employees at other times and places:

Pastor in France, earlier:

De Lery, had gone to Brazil as a missionary with Villegagnon in 1556; had later served in Belleville, France; returned to Geneva for a new assignment (*France protestante*, 1st ed., art. " Lery ").

Pastors in the canton de Vaud:

Source: H. Vuilleumier, *Hist. de l'Egl. réf. du Pays de Vaud.*

Earlier: CHEVALIER (Montreux); LE GAIGNEUX (Lausanne, acc. to *France protestante,* 1st ed., art. "Le Gaigneux," and H. Heyer, *L'Egl. de Genève,* but *not* listed in Vuilleumier).

Later: DE LERY (l'Isle).

Pastors in villages belonging to Geneva, later:

Source: H. Heyer, *L'Egl. de Genève.*

ARNAUD (Chancy); P. BADUEL (Chancy).

APPENDIX II

Beza to Bullinger, 13 November 1571, a letter describing Reformed ecclesiastical institutions in Geneva and France, and summarizing the controversy provoked by Morély's criticisms of them. This text is based on a transcript prepared by H.-V. Aubert and preserved in Geneva, MHR, collated with the signed original in Zürich, Staatsarchiv, E II 381, fols. 1304-1309. I have generally adopted Aubert's punctuation, paragraphing, and emendations of words which are incomplete in the original because of cropped margins or other flaws. Professor Henri Meylan and M. Alain Dufour, the editors of the Beza *Correspondence*, have kindly given me permission to publish this text here.

Beza to Bullinger, 13 November 1571 :

S. Etsi iampridem didicisse nos re ipsa oportuit, nullum esse tam audax aut tam impudens facinus, in quo aggrediendo, ac etiam, nisi Deus impedierit, conficiendo, Satan facile non inveniat, qui strenuam ipsi operam navent, fateor tamen nunquam me suspicatum esse, tantam hoc tempore futuram, praesertim inter meos Gallos, audaciam, ut eas Ecclesias, de quarum consensione tot tamque idoneis testimoniis liquet, inter se committere studerent. Et hoc tamen istos conatos video, quos vos quidem doctos et pios adhuc existimatis, ego vero (neque id arbitror iniuria), pro vere improbis turbatoribus, et alteris prorsus Flac[iis] habeo, ad impediendum opus Domini ab eodem spiritu compara[tis], qua in re vos mihi facile assensuros spero, ubi et qui sint ipsi, et a quibus initiis profecti, et quid moliantur plane vobis explicaro. Qu[od] si vel me quicquam hic affingere, vel ipsos vera loquutos posthac comperiatis, non recuso quin me pro viro omnium improbissimo deinceps habeatis. Repetam autem necessario rem omnem paul[o] altius. In hac Ecclesia siquando eligendi sunt ministri, serva[tur] hic ordo, ut collegium ministrorum, tum qui in urbe, tum qui in agris docent, conveniat, et in eo conventu, editis eorum nominibus qui maxime idonei putantur, accersantur quotquot caeteris videntur anteponendi. De quorum voluntate facti certiores, bis singulos audimus in nostro coetu concionantes. Sequitur deinde diligens vitae et morum inquisitio. Tande[m] qui maxime placuit, examini subiicitur omnium doctrinae christianae capitum. Hoc modo probatus, et invocato Dei nomine singulorum fratrum suffragiis delectus, Magistratui, addito conveniente testimonio, exhibetur. Is senatores duos deligit, quibus adhibitis, tertio in ministrorum coetu auditur. Senator[es] postea quid audierint et annotarint ad Senatum referunt. Senatus, si videtur, primam illam electionem ratam habet. Eius, qui sic placuit, nomen die Dominico in omnibus templis plebi editur, facta cuivis potestate ut siquid novit in eius hominis vita vel doctrina quod impediat quominus electio procedat, id intra octiduum aut Magistratui aut ministris, citra calumniam et in

Domini timore significet. Si quid delatum est, auditis, si opus est, testibus, de obiectis si Ecclesiastica sunt, in ministrorum collegio primum disceptatur, deinde Consistorium decernit, sin vero mere civilis causa est, Magistratus de re tota cognoscit. Denique qui a pastorum collegio delectus est, a Magistratu probatus, et a populo receptus, octiduo post solemnibus precibus, in duplici concione, rursum in populi conspectu Deo consecratus, in sui muneris possessionem mittitur. Et de electione quidem hactenus.

Sin vero de deponendis ministris agitur, si quidem causae sunt mere Ecclesiasticae, ut si de doctrina quaeritur, fratrum collegium de causa cognoscit, eousque ut significata Senatui sententia, Senatus ipse reum ex legibus aut absolvat aut condemnet: Sin vero causa civilis est, Magistratus cognitioni res tota relinquitur. Causae vero abrogationis, populo, nisi expediat, non significantur. Ex populo siquis fuerit observatus male de religione sentire, vocatur a ministrorum coetu, erudiendus. Si non obsequitur et prorsus se pertinacem praebet, aut etiam virus suum spargere comperitur, res tota ad Senatum defertur, et male de religione sentienti coena quoque interdicitur ex Consistorii auctoritate. Offendiculorum rei ac praesertim, qui commonefacti refractarios se praebent, ad Consistorium deferuntur, et vel eiusdem nomine a delectis duobus privatim monentur, vel etiam autoritate Magistratus citati, a Consistorio audiuntur, pro facti ratione corripiendi. Et, si quod grave et publicum offendiculum fuerit, vel reus legitime convictus prorsus malam conscientiam prodat, vel etiam peccatum agnoscere detrectet, iubetur Coena abstinere, donec resipiscentiam fuerit in Consistorio testatus. Si paruerit, rursum recipitur; sin minus, et non modo semel, sed etiam secundo vel tertio Coena abstinere maluerit, quam culpam in Consistorio deprecari, vocatus graviter increpatur ex Dei verbo, et, nisi culpam tunc demum saltem agnoscat, anno uno sic elapso, ad Senatum remittitur, qui in publicae pacis turbatorem, prout eum mereri censuerit, animadvertat. Ad excommunicationem rarissime devenitur. Id si inciderit, promulgatur excommunicatus, explicatis huius tam gravis iudicii causis, et monetur populus pro tam misero peccatore preces quotidianas concipere. Idem ubi suam poenitentiam Consistorio probarit, rursum, teste populo, adhibita gratiarum actione, in gratiam Ecclesiae recipitur citra ullam infamiae notam. Ab Apostosiae reis publica quoque satisfactio requiritur, nec tamen propterea infames habentur. Consistorium autem partim ex Ministris urbanis (quibus accedunt ex pagis pastores prout ipsis adesse licet, ac praesertim ex quorum parochiis aliquis citatus est), partim ex duodecim presbyteris constat, quorum munus annuum est, nisi iterato (quod fieri plerumque solet) in ea functione confirmentur. Ii certo die singulis annis a Senatu minore (collegio tamen ministrorum in id consilium adhibito) deliguntur, ex ipso Senatu duo, ex LX viris quatuor, ex Diacosiis sex, et quidem ex singulis urbis regionibus, ut illorum quisque suae regionis offendicula diligenter observet, et quae subito componere ipse privatim, sive solus, sive adhibito primo quoque ex ministris, non potuerit, ad consistorium singulis hebdomadibus referat. In eodem coetu de causis matrimonialibus disceptatur, quarum tamen decisio ad Senatum refertur. Praeterea hic noster mos est ut singulis annis ministri singuli urbem inter se partiti, adhibito uno ex presbyteris itemque decurione (decuriat[im] enim tota urbs distributa est), singulas familias semel aud[iant] de fidei capitibus respondentes, ne quis prorsus rudis doctrin[ae] coelestis, aut a vera fide alienus, ad Coenam admittatur. Cui labori, longe maximo, dicata est quadragesima quam voca[nt.] Hic noster ordo est, quem ut verbo Dei consentaneu[m] (absque ullo aliarum Ecclesiarum praeiudicio) adhuc non si[ne] maximo fructu observavimus, cuius etiam vindice[m] esse Dei spiritum experti sumus, quum nemo illum abrumpere sit adhuc conatus, in quem Dominus insigniter poste[a] non animadverterit. Tot annis vero duo duntaxat reper[ti] sunt qui hoc palam facere auderent, quorum unus adhuc hodie sceleratus est Apostata, et perduellionis etiam aliquot post annis damnatus, exulat, alter est Morellius quidam Parisiensis. Is quum in hanc civitatem, ut et multi alii peregrini, ascitus, aliquot annos pacate apud nos vixisset, subinde tamen melancholiae non obscura signa demonstrans, eo tandem erupit, ut hunc ordinem tanquam Tyrannicum accusaret, quod, inquit, negle[cto] populo, aut non aliter in consilium adhibito quam in comoediis κωφὸν πρόσωπον, omnia ad se ministri transtulerint. Vult enim omnia, veluti ministrorum examen et electionem, doctrinae censuras, iudicia denique Ecclesiastica in ipsius plebis oculis et conspectu, adeoque singulis ex plebe in suffragia missis exerceri, quod ni fiat, oligarchiam et tyrannidem clamitat in Ecclesiam invehi. Corrogat autem ad eam rem et verbi Divini et veteris Ecclesiae testimonia, et mirabiles rationes congregandorum coetuum et rogandarum sententiarum excogitat, adeo ut ne vetustissimis quidem Synodis parcat. Haec commenta quibuscunque argumentis potuit confirmata quum etiam perscripsisset, librum satis spissum clam excudendum curat Lugduni, et quidem addita ad P. Viretum piae memoriae praefatione, quasi librum ille inspexisset ac probasset, nempe ut lectores hoc veluti praeiudicio allectos, in suam sententiam traduceret. Sparsus est igitur per Gallicas Ecclesias hic liber prius quam Genevae quid hoc rei esset, plene patefieret, quamvis ipse ibi familiam haberet et huic reipublicae esset iure iurando addictus, neque etiam nesciret legibus cautum esse iustissimis de causis, ne quis nisi Senatui probatum quicquam edendum curaret. Quid amplius? Hunc ipsemet librum civilis belli primo initio, in quod omnes isti ipsius conatus inciderant, Aureliam adfert, quasi a Synodo diiudicandum, quam sciebat eo fuisse ante annum assignatam. Oblatus liber traditur quibusdam inspiciendus. Ii, certo die, quid complectatur, et quibus testimoniis et argumentis nitatur, sigillatim, fratrum coetui,praesente ipso Morellio, exponunt. Omnes, vix uno et altero ex pastorum numero nonnihil titubantibus, et pauculis ex populo nescio quid mussitantibus, quos postea animadversum est ab eo fuisse fascinatos, omnia illa commenta una cum libro prorsus reiiciunt. Jubetur ipse cum quibusdam delectis, ac mecum etiam, si bene memini, de suis placitis plenius conferre, ut, si fieri posset, ad mentem rediret. Ipse postea quibuscum contulerit, quo abierit, nescio. Mihi certe alioqui tum occupatissimo, vix est unquam postea conspectus. Dogmatis autem ipsius summa publice in omnibus templis refutata est, et liber ipse palam damnatus. Ipse aliquot post menses Genevam reversus, quo iam rumor istarum rerum pervenerat, tandem post varias tergiversationes in Consistorium vocatus adest. Ibi a Calvino piae memoriae rogatus ut sua tueretur, quum moras necteret, tandem damnato libro, et nisi resipisceret interdicta ipsi Coena Domini, ad Senatum remittitur, qui de violati edicti et turbatae Ecclesiae crimine cognosceret. Ipse non comparet. Senatus absentem damnat, et librum ut plane seditiose scriptum et falsae doctrinae plenum publice exurit, cuius iudicii exemplum ad te mitto. Ab eo tempore ille, relicta Geneva, ad suos reversus, vix credas quot quantisque molestiis miseram Parisiensem Ecclesiam vexarit, quibus artibus irrepere sit conatus, quoties quum sese Ecclesiae iudicio submisisset, illam fefellerit, quoties calumniator convictus et deprehensus fuerit, quorum omnium acta apud me habeo. In summa saepissime in Ecclesia Parisiensi, in Synodis provincialibus saepe, in Synodis universalibus una et altera auditus, convictus et semper damnatus, verbo quidem aliquoties et aliquatenus, reipsa vero non modo nunquam resipuit, verum etiam errores auxit et improbitate crevit, eousque semel progressus ut Ecclesiam sese periculosissimis temporibus detecturum in ipso Consistorio minaretur, et ita etiam insaniens (sicut ex deprehensis eius literus coram illustribus viris et Regina ipsa Navarrena, non sine insigni periurio reus convictus est), ut eam quam omnes Ecclesiae sequunt[ur] praedicandi verbi rationem, qua fit ut certus quispiam ad populum concionem habeat, tanquam perversam et verbo Dei repugnantem carperet, quod si forte neget, habeo exemplum literarum ipsius ex quibus convincatur.

In postrema denique Rupellana Synodo ab eius provinciae delegatis ministris accusat[us] absens, quod non modo nullum ederet resipiscentiae signum, verum etiam hoc ultimo bello, quamvis vicinam Ecclesiam haberet, oblato ad Baptismum infante, et aliis etiam rationibus non obscu[re] bonam papistarum gratiam redemisset, iudicatum est in absente[m], ut nisi plane se resipiscere testaretur, pro homine prophano e[t] prorsus extraneo haberetur. Ac ipse quidem initio commotus, in viam plane rediturus videbatur, quum Lutetiae nuper demum nactus est, per quos efficere se posse speraret, quod obtinere nullis unquam artibus toto decennio potuerat. Huic igitur sese facile adiunxit P. Ramus, de cuius ingenio, si nondum satis ex eo constat, quod nullam attigit disciplinam in qua prius non apparuerit doctor quam discipulus, nullum unquam nobilem scriptorem tractavit, quem non ut imperitum et quidem contumeliose redarguerit, at certe vel ex hoc uno cuivis constabit, ubi et qua occasione hanc, quae nunquam erumpere potuerat, flammam excitet, et quomodo in hac causa sese adhuc gessit, explicaro.

In Galliis, quum initio propter acerrimas persecutiones, constitui Ecclesiae non possent, saepe unos et eosdem et presbyteros et diaconos esse oportuit, et aliunde accersiti sunt potius quam ab ipsis Ecclesiis delecti pastores. Paulatim tamen, convocatis Synodis, aliqua est forma constituta, sicut ex ipsarum Synodorum actis (quae nunc ad te mitto, sicut Rupellae nuper disposita fuerunt) vos ipsi, si libebit, cognoscere per interpretem poteritis. Habuerunt autem semper, et adhuc nunc habent in genere aristocratiam Consistorii nobiscum communem, alioqui in exercenda disciplina multo quam nos rigidiores. Sed apud illos propter idoneorum hominum penuriam et multa pericula, composita diu fuerunt consistoria ex pastoribus, presbyteris et diaconis, quorum alioqui sic distincta semper fuerunt munera, ut soli quidem pastores verbum annuntiarent, presbyteri vero offendicula observarent, diaconi Ecclesiae aerarium tractarent. Itaque in postrema Rupellana Synodo, quum libertas maior concessa videretur, et de distiguendis muneribus ageretur, cautum est ut, nisi sicubi necessitas aliter ferat, diaconi suo proprio munere contenti sint, et quoties de doctrina quaeritur (de qua vix extra Synodos provinciales aut universales decidit[ur], ad quas etiam a singulis consistoriis provocari consuevit), liceat quidem presbyteris sententiam dicere, soli autem ministri verbi decernant. Haec illa est praeclara occasio quam homo ille tam avide corripuit, ut illum iam Morellius non comitem, sed plane ducem sit nactus, quasi oligarchiam aut Tyrannidem in Ecclesiam invehant, qui perturbatissimam et seditiosissimam Democratiam stabilire in Ecclesia recusarint. Adiunxerunt illis sese pauculi quidam, partim pro sua levitate, partim aliunde notati homines. Habes occasionem qua freti boni isti viri abhinc tres aut quatuor menses tumultuentur. Nunc vide ex ea quam sequuntur ratione, quo spiritu impellantur. Omitto quod privatos in Ecclesia homines, si verae oves essent, ac praesertim Ramum, istorum prorsus imperitum hominem, et quem scio vix ac ne vix quidem Biblia aut sacros ullos interpretes a limine salutasse, sola denique confidentia armatum in hoc certamen descendisse, certe oportuit vel ordini iam pridem a tantis viris constituto, et a Deo pene ipso coelitus comprobato assentiri, vel modeste saltem dissentire, et placide prius rogare de quibus ambigerent, quam ita arroganter, superbe, contumeliose denique vivis et mortuis maledicere, et Synodorum acta convellere, quod ipsi se fecisse si negabunt, habeo scripta ad me usque transmissa, habeo et aliorum testimonia, et vestrum etiam in primis, ex quibus coarguantur. Quid quod illum ipsum Balduinum quater Apostatam et capitalem Ecclesiae hostem, conati sunt scriptis honorificentissimis literis in suae factionis societatem pellicere? Nam ne hoc quidem possunt inficiari, quin mendacii rei peragantur. Omitto haec, inqua[m,] et illud ipsum urgeo de quo nunc agimus. Erasti dogm[a] Consistorium et excommunicationem semel evertentis, sic P. Ramo displicuit, ut quum Heidelbergae esset, libellum etiam adversus eum scripserit, cuius exemplum brevi habiturum me spero. Eius dogmatis si vos istic putant adstipulatores, quo pudore, quaeso, nos apud vos accusant? Ac cur non potius nobiscum sese adversum vos coniungunt? Nempe quoniam non hoc illis propositum est, veritatem invenire, sed ut nobis, inter quos alioqui probe convenire cousta[t,] inter nos commissis, obtineant quod cupiunt, nimirum ut per medias turbas, alteri isti plane Ismaelitae sese iactent.

Consistoria sicuti apud Bernenses constituta sunt, ac multo etiam minus vestrarum Ecclesiarum ordinem, is certe probare non potest, qui omnia ad totius populi suffragia revocet, et consistoria ex presbyteris quoque et diaconis esse constituenda contendat? Quorsum igitur illi et qua conscientia earum Ecclesiarum praeiudicia nescio quae, sub repentes emendicant, quarum instituta minime omnium comprobant? Et haec quidem de ipsis hominibus hactenus, ut illos videlicet melius notos ac perspectos posthac habeatis.

Nunc ad rem venio. Damnavit Synodus Rupellana (inquiunt isti calumniatores) eos qui disciplinam, idest excommunicationem a Coena, recipere nolu[e]rint. Primum obsecro, quod est istud glossema: disciplinam idest excommunicationem? Quasi videlicet idem sit totum atque pars totius, et quasi nullam habeant disciplinam, vel nullam ecclesiam, qui excommunicatione a Coena non utuntur, sive quod illam non probent, sive quod a se illam cum fructu exerceri non posse cred[ant.] An vero ita universus ille gravissimorum sane fratrum coetus insanierit, ut tale quicquam illis in mentem venerit? Imo si hos ipsos turbatores roges, ecquid ipsi censeant excommunicationem tollendam, vel ipso[s] impudentissime mentiri necesse fuerit, vel fateri se multo etiam severius quam Gallicarum Ecclesiarum pastores excommunicationem exerceri velle, ut qui palam omnia geri totius populi suffragiis oportere contendant. Res autem ita se habet. Nondum sane inventus est in Galliis qui excommunicationem a Coena tollendam diceret, ut adversus eiusmodi dogma quicquam constituere minime oportuerit, et hoc ausim dicere, vix ullum esse in Galliis pastorem, qui Tiguri nullam a Coena excommunicationem exerceri noverit, tantum abest ut in Tigurinam Ecclesiam quicquam decreverit Synodus, suam potius cum ea consensionem voce et literis testata. Imo ne in Erastum quidem tale decretum factum esse scio et testor, qui Synodo non tantum interfui, verum etiam praefui. Sed quum ad Synodum relatum esset ex Burdegalensi provincia, duos illic factiosos esse homines exortos, unum philosophum alterum medicum, qui sublata semel omni ministerii auctoritate, ius omne Pastores constituendi, deiiciendi, leges quasvis Ecclesiasticas condendi vel abrogandi, de ipsa quoque doctrina iudicandi, penes unum magistratum immediate esse, scriptiunculis etiam quibusdam editis, defendant, adversus illos decrevit Synodus, quod et vos ipsos facturos fuisse confido. Et ne quis hic a me confictum quicqu[am] suspicetur, habeo ego penes me illorum dogmatis summam, habeo eiusdem a Bordaeo, Burdegalensi pastore, scriptam refutationem, mihi a Synodo commissam, ut a me diligentius examinata, si opus erit, excudatur. En igitur quod res est, ex quo etiam quod sit istorum hominum ingenium, nunc tandem, ut spero, agnoscitis. Certo eos esse vos minime crediderimus qui disciplinam Ecclesiasticam abolitam velitis, aut utramque potestatem confundere, etiam si in excommunicationis usu, ac fortassis etiam nomine, non idem prorsus atque nos sentitis; nec propterea vel vos a nobis, vel nos a vobis disiungi unquam posse arbitrabimur, quos Dominus pro bonitate sua singulari, et in doctrina, et in disciplinae summa sic et nobiscum et cum Gallicis Ecclesiis coniunxit et copulavit, ut indissolubili vinculo nos colligatos, in Domino constanter per mansuros plane confidam, nedum ut tale quicquam meditatum sit, quale improbi isti homines vobis persuadere studuerunt. Et de illis quidem hactenus.

Iam ad alterum venio, in quo etiam isti idem prorsus ingenium produnt. Abhinc quadriennium Lugduni quidam Pedemontanus valde indoctus, sed admodum impudens Alamanius nomine, adiuncto sibi quodam Capone, Florentino, quem vertiginosum esse aliunde quoque constabat, inter alia portenta spargere etiam coepit, corpus Christi absurde a nobis constitui pro re Sacramenti, ex quo nihil nisi dona et merita Christi percipiamus; ac proinde expungendum substantiae vocabulum, quod ex nostra liturgia omnes Gallicae Ecclesiae initio acceptum semper retinuerunt. Huic doctrinae, quam ne ipse quidem eius author satis intelligebat, sese opposuerunt Lugdunenses, minime id quidem, ut quicquam in nostrarum Ecclesiarum consensione novarent, sed ne quid in recepta liturgia novari, vanissimi hominis importunitate, paterentur. Censuerunt igitur tantisperdum, tranquillitate Ecclesiis reddita, de hac re quoque in Synodo decerneretur, retinendam substantiae vocem, qua se declararunt, non aliud quam illud ipsum corpus traditum pro nobis et sanguinem pro nobis effusum, id est Christum ipsum, intelligere, qui ab ipsius quidem donis distingui, at nunquam separari, neque in verbi praedicatione, neque in Sacramentorum administratione possit aut debeat. Addiderunt praeterea inde non effici ipsius substantiam cum nostra uniri aut permisceri, sed ipsum Christum tamen nostrum fieri, sicut verbum et sacramenta testantur, ut spiritualiter prorsus in unum corpus mysticum cum eo coalescamus et ista arctissima ipsius spirituali per fidem nobiscum coniunctione in nobis obsignata, magis ac magis ex eo percipiamus quaecunque tum in ipso nobis imputantur, tum ab ipso in nos, subiecta ipsi membra, derivantur. De hoc postea quaeri inter nonnullos coepit, ac tandem etiam quum ad Synodum relatum esset, auditis ac postea consentientibus qui de hoc nonnihil ambigebant, tandem communi consensu decretum est, ut nihil in ipsa liturgia mutaretur, sed sententia tum vocis, tum dicti illius sic explicaretur, ut neque crasso ullo delirio (cuiusmodi est ista realis et corporea substantiarum connexio) via sterneretur (quod etiam tota ipsa liturgia satis convellit), neque istorum dogma stabiliretur, qui Christum ipsum et in verbo et in sacramentis a suis donis separant, et rem sacramenti cum ipsius fructu et utilitate inde ad nos redeunte manifeste confundunt. Ac ego quidem libenter a substantiae nomine (quo vos offendi video) abstinere, ac potius CHRISTUM IESUM dicere et scribere consuevi, quanvis certe corporis et sanguinis ipsius nominibus, quorum symbola sunt panis et vinum, res ipsas substantiales intelligi necesse sit. Sed profecto ad illorum arbitrium expungi haec vocula ex recepta liturgia non potuit, quin magnum offendiculum consequeretur, et illorum dogma stabiliri videretur. Ad rem autem ipsam quod attinet, arbitror quidem ego nos sic sentientes ac docentes, ne tantillum quidem vel a consensione vel ab illa nostra communi confessione deflectere, quod scientes prudentes nunquam faciemus. Et alium non fuisse animum Synodi scio, cui vel ego unus alioqui constantissime ad extremum usque restitissem, utcunque possit aliquis, praeiudicio ductus, nonnulla fortassis istius Synodici scripti verba alio detorquere. Deum certe testem appello, quum illa scriberentur, nunquam cuiquam (quod sciam aut quod intellexerim) in mentem venisse, ut a communi nostro consensu vel minimum discederet, nedum ut vos perstringeret, aut etiam, sicut isti falsissime scribunt, damnaret. Quod si quid tamen in illo scripto vobis displicet, gratum sane fuerit nobis quicquid illud est intelligere, ac etiam a minimis quibusque, nedum a vobis, quos non modo ut fratres amamus, verum etiam ut patres veneramur, plenius erudiri. Sic igitur ad utramque illam calumniam responsum esto.

Venio ad tertiam omnium impudentissimam, quod videlicet Lutetiam sit perscriptum, vos, scriptis ad Synodum literis, haec omnia approbasse. Obsecro vero, quis haec confingere potuit, aut cui haec confingenti creditum esset? Cui enim ex Synodo ignotum est, quid et quando scripseritis? Et quinam potuistis approbare, quae nunquam, ut opinor, a vobis sunt antehac cognita? Hoc quidem potui amico fortassis cuipiam scribere (quod tamen certo affirmare non possum), gratissimas vobis fuisse Synodi literas, quod etiam si quando illam rursum cogi cognoveritis, re ipsa testari decreveritis. Itaque vix mihi persuadere possum illa a quoquam scribi vel dici de vobis potuisse. Ac potius ut caetera alia, id quoque ab istis vanissime aut calumniosissime confictum mihi persuadeo. Huiusmodi et illud est, quod fore significant ut aliquot Ecclesiae brevi hac de re ad vos scribant. Scilicet quasi ulla sit vel minimi pagi Ecclesia, quae cum istis consentiat, nisi forte eo usque iam erupit ipsorum schisma, ut etiam aliquam Ecclesiolam a corpore caeterarum avulserint, quod tamen ego neque factum esse neque factum iri credo. Nam certe, quod antea etiam ad vos scripsi, tam pacata fuit totius Synodi disceptatio, tamque in omnibus placide consentientes omnium animi, ut nulla prorsus aut praesentis aut oriturae discordiae vel levissima suspicio apparuerit. Et de his quidem hactenus.

En igitur plenissimum, ut arbitror, ad illa omnia responsum, quod si vobis satisfecerit, ut collegae mei et ego plane confidimus, magnopere nos fueritis consolati, utpote quibus nihil unquam tristius aut acerbius accidere possit, quam si vel minima nubecula syncerae nostrae fraternitati obducatur. Duo vero nunc in summa petimus. Unum, ut quum istos (de quorum causa ineunte, ut spero, vere, in altera universali Gallica Synodo decernetur) nunc saltem animadvertatis nihil aliud quam responsi quippiam a vobis captare, quo possint quoquo modo, autoritate nominis vestri freti, incautos fallere, discordias nascentes augere, novas excitare, malo denique animo suo morem gerere. Siquidem eos ullo responso dignemini, sic eos pro vestra prudentia excipiatis, ut neque fidem suis calumniis habitam, neque sua vobis consilia probari reipsa intelligant. Alterum est, ut non nunc modo, sed deinceps quoque, undecunque aliquid intelligetis, quod ad nostrorum animorum alienationem spectet, nulli, ne levissimae quidem suspicioni indulgeatis, ac illud potius vobis magis ac magis persuadeatis, nunquam nos commissuros ut quae inter vos et nos sanctissima in veritate Domini fraternitas coaluit, totque et tam luculentis testimoniis sancita est, cuiusquam vi aut fraude ullum accipiat detrimentum. Bene vale, mi observande pater, Dominus Jesus Satanam coerceat, malorum conatus infringat, devinciat nos magis ac magis sanctae suae pacis vinculo, te una cum toto observandissimorum fratrum coetu incolumem servet, vestrisque assiduis laboribus cumulatissime benedicat. Genevae, decima tertia Novembris 1571.

Tuus Beza.

APPENDIX III

THE POLITICAL THOUGHT OF PIETRO MARTIRE VERMIGLI

Some of the most succinct and sophisticated sixteenth-century statements of Protestant political principles which I discovered in doing research for this book, are to be found in the *Loci Communes* of Pietro Martire Vermigli. This basic textbook of the entire corpus of Vermigli's thought was compiled from his voluminous works by some of his admirers well after his death, was reprinted a number of times in various countries and translated into English,[1] and probably had a considerable influence on many Protestant thinkers of the late sixteenth and early seventeenth centuries. It incorporates much of the Aristotelian philosophy which interested Vermigli from the period, before his conversion to Protestantism, when he was a student at the University of Padua, then a particularly important center for the study of Aristotelian thought. And it also incorporates much of the rather complex Biblical theology which Vermigli had worked out, on a basis laid by Zwingli, in collaboration with Bucer in Strasbourg, Cranmer in England, and Bullinger in Zurich.[2] It thus contributes in an important way to that amalgam of these two strands of thinking which is often labeled Protestant scholasticism. That amalgam also helps to explain much of the shape of Vermigli's political ideas.

These ideas are woven into Part IV of the *Loci Communes*, which shifts from more speculative theology to consider such temporal entities as the institutional Church and the Magistrate and such temporal problems as church discipline and war. I was particularly struck in this Part IV, by a passage which moves from consideration of the problem of maintaining discipline within the Church to an explicit definition of the government of the Church, expressed in the same terms used by ancient writers in defining their ideal of " mixed government " for the state, and which then bolsters this definition by an appeal to the model of republican Rome. Thus one finds in this passage the same connections between church discipline and church structure, the same arguments from analogies between Church and state, and the same appeal to an ideal of "mixed government " which figured in the controversies between Beza and Morély and between Beza and Boutilier. Vermigli himself died in 1562, before these controversies developed, and I have not found evidence that his writings figured in them, so I did not discuss his ideas in the

[1] For a description of its compilation and publication history, see C. Schmidt, *Peter Martyr Vermigli*, Vol. VII in *Leben und ausgewählte Schriften der Väter und Begründer der reformirten Kirche* (Elberfeld, 1858), pp. 295-296.

[2] For a good recent study of Vermigli and his thought, see Joseph C. McLelland, *The Visible Words of God: an exposition of the sacramental theology of Peter Martyr Vermigli, A.D. 1500-1562* (Edinburgh and London : Oliver and Boyd, 1957). It concentrates, of course, on only one aspect of his thought, but it does includes a useful general account of his career. It is based largely on materials available in Britain.

main text of this book. There remains, however, the possibility that Beza's opinions were directly influenced by Vermigli's. The two had worked together closely at the Colloquy of Poissy in 1561, where they led the group of Protestant theologians who had been invited to debate with the leaders of the Roman Catholic Church in France before the royal Court. And Morély could easily have read in Vermigli's widely available Biblical commentaries. In any event, these ideas of Vermigli's are rather interesting in themselves, as particularly neat summaries of views widely held throughout the Reformed movement. The passage defining the government of the Church:

> Ut autem recte intelligamus, quisnam excommunicare debeat, opus est excutere societatem Ecclesiae cuiusmodi sit. Non est simplex, verum ex Monarchia, Aristocratia, & Democratia composita. Removendae quippe ab illa sunt, perniciosae species rerum publicarum, Tyrannis (inquam) Oligarchia, & corruptus populi dominatus. Christum si respexeris, Monarchia dicetur: Nam ipse est Rex noster, qui sanguine suo Ecclesiam sibi acquisivit. Iam abiit in coelum, regit attamen hoc suum regnum: non quidem visibili praesentia, sed spiritu & verbo sacrarum literarum. Sunt vero in Ecclesia, qui legatione funguntur pro eo, Episcopi, Presbyteri, Doctores, & alii qui praesunt: quorum respectu merito potest dici, Aristocratia. Nam gubernationi Ecclesiarum, qui praeficiuntur tantummodo propter insignia dona Dei, quoad doctrinam & puritatem vitae, sunt ad istos gradus promovendi. Non committuntur ista munera, juxta divitiarum & census aestimationem, non ex gratia, forma & nobilitate, sed ex meritis & virtutibus: quod si non fiat, contra regular agitur. Sed quoniam in Ecclesia de negotiis gravioribus & quae sunt maximi momenti, ad plebem refertur (uti patet in Actis Apostolicis) ideo politiae rationem habet. Maximi autem ponderis habentur excommunicatio, absolutio, ministrorum electio, & alia huiusmodi: Unde concluditur, Non absque consensu Ecclesiae, quempiam excommunicari posse. Hoc pacto se habuit respublica Romana: Miseris & difficillimis temporibus, Dictatorem creabat, qui ut Monarcha se habuit, Senatum praeterea cooptabat, virtutes & merita ponderando, quo pacto Aristocratia dici potuit: caeterum in rebus gravissimis & legibus ac decretis confirmandis, ad Quirites referebat, quo pacto Democratia judicabatur.[1]

And in the English translation of the period:

> But that we maie rightlie understand, who ought to be excommunicate, it is needefull to discusse in what sort the societie of the Church is. It is not simple, but it is compounded of one alone, of manie good governours, and of the government of the people. For from it must be remooved pernitious kindes of common weales, I meane, Tyrannie, the government of a few, and the Lordshippe of corrupt people. If thou respect Christ, it shall be called a Monarchie: For he is our king, who with his owne blood hath purchased the Church unto himselfe. He is now gone into heaven, yet doeth he governe this kingdome of his, indeed not with visible presence, but by the spirit and word of the holie scriptures. And there be in the Church which doe execute the office for him: Bishops, Elders, Doctors, and others bearing rule: in respect of whom it maie justlie bee called a government of manie. For they which are preferred to the government of Churches, onlie because of the excellent gifts of God, as touching doctrine and purenesse of life, must be promoted unto these degrees. These offices are not committed unto them, according to the estimation of riches and revenewes,

[1] *Loci Communes*, 4 : 5 : 9. P. 886 in the 1576 edition, described in STC, No. 24667. This passage was first called to my attention by Ruth Wesel-Roth, *Thomas Erastus* (Lahr/Baden: Schauenburg, 1954), pp. 115-116. All my transcriptions are based on copies in the Library of the Princeton Theological Seminary. I have omitted marginalia.

not for favour, bewtie, or nobilitie sake, but in respect of merites and vertues: but if it be otherwise, it is doone against the rule. But because in the Church there be matters of verie great weight & importance, referred unto the people, (as it appeareth in the Acts of the Apostles) therefore it hath a consideration of politike government. But of the most weight are accounted excommunication, absolution, choosing of ministers and such like: so as it is concluded, that no man can be excommunicated without the consent of the Church. On this wise it stood with the common weale of Rome: In the miserable & most daungerous times. It created a Dictator, who behaved himselfe as a Monarch. It appointed also a Senate, having respect unto vertues and merites. By reason whereof it might be called a government of manie. Howbeit in the most weightie affaires and in confirming of lawes and decrees, the matter was brought unto the common people of Rome, by meanes whereof it was judged to be a government of the people.[1]

Another passage which reflects Aristotelian political thought in an even more explicit way, and, unlike the previous passage, defines " democracy " in the classic way, can be found toward the beginning of the section in which Vermigli's basic definition of the secular state is developed. That section includes this analysis of the forms of secular government:

> Forma vero Magistratuum, non una est, sed multiplex: Monarchia, Aristocratia, & Politia, vel Tyrannis, Oligarchia, & Democratia. Quarum formarum, descriptiones & naturas, Plato, Aristoteles, & caeteri Philosophi eleganter docuerunt. Ex iis omnibus formulis, optima expetenda est, & omnes ad quos id pertinet, providere debent, ne status bonus vel tolerabilis, in vitiosum degeneret. Verum si quando contigerit, ut tyranni vel flagitiosi Principes rerum potiantur, ferendum id est, quantum per verbum Dei id licet.[2]

And in English:

> Howbeit the forme of Magistrates is not of one sort but manifolde: as *Monarchia,* (the government of one) *Aristocrasia* (the rule of many good men,) and *Politia* (politike government.) Or else *Tyrannis,* (where one rules for his owne commoditie,) *Oligarchia,* (where a fewe be in authoritie,) and *Democratia,* (when the people beare the sway.) The descriptions and natures of which formes Plato, Aristotle, and other Philosophers, have elegantly described. Of all these manners of government the best is to be desired. And all men to whom it pertaineth ought to provide, that a good or tollerable estate, degenerate not into an evill one. But if it happen at any time that Tyrantes or wicked princes obtaine the governance, that must bee suffered as much as the worde of God giveth leave.[3]

Yet another section of Vermigli's *Loci Communes* which deals with problems analogous to those considered in this book, is a series of chapters devoted to the ethics of warfare. The first of these chapters develops an explicit defense of just war, coupled with a sharp refutation of the Anabaptists' Biblical arguments for pacifism.[4] A later chapter considers the legitimacy of revolt. It includes a very concise defense of armed revolt, if led by inferior magistrates, the very doctrine which was increasingly used to justify the wars of religion in France. The kernel of this defense:

---

[1] *Common Places,* 4 : 5 : 9. P. IV/60 in the 1583 English translation, described in STC, No. 24669.

[2] *Loci Communes,* 4 : 13 : 2. P. 1014 in the 1576 ed.

[3] *Common Places,* 4 : 13 : 2. P. IV/226 in the English translation.

[4] *Loci Communes,* 4 : 16 : 1-7 ; *Common Places,* 4 : 17 [sic] : 1-7.

> Alii vero sunt quidem in Repub. loco & dignitate Principibus minores: at reipsa potestatem superiorem eligunt, certisque legibus Reipub. praeficiunt, ut hodie ab Electoribus Imperii fieri videmus, & forte in aliis quibusdam Regnis idem agitur. Iis profecto licet, si Princeps pactis & promissis non steterit, eum in ordinem cogere, ac vi adigere, ut conditiones & pacta quae fuerat pollicitus, compleat, idque vel armis, cum aliter fieri non possit.[1]

And in English:

> But there be others in the Common weale, which in place and dignitie are inferiour unto Princes, and yet in verie deede doe elect the superiour power, and by certaine lawes doe governe the Commonweale: as at this day we see doone by the Electors of the Empire: And perhaps the same is doone in other kingdomes. To these undoubtedly if the Prince perfourme not his covenaunts and promises, it is lawfull to constraine and bring him into order, and by force to compell him to perfourme the conditions and covenaunts which he had promised, and that by warre when it cannot otherwise be doone.[2]

[1] *Loci Communes*, 4 : 20 : 13. P. 1087 in the 1576 ed.

[2] *Common Places*, 4 : 21[sic] : 13. P. IV/324 in the English translation.

BIBLIOGRAPHY

This bibliography lists, and sometimes describes, most of the materials that I found useful in preparing this study. It does not pretend to be a complete bibliography of the subject.

I. Source Materials

A. *Manuscript Sources*:

— in Amsterdam, Universiteits-Bibliotheek:

III E 3: includes an early copy of an important undated letter from Beza to the Admiral Coligny, formerly in the Bibliotheek, Remonstr. Kerk. I have used a photographic copy of the letter, kindly ordered by Jon C. Swan, and a full transcript, prepared and kindly loaned by Professor Henri Meylan.

— in Geneva, Archives d'Etat:

Copies de lettres: copies of official letters drafted for the city government.

Finances U, no. 1, Carnet de l'Arche, 1551-1568: re financing of the city's garrison of 1567.

Jur. Pen., Livres des Criminels, A-3 (1562-1564), A-4 (1565-1566).

Minutes et Protocoles des Notaires. Those of notary Jean Ragueau are particularly valuable.

Pièces [or portefeuilles] historiques: files of letters addressed to the city government and other documents.

Procès criminels et informations: records of investigations into criminal charges.

Registres des Baptêmes.

Registres des Morts.

Registres de la Compagnie des Pasteurs, B1 (original for 1561-1571 period), B2 (a later copy for this period), consulted with permission of the present Geneva Company of Pastors. These registers have been edited, for the entire 1546-1564 period, by Robert M. Kingdon and Jean-François Bergier.

Registres du Conseil: minutes of the daily meetings of the city's Small Council.

Registres du Consistoire: minutes of the weekly meetings of the Consistory, often very hard to decipher.

— in Geneva, Bibliothèque publique et universitaire :

Ms. fr. 406 : a file of correspondence of the Company of Pastors.

Ms. fr. 446 : " Mémoires sur les Eglises de France : papiers relatifs à Morelli. "

Ms. l. 118A and B : " Lettres diverses. " Including many from Beza to Bullinger.

Ms. l. 120 : " Lettres de Bullinger à Théod. de Bèze, de 1561-1574."

Et alia.

— in Geneva, Musée historique de la Réformation :

This is a small working library assembled for the critical edition of the correspondence of Theodore Beza. It contains recent transcripts of almost all of the known letters to and from Beza, most of them prepared by the late Hippolyte-V. Aubert ; files of notes of materials needed for the annotation of these letters, most of them assembled by H.-V. Aubert ; translations into French of the letters exchanged by Beza and Bullinger, again prepared by H.-V. Aubert. These materials are not generally available to the public, but I have been allowed to use them, by the kind permission of Professor Henri Meylan and M. Alain Dufour, the current editors of the Beza correspondence.

— in London, Public Record Office :

State Papers, Foreign, General Series, Elizabeth (S.P. 70), volume 73 : Nos. 469, Sir Thomas Smith to William Cecil, 12 July 1564 ; 469-I, minutes of the Synod of La Ferté-sous-Jouarre, 27 April 1564 ; 469-II, Pierre Denise's version of the Synod's acts ; 469-III, the refutation of Denise drafted by Chandieu, et al. I have used photographic copies of these manuscripts. Summaries of their contents can be found in the *Calendar of State Papers, Foreign Series, of the Reign of Elizabeth, 1564-1565* (London, 1870), Nos. 553, 357, 358, 359.

— in Paris, Bibliothèque de la Société de l'histoire du protestantisme français :

Collection Auzière, Ile-de-France, Syn. Prov., 563. : relatively modern transcripts of the acts of provincial synods of the Ile-de-France, including the 1564 Synod, but otherwise entirely of the seventeenth century.

— in Rotterdam, Archief der Gemeente :

Archief van de Waalsche Kerk, no. 41 (1563-1644) : copies of synodical acts, including variant copies of those edited by Kist, and French versions of those edited in Latin by Rutgers.

— in Strasbourg, copies of letters in the Sarrau Collection :

The private French Sarrau Collection contains unpublished autograph letters addressed to Calvin, but has been closed to the scholarly public. However Professor Rodolphe Peter and M. Jean Rott of Strasbourg have recently obtained copies of these letters and permission to prepare them for publication. They will probably be published in the *Revue d'histoire et de philosophie religieuses*. The collection includes one important letter from Morély to Calvin, of 10 April [1562], a transcript of which was generously supplied to me.

— in Zürich, Staatsarchiv :

E II 381 : fols. 1300-1343, 1 September 1571 to 17 June 1572, letters and other documents exchanged by Beza, Bullinger, Ramus, and others, pertaining to the decisions of the Synods of La Rochelle and Nîmes.

See also letters in vols. E I 25.8 ; E II 342a ; E II 350 ; E II 368 ; E II 441.

One can find in the Staatsarchiv extremely useful card indexes to all this ecclesiastical correspondence, classified both by author and by recipient.

— in Zürich, Zentralbibliothek :

A 44

A 84

F 47, fols. 258, 259, 263-264 : Letters to Conrad Pellican, of the 1549-1552 period, from " Janus Morellius " and " Claudius Villierius. " I have used photographic copies and transcripts, kindly supplied by Professor Henri Meylan.

B. *Printed Sources:*

— of the Sixteenth Century :

ACTES DE LA / dispute & conference / tenue à Paris, és mois / de Iuillet, & Aoust, / 1566. / ENTRE DEUX DOCTEURS / de Sorbonne, & deux Ministres de / l'Eglise reformee. / * / Distinguez selon les Iournees. / [mark] / A STRASBOURG, / Par Piere [sic] Estiart. / M. D. LXVI. (copy in Geneva, BPU ; copy of a slightly different 1568 ed. in Paris, Bibliothèque Mazarine)

Theodore Beza, *Epistolarum Theologicarum*... (Geneva, 1573).

— Geneva, 1575.

— Hanover, 1597. (I used the Princeton University Library's copy of this edition.)

(See full descriptions in Gardy, *Bibliographie*, Nos. 296, 297, 298.)

[Antoine de la Roche Chandieu],

LA CONFIR-/mation de la discipline ec-/clesisatique, obseruee es e-/glises reformees du royau-/me de France. / *Avec la response aux obiections / proposees alencontre.* / [mark : olive tree of the Estiennes] / M. D. LXVI.
(copies in Geneva, BPU ; Paris, BiblSHPF)

— another edition. [La Rochelle : Berton], 1566. (See the article by E. Droz, in BHR, XXII, 570-577.)

Pierre Charpentier,

LETTRE DE PIERRE / Charpentier Iurisconsulte, addressée à / François Portes Candiois, par laquelle / il monstre que les persecutions des E-/glises de France sont aduenues, non / par la faulte de ceux qui faisoient / profession de la Religion, mais / de ceux qui nourrissoient les / factions & conspirations, / qu'on appelle la / CAVSE. / [design] / 1572.
(copy in Geneva, BPU)

Antoine du Pinet,

LA / CONFOR-/MITE DES EGLISES / REFORMEES DE FRANCE, / Et de l'Eglise primitiue, en police / & Ceremonies, / Prouuee par l'Escriture, Con-/ciles, Docteurs, Decrets,/ & Canons anciens,/ Par ANTOINE DU PINET. / [mark] / M. D. LXIII.
(partial photographic copy lent me by Mrs. Natalie Z. Davis)

L'EXTRAICT DES / Procedures faites & / TENVES CONTRE IEAN / Morelli, natif de Paris, & n'agueres habi-/tant en la ville de Geneue : touchant vn livre composé par luy, De la discipline / Ecclesiastique, auec la sentence des ma-/gnifiques seigneurs Sindiques & Conseil / dudit Geneue, prononcée & executée le / sezieme de Septembre 1563. / [mark] / A GENEVE, / De l'Imprimerie de François Perrin. / M. D. LXIII.
(copies in Geneva, BPU ; a facsimile copy in Paris, BiblSHPF)

Gentian Hervet,

L'ANTIHVGVES, / C'est à dire, / Responce aux escrits & blasphemes de / Hugues Sureau, soy disant Ministre / Caluiniste à Orleans, contre les principaux points de la Foy & Religion Ca-/tholique. / Par Gentian Heruet Chanoine / de Rheims. / [mark] / Imprimé, & se vend à Rheims, par Iean de Foigny, à l'enseigne du Lion : / Et se vend aussi à Paris, chez Nicolas Chesneau, en la / rue saint Iacques, à l'enseigne de l'escu de Froben / & du Chesne verd. / M. D. LXVII. / AVEC PRIVILEGE DV ROY.
(copies in Paris, BiblSHPF)

— TROIS EPISTRES, / L'vne à Maistre Hugues / Sureau, Ministre des Calvinistes / à Orleans. / L'autre, à Messeigneurs les Gouuerneurs, Lieute-/nant, Bailliff, Preuost, Escheuins, & autres Magi-/strats de ladite cité d'Orleans : / La troisiesme, aux Princes, Seigneurs, Dames & Da/moiselles de ce Royaume, tendans à ce que les Mi / nistres acceptent l'offre qu'on leur fait de gager, sur le fait de prouuer la verité du corps & du sang / de Iesus Christ en l'Eucharistie, & le sacrifice / pour les pechez des viuans & des trespassez, par / le consentement de l'Eglise vniuerselle. / Par Gentian Heruet, d'Orleans, Cha-/noine de Rheims. / A RHEIMS, / Chez Iean de Foigny, à l'enseigne du Lion, deuant / le College des bons Enfans. / 1565. / AVEC PRIVILEGE.
(copy in Paris, BiblSHPF)

Lettres patentes / DV ROY, POVR L'EN-/TRETENEMENT ET ENTIE-/re execution de l'Edict & decla-/ration de la Pacification des trou-/bles de son Royaume pour le faict / de la Religion. / [mark : olive tree of the Estiennes] / A PARIS, / Par Robert Estienne Imprimeur du Roy / M. D. LXIIII. / Auec priuilege dudict Seigneur.
fol. $Biij_v$: " Donné a Roussillon le quatrieme iour d'Aoust,"
(copy in Geneva, BPU)

Joannes Morelius,

DE / ECCLESIA AB AN-/TICHRISTO PER EIVS / EXCIDIVM LIBERAN-/DA, EAQVE / Ex DEI promissis beatis-/simé reparanda / *Tractatus:* / Cui addita est ad calcem verissima / *certissimáqss ratio conciliendi* / dissidii de Coena / *Domini.* / *Ad Serenissimum Potentissimámqss An-*/gliae, Franciae, Hiberniae, & c. Reginam : Nec / *non ad caeteros pios Reges, & Principes verè Chri-*/stianos, quos Deus ab Antichristi servitute / *retraxit; de Sacrosancto Foedere ex* / *Dei mandato inter ip.* / *sos ineundo.* / LONDINI, / Impensis Georg. Bishop. / 1589
(copy in Paris, Bibliothèque Mazarine)
(See also STC, Nos. 18099, 18100.)

— Aussrottunge dess Antichrists-/ Das ist : / Ausslegung der / Offenbarung S. Johannis : / Wie vermittelst Aussrottung dess Antichrists, die Christenliche Kirche von im erle / diget, und dieselbige nach Gottes verheis-/sungen seliglichen widerumb angerich-/tet werden möge. / Deme angehenckt eine wahrhaffte unn / gewisse Mass den Streit auffzuheben vom dem / Hoch : Abendtmal dess Herrn / Erstlich durch Ioannem Morelium / der Religion halber uss

Franckreich verjagten / und seiner Gütter beraubten an die Durchleuchtigt / sternn Grossmächtigiste Königin in Engelland, & c. / in Latein beschrieben, Jetzundt aber dem gemei-/nen Mann zum besten durch Fridericum / Kranmeyr Theologiae Studiosum / in unser teutsche Sprach vertiert / und in Truck verfertigt. / M. D. XCIII.
(copy in Paris, Bibliothèque Mazarine)

Jean Morély,

TRAICTÉ / De la discipline & police / Chrestienne. / [mark] / A LYON, / PAR IAN DE TOVRNES, / M. D. LXII.
(copies in Geneva, BPU ; Paris, BiblSHPF ; the Geneva copy, Rés. 277* Dg, bears the hand-written notice, on its cover : " Ce livre a este condampne par sentence de la seigneurie contre lauteur Jo. Morelli Sr de Villier comme meschant et Resprouve. ")

Francesco Porto,

RESPONSE DE / FRANCOIS PORTUS / Candiot, aux lettres diffa-/ matoires de Pierre Car-/pentier Aduocat, / Pour l'innocence des fideles serviteurs de / Dieu, & obeissans subiets du Roy : massa-/crez le 24. iour d'Aoust 1572 : appelez fa / ctieux par ce plaidereau. / Traduite nouuellement de Latin en François. / M. D. LXXIIII.
(copy in Geneva, BPU)

RECVEIL / DES EDICTS / DE PACIFICATION, / Ordonnances & declarations fai-/tes par les Rois de France. / Sur les moyens plus propres pour appaiser les troubles / & seditions, suruenues pour le fait de la Religion, & /... Par P.D.B. Conseiller & Maistre des Requestes / de Madame sœur unique du Roy. / ... POVR IAQUES CHOVET. / M. D. XCIX.
(copy in Geneva, BPU)

Hugues Sureau, dit du Rosier,

CONFESSION / DE FOY FAICTE PAR / H. S. DV ROSIER AVEC ABIV-/ ration & detestation de la profession / Huguenotique : faicte tant par deuant / Prelats de l'Eglise Catholique & Ro-/maine, que Princes du sang Royal de / France & autres, ensemble la refutation / de plusieus [sic] poincts, mis en auant par / Caluin & Beze, contre la Foy & Eglise / Apostolique. / Le tout que dessus confirmé & signé / d'iceluy, ainsi qu'il appert par la co-/pie qu'il a baillee. / A PARIS, / Chez Sebastien Niuelle aux Cicognes, / rue sainct Iaques. / 1573. / AVEC PRIVILEGE.
(copies in Geneva, BPU ; Paris, Bibliothèque Mazarine

— CONFESSION / ET RECO-/GNOISSANCE DE HVGVES / SVREAV DIT DV ROSIER / TOVCHANT SA CHEVTE / en la Papauté, & les horribles / scandales par lui / commis, / SERVANT D'EXEMPLE A / tout le monde, de la fragilité, &/peruersité / de l'homme abandonné a soi, & de / l'infinie misericorde, & fer- / me verité de Dieu / enuers ses es-/leuz. / [mark] / A HEIDELBERG, / Par Ian Mayer. / M. D. LXXIII.
(copy in Geneva, BPU)

— SOMMAIRE / RESOLVTION / DE QVELQVES POINTS / DE LA RELIGION / CHRESTIENNE, / En forme d'Epistre responsiue aux escrits / publiez par M. Gentian Heruet con-/tre les fideles de l'Eglise d'Orleans. / Par Hugues Sureau, Ministre / en ladite Eglise. / En la page suiuante sont contenus les points / traittez en ce present Sommaire. / M. D. LXIIII.
(copy in Geneva, BPU)

— TRAITTE / DES CER-/TAINES ET INSEPARA-/bles marques de la uraye Eglise de Dieu. / Par H. S. Du Rosier. / [mark] / A HEIDELBERG, / Par Ian Mayer, l'an M. D. LXXIIII.
(copy in Geneva, BPU)

Pietro Martire Vermigli, *Loci communes...* London : Kingston, 1576.

— Zürich : Froschauer, 1580. (copy in Geneva, BPU)

— London : Vautrollerius, 1583.

— *Common Places...* London, 1583.

(See STC, Nos. 24667, 24668, 24669, on the English editions.)

— of the Seventeenth Century :

Guilielmus Apollonius, *Consideratio quarundam...* 1644. (Wing No. A-3534)

— *A consideration of certaine controversies.* 1645. (Wing No. A-3535)

Ephraim Pagitt, *Heresiography.* 4th ed., 1647. (Wing No. P-178)

— *Heresiography.* 5th ed., 1654. (Wing No. P-180)

W[illiam] R[athband], *A briefe narration of some church courses.* 1644. (Wing No. R-298)

Samuel Rutherford, *The due right of Presbyteries...* 1644. (Wing No. R-2378)

[Westminster Assembly], *Literae a conventu theologorum in Anglia.* 1644. (Wing No. W-1444)

— of the Eighteenth Century :

J. J. Rousseau, *Lettres écrites de la montagne.* 2 vols. Amsterdam : Marc Michel Rey, 1764. (presentation copy in Geneva, BPU)

C. *Reprinted and Edited Sources:*

Edward Arber, ed., *A Transcript of the Registers of the Company of Stationers of London, 1554-1640 A.D.* 5 vols. London, 1875-1894.

[Jean] Aymon, *Tous les synodes nationaux des Eglises Réformées de France.* 2 vols. The Hague, 1710. The only complete edition available of the French texts of the French synods' acts, yet uncritical, not as reliable as the English translations by Quick.

Robert Baillie, *The Letters and Journals of Robert Baillie,* ed. by David Laing. 3 vols. Edinburgh, 1841-1842.

Henry Barrow, *The Writings of Henry Barrow, 1587-1590,* ed. by Leland H. Carlson. Vol. III, *Elizabethan Nonconformist Texts.* London : Allen & Unwin, 1962.

Richard Baxter, *The Saint's Everlasting Rest.* In vol. XXIII of Baxter's *The Practical Works,* ed. by William Orme. London, 1830. Also many other editions.

Theodore Beza, *De iure magistratum,* ed. by Klaus Sturm. Vol. I, *Texte zur Geschichte der Evangelischen Theologie.* Neukirchen-Vluyn : Neukirchener Verlag des Erziehungsvereins, 1965.

— *Correspondance,* collected by Hippolyte Aubert, ed. by Fernand Aubert, Henri Meylan, Alain Dufour, Arnaud Tripet. 4 vols. to date (Nos. XL, XLIX, LXI, LXXIV, in THR), covering 1539-1563. Geneva : Droz, 1960 —

Robert Browne, *The Writings of Robert Harrison and Robert Browne*, ed. by Albert Peel and Leland H. Carlson. Vol. II, *Elizabethan Noncofonrmist Texts.* London: Allen & Unwin, 1953.

John Calvin, *Ioannis Calvini Opera quae supersunt omnia*, ed. by Baum, Cunitz, and Reuss. 59 vols. The best and most complete edition available. Reprinted in 1964 by the Johnson Reprint Corporation of New York and London.

Baldesar Castiglione, *Il Cortegiano del Conte Baldesar Castiglione*, ed. by Vittorio Cian. 2nd ed. Florence: Sansoni, 1910. The most critical ed. available. The standard English translation is by Leonard Eckstein Opdycke, several eds.

L. Cimber [pseudonym for L. Lafaist] and F. Danjou, eds., *Archives curieuses de l'histoire de France depuis Louis XI jusqu'à Louis XVIII, ou Collection de pièces rares et intéressantes...* 1re série, 15 vols. 2e série, 12 vols. Paris, 1834-1840. Reprints many polemical pamphlets of the late sixteenth century.

[Condé, Louis Ier de Bourbon], *Memoires de Condé, ou recueil pour servir à l'histoire de France, contenant ce qui s'est passé de plus mémorable dans le royaume, sous le règne de François II. & sous une partie de celui de Charles IX*, ed. by Secousse. 6 vols. London and Paris, 1743-1745. A collection of state papers, pamphlets, and the like, allegedly first collected at Condé's request.

Alfred L. Covelle, ed., *Le livre des bourgeois de l'ancienne république de Genève.* Geneva, 1897.

Charles du Moulin, *Caroli Molinaei... omnia quae extant opera...* 5 vols. Paris, 1861. Far more complete than 1612 ed. Contains Brodeau's *Vie* of du Moulin, in vol. I, and the anti-Calvinist tracts, in vol. V, most of which are missing in the earlier ed.

Francis I, *Catalogue des actes de François Ier.* 10 vols. Paris: Imprimerie Nationale, 1887-1908. In *Académie des sciences morales et politiques: collection des ordonnances des rois de France.*

Paul-F. Geisendorf, ed., *Livre des habitants de Genève.* 2 vols. Vols. XXVI and LVI in THR. Geneva: Droz, 1957, 1963.

John Greenwood, *The Writings of John Greenwood, 1587-1590*, ed. by Leland H. Carlson. Vol. IV, *Elizabethan Nonconformist Texts.* London: Allen & Unwin, 1962.

Benjamin Hanbury, *Historical Memorials Relating to the Independents or Congregationalists: from their rise to the restoration of the monarchy, A. D. MDCLX.* 3 vols. London, 1839-1844. A rather casual collection of excerpts from a great variety of sources.

Histoire ecclésiastique des églises réformées au royaume de France, ed. by G. Baum, Ed. Cunitz, Rodolphe Reuss. 3 vols. Paris, 1883-1889. An admirable critical ed., based on the first 1580 ed., of the French Protestants' extremely detailed and semi-official account of their own early history.

Robert M. Kingdon and Jean-François Bergier, eds., *Registres de la Compagnie des Pasteurs de Genève au temps de Calvin.* 2 vols. Vol. LV in THR. Geneva: Droz, 1962, 1964. Covers the period from 1546 to 1564. Also in English translation, by Philip Edgcumbe Hughes, without most of the annotation: Grand Rapids, Mich.: Eerdmans, 1966.

N. C. Kist, ed., " De Synoden der Nederlandsche Hervormde Kerken onder het kruis, gedurende de jaren 1563-1577, gehouden in Braband, Vlaaderen, enz.," *Nederlandsch Archief voor Kerkelijke Geschiedenis*, IX (*Archief voor Kerkelijke Geschiedenis*, XX), (1849), pp. 113-210. Full texts of acts of these synods, most of them in French.

A. Kluckhohn, ed., *Briefe Friedrich des Frommen, Kurfürsten von der Pfalz, mit verwandten Schriftstücken.* 3 vols. Brunswick, 1868-1872. Pub. for *Die Historische Commission bei der Königl. Akademie der Wissenschaften.*

John Knox, *The Works of John Knox*, ed. by David Laing. 6 vols. Edinburgh, 1846-1864.

L. Lafaist. See L. Cimber.

A. Lublinskaja, ed., *Documents pour servir à l'histoire des guerres civiles en France (1561-1563)*. Pub. for *Akademiia nauk SSSR, Institut istorii, Leningradskoe otdelenie.* Moscow, 1962. An edition of hitherto unpublished official letters, texts in French, critical apparatus and translations in Russian. N.B. petitions to the royal Court from Protestants, e.g. No. 98, from the Orleans Church, asking for permission to retain consistorial discipline, among other things.

John Norton, *The Answer to the Whole Set of Questions of the Celebrated Mr. William Apollonius, Pastor of the Church of Middelburg, Looking Toward the Resolution of Certain Controversies Concerning Church Government Now Being Agitated in England*, translated with introduction by Douglas Horton. Cambridge, Mass.: Belknap, 1958. Originally published in 1648, in Latin.

John Quick, ed., *Synodicon in Gallia Reformata, or the acts, decisions, decrees, and canons of those famous national councils of the Reformed churches in France.* 2 vols. London, 1692. Complete texts translated into English, based on collations of several manuscript copies, superior—especially for spellings of proper names—to the Aymon ed. in the original French, still far from a true critical edition.

[Alphonse] de Ruble, ed., *Mémoires et poésies de Jeanne d'Albret.* Paris, 1893. A memoir, with annotation, covering the 1560-1568 period, followed by random poems, manifestos, letters, and an index.

F. L. Rutgers, ed., *Acta van de Nederlandsche Synoden der zestiende eeuw.* Vol. 3 of series 2, *Werken der Marnix-Vereeniging.* Utrecht, 1889. Texts of synodical acts, beginning with the Wesel Articles of 1568.

Traugott Schiess, ed., *Bullingers Korrespondenz mit den Graubündern.* 3 vols. Vols. 23, 24, 25, in *Quellen zur Schweizer Geschichte.* Basel, 1904-1906. Texts and excerpts from a correspondence running from 1533 to 1575.

S. Stelling-Michaud, ed., *Le livre du recteur de l'Académie de Genève (1559-1878)*, vol. I, *Le texte*; vol. II, *Notices biographiques des étudiants* A-C. Vol. XXXIII in THR. Geneva: Droz, 1959, 1966. Subsequent volumes will identify fully the remaining students listed in this source.

Ch. Weiss, ed., *Papiers d'état du Cardinal de Granvelle, d'après les manuscrits de la Bibliothèque de Besançon.* 9 vols. Vol. 44 of series 1, *Collection de documents inédits sur l'histoire de France.* Paris, 1841-1852.

A. S. P. Woodhouse, ed., *Puritanism and Liberty, Being the Army Debates (1647-9)...* 2nd ed. London: Dent, 1951. Contains a particularly valuable introduction.

II. Secondary Materials

A. *Early Chronicles:*

[Louis Etienne] Arcere, *Histoire de la ville de La Rochelle et du pays d'Aulnis.* 2 vols. La Rochelle, 1756-1757.

Léon Ménard, *Histoire civile, ecclésiastique, et litteraire de la ville de Nismes.* 7 vols. Paris, 1750-1758.

Florimond de Raemond, *Histoire de la naissance, progrez et decadence de l'heresie de ce siecle.* Rouen, 1648.

Jaques-Auguste de Thou, *Histoire universelle...* [trans. by T. Carte]. 11 vols. The Hague, 1740.
Also several other editions, both in French and Latin.

B. *Works of Reference—Biographic, Bibliographic, Linguistic:*

J. P. de Bie, et al., *Biographisch Woordenboek van Protestantsche Godgeleerden in Nederland.* 5 vols. The Hague: Nijhoff, n.d.—Through " Leyendecker. "

Alfred Cartier, *Bibliographie des éditions des de Tournes, imprimeurs lyonnais.* 2 vols. Paris: Éditions des Bibliothèques Nationales de France, 1938.

Louis Desgraves, *L'imprimerie à La Rochelle.* Vol. 2: *Les Haultin, 1571-1623.* Vol. XXXIV** in THR. Geneva: Droz, 1960.

Dictionnaire de théologie catholique, ed. by A. Vacant, et al. 15 vols. Paris: Letouzey et Ané, 1903-1950.

Dictionary of National Biography, ed. by Leslie Stephen, et al. 43 vols. plus several supplementary vols. New York and London, 1885—Also other eds.

E. Droz, *L'imprimerie à La Rochelle.* Vol. 1: *Barthélemy Berton, 1563-1573;* vol. 3: *La veuve Berton et Jean Portau, 1573-1589.* Vols. XXXIV* and XXXIV*** in THR. Geneva: Droz, 1960.

Frédéric Gardy and Alain Dufour, *Bibliographie des œuvres théologiques, littéraires, historiques et juridiques de Théodore de Bèze.* Vol. XLI in THR. Geneva: Droz, 1960.

Eugène and Emile Haag, *La France Protestante, ou vies des protestants français.* 1st ed. 10 vols. Paris, 1846-1858.
— 2nd ed., revised by Henri Bordier. 6 vols. Paris, 1877-1888. Substantially better but incomplete—stops with " Gasparin. "

Hannelore Jahr, *Studien zur Uberlieferungsgeschichte der Confession de foi von 1559.* Vol. 16, *Beiträge zur Geschichte und Lehre der Reformierten Kirche.* Neukirchen-Vluyn: Neukirchener Verlag des Erziehungsvereins, 1964. Contains a lengthy bibliography of the sixteenth-century editions of the basic Calvinist confession and the Genevan catechism. To be supplemented by references in STC.

London, *British Museum: General Catalogue of Printed Books... to 1955.* 261 vols. to date. London: British Museum, 1959.

Walter J. Ong, *Ramus and Talon Inventory.* Cambridge, Mass.: Harvard, 1958.

Paris, Bibliothèque Nationale, *Catalogue général des livres imprimés de la Bibliothèque Nationale, auteurs.* 190 vols. to date. Paris, 1897.

A. W. Pollard and G. R. Redgrave, *A Short-Title Catalogue of Books Printed in England, Scotland, & Ireland, and of English Books Printed Abroad, 1475-1640.* London : Bibliographical Society, 1926. Reprinted in 1946.

Willy Richard, *Untersuchungen zur Genesis der reformierten Kirchenterminologie der Westschweiz und Frankreichs, mit besonderer Berücksichtigung der Namengebung.* Vol. 57 in *Romanica Helvetica.* Bern : Francke, 1959. Includes a useful glossary.

Donald Wing, *Short-Title Catalogue of Books Printed in England, Scotland, Ireland, Wales, and British America and of English Books Printed in Other Countries, 1641-1700.* 3 vols. New York : Columbia, 1945-1951.

C. *Other Books:*

Léonce Anquez, *Histoire des assemblées politiques des réformées de France (1573-1622).* Paris, 1859.

E. Arnaud, *Histoire des protestants du Dauphiné aux XVI*e, *XII*e, et *XVIII*e *siècles.* 3 vols. Paris, 1875-1876. Vol. 1 covers 1522-1598.

— *Histoire des protestants de Provence, du Comtat Venaissin et de la principauté d'Orange.* 2 vols. Paris, 1884.

Duc d'Aumale [Henri d'Orléans], *Histoire des princes de Condé pendant les XVI*e *et XVII*e *siècles.* 7 vols. 2nd printing. Paris, 1886-1896. Vols. 1 and 2 cover 1530-1610. N.B. extensive appendixes, containing texts of many relevant documents. There is a complete English translation of the first two volumes, including appendixes, by Robert Brown Borthwick, London, 1872.

Charles Borgeaud, *Histoire de l'Université de Genève.* Vol. I, *L'Académie de Calvin, 1559-1798.* Geneva : Georg, 1900.

P.-Daniel Bourchenin, *Etude sur les académies protestantes en France au XVI*e *et au XVII*e *siècles.* Paris, 1882.

André Bouvier, *Henri Bullinger, le successeur de Zwingli, d'après sa correspondance avec les réformés et les humanistes de langue française.* Neuchâtel : Delachaux & Niestlé ; Paris : Droz, 1940. Includes a number of previously unpublished letters in appendixes. Extremely valuable for this study, although flawed by occasional errors in transcription and in fact, and by sentimental writing.

Vittorio de Caprariis, *Propaganda e pensiero politico in Francia durante le guerre di religione. I (1559-1572).* Naples : Edizioni Scientifiche Italiane, 1959.

Eugène Choisy, *L'état chrétien calviniste à Genève au temps de Théodore de Bèze.* Geneva : Eggimann, 1902. Includes chronological and analytical sections, based on extensive archival research. Extremely valuable for this study.

— *La théocratie à Genève au temps de Calvin.* Geneva, 1897.

William Farr Church, *Constitutional Throught in Sixteenth-Century France.* Cambridge Mass. : Harvard, 1941.

Ath. Coquerel, fils, *Précis de l'histoire de l'Eglise Réformée de Paris... première époque, 1512-1594, de l'origine de l'Eglise à l'édit de Nantes.* Paris and Strasbourg, 1862.

Lucien Cramer, *La seigneurie de Genève et la maison de Savoie de 1559 à 1603.* Vols. 1 and 2 cover 1559-1580. Geneva and Paris : Kündig and Fontemoing, 1912. Vol. 3, Geneva : Jullien, 1950, covers 1580-1588. Vol. 4, by Alain Dufour, Geneva : Jullien, 1958, covers 1589-1593.

Jules Delaborde, *Gaspard de Coligny, Amiral de France.* 3 vols. Paris, 1879-1882. Includes lengthy quotations from chronicles in text ; many relevant documents in appendixes.

Emile Doumergue, *Jean Calvin, les hommes et les choses de son temps.* 7 vols. Lausanne and Neuilly-sur-Seine : Bridel and Editions de " La cause ". Nearly definitive for factual information, yet curiously naive in many judgments.

E. Droz, ed., *Aspects de la propagande religieuse.* Vol. XXVIII in THR. Geneva : Droz, 1957.

Friedrich Clemens Ebrard, *Die französisch-reformierte Gemeinde in Frankfurt am Main, 1554-1904.* Frankfurt-am-Main : Ecklin, 1906.

Philippe Erlanger, *Le massacre de la Saint-Barthélemy.* No. 12 in *Trente journées qui ont fait la France.* Paris : Gallimard, 1960. Also in English translation, New York : Pantheon, 1962. A lively, popular, narrative account, usefully documented.

H. Outram Evennett, *The Cardinal of Lorraine and the Council of Trent.* Cambridge, 1930.

Heinold Fast, *Heinrich Bullinger und die Täufer.* Weierhof, Pfalz : Mennonitischer Geschichtsverein, 1959.

G. de Félice, *Histoire des synodes nationaux des Eglises Réformées de France.* Paris, 1864. Detailed yet lacking critical apparatus.

Donald M. Frame, *Montaigne, a biography.* New York : Harcourt, Brace, and World, 1965.

Martha Walker Freer, *The Life of Jeanne d'Albret, Queen of Navarre.* London : Hurst & Blackett, n.d.

Jean-Antoine Gautier, *Histoire de Genève des origines à l'année 1691.* 8 vols. plus index vol. Geneva, 1896-1914. An annotated ed. of an eighteenth-century narrative history.

Léon Gautier, *La médecine à Genève jusqu'à la fin du XVIIIe siècle.* Vol. 30 in MDG. Geneva : Jullien and Georg, 1906.

Paul-F. Geisendorf, *Théodore de Bèze.* Geneva : Labor et Fides ; Paris : Librairie Protestante, 1949.

Robert W. Henderson, *The Teaching Office in the Reformed Tradition: a history of the doctoral ministry.* Philadelphia : Westminster, 1962.

W. M. Hetherington, *History of the Westminster Assembly of Divines.* 4th ed., ed. by Robert Williamson. Edinburgh, 1878.

Henri Heyer, *L'Eglise de Genève: esquisse historique de son organisation, suivie de ses diverses constitutions, de la liste de ses pasteurs et professeurs, et d'une table biographique.* Geneva : Jullien, 1909.

A. Huc-Mazelet, *Jean Morely et son Traicté de la discipline et police chrestienne.* Lausanne, 1866. A thèse de licence presented to the Faculté de théologie de l'Eglise libre du canton de Vaud. Contains little more than a summary of Morély's book. 49 pp.

Robert M. Kingdon, *Geneva and the Coming of the Wars of Religions in France, 1555-1563*. Vol. XXII in THR. Geneva : Droz, 1956.

August Kluckhohn, *Friedrich der Fromme, Kurfürst von der Pfalz, der Schützer der Reformirten Kirche, 1559-1576*. Nördlingen, 1879.

M. M. Knappen, *Tudor Puritanism: a chapter in the history of idealism*. Chicago : University, 1939.

L. Knappert, *Geschiedenis der Nederlandsche Hervormde Kerk gedurende de 16e en 17e eeuw*. Amsterdam : Meulenhoff, 1911.

G. V. Lechler, *Geschichte der Presbyterial- und Synodalverfassung seit der Reformation*. Leiden, 1854. Extremely valuable for this study, despite its age. Contains some useful comparative observations, as well as useful analyses, by period and by country.

Emile G. Léonard, *Histoire générale du Protestantisme*. Vol. 2, *L'établissement (1564-1700)*. Paris : Presses universitaires de France, 1961. The best available synthesis, particularly good on France, perhaps a trifle chauvinistic.

Robert Dean Linder, *The Political Ideas of Pierre Viret*. Vol. LXIV in THR. Geneva : Droz, 1964.

Erich Marcks, *Die Zusammenkunft von Bayonne: das französische Statsleben und Spanien in den Jahren 1563-1567*. Strasbourg, 1889.

Jean H. Mariéjol, *La réforme et la ligue — l'édit de Nantes (1559-1598)*. Vol. VI, part I, in Ernest Lavisse, *Histoire de France depuis les origines jusqu'à la révolution*. Paris : Hachette, 1904.

Charles Martin, *Les protestants anglais réfugiés à Genève au temps de Calvin, 1555-1560: leur église — leurs écrits*. Geneva : Jullien, 1915.

Paul-E. Martin, *Trois cas de pluralisme confessionnel aux XVIe et XVIIe siècles*. Geneva : Jullien, 1961.

Joseph C. McLelland, *The Visible Word of God: an exposition of the sacramental theology of Peter Martyr Vermigli, A.D. 1500-1562*. Edinburgh and London : Oliver and Boyd, 1957.

François Méjan, *Discipline de l'Eglise Réformée de France, annotée et précédée d'une introduction historique*. Paris : 'Je sers,' 1947.

Pierre Mesnard, *L'essor de la philosophie politique au XVIe siècle*. 2nd ed. Paris : Vrin, 1952.

E. William Monter, *Studies in Genevan Government (1536-1605)*. Vol. LXII in THR. Geneva : Droz, 1964.

Samuel Mours, *Le protestantisme en France au seizième siècle*. Paris : Librairie Protestante, 1959.

Henri Naef, *La conjuration d'Amboise et Genève*. Geneva : Jullien ; Paris : Champion, 1922. Reprinted from vol. XXXII in MDG.

Walter J. Ong, *Ramus, Method, and the Decay of Dialogue*. Cambridge, Mass. : Harvard, 1958.

Jacques Pannier, *Les origines de la confession de foi et la discipline des Eglises Réformées de France*. Fasc. 32 in *Etudes d'histoire et de philosophie religieuses publiées par la Faculté de Théologie Protestante de l'Université de Strasbourg*. Paris : Alcan, 1936.

Ludwig von Pastor, *The History of the Popes, from the close of the middle ages.* 40 vols. London : Hodges, et al., 1891-1953. Covers 1305-1799. Translated from the German.

A. F. Scott Pearson, *Thomas Cartwright and Elizabethan Puritanism, 1535-1603.* Cambridge, 1925.

Richard H. Popkin, *The History of Scepticism from Erasmus to Descartes.* Assen : van Gorcum, 1960.

Amédée Roget, *Histoire du peuple de Genève depuis la réforme jusqu'à l'Escalade.* 7 vols. Geneva, 1870-1883. Vol. 7 covers 1562-1568. Based on extensive research in Genevan archives, reported with great accuracy, although often without footnotes.

Edouard Rott, *Histoire de la représentation diplomatique de la France auprès des cantons suisses, de leurs alliés, et de leurs confédérés.* 8 vols. Berne and Paris, 1900-1923.

[Alphonse] de Ruble, *Jeanne d'Albret et la guerre civile.* Paris, 1897.

J. H. M. Salmon, *The French Religious Wars in English Political Thought.* Oxford : Clarendon, 1959.

F. de Schickler, *Les églises du refuge en Angleterre.* 3 vols. Paris, 1892.

C. Schmidt, *Peter Martyr Vermigli, Leben und ausgewählte Schriften.* Vol. VII in *Leben und ausgewählte Schriften der Väter und Begründer der reformirten Kirche.* Elberfeld, 1858.

Richard Simon, *Histoire critique des principaux commentateurs du Nouveau Testament depuis le commencement du Christianisme jusques à notre tems. ...* Rotterdam, 1693.

Leo F. Solt, *Saints in Arms: puritanism and democracy in Cromwell's army.* Stanford, 1959.

Ernst Staehelin, *Der Übertritt König Heinrichs des Vierten von Frankreich zur römisch-katholischen Kirche...* Basel, 1856.

Karl Sudhoff, *C. Olevianus und Z. Ursinus, Leben und ausgewählte Schriften.* Vol. VIII in *Leben und ausgewählte Schriften der Väter und Begründer der Reformirten Kirche.* Elberfeld, 1857.

Bard Thompson, Hendrikus Berkhof, Eduard Schweizer, Howard G. Hageman, *Essays on the Heidelberg Catechism.* Philadelphia and Boston : United Church, 1963.

Drouot Toureille, *Etude historique sur le système d'organisation ecclésiastique de Jean Morely.* Strasbourg, 1850. A bachelor's thesis presented to the Faculté de Théologie Protestante de Strasbourg. A 35 pp. sketch.

Pierre Villey, *Les sources et l'évolution des Essais de Montaigne.* 2 vols. Paris : Hachette 1908.

Herman de Vries de Heekelingen, *Genève pépinière du calvinisme hollandais.* 2 vols. Fribourg : Fragnière, 1918 ; the Hague : Nijhoff, 1924.

Henri Vuilleumier, *Histoire de l'Eglise Réformée du Pays de Vaud sous le régime bernois.* 4 vols. Lausanne : Éditions la Concorde, 1927-1933.

Charles Waddington, *Ramus (Pierre de la Ramée), sa vie, ses écrits, et ses opinions.* Paris, 1855. Recently reprinted by Wm. C. Brown Reprint Library, Dubuque, Iowa. The standard biography, reasonably complete and accurate in factual information, naive and hagiographic in judgment.

Michael Walzer, *The Revolution of the Saints: a study in the origins of radical politics.* Cambridge, Mass. : Harvard, 1965.

Ruth Wesel-Roth, *Thomas Erastus: Ein Beitrag zur Geschichte der Reformierten Kirche und zur Lehre von der Staatssouveränität.* No. XV in *Veröffentlichungen des Vereins für Kirchengeschichte in der Evang. Landeskirche Badens.* Lahr/ Baden : Schauenburg, 1954.

A. W. Whitehead, *Gaspard de Coligny, Admiral of France.* London : Methuen, 1904.

Perez Zagorin, *A History of Political Thought in the English Revolution.* London : Routledge & Kegan Paul, 1954.

D. *Articles:*

Ernest G. Atkinson, "The Cardinal of Châtillon in England, 1568-1571," *Proceedings of the Huguenot Society of London,* III (1888-1891), 172-285. Includes an appendix containing texts of relevant letters. The most detailed available study of Odet de Coligny, even though devoted to only a part of his career.

H.-V. Aubert, " Nicolas Colladon et les Registres de la Compagnie des Pasteurs et Professeurs de Genève," BSHAG, II (1898-1904), 138-163,

Jean-François Bergier, " Taux de l'intérêt et crédit à court terme à Genève dans la seconde moitié du XVIe siècle," *Studi in onore di Amintore Fanfani,* IV (Milan : Giuffrè, 1962), 89-119.

A. Bernus, " Pierre Ramus à Bâle," BSHPF, XXXIX (1890), 508-530.

P. Beuzart, "H. Sureau du Rosier (1530?-1575?)," BSHPF, LXXXVIII (1939), 249-268.

G. Bonet-Maury, " Les origines de la réforme à Beauvais (1532-1568)," BSHPF, XXIII (1874), 73-88 ; 124-137 ; 217-232. The Cardinal of Châtillon is much involved in this story.

Alfred Cartier, " ' La deffense civile et militaire des innocens et de l'Eglise de Christ,' et l' 'Apologie de Charles du Moulin,' 1563 ", *Revue des livres anciens,* 1916, II/2, 200-205.

— " Les idées politiques de Théodore de Bèze, d'après le traité *Du droit des magistrats sur leurs sujets,*" BSHAG, II (1900), 187-206. Contains texts proving Beza to be author of the treatise, which had been noticed by a number of earlier scholars, but merited further publicity.

Adrien Chopard, " Genève et les anglais (XVIe-XVIIIe siècles), " BSHAG, VII (1939-1942), 175-279.

Marguerite Christol, " Odet de Coligny, Cardinal de Châtillon, " BSHPF, CVII (1961), 1-12.

Natalie Zemon Davis, " Strikes and Salvation at Lyons." ARG, LVI (1965), 48-64.

E. Droz, " Autour de l'affaire Morély : La Roche Chandieu et Barth. Berton," BHR, XXII (1960), 570-577.

— " Pierre de Vingle, l'imprimeur de Farel," *Aspects de la propagande religieuse,* pp. 38-78.

Robert M. Kingdon, " Calvinism and Democracy : some political implications of debates on French Reformed Church government, 1562-1572," *American Historical Review,* LXIX (1964), 393-401.

— " The First Expression of Theodore Beza's Political Ideas," ARG, XLVI (1955), 88-100.

— " Genève et les réformés français : le cas d'Hugues Sureau, dit du Rosier (1565-1574)," BSHAG, XII (1962), 77-87.

— " Problems of Religious Choice for Sixteenth-Century Frenchmen," *Journal of Religious History*, IV/2 (1966), 105-112.

A. Kluckhohn, " Zwei pfälzische Gesandtschaftsberichte über den französischen Hof und die Hugenotten, 1567 und 1574," *Abhandlungen der Historischen Classe der Königlich Bayerischen Akademie der Wissenschaften*, XI/2, 179-238.

John T. McNeill, " John Calvin on Civil Government," in George L. Hunt and John T. McNeill, eds., *Calvinism and the Political Order*. Philadelphia : Westminster, 1965. Judiciously summarizes the author's substantial earlier work on this problem.

Charles Mercier, " Les théories politiques des calvinistes en France au cours des guerres de religion," BSHPF, LXXXIII (1934), 225-260 ; 381-415. Perhaps the best available single study of the subject.

Henri Meylan, " Bèze et les italiens de Lyon (1566)," BHR, XIV (1952), 235-249.

E. William Monter, " Le change public à Genève, 1568-1581," *Mélanges d'histoire économique et sociale en hommage au professeur Antony Babel*, I (Geneva, 1963), 265-290.

Patrick F. O'Mara, " L'affaire des lettres anonymes et l'agitation politique à Saint-Gervais en 1718," BSHAG, X (1951-1955), 241-279.

Richard H. Popkin, " Skepticism and the Counter-Reformation in France," ARG, LI (1960), 58-87.

Michel Reulos, " Le jurisconsulte Charles du Moulin en conflit avec les Eglises Réformées de France," BSHPF, C (1954), 1-12.

Amédée Roget, " Les propositions de Jaques Boutilier, ou discussion constitutionnelle à Genève en 1578," MDG, XVII (1872), 58-76.

Heidi-Lucie Schlaepfer, " Laurent de Normandie," *Aspects de la propagande religieuse*, pp. 176-230.

Leo F. Solt, " Puritanism and Democracy in the New Model Army," ARG, L (1959), 234-252.

Joachim Staedtke, " Bullingers Bedeutung für die protestantische Welt," *Zwingliana*, XI (1954-1958), 372-388.

Etienne Trocmé, " Une révolution mal conduite : à propos d'un centenaire et d'un livre," *Revue d'histoire et de philosophie religieuses*, XXXIX (1959) 160-168. A review article of my earlier book on *Geneva & Coming*, containing some provocative ideas, not all of which I can accept.

N. Weiss, " Une des premières écoles de théologie protestante en France (Orléans, 1561-1568)," BSHPF, LX (1911), 218-224.

INDEX

Note: This index does not include the names of people and places tabulated in Appendix I. It does cover material in the other appendixes as well as in the body of the book.

Achevé d'imprimer
sur les presses de
l'Imprimerie du « Journal de Genève »
en mai 1967